INFORMATION LITERACY AS A STUDENT LEARNING OUTCOME

INFORMATION LITERACY AS A STUDENT LEARNING OUTCOME

The Perspective of Institutional Accreditation

Laura Saunders

Foreword by Peter Hernon

 LIBRARIES UNLIMITED

AN IMPRINT OF ABC-CLIO, LLC
Santa Barbara, California • Denver, Colorado • Oxford, England

Library of Congress Cataloging-in-Publication Data

Saunders, Laura, 1975–

Information literacy as a student learning outcome : the perspective of institutional accreditation / Laura Saunders ; foreword by Peter Hernon.

   p. cm.

Includes bibliographical references and index.

ISBN 978–1–59884–852–6 (acid-free paper) — ISBN 978–1–59884–853–3 (ebook)
1. Information literacy—United States. 2. Information literacy—Standards—United States. 3. Information literacy—Study and teaching (Higher)—Evaluation. 4. Information literacy—Ability testing—United States. 5. Academic libraries—Relations with faculty and curriculum—United States. 6. Universities and colleges—Accreditation—United States. I. Title.
ZA3075.S28   2011
028.7071′173—dc22   2011011068

ISBN: 978–1–59884–852–6
EISBN: 978–1–59884–853–3

15 14 13 12 11   1 2 3 4 5

This book is also available on the World Wide Web as an eBook.
Visit www.abc-clio.com for details.

Libraries Unlimited
An Imprint of ABC-CLIO, LLC

ABC-CLIO, LLC
130 Cremona Drive, P.O. Box 1911
Santa Barbara, California 93116-1911

This book is printed on acid-free paper ∞

Manufactured in the United States of America

CONTENTS

ILLUSTRATIONS

FIGURES

TABLES

FOREWORD

It is rare that a book written in library and information science and the product of a PhD dissertation should have wide appeal to anyone interested in higher education, be that person an administrator, faculty member, member of a program or institutional accreditation organization, or member of government, from local to the national level. This book is that exception. The concept that led to the dissertation was shared with me by a well-noted authority in institutional accreditation, who underscored its importance, and I passed the topic along to Laura Saunders, who completed the research under my direction; Abbie Frost of Simmons College and Robert E. Dugan of the University of West Florida served as the other members of the dissertation committee.

The dissertation, which focuses on those academic institutions that fall within the jurisdiction of the Middle States Commission of Higher Education, examines the institutional self-reports filed for re-accreditation. Naturally, not all institutions are willing to share these reports, which provide a local perspective that is aimed at showing institutional accountability and planning—the use of data collected to improve the academic experience of students. In essence, the goal of these reports is to demonstrate that the institutions fulfill their mission statements.

With so much written about student learning outcomes, both positive and negative, the research presented in the dissertation shows how far along institutions are in embracing student learning outcomes, that is, those focused on information literacy. With this book, Dr. Saunders updates her dissertation research and expands it to include the reports that institutions in other parts of the United States make publicly available on their websites.

Obviously, a number of institutions do not practice transparency and place such information on their websites, and they question why anyone would be interested in them. The Higher Education Opportunity Act of 2008 (Public Law 110-315) calls for greater accountability and transparency, much more than many institutions are willing to provide.

The dissertation and this book represent the first snapshot of a specific point in time. A number of institutions might now have more active information literacy programs that move beyond individual courses to the program or institutional level. Further, they might be more actively engaged with student learning outcomes for areas other than information literacy. Perhaps they highlight critical thinking and problem solving over information literacy. These examples indicate that the research presented here provides a baseline and, as such, merits replication and expansion, perhaps at five-year intervals, and should include more case study research than was possible for this study. In essence, a model might be the American Customer Satisfaction Index (ACSI), a well-known national survey that

> produces indexes for 10 economic sectors, 45 industries (including e-commerce and e-business), and more than 225 companies and federal or local government agencies. In addition to the company-level satisfaction scores, ACSI produces scores for the causes and consequences of customer satisfaction and their relationships. The measured companies, industries, and sectors are broadly representative of the U.S. economy serving American households. (American Customer Satisfaction Index)

This book should help reshape the national debate and give librarians an opportunity to participate. The baseline reported here suggests that librarians have much work to do to play meaningful roles in the national dialogue. In 2002, Cecilia L. López, a nationally recognized leader on assessment, issued a challenge to librarians that apparently has gone unheeded. She points out that their voices are missing from the national debate that occurs in other fora (e.g., the American Association of Higher Education, Higher Learning Commission, and EDUCAUSE). She also explains that "it is long overdue for colleges and universities to recognize that they are losing an important resource in building and strengthening their efforts to improve student learning if they do not include librarians in those groups that have responsibility for assessment efforts at their campuses" (López, 2002, p. 356).

As Dr. Saunders well documents, there is a leadership void in higher education that librarians might be able to fulfill—that is, if they are willing to emerge as campus leaders and become an effective voice among accreditation organizations and government. Such leadership will have to come from library directors, who have institutional clout.

The area of student learning outcomes is still in its infancy and represents an excellent opportunity to advance assessment research that can improve the educational experience. It is time to stop confusing evaluation with assessment and apply the excellent literature on assessment issues that have an impact on higher education and the movement to more active learning.

Peter Hernon

Professor

Simmons College, Boston

REFERENCES

American Customer Satisfaction Index. Retrieved from http://www.theacsi.org/index.php?option=com_content&task=view&id=49&Itemid=28

López, C. L. (2002). Assessment of student learning: Challenges and strategies. *Journal of Academic Librarianship, 28*(6), 356–367.

ACKNOWLEDGMENTS

This book grew out of research undertaken for my dissertation, and would not have been possible without the input, support, and critical eye of Peter Hernon as well as Bob Dugan and Abbie Frost.

Thank you also to my boys: Dave, James, and Will.

CHAPTER 1

Introduction

Current trends in American higher education emphasize the higher-order thinking skills of evaluation, analysis, and synthesis of information as defined by Bloom's (1956) taxonomy, over the more basic skills of comprehension and recall fostered by curricula that stress rote memorization and repetition of facts. The shift toward higher-order abilities is underscored by increased attention to active learning methods such as problem-based, inquiry-based, and discovery learning, which challenge students to actively engage with information and resources to solve problems and create knowledge (Levine, 2007; Prince & Felder, 2007; Walsh & Cuba, 2009). Such approaches to instruction offer challenges that "serve as precursors to intellectual development" and "encourage students to adopt a deep approach to learning" (Prince & Felder, 2007). In a 1998 report, the Boyer Commission on Educating Undergraduates in a Research University called on universities to improve educational outcomes by offering an integrated learning experience based on inquiry and problem solving.

The goal of such an education is to produce students who do not simply absorb and regurgitate information but apply their knowledge, abilities, and skills across diverse situations and experiences. While each institution, and each program and course within an institution, emphasizes different competencies in line with their mission, values, and goals, certain abilities are applicable to all students across institutions and disciplines. Indeed, surveys of educators, business leaders, and higher-education administrators find "widespread agreement about desired outcomes of a college education already exists" (Project on Accreditation and Assessment, 2004, p. 2). Broadly speaking, these stakeholders stress the importance of a general, liberal education that emphasizes communication skills (written and oral), critical thinking, quantitative reasoning, problem solving, and lifelong learning (American Council of Trustees and Alumni [ACTA], 2009; Leef, 2003; National Leadership Council for Liberal Education and America's Promise, 2007; Project on Accreditation and Assessment, 2004).

Information literacy, broadly defined as the ability to evaluate, synthesize, and apply information (American Library Association [ALA], 1989), has been repeatedly linked to critical thinking and lifelong learning (see, e.g., Albitz, 2007; Alfino, Pajer, Pierce, & Jenks, 2008; Amudhavalli, 2008; Breivik, 2005; Ward, 2006), and as such has garnered the attention of those who support liberal education. Like other competencies highlighted as general education outcomes, the importance of information literacy centers on its applicability across fields of study and disciplines, and the fact that it is linked to critical thinking and lifelong learning. Because students who have learned information literacy skills can address their own learning needs after graduation (Breivik, 2000), information literacy is essential to lifelong learning.

The Project on Accreditation and Assessment (2004), the National Leadership Council for Liberal Education and America's Promise (LEAP, 2007), and the Lumina Foundation (2011) each include information literacy as one of the essential learning outcomes for a liberal education. Likewise, all of the regional accreditation organizations include information literacy in their standards, with three of them explicitly using the phrase "information literacy," and the others using equivalent language (Gratch-Lindauer, 2002; Saunders, 2007). The Middle States Commission on Higher Education (hereafter Middle States Commission) has the most extensive set of expectations, including the textbook *Developing Communication and Research Skills* (Middle States Commission, 2003), which discusses planning, implementing, and assessing an information literacy program.

A BRIEF HISTORY OF INFORMATION LITERACY

Information literacy is not a new concept, even though widespread recognition of its importance in higher education is relatively recent. Paul Zurkowski coined the term in 1974 to describe the skills and abilities to use information tools that he perceived would be necessary to deal with the rapid increase in information. In fact, the ability to access, evaluate, and use information to which Zurkowski referred has roots in bibliographic instruction traditionally carried out by academic librarians.

Bibliographic instruction evolved as both a concept and a practice along with the development of higher education in the United States. Academic libraries of the seventeenth, eighteenth, and early nineteenth centuries in the United States often had small collections relative to their European counterparts and offered patrons limited physical access to collections. Librarians focused on acquiring and organizing materials, leaving patrons to search on their own. Indeed, many of these libraries had closed stacks; patrons requested particular publications that the library staff retrieved for them. At this time, librarians were engaged primarily as scholars and faculty members who staffed the library in addition to their other responsibilities (Lorenzen, 2001; Weiner, 2005).

To a great extent, the development of academic libraries reflected the changes in higher education in general (Weiner, 2005). Early American colleges and universities generally applied a fixed classical curriculum, relying almost exclusively on assigned readings from textbooks (Weiner, 2005). With the birth of the modern American university in the mid-to-late nineteenth century (discussed in depth in Chapter 2), curricula expanded and graduate instruction increased, and so did the need for academic libraries to support the new curricula. The shift in curricula drove academic libraries to amass larger collections, which in turn "created a need to educate patrons in how to use these larger, more complicated collections" (Lorenzen, 2001, p. 8).

As students sought greater access to library resources and conducted more independent literature searches, librarians found that students often needed assistance in finding materials. Because librarians were usually intimately acquainted with their local collections, they might help patrons find and use the materials located there, but this was not a recognized part of their job in early years. Over time, however, many academic libraries designated staff to assist patrons with searching and show them how to use tools such as the card catalog to find and access materials. These staff members were the precursors to modern reference and instruction librarians (Rothstein, 1955).

Since most early librarians were also professors of a discipline, it is likely that these faculty incorporated use of the library into their instruction, but there is little evidence that they devoted entire courses or classes to the topic (Lorenzen, 2001). The concept of the library-teacher was realized at University of Michigan in 1875, when the Board of Regents formally requested that librarian Raymond C. Davis offer a series of lectures on the book and bibliography. This explicit request for a librarian to teach indicates that the Regents expected that some instruction on methods and tools was necessary for successful use of the library (Abbott, 1957). Indeed, Davis (1986) noted the students' limited familiarity with reference sources and the lack of understanding of basic tools such as the card catalogs and indices, and he developed his lectures to orient students to the use of the library and its resources. Several years later, the faculty approved Davis's outline for a course based on his lectures, which was offered as an elective, credit-bearing class.

Throughout the rest of the nineteenth century and into the early twentieth century, prominent proponents of academic libraries, such as Melvil Dewey and Harvie Branscomb, asserted the centrality of the library to education and promoted librarians as teachers who would leave the library and assist faculty in the classroom (Lorenzen, 2001). The idea of the academic library as the "heart of the university" is attributed to a speech given by Charles Eliot, president of Harvard University, in 1873 (Weiner, 2005). With the support of these leaders, academic libraries continued to expand their collections and services, including instruction in the use of resources.

In an address delivered at the College of William and Mary in 1912, William Warner Bishop "described the exponential growth in the production of books and recommended training in the use of books to help students and professors deal intelligently with the deluge" (Hardesty, Schmitt, & Tucker, 1986, p. 69). Shaw (1928) maintained a need to restructure what he saw as the "haphazard, unscientific teaching" taking place in most academic libraries. He proposed required courses that would meet weekly and would be supported by staff with "adequate teaching ability." Further, he asserted that colleges and universities should create departments of bibliography and "evolve and train . . . a group of bibliographic instructors, a new species which will combine . . . the librarian's knowledge of books and bibliographic procedure with the instructor's ability in teaching method" (p. 109). This is one of the first calls for librarians to systematically train and designate staff for the purpose of instruction (Lorenzen, 2001).

Hardesty et al. (1986) view the years between the two world wars as a time of support for academic libraries. The initiation of the Carnegie Corporation's book collection and support program (Carnegie Corporation of New York, 2003; Weiner, 2005)[1] encouraged institutions of higher education to view the library as more central to education. In the years following World War II, bibliographic instruction programs did not make many advances. Greater numbers of people attended college during this time, with the passage of the GI Bill. However, the funding that came with increased enrollment was not often directed toward library instruction. Instead, most of the money went to books and building projects, leaving librarians who offered instruction struggling to keep pace with demand. Hardesty et al. (1986) state that "[l]ibrary use instruction during this period can be characterized as activity without progress" (p. 148). Lorenzen (2001) notes that "articles on academic library instruction become scarce between the late 1930s and the 1960s" (p. 10), and points out that nearly 50 years passed between Shaw's (1928) call for dedicated instruction librarians and the publication of an article that described the implementation of a library position primarily focused on teaching.

Despite some stagnation during this period, Patricia Knapp (1966) conducted and wrote about the Monteith Library Project, an important study related to library use in higher education. The project took place at Wayne State University from 1960 to 1962. As director of the research, Knapp studied problem-solving techniques of undergraduates in the library, including the use of assignments involving understanding and use of the library. As a testament to the difficulties facing library instruction at this time, she and her colleagues met with strong resistance from both students and teaching faculty. Nevertheless, she argued that competency in library research is a liberal art that is often ignored by subject faculty, making intervention by the librarian important. Above all, Knapp advocated a program of guiding and instructing students in the use of library resources, sometimes called the pathfinder program, rather than just providing them with answers to questions (Hemming, 2005).

By the late 1960s, library instruction, often referred to as bibliographic instruction, "emerged as a vital force in academic librarianship" (Hardesty et al., 1986, p. 227), and this decade is typically regarded as the beginning of modern library instruction. The founding of professional associations focused on library instruction underscores the more coordinated efforts of academic librarians to offer instruction to students. In 1967, academic librarians involved in instruction founded the Instruction in the Use of Libraries Committee, later renamed the Library Instruction Round Table, under the umbrella of the American Library Association (ALA). Five years later, the Library Orientation Exchange (LOEX) was founded to serve as a clearinghouse for library instruction materials and a host for annual conferences on library instruction. The Association of College and Research Libraries (ACRL) initiated its own Instruction Section in 1977 (Salony, 1995).

Salony (1995) describes the 1980s as the second generation of bibliographic instruction, maintaining that the movement gained recognition as a public service, and that more effort was concentrated on the concepts and theories forming the foundation of the service. Indeed, she found that the number of articles on library instruction in the *Library Literature* index increased from 94 in 1955–1957 to 147 in 1967–1969 and 262 in 1984–1985. By the late twentieth century, library instruction had become "mainstream, occupying an accepted, respected, and expected place in librarianship (especially in academic librarianship)" (Martin & Jacobson, 1995, p. 5), with 65 percent of academic libraries offering some sort of library instruction in 1987 as compared to 24 percent in 1979 (Salony, 1995).

Developments in higher education and in technology have had vast influence on the evolution of library instruction. In particular, the advent of the Internet and the widespread access to information it engenders has forced librarians to rethink both the content and the purpose of their instruction. Historically, bibliographic instruction seems to have focused largely on skills-based instruction. As instruction shifts to dealing with online resources, students need to learn how to find and access a more expansive variety of information, and to develop the transferable and critical thinking skills of evaluation and synthesis of information (Salony, 1995). In essence, information literacy is "more ambitious instructional engagement" than traditional library instruction because it seeks to "go beyond teaching mainly retrieval skills, to addressing a more total research environment in the course of finding and using information/knowledge" (Owusu-Ansah, 2004, p. 5). In refocusing their instruction, librarians also reexamine pedagogical practices. Like other teaching faculty, librarians are shifting from traditional lecture-based instruction to incorporation of active learning techniques (e.g., Downey, Ramin,

& Byerly, 2008; Munro, 2006; Smith, 2007), a widely accepted approach in which students are engaged in discovering and creating knowledge, based on a constructivist approach to learning (Allen, 1995). The shift in content and pedagogy from skills-based to concept-based instruction marked the beginning of the shift in focus away from library instruction and toward information literacy.

DEVELOPMENT OF INFORMATION LITERACY

Librarians led the way in defining and promoting the concept of information literacy. In 1989, ALA convened a committee of education and library leaders that outlined the concept of information literacy. The committee's *Final Report* describes an information-literate person as one who can "recognize when information is needed and have the ability to locate, evaluate, and use effectively the needed information," and asserted that to achieve "such a citizenry will require that schools and colleges appreciate and integrate the concept of information literacy into their learning programs" (American Library Association, 1989, para. 3). The report details the need for and benefits of an information-literate society, asserting that information-literate individuals have a capacity for lifelong learning, and suggesting that the abilities to access and use information could help balance some socioeconomic disparities. Although the focus of this report is on the need for information literacy, and the definition laid out remains broad, this seminal report helped bring information literacy to the attention of various education and government stakeholders.

In response to the ALA Committee report, the National Forum on Information Literacy was convened in 1989. This coalition of organizations includes representatives from business, government, and education who are committed to promoting information literacy globally. While interest in information literacy grew, discussion on the definition continued. A paper presented at the 1989 LOEX Conference defined information literacy as "understanding the role and power of information, having the ability to locate it, retrieve it, and use it in decision making, and having the ability to generate and manipulate it using electronic processes" (Olsen & Coons, 1989, p. 8). The same year, Breivik and Gee (1989) called information literacy "a survival skill in the information age" (p. 12), and a 1992 report to the National Forum on Information Literacy made an explicit connection among information literacy, critical thinking, and problem solving (Doyle, 1992). In 1998, the American Association of School Libraries (AASL) and the Association of Educational Communications and Technology (AECT) published *Information Literacy Standards for Student Learning*, which outlined the skills and knowledge considered necessary for K–12 students (American Library Association, American Association of School Libraries, and Association of Educational Communications and Technology, 1998).

Within higher education, however, ALA's Association of College and Research Libraries (ACRL) created the most widespread and influential definition of information literacy with the publication of *Information Literacy Competency Standards for Higher Education* in 2000. Acknowledging the lack of national standards for information literacy, ACRL established a task force to build on the work of AASL/AECT and develop a set of standards for higher education, which was approved on January 18, 2000 (American Library Association, Association of College and Research Libraries, Task Force on Information Literacy Competency Standards, 2000).

The standards outlined in *Information Literacy Competency Standards for Higher Education* offer a "framework for assessing the information literate individual ... [and] outline the process by which faculty, librarians, and others pinpoint specific indicators that identify a student as information literate" (American Library Association, Association of College and Research Libraries, Task Force on Information Literacy Competency Standards, 2000, p. 212). The definition presents five competency areas[2] along with 22 performance indicators, which offer further detail on the competencies. Finally, possible outcomes are listed for each performance indicator to assist instructors in assessing learning for each area. According to the standards, an information-literate individual:

- Determines the nature and extent of an information need
- Accesses needed information efficiently and effectively
- Evaluates information and its sources critically and incorporates selected knowledge into his or her knowledge base and value system
- Uses information to accomplish a specific purpose
- Understands the legal, economic, social, and ethical implications of information

These general standards are now supplemented by more discipline-specific standards. As discussed in Chapter 11, ACRL offers standards for several disciplines, including anthropology, science, and English literature. The new sets of standards adapt the general standards by offering objectives and performance indicators specific to the subject area. Acceptance of the definition provided by ALA and ACRL has been widespread. Both the American Association of Higher Education (Breivik, 2000) and the Council of Independent Colleges (2004) endorse the ACRL *Information Literacy Competency Standards*.

INFORMATION LITERACY AS A LEARNING OUTCOME

Researchers and higher-education policymakers have identified certain broad areas of knowledge as essential for all college graduates, regardless of a specific major or field of study. Sometimes called learning outcomes, these areas describe "not only the knowledge leading to understanding but also abilities, habits of mind, ways of knowing, attitudes, values, and other dispositions" (Maki, 2004, p. 3) expected of students. Information literacy is included along with other outcomes such as critical thinking, written and oral communication skills, and quantitative reasoning as an essential learning outcome applicable to all students across disciplines (National Council on Liberal Education and America's Promise, 2007; Project for Accreditation and Assessment, 2004). Breivik (2005) describes information literacy as a "kind of critical thinking ability ... but a person who is information literate specifically uses critical thinking to negotiate our information-overloaded existence" (p. 23). Amudhavalli (2008) calls information literacy a "survival skill in the information age" (p. 48).

In the same vein, the U.S. Department of Labor (1991) identifies the ability to acquire and evaluate data and interpret and communicate information as core competencies necessary to be successful in the workplace. Similarly, the National Center for Education Statistics (NCES) names critical thinking skills, including the ability to find and evaluate information, as among the most important skills for college graduates to possess (Jones, 1995). The Association of American Colleges and Universities Board of Directors (2004) identifies "strong analytical communication, quantitative and *information skills* [emphasis added]" as the first of their five key educational outcomes for higher education (p. 5).

Accreditation organizations also underscore the importance of information literacy as a learning outcome to college graduates by including such outcomes in their standards. Successive studies (Gratch-Lindauer, 2000; Saunders, 2007) show that regional accreditation organizations, the six organizations that oversee the accreditation of organizations in specific geographic regions of the United States, give increased attention to information literacy outcomes in recent versions of their standards. Indeed, of the six accreditation organizations, only one offers minimal coverage of information literacy within its standards, four have significant coverage, and one falls in between (Saunders, 2007).

Of the six regional accreditation organizations, the Middle States Commission (2002) has the most explicit and comprehensive set of standards related to information literacy as a learning outcome. In fact, Oswald Ratteray, formerly the assistant director of constituent services and special programs at the Middle States Commission, served on the task force that developed the ACRL *Information Literacy Competency Standards*. His work on the task force helped to extend the influence of the standards beyond librarians. Indeed, two years after the publication of the *Information Literacy Competency Standards*, the Middle States Commission revised its own standards for accreditation to include more specific and extensive requirements for information literacy.

The Middle States Commission was an early proponent of information literacy, having first implemented a standard on information literacy in

1994 that supports library orientation and instruction in the access and use of resources. A year later, the Middle States Commission sponsored two events for institutions with successful information literacy programs. These symposia resulted in a commitment to help institutions share experiences in developing information literacy programs, and a belief that information literacy is a component of lifelong learning (Eisenberg, Lowe, & Spitzer, 2004).

The 2002 edition of the Middle States Standards for Accreditation is not the first to include information literacy, but it is even more explicit in the commission's expectation that information literacy must be included as a student learning outcome. In addition, these standards are supported by other publications aimed at assisting institutions in implementing information literacy programs, namely *Developing Research and Communication Skills* in 2003, and *Student Learning Assessment*, which was updated in 2007. *Developing Research and Communication Skills* serves as a handbook for implementing standards related to learning outcomes for information literacy into the curriculum. Created by Middle States Commission staff, along with an advisory panel made up of academic librarians and library and information science faculty, this publication makes reference to the influence of the ACRL standards. The first part of the book argues for the importance and relevance of information literacy to student success, aligning it with critical thinking and lifelong learning, and calling it "a metaphor for the entire learning experience" (Middle States Commission, 2003, p. 2).

While the other regional accreditation organizations are not as detailed in their coverage of information literacy, each still offers some support for it as a learning outcome. The North Central Association of Colleges and Schools (NCACS, 2003), for example, does not use the phrase information literacy but contends that college graduates must be prepared to be "knowledge workers" in the sense that they must not just master certain information, but they must also comprehend, synthesize, and apply that information. The NCACS maintains that such workers will be valued for their "capacity to sift and winnow massive amounts of information in order to discover or create new or better understandings" (North Central Association of Schools and Colleges, 2003, 3.2–12). Likewise, the Northwest Commission on Colleges and Universities (NWCCU, 2003) emphasizes the library's instructional role, including services that help patrons learn to use resources effectively. The Western Association of Schools and Colleges (WASC, 2001, p. 27), on the other hand, specifically lists information literacy as one of the core learning abilities of a baccalaureate degree. The New England Association of Schools and Colleges (NEASC, 2005, p. 9) links information literacy to lifelong learning and critical thinking, stating within its standards that graduates should exhibit the abilities of "critical analysis and logical thinking; and the capacity for continuing learning, including the skills of information literacy." The Southern Association of Colleges and Schools (SACS) emphasizes the instructional role of the library, indicating that students should receive "regular and timely instruction in the use of library and other learning/information resources" (2008, 3.8.2).

Because the information literacy skills traditionally taught through bibliographic instruction are relevant across the curriculum, the regional accreditation organizations call for partnerships and collaboration between teaching faculty and librarians to integrate information literacy seamlessly into the curriculum. *Developing Research and Communication Skills* (Middle States Commission, 2003) maintains that collaboration can facilitate creativity and help instructors avoid redundancies across the curriculum. The text warns that those institutions that relegate information literacy to one-shot sessions will be "placing itself at the lower end of information literacy delivery" (p. 21).

In support of and to help facilitate such collaboration, *Developing Research and Communication Skills* presents a framework suggesting how faculty and librarians might divide responsibilities for information literacy instruction. The framework lists the five competencies drawn directly from the ACRL standards, and, for each competency area, it indicates who should lead and who should support instruction in that area. The rest of the publication offers detailed advice on steps to integrate information literacy into the curriculum as well as suggestions for developing and assessing specific program and course-related learning outcomes.

Student Learning Assessment (Middle States Commission, 2007) is a general text providing resources and advice for assessing learning, but it too demonstrates the Middle States Commission's support for information literacy as a learning outcome. This publication addresses the five competencies of information literacy, acknowledges the role library research plays in information literacy, and stresses the importance of collaboration between faculty and librarians in information literacy instruction and assessment. Indeed, the publication reminds institutions of the importance of sharing assessment feedback with the librarians who "design and deliver significant components of the information literacy requirement" (p. 60).

In a related article, Ratteray (2002) offered institutions further guidance on how to address information literacy outcomes within their self-studies as they prepare for accreditation reviews. While upholding institutional autonomy in deciding on specific outcomes and assessment measures for information literacy, he also stresses the need to address information literacy as a general student learning outcome, and not only as a library skill or responsibility. As such, he asserts the need for high levels of collaboration between teaching faculty and librarians. In support of such collaboration, Ratteray presents a framework similar to that in *Developing Research and Communication Skills* (see Figure 1.1). In addition to offering information literacy competencies, and suggestions for lead and supporting roles, this framework identified "critical loci for instruction," or possible areas in

Figure 1.1 Middle States Commission Framework for Information Literacy*

Potential Objectives for an Assessment Plan	Lead Instructional Responsibility	Critical Loci of Instruction (Potential Sources for Data)
Determining nature and extent of an information need	Faculty lead; Librarians support	Classroom discussions; Individual consultations; Online tutorials; Peer-group discussions; Other mentors
Accessing information effectively and efficiently	Librarians lead; Faculty support	Classroom discussions; Individual consultations; Online tutorials; Peer-group discussions; Other mentors
Evaluating critically sources and content of information	Librarians lead on critique of sources; Faculty lead on critique of content	Classroom discussions; Individual consultations; Online tutorials; Peer-group discussions; Other mentors
Incorporating information in learner's knowledge base and value system	Faculty lead; Librarian may be asked to support	Classroom discussions; Individual consultations; Online tutorials; Peer-group discussions; Other mentors
Using information to effectively accomplish a specific purpose	Faculty lead; Librarians may be asked to support	Artistic performance; Project demonstration; Classroom discussions; Individual consultations; Online tutorials; Peer-group discussions; Other mentors
Understanding economic, legal, and social issues in the use of information and technology	Faculty and librarians (individually, jointly, and continuously)	Plans or rehearsals for projects/performances; Classroom discussions; Individual consultations; Online tutorials; Peer-group discussions; Other mentors

* Reprinted from "Information literacy in self-study and accreditation," by O. M. T. Ratteray, 2002, *Journal of Academic Librarianship. 28*(6), p. 371, with permission from Elsevier.

which learning might occur and data might be produced that could be used for assessment of student learning (p. 371).

ASSESSMENT OF INFORMATION LITERACY LEARNING OUTCOMES

Regional accreditation organizations focus assessment of student learning outcomes on the institutional and program levels more than on the course level. Course-level learning outcomes define the specific content and skills that students should attain within a course. Those course-level learning outcomes in aggregate, including other program experiences such as internships and cocurricular activities, spell out the program-level goals. Program-level goals, integrated with general education and other institutional outcomes, lead to institutional goals. Thus, program-level assessment offers insight into student learning at the macro level and indicates how well programs are achieving their learning outcome goals. Each institution needs a coherent hierarchy of outcomes, where "goals at the subordinate levels contribute to attainment of goals at the higher levels" (Middle States Commission, 2007, p. 12). The Middle States Commission (2007) offers suggestions for gathering evidence to apply to program-level assessment, such as senior capstone projects, student portfolios, surveys, and standardized tests.

By including information literacy as a learning outcome within their standards, regional accreditation organizations expect student learning to be assessed at the program and institutional levels. Such assessment entails information literacy learning outcomes defined at both the program level and the institutional level. The Middle States Commission (2007) contends that librarians can contribute to assessment of information literacy learning outcomes as they play "a critical role in the process of enhancing student learning" (p. 6). However, since faculty set course- and program-level goals and conduct most of the instruction, such assessment ideally requires a partnership between both faculty and librarians.

Some librarians have been able to work with faculty to assess information literacy within the general education program (Diller & Phelps, 2008; Scharf, Elliot, Huey, Briller, & Joshi, 2007). In such instances, librarians work with general education faculty to establish learning goals for information literacy, sometimes related to rubrics,[3] and develop assignments or projects against which to measure learning. Since general education classes are usually taken within the first two years of study, the results of these assessment projects set a baseline for future evaluations as students continue through their major programs of study.

Examples of program-level assessment, even for general education programs, are rare, however. The majority of institutions assessing information literacy are doing so at the course or session level, rather than at the program level (e.g., Houlson, 2007; Sharma, 2006). For instance, librarians who teach information literacy courses embed assignments such as papers, portfolios, or tests and quizzes. Although these instructors often link the learning-outcome goals of the class to those of the general education program, the assessment does not extend beyond the course. Indeed, during an ACRL OnPoint (American Library Association, Association of College and Research Libraries, 2009) session, "What Really Are Student Learning Outcomes?" convened by Peter Hernon, the majority of participants indicated that assessment of information literacy outcomes was taking place at the course level, and some expressed confusion about what is program-level assessment. Others noted that without the faculty cooperation to integrate information literacy into the wider curriculum, librarians could not move forward with program-level assessment. Nevertheless, Figure 1.1 indicates that collaboration is expected and essential to achieving thorough assessment of learning outcomes for information literacy beyond the course or session level.

DEBATING DEFINITIONS

Despite apparent agreement on the necessity of students having information literacy abilities and the widespread acceptance of the ACRL definition, "discussions on the topic are still plagued with concerns of whether the concept of information literacy has been defined clearly and adequately enough to permit deliberations on how to achieve information literacy" (Owusu-Ansah, 2003, p. 219). For instance, some librarians lament the skills-based emphasis of the ALA and ACRL definitions as reductionist and argue that information literacy should be viewed as "a phenomena more deeply connected with people's formal and informal meaning-making activities in all contexts" (Lloyd, 2005, p. 570). Budd (2008) likewise sees current conceptualizations as too formulaic and process-based and proposes a more constructivist approach he calls the "phenomenological cognitive approach," which emphasizes the students' meaning-making interactions with information and with each other. Owusu-Ansah (2005) mentions a number of examples of cognitive views of information literacy, including:

- Doyle's (1992) description of information literacy as a 10-step progression through an information task
- Kuhlthau's (1993) assertion that information literacy is not a set of skills but a way of learning characterized by a six-stage process: task initiation, topic selection, prefocus exploration, focus formulation, information collection, and search closure
- Bruce's (1997) characterization of information literacy within a thinking-reasoning framework

Other librarians object to the generic nature of the original ACRL definition, indicating that it is overly broad (Lloyd, 2005; Manuel, 2004; Simmons, 2005). In their view, by being overly broad, the *Information Literacy Competency Standards* create a "tension between generality/universality and discipline-specificity" (Manuel, 2004, p. 280). While most discussions of information literacy are "ahistorical and decontextualized" (Manuel, 2004, p. 280), information literacy can also be seen as context dependent. The implication is that individuals who are considered information literate in one area may not be so in another area, depending on their areas of expertise (Lloyd, 2005). In this view, it is necessary to place information literacy in the context of academic disciplines and have instruction librarians function as discourse mediators who help students to recognize and transition among the information-seeking practices of different disciplines (Simmons, 2005).

While many librarians argue over the definition of information literacy, others suggest the term *information literacy* is limiting because it is so strongly associated with librarians (Ratteray, 2002). Indeed, within its 1994 standards, the Middle States Commission included information literacy only within the library sections. However, Ratteray (2002) posits that the strong link between information literacy and libraries may lead some faculty and administrators to "marginalize information literacy as the librarian's 'turf,' " leading some faculty to "feel absolved of any need to take a great interest in, or to feel a responsibility for, information literacy in the curriculum" (p. 369). While some faculty may be slow to adopt information literacy in their classrooms, not all librarians are eager to share information literacy with teaching faculty.

Because information literacy offers librarians a vehicle for becoming involved in instruction and curriculum planning, some librarians limit their focus to those aspects of information literacy that apply to the library. In an e-mail posting to the information literacy listserv ILI-l hosted by ALA, Ratteray (2005) lamented the tendency in librarians to reduce information literacy to "a subset of its components (effectively Standards 1, 2, and part of 5 from a librarian's perspective)."[4] He further asserted that the Middle States Commission "dropped the ball in 2002" by not including discipline faculty on the advisory board that created *Developing Research and Communication Skills* (Middle States Commission, 2003), thereby further implying that information literacy "belongs" to librarians. Finally, Ratteray reiterates the Middle States Commission's stance that "real" information literacy goes "way beyond anything having to do with the library or 'research' in its technical library-based sense," and that "faculty and students are at the center of this learning universe, and librarians are important supporters and facilitators" (2005, para. 3).

Despite such support for collaboration, tensions between librarians and faculty persist. Librarians frequently refer to faculty reticence as a barrier to collaboration, and indeed, evidence of such hesitance on the part of the faculty exists. On the other hand, not all librarians are anxious to collaborate with faculty. While Ratteray suggests that librarians play a largely supportive role in information literacy instruction, some librarians seem to promote library ownership of information literacy. Owusu-Ansah (2004, 2007) argues repeatedly for academic libraries to be given status as academic departments so librarians can offer stand-alone, credit-bearing information literacy courses.

In response to these debates over definitions and roles and responsibilities, some writers have suggested alternate terms for describing information literacy. In the same listserv posting of 2005, Ratteray applauded librarian Kathy DeMay for suggesting that the subset of components of information literacy having to do with the library could be renamed "research fluency." However, in many fields, the word research denotes empirical research or research studies, rather than library research. As such, "research fluency" may not be a suitable substitute, but might in fact confuse the issue further. The Associated Colleges of the South (2006) created programs around "information fluency," which it defines as "the optimal outcome when critical thinking skills are combined with information literacy and relevant computing skills" (final paragraph). Instead of describing individuals as information literate, Lloyd (2005) suggests the terms "engaged, enabled, enriched, and embodied" (p. 570). Thus far, however, no other term has achieved the widespread use or recognition that information literacy has. Further, Owusu-Ansah (2005) argues that from a library perspective, none of these terms strays far from the initial definition proposed by ALA in 1989, and that the continued "debates create impressions of potential conflict when really there are none" (p. 367). Rather than arguing the fine points of the definition, librarians should view the ACRL standards as a living document that can be amended and changed. Indeed, ACRL (2000) intends for those using the standards to adapt them in light of the mission and values of the institution and/or discipline or program in which they are being used. As such, the standards are less a fully realized definition, and more a framework to be manipulated within the context of their application.

CONCLUSION

Attention to the topic of information literacy outside of library and information science is relatively recent. Although various groups identify information literacy as an important learning outcome, acceptance is not universal. Indeed, the concept of information literacy continues to be associated largely with librarians and library skills, and many faculty have been reluctant to embrace it. In some cases, faculty assume that students already have the competencies, and in other cases, they regard it as the responsibility of the student and the librarian to be addressed outside of a course. Although accreditation organizations assert the importance of information literacy, it is unclear how deeply information literacy–learning outcomes have permeated institutional cultures and have been adopted and promoted by administrators and faculty. Likewise, while accreditation organizations clearly support collaboration between faculty and librarians in information literacy, librarians identify many barriers to such collaboration. The role of accreditation organizations is to establish standards such as those related to information literacy, and to facilitate quality improvement in higher education by assisting institutions in identifying and assessing progress toward learning outcomes. The next chapter examines the role of accreditation organizations within the history of higher education in the United States, and how these organizations affect the development of learning outcomes like information literacy.

NOTES

1. In the 1930s and 1940s, the Corporation spent nearly $2.5 million in grants to develop libraries and purchase books at 200 liberal arts colleges. Two hundred and forty-eight libraries received money to build collections, and 108 institutions received money to use toward building projects. The corporation focused on institutions that were willing to provide adequate financial support to their libraries.

2. The third competency area—evaluating information and incorporating selected information into the knowledge base—is often separated into two separate competencies (Middle States Commission, 2003). Throughout the rest of this study, the author refers to six information literacy competency areas.

3. Rubrics are tools that define the ability or knowledge expected of students at different levels, such as novice, intermediate, and proficient. Such rubrics can be used as scoring tools for assignments.

4. American Library Association, Association of College and Research Libraries (2000). Standard One provides a general overview of "the need for information." Standard Two covers locating and accessing information, and Standard Five is the ethical use of information.

REFERENCES

Abbott, J. C. (1957). *Raymond Cazallis Davis and the University of Michigan general library 1877–1905*. Retrieved from Proquest Research.

Albitz, R. S. (2007). The what and who of information literacy and critical thinking in higher education. *portal: Libraries and the Academy, 7*(1), 97–109. Retrieved from Project MUSE.

Alfino, M., Pajer, M., Pierce, L., & Jenks, K. O. (2008). Advancing critical thinking and information literacy skills in first year college students. *College and Undergraduate Libraries, 15*(1–2), 81–98. Retrieved from H. W. Wilson.

Allen, E. E. (1995). Active learning and teaching: Improving postsecondary library instruction. *Reference Librarian, 51–52*, 89–103. Retrieved from Haworth Press Journals.

American Library Association. (1989). *Presidential committee on information literacy: Final report*. Chicago, IL: Author. Retrieved from http://www.ala.org/ala/mgrps/divs/acrl/publications/whitepapers/presidential.cfm

American Library Association, American Association of School Librarians, and Association for Educational Communications and Technologies National Guidelines Vision Committee. (1998). *Information literacy standards for student learning*. Retrieved from http://www.ala.org/ala/mgrps/divs/aasl/aaslarchive/pubsarchive/informationpower/InformationLiteracyStandards_final.pdf

American Library Association, Association of College and Research Libraries. (2000). *Information literacy competency standards for higher education*.

Retrieved from http://www.ala.org/ala/mgrps/divs/acrl/standards/informationliteracycompetency.cfm

American Library Association, Association of College and Research Libraries. (2009, January 14). *Student learning outcomes, the culture of assessment, and accrediting agencies.* Retrieved from http://www.ala.org/ala/mgrps/divs/acrl/events/onpoint/archives/2009-01-14.cfm

American Library Association, Association of College and Research Libraries, Task Force on Information Literacy Standards. (2000). Information literacy competency standards for higher education: The final version, approved January 2000. *College and Research Libraries News, 61*(3), 207–215. Retrieved from H. W. Wilson.

Amudhavalli, A. (2008). Information literacy and higher education competency standards. *DESIDOC Journal of Library and Information Technology, 28*(2), 48–55.

Associated Colleges of the South. (2006). *Information fluency working definition.* Retrieved from http://www.colleges.org/techcenter/if/if_definition.html

Association of American Colleges and Universities Board of Directors. (2004). *Our students' best work: A framework for accountability worthy of our mission.* Washington, DC: Association of American Colleges and Universities.

Boyer Commission on Educating Undergraduates in the Research University. (1998). *Reinventing undergraduate education: A blueprint for America's research universities.* Stony Brook, NY: State University of New York.

Breivik, P. S. (2000). Information literacy and the engaged campus. *AAHE Bulletin, 53*, 3–6. Retrieved from http://www.aahea.org/bulletins/articles/nov2000_1.htm

Breivik, P. S. (2005). Twenty-first century learning and information literacy. *Change, 37*(2), 20–27. Retrieved from Ebsco.

Breivik, P. S., & Gee, G. E. (1989). *Information literacy: Revolution in the library.* New York, NY: MacMillan.

Bruce, C. (1997). *The seven faces of information literacy.* Adelaide, Australia: Auslib Press.

Budd, J. M. (2008). Cognitive growth, instruction, and student success. *College and Research Libraries, 69*(4), 319–330. Retrieved from H. W. Wilson.

Carnegie Corporation of New York. (2003). *A short history of Carnegie Corporation's library program.* Retrieved from http://carnegie.org/publications/carnegie-reporter/single/view/article/item/100/

Council of Independent Colleges. (2004). CIC endorses ACRL Information literacy competency standards. *Independent Online Newsletter.* Retrieved from http://www.cic.edu/publications

Davis, R. C. (1986). Teaching bibliography in colleges. In L. L. Hardesty, J. P. Schmitt, & J. M. Tucker (Eds.), *User instruction in academic libraries: A century of selected readings* (pp. 35–45). Metuchen, NJ: Scarecrow Press.

Diller, K. R., & Phelps, S. F. (2008). Learning outcomes, portfolios, and rubrics, oh my! Authentic assessment of an information literacy program. *portal: Libraries and the Academy, 8*(1), 75–89. Retrieved from Project MUSE.

Downey, A., Ramin, L., & Byerly, G. (2008). Simple ways to add active learning to your library instruction. *Texas Library Journal, 84*(2), 52–54. Retrieved from H. W. Wilson.

Doyle, C. S. (1992). *Final report to the National Forum on Information Literacy.* Syracuse, NY: ERIC Clearinghouse on Information and Technology.

Eisenberg, M., Lowe, C. A., & Spitzer, K. L. (2004). *Information literacy: Essential skills for the information age.* Westport, CT: Libraries Unlimited.

Gratch-Lindauer, B. (2002). Comparing the regional accreditation standards: Outcomes assessment and other trends. *Journal of Academic Librarianship, 28* (1–2), 14–25. Retrieved from H. W. Wilson.

Hardesty, L. L., Schmitt, J. P., & Tucker, J. M. (1986). *User instruction in academic libraries: A century of selected readings.* Metuchen, NJ: Scarecrow Press.

Hemming, W. (2005). Online pathfinders: Toward an experience-centered model. *Reference Services Review, 33*(1), 66–87. Retrieved from Emerald.

Houlson, V. (2007). Getting results from one-shot instruction: A workshop for first-year students. *College and Undergraduate Libraries, 14*(1), 89–108. Retrieved from Informaworld.

Jones, E. A. (1995). *National assessment of college student learning: Identifying college graduates' essential skills in writing, speech and listening, and critical thinking.* Washington, DC: National Center for Education Statistics.

Knapp, P. (1966). *The Monteith College library experiment.* New York, NY: Scarecrow Press.

Kuhlthau, C. C. (1993). *Seeking meaning: A process approach to library and information services.* Norwood, NJ: Ablex Publishing.

Leef, G. (2003). *Becoming an educated person.* Retrieved from https://www.goacta.org/publications/downloads/BEPFinal.pdf

Levine, M. (2007). The essential cognitive backpack. *Educational Leadership, 64*(7), 16–22. Retrieved from Ebsco.

Lloyd, A. (2005). Information literacy: Different contexts, different concepts, different truths? *Journal of Librarianship and Information Science, 37*(2), 82–88. Retrieved from Emerald.

Lorenzen, M. (2001). A brief history of library information in the United States of America. *Illinois Libraries, 83*(2), 8–18. Retrieved from H. W. Wilson.

Lumina Foundation. (2011). *The degree qualifications profile.* Indianapolis, IN: Author. Retrieved from http://www.luminafoundation.org/publications/The_Degree_Qualifications_Profile.pdf

Maki, P. (2004). *Assessing for learning: Building a sustainable commitment across the institution.* Sterling, VA: Stylus.

Manuel, K. (2004). Generic and discipline-specific information literacy competencies: The case of the sciences. *Science and Technology Libraries, 24*(3–4), 279–308. Retrieved from Haworth Press Journals.

Martin, L. M., & Jacobson, T. E. (1995). Reflections on maturity: Introduction to "Library instruction revisited: Bibliographic instruction comes of age." *Reference Librarian, 51–52,* 5–13. Retrieved from Haworth Press Journals.

Middle States Commission on Higher Education. (2002). *Characteristics of excellence in higher education.* Philadelphia, PA: Author. Retrieved from http://www.msche.org/publications/CHX06_Aug08REVMarch09.pdf

Middle States Commission on Higher Education. (2003). *Developing research and communication skills: Guidelines for information literacy in the curriculum.* Philadelphia, PA: Author.

Middle States Commission on Higher Education. (2007). *Student learning assessment: Options and resources*. Philadelphia, PA: Author. Retrieved from http://www.msche.org/publications/SLA_Book_0808080728085320.pdf

Munro, K. (2006). Modified problem-based library instruction: A simple reusable instructional design. *College and Undergraduate Libraries, 13*(3), 56–61. Retrieved from Haworth Press Journals.

National Leadership Council for Liberal Education and America's Promise. (2007). *College learning for the new global century*. Washington DC: Association of American Colleges and Universities.

New England Association of Schools and Colleges. (2005). *Standards for accreditation*. Bedford, MA: Author. Retrieved from http://www.neasc.org

North Central Association of Schools and Colleges, Higher Learning Commission. (2003). *Handbook of accreditation* (3rd ed.). Chicago, IL: Higher Learning Commission. Retrieved from http://www.ncahlc.org/download/Handbook03.pdf

Northwest Commission on Colleges and Universities. (2003). *Accreditation handbook*. Redmond, WA: Author. Retrieved from http://www.nwccu.org

Olsen, J. K., & Coons, B. (1989). Cornell University's information literacy program. In *Coping with information illiteracy: Bibliographic instruction for the information age*. Papers presented at the 17th national LOEX library instruction conference held in Ann Arbor, Michigan, May 4–5, 1989.

Owusu-Ansah, E. K. (2003). Information literacy and the academic library: A critical look at a concept and the controversies surrounding it. *Journal of Academic Librarianship, 29*(4), 219–230. Retrieved from H. W. Wilson.

Owusu-Ansah, E. K. (2004). Information literacy and higher education: Placing the academic library in the center of a comprehensive solution. *Journal of Academic Librarianship, 30*(1), 3–16. Retrieved from H. W. Wilson.

Owusu-Ansah, E. K. (2005). Debating definitions of information literacy: Enough is enough! *Library Review, 54*(6), 366–374. Retrieved from Emerald.

Owusu-Ansah, E. K. (2007). Beyond collaboration: Seeking greater scope and centrality for library instruction. *portal: Libraries and the Academy, 7*(4), 415–429. Retrieved from Project MUSE.

Prince, M., & Felder, R. (2007). The many faces of inductive teaching and learning. *Journal of College Science Teaching, 36*(5), 14–20. Retrieved from Ebsco.

Project on Accreditation and Assessment. (2004). *Taking responsibility for the quality of the baccalaureate degree*. Washington, DC: Association of American Colleges and Universities.

Ratteray, O. M. T. (2002). Information literacy in self-study and accreditation. *Journal of Academic Librarianship, 28*(6), 368–375. Retrieved from H. W. Wilson.

Ratteray, O. M. T. (2005, November 20). RE: What to call what we do: Information literacy vs. research fluency (electronic mailing list message). Retrieved from Information Literacy Listserv, http://lists.ala.org/wws/arc/ili-l

Rothstein, S. (1955). *The development of reference services through academic traditions, public library practice, and special librarianship*. Chicago, IL: Association of College and Reference Librarians.

Salony, M. F. (1995). The history of bibliographic instruction: Changing trends from books to the electronic world. *Reference Librarian, 51–52*, 31–51. Retrieved from Haworth Press Journals.

Saunders, L. (2007). Regional accreditation organizations' treatment of information literacy: Definitions, collaboration, and assessment. *Journal of Academic Librarianship, 33*(3), 317–326. Retrieved from H. W. Wilson.

Scharf, D., Elliot, N., Huey, H. A., Briller, V., & Joshi, K. (2007). Direct assessment of information literacy using writing portfolios. *Journal of Academic Librarianship, 33*(4), 462–477. Retrieved from H. W. Wilson's Library Literature.

Sharma, S. (2006). From chaos to clarity: Using the research portfolio to teach and assess information literacy skills. *Journal of Academic Librarianship, 33*(1), 127–135. Retrieved from H. W. Wilson's Library Literature.

Shaw, C. B. (1928). Bibliographic instruction for students. *Library Journal, 53*, 300–301.

Simmons, M. H. (2005). Librarians as disciplinary discourse mediators: Using genre theory to move toward critical information literacy. *portal: Libraries and the Academy, 5*(3), 297–311. Retrieved from Project MUSE.

Smith, F. A. (2007). Perspectives on the . . . pirate-teacher. *Journal of Academic Librarianship, 33*(2), 376–388. Retrieved from H. W. Wilson.

Southern Association of Colleges and Schools. (2008). Principles of accreditation: Foundations for quality enhancement. Decatur, GA: Author. Retrieved from http://www.sacscoc.org/pdf/2008PrinciplesofAccreditation.pdf

US Department of Labor. (1991). *What work requires of schools.* Washington, DC: Author. Retrieved from http://wdr.doleta.gov/SCANS/whatwork/whatwork.pdf

Walsh, D. C., & Cuba, L. (2009). Liberal arts education and the capacity for effective practice: What's holding us back? *Liberal Education, 95(4)*, 32–38. Retrieved from ProQuest.

Ward, D. (2006). Revisioning information literacy for lifelong meaning. *Journal of Academic Librarianship, 32*(4), 396–402. Retrieved from H. W. Wilson.

Weiner, S. G. (2005). The history of academic libraries in the United States: A review of the literature. *Library Philosophy and Practice, 7*(2), 1–12. Retrieved from Ebsco.

Western Association of Schools and Colleges. (2001). *Handbook of accreditation.* Alameda, CA: Author. Retrieved from http://www.wascsenior.org/

Zurkowski, P. B. (1974). *The information service environment relationships and priorities.* Washington, DC: National Commission on Libraries and Information Science.

CHAPTER 2

Accreditation and Higher Education in the United States

Accreditation of higher education provides an important opportunity for the continued development of information literacy as a student learning outcome. Although accreditation organizations serve a number of purposes, one of their core responsibilities is to set standards for quality in education. The self-studies that institutions prepare for accreditation review offers the institutions a chance to reflect on practices, identify areas for improvement, and begin planning for change. By requiring institutions to report on activities in this way, accreditation organizations facilitate the assessment and improvement of learning. As noted in the previous chapter, many accreditation organizations now include information literacy as a possible learning outcome, setting the expectation that institutions might define learning goals for information literacy in their curriculum and assess student progress for learning in this area.

OVERVIEW OF ACCREDITATION

Accreditation of institutions of higher education in the United States, be it program or institutional, is the "primary means by which the quality of higher education institutions and programs is assured in the United States. Accreditation is a form of self-regulation in which colleges, universities and programs have come together to develop standards, policies and procedures for self-examination and judgment by peers" (Council for Higher Education Accreditation [CHEA], 2006b, p. 1). Nongovernmental accreditation organizations oversee the process and are responsible for granting accreditation status to institutions within a specific geographic area, or for a particular professional program or field of study. These accreditation organizations are themselves reviewed for quality and effectiveness by either the federal government, which grants them the authority to operate, or the Council for Higher Education Accreditation (CHEA), an association of colleges, universities, and accreditation organizations that oversees and advocates for higher education accreditation in the United States, or both (Council for Higher Education Accreditation, 2006a).

While professional associations (e.g., the Accreditation Board for Engineering and Technology) and faith-related accreditation organizations (e.g., the Association for Biblical Higher Education) accredit individual programs within a college or university, regional accreditation takes place at the institutional level, offering an overview of the quality and integrity of the overall institution. It is assisted by six affiliated organizations that administer the accreditation process within specific geographic regions (see Table 2.1 for jurisdiction information):

1. Middle States Commission
2. New England Association of Schools and Colleges (NEASC)
3. North Central Association of Colleges and Schools (NCACS)
4. Northwest Commission on Colleges and Universities (NWCCU)
5. Southern Association of Colleges and Schools (SACS)
6. Western Association of Schools and Colleges (WASC)

Each of these organizations publishes standards that establish the criteria by which they assess institutions within their jurisdiction. In addition, accreditation organizations sometimes supplement these standards with additional documents that interpret or expand on the basic standards. For instance, NEASC offers its constituents a document entitled *Student Success S-series* (NEASC, 2008), which gives explanations and examples to guide institutions in documenting student learning outcomes. Likewise, SACS publishes a series of guidelines and position statements intended to assist institutions in fulfilling accreditation requirements by giving examples of accepted practices.

In setting standards and administering the process to gain or retain accredited status, these organizations ensure the quality of the education offered, ascertain that the educational goals match the institutional mission, and assist institutions in ongoing improvement of programs and services in relationship to the institutional mission.

A BRIEF HISTORY OF ACCREDITATION IN THE UNITED STATES

An understanding of the history and evolution of higher education and of accreditation organizations is essential for setting the context for the role

Table 2.1   Regional Accreditation Organizations' Jurisdiction

Name	Regional Authority	URL
Middle States Commission on Higher Education	Washington, DC, New York, Pennsylvania, Delaware, Maryland, New Jersey, Puerto Rico, U.S. Virgin Islands	http://www.msche.org
New England Association of Schools and Colleges	Connecticut, Maine, Massachusetts, New Hampshire, Rhode Island, Vermont, Canada	http://www.neasc.org
North Central Association of Colleges and Schools	Arizona, Arkansas, Colorado, Illinois, Indiana, Iowa, Kansas, Michigan, Minnesota, Missouri, Nebraska, New Mexico, North Dakota, Ohio, Oklahoma, South Dakota, West Virginia, Wisconsin, Wyoming	http://www.ncahigher learningcommission.org
Northwest Commission of Colleges and Universities	Alaska, Washington, Oregon, Idaho, Montana, Nevada, Utah	http://www.nwccu.org
Southern Association of Colleges and Schools	Alabama, Florida, Georgia, Kentucky, Louisiana, Mississippi, North Carolina, South Carolina, Tennessee, Texas, Virginia	http://www.sacscoc.org
Western Association of Schools and Colleges	California, Hawaii, Guam, Pacific Basin	http://www.wascsenior .org/wasc

that accreditation organizations play today in overseeing and setting standards for higher education. This section, which outlines the history and development of regional accreditation within the United States, offers an overview of the current system with its emphasis on assessment for accountability and program improvement.

Overview

Higher education has been embedded in American culture since the colonial period. Nine institutions of higher learning, beginning with Harvard in 1636, were founded in colonial America. As the country grew and expanded after the Revolutionary War, so did the system of higher education. Most institutions based their curriculum largely on those in Western Europe with which Americans were familiar. Still, these institutions developed uniquely American attributes (Church & Sedlak, 1989).

The United States never established a government-sponsored national university similar to those in most European countries. Indeed, early in the nation's history, plans for a national university placed in Washington, D.C., were discussed but never implemented. As a result, the higher-education system in the United States has remained decentralized (Domonkos, 1989). In the absence of a coordinated system, each institution developed strong ties to its surrounding community. One reason for these ties is that it was seen as the primary role of the institution at the undergraduate level to prepare students for jobs, professional positions, and leadership roles within the community. In addition, nearly all institutions relied on the surrounding community for financial support in the form of donations or endowments, resulting in institutions that were "peculiarly regional, in the sense of having 'relevance to a special community' " (Gruber, 1989, p. 188). The strength and extent of this relationship are perhaps best exemplified by the fact that this relationship "led to a system of governance whereby community leaders assumed financial and educational responsibility" (Church & Sedlak, 1989, p. 97) for these institutions. The result is a uniquely American form of institutional governance based on a board of trustees that broadly oversees the functions of the institution.

Despite the ostensible focus on preparing students for work in the community, the programs within higher education were not vocational but instead were classically based. Indeed, until the late nineteenth century, educational programs were "prescribed and reflected the view that knowledge was a fixed body of truth to be acquired by rote" (Gruber, 1989, p. 181). As such, the curriculum did not differ greatly from one institution to another. In fact, often little difference could be found between the curricula of high schools and institutions of higher education. Further, since teaching relied mainly on memorization and recitation, the position of the faculty was not considered a profession, and thus was often held by young men who were finishing their own studies or waiting for an opportunity to take a minister's role in a congregation (Church & Sedlak, 1989).

After the Civil War, however, the classically based liberal-arts programs began to grow in size and scope, giving rise to the modern university modeled after the German system. Passage of the Morrill Act by Congress in 1862, which granted public lands to the states for the express purpose of establishing institutions of higher learning, spurred some of this growth (Domonkos, 1989). Heavily influenced by developments in science, education moved toward a more empirically based model, in response to "a demand for scientific and technical knowledge by both business and the federal and state governments" (Gruber, 1989, p. 182). Indeed, the founding of Johns Hopkins

University as America's first research university in 1876 represents the birth of the modern American university (Brough, 1972, p. xi). These changes in the curriculum were accompanied by an increasing professionalization of academia. Faculty jobs expanded beyond teaching into areas of research and scholarship, and PhD degrees were established, following the German model. Perhaps the most obvious indication of the solidification of college teaching as a profession in its own right was the founding of the American Association of University Professors (AAUP) in 1915. Although the AAUP maintained that it was not a trade union and staunchly refused to address issues of salary, it did help to define the role of faculty and facilitate relationships with the government and local communities (Hawkins, 1989).

The rapid growth in numbers of institutions, as well as in the breadth and depth of programs as institutions expanded curricula to include empirically based science and graduate programs, highlighted the need for greater oversight of the system of higher education. By the end of the nineteenth century, academia faced a host of issues that needed to be addressed on a wider scale. Whereas classically based programs did not vary greatly from one institution to another, new curricula resulted in variability not only in the programs offered by different institutions, but also in the quality of those programs. The movement of students from one institution to another further complicated the issue. Admissions boards had to decide whether to accept the credits these students earned at other institutions. In addition, there was a lack of distinction between high school and college curricula such that in some cases, undergraduate programs merely repeated secondary-school curricula. Finally, without an entity to establish a set of criteria for entrance into college, the requirements and expectations for incoming undergraduates varied greatly among institutions.

In order to address these differences and establish some degree of standardization, the universities developed independent boards, which were early incarnations of regional accreditation organizations. The first such organization was founded in 1884 in New England, when a group of secondary-school teachers together with Harvard president Charles Eliot formed the New England Association of Schools and Colleges (Stoops & Parsons, 2003), followed by the Middle States Commission in 1887. The North Central Association of Colleges and Schools and the Southern Association of Colleges and Schools were both established in 1895, the Northwest Association of Schools and Colleges in 1917, and the Western Association of Schools and Colleges in 1962.

Initially, these institutions were concerned with standardizing requirements for movement from high school to undergraduate study and from undergraduate to graduate programs, as well as facilitating the transfer of credit from one institution to another. Before long, they turned their attention to establishing standards of quality (Alstete, 2004), defined as fitness for the purposes of teaching and learning (Hayward, 2002). They favored seeking a "voluntary method for identifying institutions capable of [meeting] their objectives and worthy of trust" (Stoops & Parsons, 2003, p. 28). The NCACS was the first to develop a set of accreditation standards for postsecondary institutions, publishing the first list of accredited institutions in 1913 (Alstete, 2004, p. 44), with the other regional accreditation organizations soon following.

Accreditation organizations and college and university administrators needed an entity to provide coordination and engage in advocacy with the government and the public. In order to coordinate their efforts, the organizations created the Federation of Regional Accrediting Commissions of Higher Education (FRACHE) in 1949. Shortly thereafter, in 1952, legislation was enacted mandating the Department of Education to publish a list of recognized accreditation organizations. By recognizing accreditation organizations, the Department of Education implicitly endorsed the nongovernmental system of accreditation and its ability to ensure quality in higher education.

To further improve this process, in 1975, FRACHE merged with the National Commission on Accrediting to form the Council on Postsecondary Accreditation (COPA). COPA's mission was to promote and ensure the quality of higher education accreditation. However, in 1993, tensions among the different types of accreditation organizations led to COPA's dissolution and its replacement with the Council for Recognition of Postsecondary Accreditation (CORPA), and, in 1996, CHEA (Stoops & Parsons, 2003). The purpose of these successive organizations is "to provide a unified process of recognizing accreditation agencies through peer-review evaluation, and to improve quality assurance amongst member institutions in the United States" (Accrediting Council for Independent Colleges and Schools, 2008, para. 7).

Presently, the six regional accreditation organizations perform a number of functions. Each publishes a set of standards intended to promote quality and improvement in member institutions, oversees the administration of the accreditation process, and makes determinations on accredited status. In addition, the accreditation organizations facilitate communication with the public by reporting on accreditation actions and maintaining databases of accredited institutions within their jurisdiction. As NEASC notes, the regional accreditation organizations operate independently of one another, but "they cooperate extensively and acknowledge one another's accreditation" (New England Association of Schools and Colleges, 2008a, question 2).

The Council on Higher Education Accreditation

Because the regional organizations are independent of one another, policies and processes vary considerably from one region to another. This lack of standardization has led different stakeholders to question how effective such organizations can be. Throughout the 1990s, tensions between colleges and universities on the one hand and Congress on the other rose as the latter questioned the viability of the self-regulated accreditation process and considered moving oversight to the government. Congress wanted the Department of Education to set national standards for accountability and thereby to provide stricter oversight than Congress believed the regional accreditation organizations offered. The majority of higher-education administrators and associations such as the AAUP objected that direct government regulation threatens academic freedom and diversity (Bloland, 2001).

CHEA advocates for the self-regulatory and voluntary system of accreditation, and it provides general oversight of the accreditation process. CHEA facilitates relationships between accreditation organizations and the government by communicating with, lobbying to, and offering information about accreditation for the government and the public. CHEA also ensures the necessary oversight of accreditation that Congress expects through a process of review and recognition of accrediting organizations meant to ensure their quality and effectiveness (Stoops & Parsons, 2003).

In addition to dealing with the six regional accreditation organizations, CHEA oversees 52 different faith-related, career-related, and programmatic accreditation organizations (see Table 2.2). In addition, approximately 3,000 higher-education institutions have membership. As a service to the public, CHEA maintains a searchable database of approved accreditation organizations, as well as accredited schools or those in the process of gaining accreditation. Finally, CHEA conducts surveys and publishes reports to inform the public about accreditation processes, current issues, and trends.

ACCREDITATION PROCESS

The process of gaining or retaining accreditation involves three main stages: the self-study, the external review, and the decision (see Figure 2.1). Despite variance in approach and emphases, the standards of each regional accreditation organization address similar areas, including facilities (the equipment and supplies provided by the college or university in support of students), fiscal capacity, and recruiting and admissions practices, as well as student learning outcomes (Council on Higher Education Accreditation, 2006a, p. 1). While standards outline important areas to be addressed and set levels of expectations for institutions to meet, they typically address a broad level. As a result, institutions have some leeway in how they interpret and implement the criteria set forth in the standards. One of the hallmarks of accreditation is the centrality of individual institutional missions in defining quality, effectiveness, and compliance with accreditation criteria. With this in mind, regional accreditation organizations recognize "an institution's mission, goals, and objectives as guideposts for all aspects of accreditation protocol. The . . . mission provides a lens through which the institution and

Table 2.2 Programmatic, Faith-Based, and Career Accreditation Organizations Recognized by the Council for Higher Education Accreditation

Name	Program/Area of Accreditation	URL
	Programmatic	
Association to Advance Collegiate Schools of Business (AACSB)	Business administration; accounting	http://www.aacsb.edu
Accreditation Board for Engineering and Technology (ABET)	Engineering; engineering technology; computing programs; applied science	http://www.abet.org
Accreditation Council for Pharmacy Education (ACPE)	Pharmacy	http://www.acpe-accredit.org
Accreditation Review Commission on Education for the Physician Assistant, Inc. (ARC-PA)	Physician assistant	http://www.arc-pa.org
Accrediting Council on Education in Journalism and Mass Communications (ACEJMC)	Journalism; mass communications	http://www2.ku.edu/~acejmc
American Association for Marriage and Family Therapy Commission on Accreditation for Marriage and Family Therapy Education (AAMFT/COAMFTE)	Clinical training programs in marriage and family therapy	http://www.aamft.org
American Association of Family and Consumer Sciences (AAFCS) Council for Accreditation	Family and consumer sciences	http://www.aafcs.org

American Association of Nurse Anesthetists Council on Accreditation of Nurse Anesthesia Education Programs (CoA-NA)	Nurse anesthesia	http://www.aana.com
American Board of Funeral Service Education (ABSFE) Council on Accreditation	Funeral service education	http://www.abfse.org
American Council for Construction Education (ACCE)	Construction; construction science; construction management; construction technology	http://www.acce-hq.org
American Culinary Federation Foundation, Inc. (ACFF) Accrediting Commission	Culinary management; culinary arts	http://www.acfchefs.org
American Dietetic Association Commission on Accreditation for Dietetics Education (CADE-ADA)	Dietetic technician; dietetics	http://www.eatright.org/cade
American Library Association (ALA) Committee on Accreditation (CoA)	Library and information studies	http://www.ala.org/accreditation/
American Occupational Therapy Association (AOTA) Accreditation Council for American Occupational Therapy Education (ACOTE)	Occupational therapy; occupational therapy assistant	http://www.aota.org
American Optometric Association (AOA) Accreditation Council on Optometric Education (ACOE)	Optometric degree programs; optometric technician programs; optometric residency programs	http://www.theacoe.org

(Continued)

Table 2.2 (Continued)

Name	Program/Area of Accreditation	URL
American Physical Therapy Association (APTA) Commission on Accreditation in Physical Therapy Education (CAPTE)	Professional physical therapy; paraprofessional physical therapy assistant	http://www.capteonline.org
American Podiatric Medical Association (APMA) Council on Podiatric Medical Education	Doctor of podiatric medicine	http://www.cpme.org
American Psychological Association (APA) Council on Accreditation (CoA)	Clinical, counseling, school, and combined professional-scientific psychology; internships; post-doctoral residency programs;	http://www.apa.org
American Society of Landscape Architects (ASLA) Landscape Architectural Accreditation Board (LAAB)	Professional programs	http://www.asla.org
American Speech-Language- Hearing Association (ASHA) Council on Academic Accreditation in Audiology and Speech Language Pathology	Speech language pathology; audiology	http://www.asha.org/academic/accreditation/default.htm
American Veterinary Medical Association (AVMA) Council on Education	Doctor of veterinary medicine	http://www.avma.org
Association of Collegiate Business Schools and Programs (ACBSP)	Business-related fields	http://www.acbsp.org
Aviation Accreditation Board International (AABI)	Nonengineering aviation	http://www.aabi.aero

Commission on Accreditation of Allied Health Education Programs (CAAHEP)	Anesthesiologist assistant; cardiovascular technologist; cytotechnologist; diagnostic medical sonographer, electroneurodiagnostic technologist, emergency medical technician-paramedic, exercise science professional, kinesiotherapist, medical assistant, medical illustrator, ortholist and prosthetist, perfusionist, polysomnographic technologist, respiratory therapist, specialist in blood bank technology, surgical assistant and surgical technologist	http://www.caahep.org
Commission on Accreditation of Healthcare Management Education (CAHME)	Professional programs	http://www.cahme.org
Commission on Collegiate Nursing Accreditation (CCNE)	Nursing	http://www.aacn.nche.edu/accreditation
Council for Accreditation of Counseling and Related Educational Programs (CACREP)	Career counseling; college counseling; community counseling; gerontological counseling; marital, couple and family counseling/therapy; mental health counseling; school counseling; student affairs; and doctoral degree programs in counselor education and supervision	http://www.cacrep.org
Council for Interior Design Accreditation (CIDA)	Interior design	http://www.accredit-id.org
Council on Chiropractic Education (CCE) Commission on Accreditation	Solitary purpose chiropractic institutions	http://www.cce-usa.org

31

(Continued)

Table 2.2 (Continued)

Name	Program/Area of Accreditation	URL
Council on Rehabilitation Education (CORE) Commission on Standards and Accreditation	Graduate programs in rehabilitation counseling	http://www.core-rehab.org
Council on Social Work Education (CSWE) Commission on Accreditation	Social work	http://www.cswe.org
Joint Review Committee on Education Programs in Radiologic Technologies (JRCERT)	Radiography; radiation therapy; magnetic resonance; medical dosimetry	http://www.jrcert.org
Joint Review Committee on Educational Programs in Nuclear Medicine Technology (JRCNMT)	Nuclear medicine technology	http://www.jrcnmt.org
National Accreditation Agency for Clinical Laboratory Sciences (NAACLS)	Clinical laboratory science/medical technology, clinical laboratory technician/medical laboratory technician, histotechnologist, histotechnician, pathologist assistant, and diagnostic molecular scientist	http://www.naacls.org
National Association of Industrial Technology (NAIT)	Nonengineering degrees in industrial technology	http://www.nait.org
National Association of Schools of Art and Design (NASAD) Commission on Accreditation	Art/design; art/design related disciplines	http://www.arts-accredit.org
National Association of Schools of Dance (NASD) Commission on Accreditation	Dance; dance-related disciplines	http://www.arts-accredit.org

National Association of Schools of Music (NASM) Commission on Accreditation	Music; music-related disciplines	http://www.arts-accredit.org
National Association of Schools of Public Affairs and Administration (NASPAA) Commission on Peer Review and Accreditation (CORPA)	Public affairs; public policy and administration	http://www.naspaa.org
National Association of Schools of Theater (NAST) Commission on Accreditation	Theater; theater-related disciplines	http://www.arts-accredit.org
National Council for Accreditation of Teacher Education (NCATE)	Preparation programs for teachers and other personnel of elementary and secondary schools	http://www.ncate.org
National League for Nursing Accreditation Commission, Inc. (NLNAC)	Nursing	http://www.nlnac.org
National Recreation and Park Association (NRPA/COA) Council on Accreditation	Recreation; park resources; leisure studies	http://www.nrpa.org/coa/
Planning Accreditation Board (PAB)	Urban and regional planning	http://www.planningaccreditationboard.org/
Society of American Foresters (SAF)	Forestry	http://www.safnet.org
Teacher Education Accreditation Council, Inc. (TEAC)	Teacher education	http://www.teac.org
Faith-based		
Association for Biblical Higher Education (ABHE)	Christian ministries through biblical, vocational, and general studies	http://www.abhe.org

(Continued)

Table 2.2 (Continued)

Name	Program/Area of Accreditation	URL
Association of Advanced Rabbinical and Talmudic Schools (AART) Accreditation Commission	First rabbinic; first Talmudic	n/a
Commission on the Accrediting of the Association of the Theological Schools of the United States and Canada (ATS)	Professional and graduate theological education	http://www.ats.edu
Transnational Association of Christian Colleges and Schools (TRACS) Accreditation Commission	Post-secondary institutions	http://www.tracs.org
	Career	
Accrediting Council for Independent Colleges and Schools (ACICS)	Institutions educating for professional, technical, or occupational careers	http://www.acics.org
Distance Education and Training Council (DETC) Accreditation Commission	Programs of study that are primarily (51 percent or more) offered by distance	http://www.detc.org

Figure 2.1   Accreditation Process

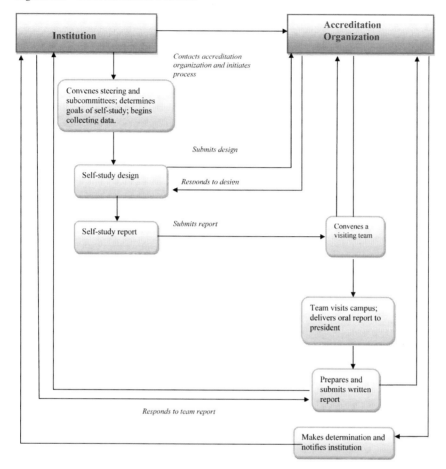

the Commission's evaluation team view the standards and apply them to that institution" (Middle States Commission, 2002, p. 2). The organizations recognize that each institution has different goals, serves different communities, and has different facilities and budgets with which to work. As such, "quality cannot always be defined in precisely the same terms for all institutions" (Baker, 2004, p. 7).

Colleges and universities wanting to retain their accredited status undertake a decennial review that begins with a self-study. This document, which details the institution's mission and goals, outlines the ways in which the institution meets the standards set by the accreditation organization, thus reconciling and aligning the institution's mission and goals. A committee composed of administrators, faculty, and staff from across campus steer the self-study, which typically takes between 18 months and two years to complete. The purpose of the self-study is to review the policies and processes of the institution, produce data and documentation to demonstrate how the institution meets its mission and goals, and set new goals and objectives or identify areas of improvement.

Although self-studies are usually general documents that review all aspects of the institution, some regional accreditation organizations offer their constituents the option of completing a focused study, which centers on one aspect, program, or area of the institution. Often the focus is on a new program or an area identified previously as one requiring improvement. For instance, the Middle States Commission's process allows a choice of three broad self-studies models: comprehensive, selective topics, and collaborative. All first-time candidates for accreditation, and all institutions being reviewed for the first time after their initial accreditation, must complete a comprehensive self-study, which covers all aspects of the institution from programs and services to governing and outcomes. Such a study tends to follow the outline of the Middle States' standards, although institutions can reorder, group, or combine standards in their response. In a selective topics self-study, the institution can "devote concentrated attention to topics it selects and concentrate solely on those topics in its self-study" (Middle States Commission, 2007a, p. 25). Finally, in the collaborative model, institutions that are accredited by other accreditation organizations in addition to the Middle States Commission have the option to combine their Middle States Commission review with those of other organizations. Those other accreditation organizations may choose whether or not to participate, but if they do, the institution can reduce duplication of effort by producing a single self-study for both reviews (Middle States Commission, 2007a).

The self-study phase is followed by a peer review conducted by an external team convened by the accreditation organization. The team visits the campus of the institution under review, observes operations and processes, conducts interviews with numerous institutional stakeholders, and reads the self-study and other documentation. The team then creates its own report that summarizes its observations, responds to the self-study, and offers any recommendations it may have. The institution has the opportunity to respond to the team report. In the final stage of the process, the accreditation organization issues its decision about the institution's status. Besides granting accreditation, the organization can also submit recommendations to the institution, issue warnings, put an institution on probation as it works to improve problem areas, or revoke accredited status.

While accreditation organizations maintain that the voluntary, nongovernmental nature of accreditation helps to ensure academic freedom and promote quality improvement, many critics question the ability of the accreditation organizations to accomplish their aims (Reindl, 2007; Schneider, 2005). They believe that the push for assessment has not resulted in students graduating with the skills necessary for success in the workplace and personal life. One obstacle for accreditation organizations and institutions is that the accreditation process is intense, and it incurs large expenses in terms of both staff time and money. Indeed, the self-study should be a purposeful reflection on the practices and policies of the institution. The results of the study should inform institutional decision making and help administrators plan improvements to increase accountability. However, if institutions view the process as burdensome, they may not engage fully, meaning these potential benefits go unrealized (Kells, 1994).

Ideally, once completed, the assessment reported in the self-study should be integrated into the organization and form the basis of an ongoing process that leads to continuous quality improvement in student knowledge, skills, and abilities. As such, the self-study provides an opportunity for the institution to engage in reflection and implement change; the institution can use the process "as part of an informed procedure to clarify institutional goals to stakeholders, assess goal achievement, and present the organization's true capabilities" (Alstete, 2004, p. 32). However, critics note that too often, institutions view the self-study report as simply one more set of documentation to be compiled for outside observers. In this spirit, institutions may complete the report, move through the accreditation process, and not use or refer to it again. This means that the "infusion of continuous self-study as part of a continuous improvement strategy . . . [may not be] attempted" (Alstete, 2004, p. 6).

Further, some observers (Gelmon, 1997; Trow, 1994) maintain that accreditation processes actually limit or inhibit change and innovation. One possible reason is that institutions tend to conform too rigidly to accreditation standards. Institutions may plan programs to align with external standards, rather than considering the unique needs and concerns of their own communities (Trow, 1994). Similarly, the risk of losing accreditation might make some institutions afraid to be creative or make changes (Gelmon, 1997). They may simply view the risks of a failed program as greater than the potential benefits.

Suskie (2006) notes the inherent contradiction in reporting for both accountability and quality improvement. The former demands that institutions offer proof that they are performing well, while the latter asks them to admit and point to areas where they are not doing well enough and can improve. The fact that institutions must address demands to make accreditation information such as the self-study public only adds to the pressure they face. In response, many institutions might be tempted to be incomplete in responding to quality improvement initiatives or to focus on minor areas of improvement, for fear that admitting to greater needs for improvement reflects badly on them and discourages students from applying for admission. Suskie (2006) suggests combining assessment for accountability and quality improvement to reduce the burden of cost and staff effort, but allowing institutions to report on accountability and quality improvement separately in order to avoid underreporting on areas of improvement.

The fact remains that accreditation organizations emphasize assessment in accreditation standards. The North Central Association of Colleges and Schools incorporated an assessment initiative into its standards in 1989. This initiative outlined a 10-year implementation in which institutions were asked to develop a plan for assessing student learning outcomes within the first five years and to begin to use those data for quality improvement in the subsequent five years. A review of 100 self-studies and team reports for NCACS constituents led López (2004) to conclude, "it is not easy to gain universal acceptance of the efficacy of assessing student learning" (p. 30). The number of those institutions meeting the 10-year goal, she pointed out, was small, whereas the number of institutions that had yet to obtain faculty and program support was "disappointingly large" (p. 31). Indeed, both Ewell (1997) and Miller (1997) acknowledge that faculty resistance to assessment initiatives, especially externally imposed ones, is often high. Still, López (2004) notes that although NCACS institutions may not have fully achieved the goal of an assessment initiative, the accreditation organization has been successful in communicating its message and familiarizing its constituents with assessment. As a result, all institutions of higher education are aware of the initiative and what it means.

STAKEHOLDERS INTERESTED IN LEARNING OUTCOMES

The majority of college and university administrators and accreditation organizations consider academic freedom and diversity of institutional missions to be the cornerstone of higher education in the United States. While some writers (Alstete, 2004; Eaton, 2007a) argue that the excellence and worldwide reputation of American higher education is due in part to the system of limited government oversight, the authority and effectiveness of regional accreditation organizations have not been completely unchallenged.

As the cost of attending institutions of higher education rises, and as more careers in the United States require at least an undergraduate degree, stakeholder groups demand evidence that colleges and universities achieve the goals of providing a quality education and of preparing students to succeed in work and personal life. The groups directly interested in the assessment of higher education are varied, but include government, students, parents, employers, professional associations, higher-education researchers, and policy makers

Figure 2.2   Stakeholders Interested in Accreditation

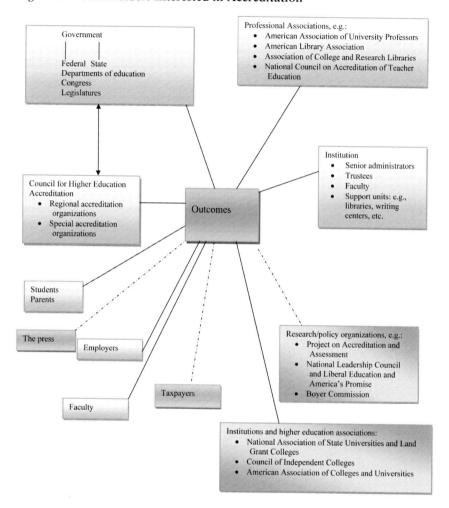

(see Figure 2.2). Although each of these groups is concerned generally with the quality of education as demonstrated by the knowledge and abilities of graduating students, each has its own particular concerns. As noted in the previous chapter, several of these groups have explicitly or implicitly endorsed information literacy as a learning outcome. This array adds another layer of complexity for institutions attempting to demonstrate success in meeting both student outcomes and student learning outcomes, in that these institutions are trying to satisfy various concerns of each stakeholder. The following section outlines the primary concerns of each of these groups.

Direct Stakeholders

The following groups are directly involved in or affected by institutions of higher education. They have an interest in the quality and effectiveness of the programs offered by these institutions.

Government

Although not directly involved in the oversight of institutions, federal and state governments provide substantial financial support for higher education, both directly and indirectly, in the form of grants, tax benefits, and student financial aid. As such, both levels of government want assurance of a return on investments. The enactment of the Servicemen's Readjustment Act, also called the GI Bill of Rights, in 1944 provided for veterans to attend college and led to the establishment of new colleges and universities, some of which were of questionable quality. As a means of protecting the investment it made in terms of funding veterans' education, financial aid to other students, and tax breaks to the institutions, the federal government increased its scrutiny of accreditation organizations. In part, the government decided that, in order to qualify for federal funds, institutions had to be accredited by one of the organizations recognized by the Department of Education.

Beginning in 1952, Congress required the Department of Education to publish a list of recognized accreditation organizations. Although the department initially relied on existing lists provided by the accreditation organizations themselves, over time, it developed its own increasingly elaborate set of regulations for recognizing accreditation organizations. The standards for recognition of an accreditation organization by the Department of Education, written into public law and regulations, encompass areas such as curricula, faculty, grading, courses, calendars, job placement rates, and records of student complaints (Wellman, 1998). In addition, Neal (2008) further argues that colleges and universities should not receive tax-exempt status and federal money without demonstrating achievement, a sentiment that was espoused by the then secretary of education Margaret Spellings (Yudof & Ruberg, 2007).

Although accreditation is ostensibly voluntary and is not government mandated or administered, it is required for those institutions wanting to receive federal funding (e.g., financial aid for students). As such, accreditation serves as a "gatekeeper for federal dollars" (Neal, 2008, p. 25), rendering the process virtually mandatory.

Some of the regulations governing federal support of higher education are contained in the Higher Education Act (P.L. 110-315), parts of which were set to expire in 2003. As Congress prepared to reauthorize the act, considerable debate ensued about how best to hold higher-education institutions accountable and who should oversee that accountability. In the past, state government has largely concerned itself with ensuring the proper spending of government money. More recently, however, states have echoed the wider concern for accountability and assessment. The result has been "*a public agenda for higher education* [emphasis original]—a set of state policy goals that are systematically woven throughout finance, governance, and accountability policies" (Ewell & Jones, 2006, p. 12). Examples include Tennessee's performance-based funding and Oklahoma's incentive program that rewards institutions for each graduate produced (Ewell & Jones, 2006). Similar discussions have taken place at the federal level. Indeed, early discussions of the reauthorization of the Higher Education Opportunity Act considered trying to link funding to school performance overseen by the federal government, much as is done in elementary and secondary education. Specifically, Congress proposed fundamentally restructuring the relationships between institutions and accreditation organizations, and accreditation organizations and the government, by requiring accreditation organizations to establish single sets of standards for institutional quality, faculty performance, and student success, while the government would establish definitions of quality.

The final version of the Higher Education Opportunity Act of 2008 (P.L. 110-315) does not substantially alter the relationship between accreditation organizations and government, but it does impose some new requirements. To begin with, in order to earn federal recognition, accreditation organizations must ensure that their institutions have published transfer policies that detail how they address course credits from other institutions. In addition, while previously accreditation organizations made information public "upon request," they are now required to routinely publish information such as summaries of the actions they take. When accreditation organizations take negative action against an institution, they must make their reasons available in writing (Council for Higher Education Accreditation, 2008).

Accreditation Organizations

Accreditation organizations—regional, faith-related, and program—have a stake in student learning and student outcomes assessment, and many of them react negatively to the prospect of government oversight. They assert that government oversight hinders academic freedom and ultimately undercuts the quality of education that such oversight was intended to ensure, and they lobbied to retain their autonomy. As president of CHEA, Eaton (2007a) opposes government oversight, describing it as a "fundamental assault" and a "deliberate political choice." She warns that "institutional autonomy, academic freedom, and peer review—hallmarks of our enterprise—would be sacrificed in the name of accountability" (p. 2).

While acknowledging the need for quality assurance and accountability, Eaton (2007a) questions the appropriateness and effectiveness of involving the government in the process. Specifically, she argues that the "federal vision of accountability [is] so rigid and bureaucratic that it leaves no room for the driving force of institutional mission" (p. 2). In a joint statement issued by the regional accreditation organizations, representatives emphasized that institutions should be responsible for setting and defining educational outcomes within the scope of their mission. They should be free from government mandates (Beno, 2007). Ultimately, lobbying efforts from the higher-education community were successful, and the act was renewed without significant changes to the accreditation process. Indeed, the Higher Education Opportunity Act of 2008 specifically states that "nothing in this section shall be construed to permit the secretary to establish any criteria that specifies, defines, or prescribes the standards that accrediting agencies or associations shall use to assess any institution's success with respect to student achievement" (P.L.110-315; Stat. 3327 [3] [g]). Nevertheless, the intense debate and scrutiny surrounding the Higher Education Opportunity Act underscored the need for accreditation organizations to ensure the centrality of assessment going forward. The president of CHEA acknowledges the need for a strong response to demands for accountability. She notes that "more than any other single factor, what we do about accountability will drive the future credibility of accreditation, as well as confidence in our work" and indicates that accountability should include "evidence of student achievement, transparency, a willingness to engage comparability and ranking issues" (Eaton, 2007b, section: price of credibility, para. 2).

Institutions and Higher Education Associations

Institutions generally want exclusion from government oversight. In their own response to the 2005 proposed Higher Education Opportunity Act, the National Association of State Universities and Land-Grant Colleges (NASULGC), which represents more than 200 large research universities, and the American Association of State Colleges and Universities (AASCU), representing more than 400 public higher-education institutions, urged their members to develop and implement their own systems of assessment. Both associations "rejected the idea of federally mandated standardized tests," maintaining that the federal government would not be flexible enough to accommodate the vast differences between individual institutions (Klein, 2006, p. 9).

Nevertheless, institutions of higher education recognize the importance of accountability and assessment both for their own internal improvement and for communication with the public. In New Leadership for Student Accountability, the American Association of Colleges and Universities (AACU) and the Council for Higher Education Accreditation (2008) affirm that institutions of higher education have a responsibility to the public to promote democracy by graduating students who are prepared to become active, informed, productive citizens. Further, they assert that, while the responsibility for achieving quality in education is shared by accreditation organizations, governing boards, and the federal government, the primary responsibility for setting standards and achieving quality rests with institutions themselves. *New Leadership for Student Accountability* calls on institutions to gather data about student achievement and performance and to use those data to inform and improve teaching practices.

Institutional commitment to accountability and assessment was also underscored at the 2008 CHEA conference, in which the presidents of CHEA and the AACU, as well as leaders of seven other associations representing more than 3,000 colleges and universities, pledged to continue promoting the assessment of student learning outcomes. Also participating in this pledge were the presidents of the American Council on Education, National Association of State Universities and Land-Grant Colleges, American Association of Community Colleges, the Council of Independent Colleges, American Association of State Colleges and Universities, the Association of American Universities, and the National Association of Independent Colleges and Universities (Humphreys & Porter, 2008).

Specialized Professional Associations

Professional associations, which often accredit degree programs within a college or university, are likewise concerned with accountability and assessment. Currently, CHEA recognizes 52 programmatic accreditation organizations, most of which, like regional accreditation organizations, respond to calls for accountability by increasing their focus on student learning outcomes. In a recent press release, the American Library Association (ALA, 2008) announced the adoption of revised standards for accreditation of master's programs with "stronger emphasis on systematic planning, student learning outcomes, assessment and diversity." In 2008, the Commission on Collegiate Nursing Education (CCNE) also adopted new standards that promote a "value-based initiative," in which the commission aims to foster accountability to interested communities. Both the ALA and CCNE standards stress the importance of individual and aggregate student outcomes and student learning outcomes, and consistent assessment of those outcomes (Commission on Collegiate Nursing Education, 2008). Finally, the National Council for Accreditation of Teacher Education (NCATE) voted unanimously to redesign its accreditation process. Among its goals is to "raise the bar for teacher education" by fostering continuous improvement and recognizing innovative and high-quality programs that have different tracks for novice teachers, mentor teachers, and specialists (National Council for Accreditation of Teacher Education, 2008).

Trustees

As noted previously, higher-education institutions in the United States are governed by trustees, a board of external community members whose role is to oversee and approve most major decisions. Trustees are concerned with the quality and reputation of the institutions they serve, and of higher education in general. While acknowledging that faculty are best suited to make decisions about (and are ultimately responsible for) the curriculum, the American Council of Trustees and Alumni (ACTA) stresses that "trustees have legal and fiduciary responsibilities for the educational, as well as the fiscal, health of their institutions" (Leef, 2003, p. 21). Furthermore, ACTA has been extremely critical of accreditation organizations, flatly stating that "nothing in the accreditation process concretely measures student learning, instructional quality or academic standards" (American Council of Trustees and Alumni, 2007, p. 6).

Students and Parents

Those with the most direct stake in the quality of higher education perhaps are the students who will attend these institutions and their parents, who often pay part or all of the tuition. While students and parents weigh a number of factors in judging the quality of a school (e.g., admission rates, graduation rates, and independent rankings) they often look for tangible results in the form of employment in the graduate's field of choice or perhaps entry into a graduate program for further education. Those students who are studying in fields requiring licensure to practice are interested in passing rates on qualifying examinations.

Employers

Employers hiring graduates look for assurance that their new employees possess the skills and qualities that enable them to perform their job well and to contribute to the organization. The importance of a college degree in the workforce is underscored by the fact that the U.S. Bureau of Labor Statistics predicts that 90 percent of the fastest-growing jobs in the next decade will require some postsecondary education (U.S. Department of Education, 2006). Jobs requiring a college degree will comprise about half of the projected job growth in the United States. Such a growth could lead to a degree gap in which there are more high-skilled jobs than people to fill them (Reindl, 2007). While grades or pass rates on licensure examinations are useful, many employers want further proof that the programs their future employees attend are rigorous and produce qualified candidates.

The Business Higher Education Forum (2004), a panel of business leaders and higher-education administrators, notes that employers "look for something beyond degree attainment in new hires" (p. 10). They are looking for a complex set of competencies that includes the ability to think critically, solve problems, and work in teams. Hewlett Packard vice president Wayne Johnson indicates that beyond technical skills, new graduates need the ability to think creatively (Marklein, 2007). Rockman (2002) notes that business leaders (e.g., Bank of Montreal president Anthony Comper, and America Online vice president Terry Crane) express similar sentiments about the importance of problem solving, using information effectively, and having strong technology skills. Ewell (2001) sums up a concern "among employers and business leaders increasingly focused on the need to develop a '21st Century' workforce that was highly literate, well-versed in problem-solving and collaborative skills, and equipped with appropriate technology skills to meet the needs of an emerging 'knowledge economy' " (p. 2).

As employers attempt to find the most qualified candidates, the Business Higher Education Forum (2004) indicates that a lack of transparency on the part of many institutions about how they define and measure student success has led some employers to supplement applicants' educational information with in-house tests of literacy and quantitative skills. Further, some businesses are developing their own solutions to a perceived inadequacy in higher education by producing their own education programs, both for in-house and external customers, marking a shift in employers' relationship with higher education from customer to producer. As a result, businesses influence educational outcomes (Lingenfelter, 2003).

Faculty

As the party most directly responsible for curricula, instruction, and ultimately student learning, faculty have a strong stake in outcomes assessment. While much of the scrutiny by the government has been directed at accreditation organizations or institutions, faculty typically set learning outcomes for the courses and programs in which they teach, and as such, student achievement reflects directly on them. Further, faculty tend to develop and implement the assessment or evaluation measures used to gauge student learning, such as tests, quizzes, and assignments. As such, the faculty are often the most directly involved in assessment of student learning outcomes.

Indirect Stakeholders

Although the following groups do not participate directly in the programs and services of higher education, they still share an intellectual or monetary interest in the performance of these institutions. They also produce research studies and products related to higher education.

Research Institutions and Policy Makers

Education researchers and policy makers have issued reports that emphasize the importance of assessment and accountability for ensuring quality in higher education. Noting the shift from input and output measures to outcomes (e.g., changes in student learning), the Project on Accreditation and

Assessment (2004) asserts that "the higher education community as a whole is coming to view the achievement by students of desirable learning outcomes as the key indicator of quality" (p. 1). The National Leadership Council for Liberal Education and America's Promise (2007) likewise maintains that input and output measures "miss entirely the question of whether students who have placed their hopes for the future in higher education are actually achieving the kind of learning they need for a complex and volatile world" (p. 1).

Taxpayers

Government support for institutions of higher education, whether in the form of financial aid, grants, or tax breaks, ultimately comes from taxpayers. Whether or not they attend a college or university, taxpayers also have a stake in the quality of higher education because they are indirectly investing in it. In a speech to the National Advisory Committee on Institutional Quality and Integrity in which she called for greater transparency and accountability in colleges and universities, then secretary of education Spellings intimated that the government has a "fiduciary duty and a statutory duty to serve consumer and taxpayer interest in higher education" (Yudof & Ruberg, 2007, para. 9). Similar concerns have been voiced at the state level. For instance, the states of Tennessee (Noland, Johnson, & Skolits, 2004) and Oklahoma (Oklahoma State Regents for Higher Education, 2008) have merit-based funding systems, in which state money is awarded to institutions based on performance. In Texas, Governor Rick Perry instituted an accountability system for higher education, asserting that "our institutions of higher education should be held accountable to taxpayers for the billions of dollars in state funding they receive each year" (Office of the Governor, Rick Perry, 2004, para. 2).

The Press

Many news outlets, most notably the *Chronicle of Higher Education*, *Inside Higher Ed*, and *U.S. News and World Report*, have covered accreditation and accountability in higher education extensively. An op-ed in the *Chronicle of Higher Education* acknowledges some efforts to establish transparency, but questions how committed most institutions of higher education really are to "deliver truly useful information" (Vedder, 2008, p. A64). Another article in the same newspaper criticized the Higher Education Opportunity Act of 2008 as a missed opportunity for its failure to increase oversight and accountability. It claimed that by limiting government oversight, the act does not provide for adequate controls on the quality of education (Miller, 2008).

U.S. News and World Report is perhaps best known for its yearly rankings of top colleges and universities. Many institutions and accreditation organizations question the criteria that the publication uses to devise its ranking system. They complain that it relies too heavily on perceptions, inputs, and outputs. In addition, the rankings do not take into account the varied missions of individual institutions, instead treating institutions as if they all have the same vision and goals. Nevertheless, the *U.S. News and World Report* website (http://colleges.usnews.rankingsandreviews.com/college) logged over 70 million hits within 72 hours of posting its 2008 rankings (Yudof & Ruberg, 2007). Furthermore, Kingsbury (2007) notes that the publication has to rely on inputs and outputs for rankings because most colleges and universities do not release other information. He suggests that, if such data were more accessible, they might change the rankings and lend support to calls for greater openness and transparency.

PURPOSES OF ACCREDITATION

Accreditation organizations serve a dual purpose: they ensure quality through accountability, and they promote continuous improvement among their constituency and organizations. As defined within higher education, accountability is "the public presentation and communication of evidence about performance as related to [the accomplishment of mission and] goals" (Hearn & Holdsworth, 2002, p. 29). Quality improvement, on the other hand, requires analyzing data gathered for accountability and about learning and using the data to address weaknesses, build on strengths, and engage in continuous improvement in student learning.

Accountability

The increased attention to accountability from stakeholders is due in part to the increasing number of jobs that require postsecondary education. A college degree has become a precondition of gainful employment for many positions, while employers demand "an increasingly specific set of higher-order literacies and communication skills" (Council on Higher Education Accreditation, 2003, p. 4). As Suskie (2006) notes, "the increased need for higher education has increased public attention to it" (p. 15). By establishing expectations for institutions within their constituency, and demanding documentation and reporting of achievement of these expectations, accreditation organizations assist their constituents in answering stakeholders' calls for accountability and for an educated graduate, one well prepared to enter the workforce.

In general, the standards set by regional accreditation organizations establish a baseline of quality for their constituents and "minimum standards of performance, to ensure that practitioners are capable of meeting at least the minimum threshold of acceptable practice" (Gelmon, 1997, p. 53). When a college or university meets these standards and gains or retains accreditation, the public knows that the institution meets those quality standards and that graduates of the program possesses certain knowledge, skills, and abilities and can perform at a certain level. Baker (2004) maintains that accredited status "warrants confidence of the educational community and the public with regard to the institution's performance, quality, and integrity" (p. 6).

Improving the Quality of the Educational Experience

While accreditation standards ensure the public of a certain level of quality, they are not an end in themselves. To begin with, because these standards focus on a minimum threshold, they normally do not present a challenge to many institutions (Alstete, 2004). In addition, the evidence produced for meeting accreditation standards indicates an institution's current level of quality and effectiveness, but it does not necessarily ensure the institution's ability to maintain that level into the future. Most undergraduate degree programs are designed to be completed in approximately four to five years, but many students actually take longer to complete their degrees. As such, a student's interest in the quality of the institution persists beyond their date of admission. Further, the reputation of one's institution continues to be important even after graduation, as one seeks employment or admission to graduate programs. Enrolling students want assurance that their chosen college or university not only has a good reputation and meets current standards for quality, but that the institution also has the need and motivation to persist in their achievements (Baker, 2004). Accreditation organizations assist institutions in meeting stakeholder demands by facilitating quality improvement through preparing a self-study report and requiring assessment.

One of the hallmarks of higher education accreditation is that it does not try to hold all institutions to a single, inflexible set of standards. In order to accommodate the differences reflected in institutional mission statements, accreditation organizations seek to strike a balance between setting specific standards or expectations for all institutions to meet, and offering individual institutions the freedom to adapt or interpret standards within the context of their own mission and culture. Alstete (2004) maintains that this emphasis on self-evaluation over external review means that the accreditation organizations are seen less as judges and more as "facilitator[s], guide[s], and mentor[s] for assisting the educational institution in self-improvement" (p. 2).

In order to move beyond baseline quality toward excellence through continuous assessment, individual institutions are expected to use accreditation standards as a starting point to create their own improvement plans; they may use their missions and goals to set institution-specific outcomes (Alstete, 2004). There is great variety across institutions of higher education. Missions and values vary among institutions, with some espousing certain religious tenets and others focusing on certain fields such as engineering or technology. Some institutions exclusively offer bachelor's degrees, while others have graduate programs of varying number and size. In addition, different admissions criteria result in differing student bodies from one institution to another. By adapting baseline standards, institutions can set goals consistent with their unique missions and communities.

By allowing institutions to use their missions as a lens through which to view standards, accreditation organizations "provide a means to judge an institution in terms of its own expectations of itself" and to set external measures of quality and effectiveness (Baker, 2004, p. 7). It is important to note, however, that the flexibility to address standards in terms of individual missions that is given to colleges and universities is not meant to make it easier for these institutions to achieve accreditation. Rather, the use of the mission as a guide for interpreting standards is meant to challenge institutions to find opportunities to grow and improve in ways consistent with their mission, values, and goals. As Miller (1997) points out, the use of institutional missions is not "just a matter of accreditors helping each institution develop an individual set of measures that will make it look good" (p. 26). Instead, by linking accreditation standards with assessment practices, individual institutions can identify areas for improvement or "begin to work on setting and achieving 'stretch' goals that move [them] toward [achievement of] excellence" (Gelmon, 1997, p. 53). Accreditation organizations expect institutions to have a clearly defined mission, to set goals that align with that mission, and to collect and analyze data to demonstrate achievement of these goals. The balance between external standards and internal mission is the vehicle through which accreditation organizations accomplish their dual purpose.

ASSESSMENT

The term assessment refers to the processes that institutions use to gather and analyze evidence about outcomes. Suskie (2004) defines assessment of student learning as an ongoing process involving four steps:

1. Establishing clear, measurable expected *outcomes* of student learning
2. Ensuring that students have sufficient *opportunities* to achieve those outcomes
3. Systematically gathering, analyzing and interpreting *evidence* to determine how well actual student learning matches stated expectations
4. Using the resulting information to understand and *improve* student learning (p. 4)

As with other accreditation expectations, how institutions employ and apply assessment standards varies. While regional accreditation organizations insist that institutions within their jurisdiction engage in assessment, they do not specify the particular outcomes, methods of data collection, or measures to use. The mission of the college or university determines the particular outcomes to assess, and whatever measures are used for evidence gathering should be appropriate to the goals of the institution and its programs and the type of data that the institution seeks to uncover.

Miller (1997) enumerates the functions ascribed to assessment as:

- Refining understanding of learning and tracking the impact on students
- Using that understanding to discover and employ the most effective learning strategies
- Addressing public concerns and answer public questions

She cautions that to be effective, assessment cannot be reactive or undertaken simply to comply with external demands, but it must become an integral part of the institution. Similarly, the Project on Accreditation and Assessment (2004) offers numerous guidelines for good assessment practice, suggesting, for instance, that assessment should be formative and, when appropriate, summative. Formative assessment gives institutions insight into program goals and allows them to make adjustments as necessary. Summative assessment offers an overview of a program ending, which can be measured against initial goals and used for planning future programs. The Project also encourages the use of both quantitative and qualitative data. Further, it advises that assessment should be student-centered, not externally imposed. In other words, faculty and institutions should engage in assessment to determine how well students are learning and how to improve learning. In this way, evidence for external accountability will be generated, and assessment becomes an integrated part of the institutional culture.

The importance of establishing an institution-wide commitment to assessment finds nearly unanimous support throughout the literatures of both higher education and library and information science. Indeed, the link between classroom assessment and improved teaching and learning has strong support (e.g., Allen, 2004; Angelo & Cross, 1993; Christoforou & Yigit, 2008; Ford, 2006). Program-level assessment indicates how well departments achieve their learning goals, in particular how well students learn, which includes "not only the knowledge leading to understanding but also abilities, habits of mind, ways of knowing, attitudes, values, and other dispositions" (Maki, 2004, p. 3). At the institutional level, assessment produces the evidence of student learning and increased knowledge demanded by the public as well as impacts the internal organization. Rice (2006) mentions accountability and assessment as one of the main reasons why higher education in the United States is consistently ranked the best in the world. While acknowledging the importance of outcomes assessment for satisfying accreditation and other external demands, Shupe (2007) also offers numerous internal benefits for institutions committed to assessment, including a more dynamic curriculum, more engaged student support services, and the ability to understand and address individual student needs. Simply put, an institution that fosters a culture of assessment, in which assessment practices permeate all levels and areas of the institution, "can become significantly better" (Shupe, 2007, p. 8).

Outcomes Assessment

Quality, which can be assessed with respect to various aspects of an institution and its programs, can relate to student learning as well as factors such as faculty productivity in terms of classes taught, publications, or grants received; facilities; student services; and the role of the library. One difficulty with the concept of quality is that it is often left undefined or only vaguely defined. Baker (2004) notes the lack of consensus, maintaining "the considerable variance in constituent perspectives and institutional philosophies, characteristics, cultures, and missions makes it difficult to articulate common operational definitions" (p. 2). Nevertheless, the Middle States Commission (2007b) defines a quality institution as follows:

> Institutions identify student learning goals for educational offerings that are appropriate to ... [their] higher education mission; that ... [their] offerings display appropriate academic content, rigor, and coherence; that ... [their] curricula are designed so that students demonstrate college-level proficiency in general education and essential skills, including oral and written communication skills, scientific and quantitative reasoning, critical analysis and reasoning, technological competence, and information literacy; and that assessment demonstrates that students at [the time of] graduation have achieved appropriate higher education goals. (p. 1)

In assessing quality, the focus is on outcomes. With respect to students, outcomes encompass student outcomes and student learning outcomes. Though similar, student outcomes and student learning outcomes are not the same thing. The former are really output measures, based on aggregate statistics (e.g., graduation and retention rates, transfer rates, and employment placement upon graduation). Student outcomes may also comprise benefits garnered after graduation, such as increased income or employment opportunities and mobility, or access to postgraduate education (Ewell, 2001). As such, these statistics report on what an institution has accomplished, but they neither account for individual student differences nor measure changes within students over the course of their college experience (Dugan & Hernon, 2002). Such measures traditionally comprised the bulk of institutional reporting "as a proxy for institutional effectiveness" (Ewell, 2001, p. 5).

On the other hand, student learning outcomes indicate how well students learn within specified contexts. The assessment of student learning outcomes "focuses on the extent to which students construct their own meaning from what their instructors present, that is, the extent to which they can apply, synthesize, demonstrate, and translate what they have learned" (Dugan & Hernon, 2006, p. 2). Student learning outcomes can be established at various levels: course, program, college/school, and institutional. For instance, course outcomes identify the skills and knowledge students should gain by the end of a single course, whereas program outcomes do the same for a degree program or full course of studies. Each academic program should have student learning outcomes. Likewise, the library and other academic support units, presumably in conjunction with faculty, can participate in those outcomes. Information literacy might be one area for student learning outcomes. For instance, using the framework depicted in Figure 1.1, institutions may define expectations of student knowledge and abilities at various levels. Institutional outcomes identify a broader set of goals, establishing the general expectations for graduates of that institution, regardless of the particular courses or programs they take.

Historically, accreditation self-studies include input measures (e.g., budget, size of the library, and other facility measures), outputs (e.g., levels of satisfaction), and student outcomes. These procedures assume that "institutional infrastructure and resources (inputs) were directly responsible for institutional outcomes" (Baker, 2004, p. 8). Such measures largely consist of counting and percentages. Because they are quantitative, these measures were thought to be more objective, but are now being criticized as reductionist and incapable of providing an overview of an institution's effectiveness and quality. Over time, the public has become skeptical of the validity of these measures, and the focus has now shifted to assessing outcomes, particularly student learning outcomes, as "the primary means by which institutions demonstrate their . . . effectiveness" (Maki, 2004, p. 89).

Baker (2004) writes that "in response to shifting societal expectations, regional accrediting agencies have recently revised their accreditation criteria to more clearly emphasize assessment of achievements of institutional and student learning outcomes, as well as judgments of institutional intentions and capacity, in making accreditation decisions," as a means to "[respond] to current societal expectations for accountability and quality assurance" (pp. 10–11). Indeed, the Southern Association of Colleges and Schools initiated the Quality Enhancement Plan (QEP), whereby all institutions within its jurisdiction must develop a quality enhancement plan as part of their accreditation process. Similarly, the Middle States Commission issued a new set of standards in 2002 that incorporated assessment into its 14 standards. One standard is devoted entirely to student learning outcomes. These standards do not exclude input and output measures, but place greater emphasis on assessing student learning.

Assessment for Quality Improvement

While Miller (1997) presents assessment primarily as a way to provide a description of institutional activities, assessment also contributes to the quality improvement efforts of accreditation organizations and their constituents. When the data describe the current state of student learning, they relate to accountability in that they offer evidence of the quality of the existing programs in meeting the stated mission. When those data are used to make decisions about how to improve or enhance programs, institutions are moving to quality improvement.

Indeed, many authors (e.g., Lopéz, 2004; Maki, 2004; Suskie, 2006; Wiggins, 1997) describe assessment activities as circular, starting with the identification of learning outcomes, followed by the gathering and interpreting of data, and completed by using information to inform decisions and make changes to improve learning. They underscore the importance of closing the feedback loop by using assessment data for quality improvement. Wiggins (1997) maintains that feedback is essential to learning and improvement, from the individual to the institutional level, claiming "you don't get good at anything without feedback" (p. 31). He laments that too often, educators do not close the feedback loop. Instead, institutions gather enormous amounts of data for reporting to various governmental, nongovernmental, and accreditation organizations, and do not use the data beyond those reports. This leaves the institutions with the problem of being data rich and information poor. As Suskie (2006) notes, the work undertaken for accountability and accreditation is virtually useless if it is not used to improve programs. Dugan and Hernon (2006) state that the "the goal is to improve overall instruction, advance or deepen learning" (p. 2).

For the accreditation process to work as it is intended, each institution must develop a mission statement and a set of clearly stated goals that are based on the mission and that indicate what students will learn from their program of study, or that describe learning outcomes at the institutional level. Next, the institution must formulate an assessment plan for how it will gather data to demonstrate student learning, and how it will further analyze and use that data to improve teaching and learning continuously. Maki (2004), who offers a model of the feedback loop, outlines four steps of the planning process: (1) identify outcomes; (2) gather evidence; (3) interpret that evidence; and (4) implement change. She indicates that the entire cycle should be repeated after the changes identified in the last step have been made. She also offers suggestions for how evidence can inform decisions (e.g., developing a more effective orientation or revising the sequence of courses). The purpose of making changes based on assessment evidence is to improve student learning. Ideally, these efforts will not be tied solely to accreditation; they should be organic and ongoing. The goal is to create an institutional culture that embraces outcomes assessment and student learning. Dwyer (2006) describes institutions that address learning goals as "learning organizations" (p. 165), in that they use assessment data to isolate areas for improvement and implement changes to increase student learning.

Information Literacy as a Learning Outcome

While individual institutions are expected to establish their student learning outcomes in terms of their missions, certain broad expectations have been identified as essential to all college or university graduates. Because regional accreditation organizations set standards at the institutional level, student learning outcomes are usually defined as part of general education at the undergraduate level, applicable across disciplines and programs. In large part, these student learning outcomes are associated with the higher-order thinking skills of evaluation and synthesis as defined by Bloom's taxonomy, a model that identifies domains of learning and abilities such as evaluation and synthesis as higher level (Bloom, 1956). According to Bloom, the lower-order skills of knowledge and understanding require only that individuals understand and recall information. Synthesis and evaluation, on the other hand, are more complex and abstract applications of knowledge through which individuals use knowledge to accomplish a purpose or create new information. Because of its emphasis on evaluation and use of information, information literacy incorporates aspects of the higher-order thinking abilities.

Although several stakeholder groups evince support for information literacy, much of the writing on the topic originates from library and information science (LIS). Indeed, in 1989, the ALA convened a presidential committee to comment on the importance of information literacy. The committee's *Final Report* underscores the importance to a democratic society of developing the knowledge and skills to "appreciate and integrate the concept of information literacy into their learning programs" (American Library Association, 1989, para. 3). In an effort to clarify the term, the ALA's Association of College and Research Libraries (ACRL) developed one of the most widely accepted definitions of information literacy. An information-literate person, ACRL asserts, is one who can find information efficiently and effectively, evaluate the information, and use it to accomplish a purpose in an ethical and legal manner (American Library Association, Association of College and Research Libraries, 2000).

While librarians have taken the lead in promoting information literacy as a student learning outcome in higher education, the competencies encompassed under information literacy reach far beyond library research skills. Within *Developing Research and Communication Skills*, the Middle States Commission (2003) underscores the scope of information literacy by describing it as "a metacognitive device for students to better manage the learning process," and by asserting that "in any learning endeavor, the student invokes some aspect(s) of the information literacy process" (p. 2). Ratteray (2002) further underscores the portability of information literacy by asserting that it is "invoked any time a student attempts to learn anything in any discipline" (p. 370).

MIDDLE STATES COMMISSION ON HIGHER EDUCATION

Information literacy has been widely acknowledged as an important student learning outcome, but the Middle States Commission remains one of the strongest supporters of information literacy as an important program or institutional outcome. In order to further assist its constituents in achieving standards related to learning assessment, and as further proof of its commitment to integrating learning assessment fully into the accreditation process, the Middle States Commission created a series of guides to assessment. *Assessing Student Learning and Institutional Effectiveness* (Middle States Commission, 2005) is a brief guide that outlines the major changes to the 2002 standards, and offers institutions practical advice on meeting those standards. *Student Learning Assessment: Options and Resources* (Middle States Commission, 2007b), first published in 2002, explains the standards and the roles and expectations of the Middle States Commission. It also offers advice on developing, promoting, and integrating assessment into the campus culture. This monograph incorporates *Assessing Student Learning and Institutional Effectiveness* as a separate chapter. A third monograph, *Developing Research and Communication Skills* (Middle States Commission, 2003), as noted in the previous chapter, is devoted entirely to information literacy as a learning outcome.

CONCLUSION

As a college education becomes a prerequisite for many careers, and the cost of higher education makes a baccalaureate or graduate degree harder for many individuals to attain, government, employers, and the general public demand that colleges and universities, and the organizations that accredit them, demonstrate the quality of their degrees. Increasingly, accreditation organizations rely on student learning outcomes or demonstrable gains in student "knowledge leading to understanding but also abilities, habits of mind, ways of knowing, attitudes, values, and other dispositions" (Maki, 2004, p. 3) to demonstrate that quality; such learning is a good indicator of institutional effectiveness. Information literacy is one student learning outcome important for students to achieve.

Despite wider recognition of the importance of information literacy as a learning outcome in recent years, and a greater emphasis on assessment of student learning, it is unclear how institutions are responding to these expectations. To what extent are institutions, especially those accredited by the Middle States Commission, incorporating learning outcomes for information literacy at the course, program, and institutional levels? Further, how are they assessing student learning? The next chapter presents the study's reflective inquiry, including the methods undertaken to answer these questions.

REFERENCES

Accrediting Council for Independent Colleges and Schools. (2008). *History of accreditation*. Retrieved from http://www.acics.org/accreditation/content .aspx?id=2258

Allen, J. (2004). The impact of student learning outcomes assessment on technical and professional communication programs. *Technical Communication Quarterly, 13*(1), 93–108. Retrieved from ProQuest.

Alstete, J. W. (2004). *Accreditation matters: Achieving academic recognition and renewal*. San Francisco, CA: Jossey-Bass.

American Council of Trustees and Alumni. (2007). *Why accreditation doesn't work and what policymakers can do about it*. Retrieved from https://www.goacta .org/publications/downloads/Accreditation2007Final.pdf

American Library Association. (1989). *Presidential committee on information literacy: Final report*. Chicago, IL: Author. Retrieved from http://www.ala.org/ala/ mgrps/divs/acrl/publications/whitepapers/presidential.cfm

American Library Association. (2008). *ALA Council adopts revised standards for application*. Retrieved from http://www.ala.org/Template.cfm?Section=archive& template=/contentmanagement/contentdisplay.cfm&ContentID=171135

American Library Association, Association of College and Research Libraries. (2000). *Information literacy competency standards for higher education*. Retrieved from http://www.ala.org/ala/mgrps/divs/acrl/standards/informationliteracy competency.cfm

Angelo, T. A., & Cross, K. P. (1993). *Classroom assessment techniques: A handbook for college teachers* (2nd ed.). San Francisco, CA: Jossey-Bass.

Association of American Colleges and Universities. (2008). *New leadership for student learning and accountability*. A joint report with the Council for Higher Education Accreditation. Retrieved from http://www.chea.org/pdf/ 2008.01.30_New_Leadership_Statement.pdf

Baker, R. L. (2004). Keystones of regional accreditation: Intentions, outcomes, and sustainability. In P. Hernon & R. E. Dugan (Eds.), *Outcomes assessment in higher education: Views and perspectives* (pp. 1–16). Westport, CT: Libraries Unlimited.

Beno, B. (2007). *C-RAC letter on negotiated rule making*. Washington, DC: Council of Regional Accrediting Commissions. Retrieved from http://www.ncahlc.org /download/CRAC_Negreg.pdf

Bloland, H. G. (2001). *Creating the Council for Higher Education Accreditation (CHEA)*. Phoenix, AZ: Oryx Press.

Bloom, B. S. (1956). *Taxonomy of educational objectives: The classification of educational goals*. New York, NY: McKay.

Boyer Commission on Educating Undergraduates in the Research University. (1998). *Reinventing undergraduate education: A blueprint for America's research universities.* Stony Brook, NY: State University of New York.

Brough, K. (1972). *Scholar's workshop: Evolving conceptions of library service.* Boston, MA: Gregg Publishers.

Business Higher Education Forum. (2004). *Public accountability for student learning in higher education: Issues and options.* Retrieved from http://www.bhef.com/publications/documents/public_accountability_04.pdf

Church, R. L., & Sedlak, M. W. (1989). The antebellum college and the academy. In L. S. Goodchild & H. S. Wechsler (Eds.), *The history of higher education* (pp. 95–108). Needham Heights, MA: Ginn Press.

Christoforou, A. P., & Yigit, A. S. (2008). Improving teaching and learning in engineering education through a continuous assessment process. *European Journal of Engineering Education, 33*(1), 105–116. Retrieved from Ebsco.

Commission on Collegiate Nursing Education. (2008). *Standards for accreditation of baccalaureate and graduate degree nursing programs.* Retrieved from http://www.aacn.nche.edu/accreditation/pdf/standards.pdf

Council for Higher Education Accreditation. (2003). *Statement of mutual responsibilities for student learning outcomes: Accreditation, institutions, and programs.* Washington, DC: Author. Retrieved from http://www.chea.org/pdf/StmntStudentLearningOutcomes9-03.pdf

Council for Higher Education Accreditation. (2006a). *CHEA at a glance.* Washington, DC: Author. Retrieved from http://www.chea.org/pdf/chea_glance_2006.pdf

Council for Higher Education Accreditation. (2006b). *Fact Sheet #5.* Washington, DC: Author. Retrieved from http://www.chea.org/pdf/fact_sheet_5_operation.pdf

Council for Higher Education Accreditation. (2008, September 19). Accreditation and the Higher Education Opportunity Act of 2008. *CHEA Update*, 45. Retrieved from http://www.chea.org/Government/HEAUpdate/CHEA_HEA45.html

Domonkos, L. S. (1989). History of higher education. In L. S. Goodchild & H. S. Wechsler (Eds.), *The history of higher education* (pp. 3–24). Needham Heights, MA: Ginn Press.

Dugan, R. E., & Hernon, P. (2002). Outcomes assessment: Not synonymous with inputs and outputs. *Journal of Academic Librarianship, 28*(6), 376–380. Retrieved from H. W. Wilson.

Dugan, R. E., & Hernon, P. (2006). Institutional mission-centered student learning. In P. Hernon, R. E. Dugan, & C. Schwartz (Eds.), *Revisiting outcomes assessment in higher education* (pp. 1–12). Westport, CT: Libraries Unlimited.

Dwyer, P. M. (2006). The learning organization: Assessment as an agent of change. In P. Hernon, R. E. Dugan & C. Schwartz (Eds.), *Revisiting outcomes assessment in higher education* (pp. 165–180). Westport, CT: Libraries Unlimited.

Eaton, J. S. (2007a). Assault on accreditation: Who defines and judges academic quality? *Liberal Education, 93*(2), 2–3. Retrieved from Ebsco.

Eaton, J. S. (2007b). Federal policy events and reflections on the accreditation-government relationship: Four points. *Inside Accreditation, 3*(4). Retrieved from http://www.chea.org/ia/IA_08-13-07.html

Ewell, P. T. (1997). Accountability and assessment in a second decade: New looks or the same old story? In *Assessing Impact: Evidence and Action, Presentations from the 1997 AAHE Conference on Assessment and Quality* (pp. 7–21). Washington, DC: American Association of Higher Education.

Ewell, P. T. (2001). *Accreditation and student learning outcomes: A proposed point of departure.* Washington, DC: Council for Higher Education Accreditation. Retrieved from http://www.chea.org/award/StudentLearningOutcomes2001 .pdf

Ewell, P. T., & Jones, D. P. (2006). State-level accountability for higher education: On the edge of transformation. *New Directions for Higher Education, 135,* 9–16. Retrieved from Ebsco.

Ford, L. E. (2006). *Assessment from the inside out: How we used a student's experience in the major as a way to examine our own teaching, judge student learning outcomes, and reevaluate our goals.* Paper presented at the annual meeting of the American Political Science Association, Marriott, Philadelphia, PA. Retrieved from http://www.allacademic.com/

Gelmon, S. B. (1997). Intentional improvement: The deliberate linkage of assessment and accreditation. In *Assessing impact: Evidence and action, Presentations from the 1997 AAHE Conference on Assessment and Quality* (pp. 51–65). Washington, DC: American Association of Higher Education.

Gratch-Lindauer, B. (2002). Comparing the regional accreditation standards: Outcomes assessment and other trends. *Journal of Academic Librarianship, 28* (1–2), 14–25. Retrieved from H. W. Wilson.

Gruber, C. S. (1989). Backdrop. In L. S. Goodchild & H. S. Wechsler (Eds.), *The history of higher education* (pp. 181–196). Needham Heights, MA: Ginn Press.

Hawkins, H. (1989). University identity: The teaching and research functions. In L. S. Goodchild & H. S. Wechsler (Eds.), *The history of higher education* (pp. 265–279). Needham, MA: Ginn Press.

Hayward, F. (2002). *Glossary of key terms.* Washington, DC: Council for Higher Education Accreditation. Retrieved from http://www.chea.org/international/ inter_glossary01.html#qa

Hearn, J. C., & Holdsworth, J. M. (2002). Influences of state-level policies and practices on college students' learning. *Peabody Journal of Education, 77*(3), 6–39. Retrieved from Ebsco.

Humphreys, D., & Porter, R. (2008). *Major higher education associations pledge new leadership for student learning and accountability at CHEA Annual Conference.* Press Release Memo. Retrieved from http://www.chea.org/pdf/ 2008.01.30_Leadership_Statement_News_Release.pdf

Kells, H. R. (1994). *Self-study processes: A guide for postsecondary and similar service-oriented institutions and programs.* Phoenix, AZ: Oryx Press.

Kingsbury, A. (2007). The measure of learning. *U.S. News and World Report, 142* (9), 52–57. Retrieved from Ebsco.

Klein, A. (2006). Accountability key, groups tell colleges. *Education Week, 25*(32), 9. Retrieved from ProQuest.

Leef, G. (2003). *Becoming an educated person.* Retrieved from https://www.goacta .org/publications/downloads/BEPFinal.pdf

Lingenfelter, P. E. (2003). Educational accountability. *Change, 35*(2), 18–24. Retrieved from ProQuest.

López, C. L. (2004). A decade of assessing student learning: What we have learned, and what is next. In P. Hernon & R. E. Dugan (Eds.), *Outcomes assessment in higher education: Views and perspectives* (pp. 29–72). Westport, CT: Libraries Unlimited.

Maki, P. (2004). *Assessing for learning: Building a sustainable commitment across the institution.* Sterling, VA: Stylus.

Marklein, M. B. (2007, January 11). Panel urges collegians to focus on liberal arts. *USA Today.* Retrieved from Ebsco.

Middle States Commission on Higher Education. (2002). *Designs for excellence: Handbook for institutional self-study.* Philadelphia, PA: Author. Retrieved from http://www.umaryland.edu/self_study/documents/middles_%20states_%20designs.pdf

Middle States Commission on Higher Education. (2003). *Developing research and communication skills: Guidelines for information literacy in the curriculum.* Philadelphia, PA: Author.

Middle States Commission on Higher Education. (2005). *Assessing student learning and institutional effectiveness.* Philadelphia, PA: Author. Retrieved from http://www.msche.org/publications/Assessment_Expectations051222081842.pdf

Middle States Commission on Higher Education. (2007a). *Self-study: Creating a useful process and report.* Philadelphia, PA: Author. Retrieved from http://www.msche.org/publications/SelfStudy07070925104848.pdf

Middle States Commission on Higher Education. (2007b). *Student learning assessment: Options and resources.* Philadelphia, PA: Author. Retrieved from http://www.msche.org/publications/SLA_Book_0808080728085320.pdf

Miller, C. (2008). The new higher education act: Where it comes up short (Commentary). *Chronicle of Higher Education, 54*(48), A19–A20.

Miller, M. (1997). Looking for results: The second decade. In *Assessing impact: Evidence and action, Presentations from the 1997 AAHE Conference on Assessment and Quality* (pp. 23–30). Washington, DC: American Association of Higher Education.

National Council for Accreditation of Teacher Education. (2008). *NCATE to develop options within the accrediting process.* Retrieved from http://www.ncate.org/Public/Newsroom/NCATENewsPressReleases/tabid/669/EntryId/72/NCATE-to-Develop-Options-within-Accrediting-Process.aspx

National Leadership Council for Liberal Education and America's Promise. (2007). *College learning for the new global century.* Washington, DC: Association of American Colleges and Universities.

Neal, A. D. (2008). Seeking higher-ed accountability: Ending federal accreditation. *Change, 40*(5), 24–31. Retrieved from ProQuest.

New England Association of Schools and Colleges. (2008a). *FAQs.* Retrieved from http://cihe.neasc.org/information_for_the_public/faq_about_accreditation

New England Association of Schools and Colleges. (2008b). *Student success S-series.* Retrieved from http://cihe.neasc.org/standards_policies/commission_policies/

Noland, B. E., Johnson, B. D., & Skolits, G. (2004). *Changing perceptions and outcomes: The Tennessee performance funding experience.* Retrieved from http://tennessee.gov/thec/Divisions/AcademicAffairs/performance_funding/Research%20Noland%20DandridgeJohnson%20Skolits%202004.pdf

Office of the Governor, Rick Perry. (2004). *Governor Rick Perry directs university regents to set accountability standards.* Retrieved from http://governor.state. tx.us/news/press-release/4327/

Oklahoma State Regents for Higher Education. (2008). *Brain gain 2010.* Retrieved from http://www.okhighered.org/studies-reports/brain-gain/.

Project on Accreditation and Assessment. (2004). *Taking responsibility for the quality of the baccalaureate degree.* Washington, DC: Association of American Colleges and Universities.

Ratteray, O. M. T. (2002). Information literacy in self-study and accreditation. *Journal of Academic Librarianship, 28*(6), 368–375. Retrieved from H. W. Wilson.

Reindl, T. (2007). *Hitting home: Quality, cost and access challenges confronting higher education today.* Indianapolis, IN: Lumina Foundation. Retrieved from http://www.eric.ed.gov/PDFS/ED497037.pdf

Rice, R. E. (2006). Enhancing the quality of teaching and learning: The U.S. experience. *New Directions for Higher Education, 133*, 13–22. Retrieved from ProQuest.

Rockman, I. F. (2002). Strengthening connections between information literacy, general education, and assessment efforts. *Library Trends, 51*(2), 185–198. Retrieved from H. W. Wilson.

Saunders, L. (2007). Regional accreditation organizations' treatment of information literacy: Definitions, collaboration, and assessment. *Journal of Academic Librarianship, 33*(3), 317–326. Retrieved from H. W. Wilson.

Schneider, M. (2005). *2003 National Assessment of Adult Literacy (NAAL) results.* Retrieved from http://nces.ed.gov/whatsnew/commissioner/remarks2005/ 12_15_2005.asp

Shupe, D. (2007). Significantly better: The benefits for an academic institution focused on student learning outcomes. *On the Horizon, 15*(2), 48–57. Retrieved from ProQuest.

Stoops, J. A., & Parsons M. D. (2003). Higher education and accreditation. In J. W. Guthrie (Ed.), *Encyclopedia of education* (2nd ed., Vol. 1, pp. 28–35). New York, NY: MacMillan Reference. Retrieved from Gale Virtual Reference Library.

Suskie, L. (2004). *Assessing student learning: A common sense guide.* Bolton, MA: Anker Publishing.

Suskie, L. (2006). Accountability and quality improvement. In P. Hernon, R. E. Dugan, & C. Schwartz (Eds.), *Revisiting outcomes assessment in higher education* (pp. 13–38). Westport, CT: Libraries Unlimited.

Trow, M. (1994). Managerialism and the academic profession: The case of England. *Higher Education Policy, 7*(2), 11–18.

US Department of Education. (2006). *A test of leadership: Charting the future of U.S. higher education.* Washington, DC: Author. Retrieved from http:// www.ed.gov/about/bdscomm/list/hiedfuture/reports/final-report.pdf

Vedder, R. K. (2008). Colleges should go beyond the rhetoric of accountability. *Chronicle of Higher Education, 54*(42), A64. Retrieved from Ebsco.

Wellman, J. (1998). *Recognition of accreditation organizations.* Washington, DC: Council for Higher Education Accreditation. Retrieved from http:// www.chea.org/pdf/RecognitionWellman_Jan1998.pdf

Wiggins, G. (1997). Feedback: How learning occurs. In *Assessing impact: Evidence and action, Presentations from the 1997 AAHE Conference on Assessment and Quality* (pp. 31–39). Washington, DC: American Association of Higher Education.

Yudof, S., & Ruberg, C. (2007). *Secretary Spellings encourages greater transparency and accountability in higher education at the national accreditation meeting* (Press Release). Retrieved from http://www.ed.gov/news/pressreleases/2007/12/12182007.html

CHAPTER 3

The Study's Reflective Inquiry and Procedures

Institutional self-studies and team visiting reports, generated for and during the accreditation process, demonstrate the extent to which an institution achieves accreditation standards. While institutions have some flexibility in how they interpret them, the accreditation standards set broad expectations of general student learning outcomes such as critical thinking abilities, the capacity for lifelong learning, and information literacy. In their self-study reports, institutions offer evidence of achievement of those student learning outcomes as well as provide inputs, outputs, and student outcomes as specified in the standards. After reading the self-study, a team convened by the accreditation organization visits the campus to conduct observations and interviews. This team generates a report that summarizes its responses to the institutional self-study and the observations made during the campus visit, as well as provides any recommendations the team has for the institution. The institution then has an opportunity to respond to the visiting team's report before the accreditation organization renders a decision on accreditation status.

PROBLEM STATEMENT

Accreditation standards, and the self-studies and team reports produced as part of the accreditation process, serve as valuable sources of insight into how institutions interpret and incorporate the expectations of accreditation organizations into their missions, goals, and assessment practices. While a self-study and its related committee report is specific to the institution under review, taken as a whole, the group of documents produced within a certain time span indicate trends, highlight which focus areas receive the most attention, and create a snapshot of the current state of higher education across institutions.

By detailing how institutions interpret and apply standards in their programs and practices and align those standards with their individual goals and missions, the self-studies and team reports reveal the extent to which institutions treat information literacy as a student learning outcome and how that outcome is framed in practice. No study has examined the self-study reports of individual institutions in light of information literacy as an outcome to determine how and to what extent colleges and universities acknowledge and address such an outcome.

The results of this study have implications for accreditation organizations—both regional and specialized as well as CHEA—that have incorporated information literacy learning outcomes into their standards. By demonstrating the extent to which these institutions addresses outcomes for information literacy, this study offers some evidence of the level of importance institutions actually afford to those outcomes. Those individuals serving as team members for accreditation review, and administrators of institutions seeking to gain or renew their accreditation, will also be interested to see how institutions and evaluators assess one particular student learning outcome with regard to regional standards. The results might inform the development of training programs for visiting team members as well.

Likewise, stakeholders such as government agencies and state legislatures concerned with accountability in higher education can see how accreditation organizations and institutions hold themselves responsible for one student learning outcome. Because information literacy is often intertwined with and supported by library instruction, library directors and instruction librarians who are managing or implementing an information literacy program will also be interested in these results, as will those professional library associations directly concerned with information literacy such as the ACRL. Finally, teaching faculty, who are ultimately most directly responsible for achievement of student learning outcomes, might be interested to see how such outcomes are being interpreted, implemented, and assessed.

LITERATURE REVIEW

By setting expectations and facilitating assessment for improvement, accreditation organizations can act as catalysts for change. For instance, Saunders (2007) conducted a case study of an institution seeking renewal of its regional accreditation and found that 7 of the 10 participants interviewed thought the accreditation process had a positive impact on program quality, whereas only one respondent believed that accreditation undermined quality. This respondent contended program quality was not discussed during the process, and that by focusing so much attention on outcomes, the institution impeded academic improvement. On the other hand, those participants who saw a positive impact cited the self-study and peer review, as well as the accreditation organization's "new emphasis on assessment of educational outcomes" (p. 192), as the aspects of the process having the greatest impact.

A statement of principles issued by the Association of American Colleges and Universities in conjunction with the Council for Higher Education Accreditation (Association of American Colleges and Universities, 2008) asserts that individual institutions must take primary responsibility for student learning assessment. While acknowledging the continued importance of the role of accreditation organizations in initiating and maintaining such assessment, both organizations assert that "colleges and universities must themselves take the lead in seeing that American higher education maintains its position of global leadership" (p. 2). This idea of leadership was expounded in a study of specialized and program accreditation at Farleigh Dickinson University, in which the researcher (Ferrara, 2007) found that the president and program leaders used accreditation assessment as a means for institutional improvement. Six programs had specified student learning outcomes, and university leaders leveraged accreditation requirements to advance the inclusion of student learning outcomes in other programs. In this case, accreditation provided an external impetus, but was not the driving force of change.

In the *Project on the Future of Higher Education*, Guskin and Marcy (2003) stress the need for colleges and universities to make fundamental and transformative changes in how they educate students in response to increasing budgetary and financial pressures. They lay out a framework comprising three organizing principles and seven transformative actions to assist institutions in making the requisite changes. Two of the areas specifically addressed in this publication are assessment of learning outcomes and the role of the library. Guskin and Marcy (2003) challenge institutions to use student learning outcomes rather than credit hours earned as the basis for awarding degrees. They also argue for restructuring the academic library, including "assignment to a more prominent role in educational delivery," maintaining that the "library of the future will need to become a true learning center for students and faculty ... both the symbolic and concrete heart of the learning-centered campus" (p. 20).

The Library: Roles and Responses

Although Guskin and Marcy (2003) do not specifically discuss information literacy, their emphasis on the library as a partner in teaching and learning alludes to the role that academic libraries can play in developing and assessing information literacy learning outcomes. The definition of information literacy developed by ACRL has been one of the most widely accepted throughout higher education, and could be used as the foundation for the library's role. While several accreditation organizations use language similar to ACRL in their standards, the Middle States Commission explicitly draws on the ACRL definition to form the basis of its framework for implementing information literacy programs in *Developing Research and Communication Skills* (Middle States Commission, 2003).

As discussed in Chapter 1, library instruction, often focused on finding and evaluating information sources and properly citing sources from which students have drawn intellectual content, has been a core service of academic libraries since at least the 1970s. However, traditional library instruction was often regarded as a service or a supporting role, while current library mission statements show libraries redefining their role by using phrases such as teaching library, learning library, and learner's library. Gilchrist (2007) contends that this shift to a learning library entails "a deeper philosophic and programmatic intention. This means a more direct, deliberate, and systematic connection to the curriculum" (p. 16).

Indeed, librarians have written extensively on many aspects of librarians as instructors, including discussions of pedagogy and teaching practice (Accardi, Drabinski, & Kumbier, 2010; Albrecht & Baron, 2002; Elmborg, 2006; Grassian & Kaplowitz, 2001, 2005; Keyser, 1999; Swanson, 2005), addressing learning styles (Bodi, 1990; Costello, Lenholt, & Stryker, 2004; Holmes, 2003), and learning outcomes assessment (Lindauer, 2004; Neely, 2006; Oakleaf, 2008; Radcliff, 2007). Some authors have also focused on the roles and opportunities for the librarian within the context of information literacy instruction (O'Hanlon, 2007; Scales, Matthews, & Johnson, 2005; Stamatoplos, 2009). Walter (2008) explored the extent to which instruction librarians identify themselves as teachers, and what graduate programs can do to prepare librarians more fully for a teaching role. Thompson (2002) emphasizes the role of librarian as teacher and curriculum developer, and likewise stresses the importance of professional development in gaining or strengthening teaching skills.

Librarians have acknowledged the role of accreditation in fostering information literacy on campus. In a literature review, Johnson (2003) noted increased discussion of the role of accreditation in the literature of library and information science (LIS). Librarians' interest in accreditation for information literacy is evidenced by the attention to detail they display in the review of various standards. In a number of cases, specialized accreditation organizations are not explicit in their expectations for information literacy learning outcomes. But through a careful reading and extrapolation, it is possible to draw clear connections between the specialized standards and ACRL competency areas. For instance, Ruediger and Jung (2007) offer an in-depth analysis that draws comparisons between the recently revised standards of the Accrediting Council on Education in Journalism and Mass

Communications (ACEJMC) and the ACRL standards. In particular, they draw attention to ACEJMC's expectation that students be able to conduct research and evaluate the information they find. Trussell (2004) notes similarities between the Accreditation Board for Engineering and Technology's (ABET) focus on ethics in its most recent standards and ACRL's emphasis on the ability to use information in ethical, legal, and socially responsible ways. Trussell outlines ways in which librarians could support engineering faculty in instruction and assessment for this outcome. Likewise, VanderPol and Taranto (2002) equate information literacy abilities with the language used by the National Association of Schools of Music and the American Chemical Society, which underscore a student's need to keep current and engage in lifelong learning.

In general, LIS articles mentioning accreditation tend to focus on the role of librarians in instruction and assessment of information literacy, and using accreditation standards as leverage for justifying that role (Tunon, 2003). Several authors suggest that accreditation standards offer opportunities for librarians to take on a broader role within the campus. For instance, Jacobson and Germain (2006) discuss their involvement on a campus-wide curriculum committee established to integrate new standards, including information literacy outcomes, at SUNY Albany. This committee offers workshops for faculty and conducts syllabus reviews to assist faculty in designing assignments that integrate information literacy competencies. Thompson (2002) emphasizes the centrality of the library in information literacy, asserting that the shift in focus to critical thinking abilities and lifelong learning means that "the time is ripe for a transformation of the traditional mission for teaching 'library skills' into a broader mandate for teaching '*information literacy*' " (p. 218).

Collaboration/Partnerships for Instruction and Assessment

While librarians have actively promoted information literacy outcomes and recognized the opportunities for leadership, accreditation organizations and other stakeholders stress that information literacy is neither synonymous with library research skills nor is it solely the domain of librarians. The Middle States Commission, in particular, underscores this point by calling for seamless integration of information literacy skills within the curriculum. Acknowledging the roots of information literacy in LIS, the Middle States Commission (2003) contends that "the concept now has been extended to describe a more comprehensive vision of teaching and learning" (p. 3). As such, information literacy as an outcome specified by the various regional accreditation organizations is largely written into general education standards, rather than library-related standards. This is not to suggest that librarians have no role to play in information literacy instruction and assessment. Rather, teaching faculty and librarians should partner in these endeavors, an idea supported, to a greater or lesser extent, by all of the regional accreditation organizations (Saunders, 2007).

As with any other learning outcomes, institutions are expected to assess and provide evidence of achievement in the area of information literacy. Ideally, both faculty and librarians participate in the assessment. The fact that information literacy extends beyond the library and general education to all disciplines implies the necessity of collaboration among faculty of different disciplines and between faculty and librarians in instructing and assessing students in these competencies.

Several regional accreditation organizations echo the call for partnerships evident in the Middle States Commission's standards. For instance, the New England Association of Schools and Colleges (NEASC, 2005) states that, in assessing student learning outcomes, institutions must evaluate what is happening both inside and outside the classroom, with particular attention to the "impact of its library, information resources and services" (standard 7.12). The Northwest Commission on Colleges and Universities (2003) also underscores the importance of collaboration between librarians and faculty by suggesting that librarians should be included in curriculum planning, in order to ensure that information resources are meaningfully integrated into students' learning processes.

The obstacles to such collaboration can be numerous, however. Librarians often lament that campus cultures of academic freedom and faculty autonomy mean that faculty tend to "own" their courses, and librarians depend on faculty buy-in and support for information literacy programs (Saunders, 2009). Such buy-in is not widespread. Gilchrist (2007) notes that, while librarians have been active both in promoting information literacy and in redefining the library's role as a teaching partner, others in higher education rarely acknowledge the possibilities or contributions of the library. In particular, she points out that, while many studies assert the benefits of collaboration for teaching and learning, few of these include librarians among the collaborators.

Due to this reticence on the part of faculty, some authors suggest that the onus is on the librarians to initiate and develop such partnerships. Smith (2001) encourages librarians to develop an ongoing dialogue with faculty about integrating information literacy into the curriculum. Faculty, he maintains, are more likely to be receptive to ideas that align with their teaching areas and expertise. He warns that librarians will likely have to take the initiative in starting these conversations and looking for opportunities to collaborate. A number of writers (Rader, 2004; Thompson, 2002; Tunon, 2003) assert that attention to information literacy in accreditation standards offers librarians an opportunity to engage in dialogues with faculty and to assume a leadership role.

Gilchrist (2007) documents the way in which instruction librarians in one institution took initiative in advocating for, creating, and implementing an information literacy program on campus. Under the leadership of the librarians, a partnership was established with teaching faculty. Rader (2004), who stresses the current culture as a time of opportunity, encourages librarians to use their expertise and knowledge to take a more active educational role on campus. In fact, other authors echo the leadership potential offered by information literacy. Fowler and Walter (2003) maintain that "the rise of information literacy instruction as a strategic direction for many libraries increasingly requires the instruction coordinator to act as a leader both within the library and across campus" (p. 465).

Accountability and Transparency

Assessment of learning outcomes such as information literacy is important because it addresses the various stakeholder groups' demands for accountability and transparency outlined in Chapter 2. As noted in that chapter, many of these groups seek assurance of a return on the direct or indirect investments they make in higher education, and ask institutions to provide evidence of student learning as one measure of achievement. While much of the scrutiny focuses on parent institutions, in an address to the Association of Christian Librarians, Smith (2009) warns librarians "you're being watched" (p. 78). He notes that references to accountability have increased threefold in the last two decades within the LIS literature, and he warns that librarians must gather data to measure the contribution they make to the overall institution. Dougherty (2009) agrees that in the face of the current recession, it is incumbent upon librarians not only to assess their services, but to analyze the results both for continued improvement and in order to explain how the library supports overall institutional efforts at accountability.

Institutional Culture

Whether or not institutions foster collaboration, assessment, accountability, and transparency depends to some extent on the culture of the institution. Institutional culture describes the patterns of behavior, norms, beliefs, and values that make up the institution and guide the actions and interactions of individuals within that institution (Lakos & Phipps, 2004; Scott & Marshall, 2005). In other words, certain behaviors, attitudes, and actions that are valued by the institution will be encouraged, while others will be discouraged. Institutional cultures are often historically rooted and deeply ingrained, and, as Devlin, Burich, Stockham, Summey, and Turtle (2006) note, that culture can "thwart or facilitate change" (p. 162). In relation to information literacy, Bennett (2007) identified three elements that support the integration of information literacy into the culture of the institution. First, integration tends to coincide with curricular review or redesign.

Institutions that create dialogues about the curriculum and involve faculty and staff in discussions about curricular reform tend to be "extraordinarily fertile ground for advancing programs of information literacy" (p. 164). Second, institutions that promote undergraduate research, where students are expected to find and use information independently, tend to support information literacy. Finally, institutions that value information literacy view the library as a place for learning and instruction, rather than just a place to house resources.

Leadership

The broad-based, collaborative information literacy programs described in Figure 1.1 depends on buy-in from faculty and senior administrators, and may require substantial changes to the culture of some institutions, a challenging undertaking. To influence such changes, librarians may need to assume leadership roles on their campuses. In its *Standards for Proficiencies for Instruction Librarians and Coordinators*, ACRL (American Library Association, Association of College and Research Libraries, 2007) identifies leadership skills as essential, suggesting that instruction librarians must take initiative to promote and advocate for information literacy on their campuses. As Walter (2008) notes, instruction librarians are beginning to describe themselves as teachers, and the education literature has identified attributes that tend to characterize teacher leaders. Since classroom teachers tend to work alone, in order to effect change within their organizations, they must be adept at making connections with colleagues outside the classroom and at working collaboratively (Dozier, 2007; Fowler & Walter, 2003; Frost & Harris, 2003; York-Barr & Duke, 2004). They also must have a strong understanding of the organizational culture, including knowledge of the policies and procedures that support and facilitate their work, and of the key players who can help them achieve their goals (Frost & Harris, 2003). Using their ability to build relationships and their understanding of the organization, teacher leaders can create a base of followers who share their vision and are willing to work toward making that vision a reality.

PROCEDURES

The Middle States Commission has the most detailed and comprehensive set of standards regarding information literacy outcomes of the six regional accreditation organizations. In addition to specific learning outcomes for information literacy within its standards, the Middle States Commission (2003) also developed *Developing Research and Communication Skills*, which offers its constituents extensive guidelines on how and why to implement an information literacy program on their campuses. Because of this emphasis on information literacy, and former assistant director of the Middle

States Commission Oswald Ratteray's (2002) support for information literacy as a learning outcome, the bulk of this study centers on the accreditation documents produced by institutions within the jurisdiction of the Middle States Commission, specifically the institutional self-study.

Population

The population for this study is comprised of the colleges and universities accredited by the six regional accreditation organizations (see Table 2.1). Although these organizations accredit some institutions in US territories and overseas, these are excluded. The list of institutions accredited by each accreditation organization was obtained from directories maintained by the organization and accessible from the individual organization's website. After removing community colleges, institutions outside of the United States (including those located in Puerto Rico and other islands), specialized and online-only institutions, for-profit institutions, and those institutions undergoing accreditation review for the first time at the time of this study, the population is 1,520 colleges and universities.

To compile a preliminary list of self-studies, the home page of each institution was searched to determine if the documents were publicly available. If a search box was available, the site was searched for particular keywords including "accreditation," "self-study," and terms representing the regional accreditation organization such as "middle states," "neasc," and "sacs." If no search option was available, or if these searches were unsuccessful, other navigational tools (e.g., a site map) were used to locate institutional research offices or provost offices, and those pages were reviewed for documentation. In addition to recording the availability of documents for each of the 1,520 institutions, information about Carnegie classification of institutions of higher education (see Table 3.1), accreditation status, and latest accreditation update for each institution was noted.

Because the Middle States Commission has the most extensive set of standards and guidelines related to information literacy, its region was chosen for further analysis. In addition to documents available publicly online, documents were solicited from institutions, and case study institutions were selected from the group accredited by this organization. In order to access documents not publicly available, the author first sent a letter to the Middle States Commission to request access to self-study documents. Although the Middle States Commission encourages its constituents to make accreditation documentation, specifically the self-study, available to the public, institutions are not required to do so. In some cases, reports are posted to the web, but are password-protected so as to limit access to members of the institution's community. In other cases, the reports are held in paper copy, perhaps in the provost's office or in the library. Thus, it is necessary to request access to reports that were not publicly posted online.

Table 3.1   Search Results for Accreditation Documents

Institutions by Carnegie Classification*	Middle States	Other Regions
Baccalaureate**	7	60
Master's smaller programs**	3	16
Master's medium programs**	6	17
Master's larger programs**	20	48
Doctoral/ Research**	24	88
Not classified	3	
Total no. of institutions	63	229

*The classification system was first developed by the Carnegie Foundation in 1970 to "support its program of research and policy analysis." The recently updated 2005 edition has been expanded to include more categories, and is "the leading framework for describing institutional diversity in U.S. higher education" (Carnegie Foundation for the Advancement of Teaching, 2007, para. 1)
**Definitions:

- Baccalaureate: bachelor's degrees accounted for at least 10 percent of all undergraduate degrees and they awarded fewer than 50 master's degrees;
- Master's smaller: Institutions awarding 50-99 master's degrees;
- Master's medium: Institutions awarding at least 100-199 master's degrees, but fewer than 20 doctorates;
- Master's larger: Institutions awarding at least 200 master's degrees, but fewer than 20 doctorates; and
- Doctoral/Research: institutions that awarded at least 20 doctorates in a year; further subdivided by level of research activity.

   The letter to the Middle States Commission serves a dual purpose. First, it alerts staff members to the scope and nature of the work. Because this research focuses on the Middle States Commission's constituents extensively, and because it investigates institutional responses to specific accreditation requirements, it is assumed that the Middle States Commission would be interested in the study, and should be informed of it. In addition, the Middle States Commission also keeps copies of all documents at its headquarters in Pennsylvania, which could serve as another point of access for missing documents. Thus, the letter inquired as to whether the Middle States Commission could allow access to those documents. Such a step precludes the need to collect documents individually from each institution.

   Because the Middle States Commission considers self-studies confidential, it will not release them to researchers or others without consent from the institution. The next step was to send individual letters to each institution without publicly posted self-studies and team reports to request access to these documents. The letter introduced the topic area of the research, outlined the design, and asked institutions to share their self-study documents. The letter stressed that the research focuses on institutional activity in relation to assessment of student learning outcomes for information literacy and would not expose institutions to criticism or punitive actions. The letter assured anonymity for all individuals and institutions. Respondents are asked to send reports digitally if possible.

Methodology

This study was conducted in four phases, each of which uses a separate methodology. Through content analysis, phase one developed a codebook of institutions' characteristics to be used in the following phase. Phase two relies on content analysis to uncover patterns or themes in the treatment of information literacy within the sets of documents reviewed. The third phase centers on case studies chosen from the results of phase two, and phase four extends the review of self-studies nationwide.

Phase One

The first stage consists of a pretest, in which the researcher uses a subset of documents not included in the final study. These documents were drawn from institutions that are accredited by the Middle States Commission, but are located outside of the continental United States. These institutions include universities located in American territories such as Puerto Rico and the US Virgin Islands. Only self-contained universities were included in this stage, and not branch campuses of institutions located within the United States. Further, only documents that were freely accessible on the web were included.

Using content analysis, the retrieved documents were analyzed for patterns about coverage of information literacy. In particular, instances of the use of the phrase "information literacy" or language from the ACRL definition were noted. These instances are then reexamined to determine if there are patterns in how the institutions use the terminology:

- In what context is information literacy discussed (general education outcomes, libraries, other)?
- Which ACRL competencies are mentioned? If ACRL competencies are not mentioned, is equivalent language used?
- How is the outcome phrased and assessed?
- Do these institutions share common characteristics (for-credit information literacy classes, mission statements identifying information literacy as an outcome, and an assessment person on staff)?

The findings are used to generate a list of categories for institutional characteristics and information literacy implementation to help address phase two questions and to be used for coding documents in phase two.

Phase Two

This phase concentrates on accreditation documents from the 264 institutions accredited by the Middle States Commission. It begins with the 63 institutions for which accreditation documents are freely posted on the web and continues with documentation received from the remaining 201 institutions, which were contacted directly. Using the framework of categories developed during the pretest, this study determines how many institutions include information literacy as a student learning outcome within their self-studies, how and to what extent these institutions address these outcomes, and whether certain traits characterize these institutions. Specifically, using content analysis, this phase addresses the following questions:

- Coverage of information literacy in accreditation documents:
  - Is information literacy mentioned?
  - How is information literacy defined?
  - Is information literacy identified as an outcome?
  - If so, in what context (i.e., general education, library, other)? Is information literacy listed as a separate learning outcome, or as a subset of critical thinking?
- ACRL competencies mentioned:
  - Are ACRL competencies included? If yes, which ones?
  - Are Middle States Commission documents (e.g., *Developing Research and Communication Skills*) referred to?
  - If not, is some equivalent language used?
- Assessment of information literacy outcomes:
  - Are information literacy learning outcomes being assessed?
  - If so, at what level?
    - Institutional level? Program level? Course level?
    - What methods are employed (Direct or indirect; tests, bibliography reviews, portfolios, etc.)?
- Use of assessment data:
  - Is there any indication of whether/how assessment data are used for educational improvement?
- Pretest categories:
  - Which pretest categories are identified in the institutions?
  - Are there differences in categories between those institutions whose documents were posted freely on the web, and those whose documents had to be requested?
  - Are other, previously unidentified, characteristics evident in these institutions?
- Leadership for information literacy:
  - Is there an indication of who initiated/promoted planning for information literacy?

○ Who takes responsibility for instruction and assessment?
○ Is there evidence of collaboration?

Content analysis can be either a quantitative or qualitative method, or both. In quantitative content analysis, documents are scanned either automatically or manually to find instances of preselected keywords related to the topic under study. The researcher then tallies the counts within and across documents in order to make deductions about the importance, weight, or depth of feeling that can be attributed to the document or its author based on the frequency of word occurrence (Babbie, 2002). Likewise, the researcher compares word usage among documents and looks for patterns within and among documents.

In qualitative content analysis, the researcher looks at documents more holistically, analyzes meanings of words and phrases, and attempts to make "specific inferences from text to other states or properties of its source" (Krippendorff, 1980, p. 103). Such analysis requires careful reading and rereading of documents in order to decipher both overt and underlying meanings of the text, and identified parts of the text relating to themes or ideas are then categorized. The researcher may choose to use either inductive category development, in which tentative categories are devised from the research questions, and theoretical framework and revised as data are analyzed; or from deductive category application, in which categories are predetermined along with clear definitions and strict rules for determining when document text are entered into a specific category.

This study primarily employed inductive category application, using categories developed during the pretest phase to identify common themes in accreditation documents. Secondary quantitative analysis was conducted to investigate the use of particular words and phrases: "information literacy," "partnership," *or* "collaboration" within the documents. In this secondary analysis, the number of times a word was used suggests the importance attached to that concept.

Phase Three

Based on the results of phase two, four institutions accredited by the Middle States Commission are selected to serve as case studies for more in-depth analysis, which constitutes the third stage of research. A case study is a type of field research defined as "the in-depth examination of a single instance of some social phenomenon" such as an institution (Babbie, 2005, p. 480). The aspects of studies can vary. For instance, the actual phenomena that constitute the case can be many different things, but, for the purposes of this study, they encompass the information literacy program, however it is defined within the institution, and all persons associated with that program. If the information literacy program widely involves faculty, a key department was selected. In addition, within the broad context of a case study, the researcher can adopt many roles, from impartial observer to active participant. This particular project uses qualitative interviews, in which participants are asked open-ended questions. The researcher interacts with the participants, but uses neutrally worded questions. Finally, the observations made in case studies can be used for exploratory or explanatory purposes. In this case, data from case studies explains emerging patterns from the content analysis in phase two.

The format for this stage is a qualitative interview, meaning that questions and format may not be exactly the same in each case, but in general they relate to programming, roles and responsibilities, and assessment. All participants signed an informed consent form, which was approved by the Simmons College Institutional Review Board. Case studies allow for extended observations of the settings, interactions, and processes of people and phenomena, and can allow for a more in-depth analysis. Observing the processes and programs of these institutions and conversing with faculty and staff directly involved in the planning and implementation helps to set the context for the programs described in accreditation documents.

Further, while the content analysis of phase two identifies institutional responses to accreditation standards, the case studies may offer some explanation about how and why certain institutions chose to implement the standards in specific ways (Babbie, 2005). The purpose of these case studies is to combine observation and interviews to probe more deeply into the findings of the content analysis. Characteristics for choosing case studies might include institutions with a national reputation for information literacy, those with publications related to information literacy as a learning outcome, and/or robust assessment programs for information literacy as a student learning outcome. This phase investigates the following questions:

- Is there acknowledgement and agreement about who leads information literacy efforts on campus?
- Is there evidence of collaboration?
  - If so, who is involved?
  - How are responsibilities divided (e.g., as in Figure 1.1)?
  - At what level are programming/planning decisions made (institutional/program/course)?
  - Who is involved in planning the curriculum?
- What characteristics from pretest or phase one categories might account for the successful implementation of information literacy programs?

Phase Four

While the Middle States Commission has the most extensive set of standards related to information literacy, other regional accreditation organizations also address the competencies of information literacy. In order to compare institutions across regions and establish a nationwide baseline for how institutions are addressing learning outcomes for information literacy, the fourth phase of this study involves a cursory overview of publicly available self-studies from institutions in the five remaining regions. Procedures for this phase are similar to those in phase two. To begin with, the author searched membership directories of each of the five accreditation organizations to compile a list of 1,256 institutions nationwide, excluding for-profit, online-only, and specialized institutions. The website of each institution was then searched to discover any publicly posted decennial self-studies, using keywords such as "self-study," "accreditation," or the name of the relevant accreditation organization. If the site did not support searching, a manual search of administrator pages such as the provost or president was conducted. These searches resulted in a total of 229 self-studies from across the nation. Using the same codebook from phase two, these documents were analyzed for the same themes and patterns relating to information literacy.

LIMITATIONS

Qualitative content analysis is often criticized because the subjectivity of the analysis calls reliability and validity into question (Babbie, 2005; Creswell, 2003). Within this study, the author corrects for these limitations by testing her own analysis against that of another coder. A colleague was given a self-study from the sample population, along with coding categories and criteria developed during the pretest. The colleague then independently reviewed and categorized documents. Both sets of data were tested for intercoder reliability using Cohen's kappa, which was found to be .73. This falls within the 95 percent confidence rate for Cohen's kappa, meaning that the results are reliable.

In addition, although accreditation organizations encourage institutions within their jurisdiction to make public accreditation documents, including self-reports, each college and university decides whether to share that information. As a result, this study was limited to those institutions that either posted accreditation documents publicly on their websites or agreed to send copies to the author on request.

Knowing the purpose of the study and intentions of the authors, those institutions that were contacted directly may have chosen to participate only if they believe that their accreditation documents were generally positive, particularly in the area of information literacy. Possibly, institutions with more robust information literacy programs are more likely to participate, and therefore might skew the data. Likewise, institutions with more positive self-studies might be more likely to post their documents publicly online.

Support for and expectations of information literacy as a student learning outcome vary among the regional accreditation organizations, and have changed over time as each organization issues new sets of standards. For instance, although the Middle States Commission has supported information literacy as an important concept since at least the early 1990s, information literacy as a learning outcome was only written into the most recent version of its standards, which went into effect in 2002. Since accreditation reviews are on a 10-year cycle, unless they undergo a periodic review, some institutions may have had their last review before the current standards went into effect. As a result, those institutions cannot be expected to have placed as much emphasis on information literacy as those reviewed since the current standards went into effect.

CONCLUSION

Information literacy abilities are critical to success in an information-rich world. Accreditation organizations acknowledge the importance of information literacy along with other liberal arts competencies such as critical thinking and quantitative reasoning. However, the extent to which colleges and universities have addressed information literacy as a learning outcome is unclear. In fact, the skills and knowledge associated with information literacy (e.g., locating and accessing information, and evaluating of information) often are already addressed in the curriculum and through cocurricular activities such as library instruction. Nevertheless, institutions do not always acknowledge these areas as information literacy.

An institution may name information literacy specifically as a student learning outcome, or address generic information literacy competencies within other competencies. How explicit the institution is in addressing information literacy as a student learning outcome might affect related areas such as the level of collaboration between faculty and librarians, and the extent to which information literacy is assessed at the program level. Characteristics such as librarian involvement in curricular planning, high levels of collaboration, and specific institutional goals for information literacy as a student learning outcome may be common to institutions with robust information literacy programs.

REFERENCES

Accardi, M. T., Drabinski, E., & Kumbier, A. (2010). *Critical library instruction: Theories and methods.* Duluth, MN: Library Juice Press.

Albrecht, R., & Baron, S. (2002). The politics of pedagogy: Expectations and reality for information literacy in librarianship. *Journal of Library Administration, 36*(1–2), 71–96. Retrieved from Haworth Press Journals.

American Library Association, Association of College and Research Libraries. (2007). *Standards for proficiencies for instruction librarians and coordinators.* Retrieved from http://www.ala.org/ala/mgrps/divs/acrl/standards/profstandards.cfm

Association of American Colleges and Universities. (2008). *New leadership for student learning and accountability.* A joint report with the Council for Higher Education Accreditation. Retrieved from http://www.chea.org/pdf/2008.01.30_New_Leadership_Statement.pdf

Babbie, E. R. (2002). *The basics of social research* (2nd ed.). Belmont, CA: Wadsworth Thomson Learning.

Bennett, S. (2007). Campus cultures fostering information literacy. *portal: Libraries and the Academy, 7*(2), 147–167. Retrieved from ProjectMUSE.

Bodi, S. (1990). Teaching effectiveness and bibliographic instruction: The relevance of learning styles. *College and Research Libraries, 51,* 113–119. Retrieved from H. W. Wilson.

Carnegie Foundation for the Advancement of Teaching. (2007). *The Carnegie classification of institutions of higher education.* Retrieved from http://www.carnegie foundation.org/classifications/

Costello, B., Lenholt, R., & Stryker, J. (2004). Using blackboard in library instruction: Addressing the learning styles of generations X and Y. *Journal of Academic Librarianship, 30*(6), 452–460. Retrieved from H. W. Wilson.

Creswell, J. W. (2003). *Research design: Qualitative, quantitative, and mixed methods approaches.* Thousand Oaks, CA: Sage Publications.

Devlin, F. A., Burich, N. J., Stockham, M. G., Summey, T. P., & Turtle, E. C. (2006). Getting beyond institutional cultures: When rivals collaborate. *Journal of Library Administration, 45*(1), 149–168. Retrieved from InformaWorld.

Dougherty, R. M. (2009). Assessment + analysis = accountability. *College and Research Libraries, 70*(5), 417–418. Retrieved from H. W. Wilson.

Dozier, T. K. (2007). Turning good teachers into great leaders (cover story). *Educational Leadership, 65*(1), 54–58. Retrieved from Academic Search Complete.

Elmborg, J. (2006). Critical information literacy: Implications for instructional practice. *Journal of Academic Librarianship, 32*(2), 192–199. Retrieved from H. W. Wilson.

Ferrara, H. (2007). *Accreditation as a lever for institutional change: Focusing on student learning outcomes.* Retrieved from ProQuest Digital Research (AAT 3255872).

Fowler, C. S., & Walter, S. (2003). Instructional leadership: New responsibilities for a new reality. *College and Research Libraries News, 64*(7), 465–468. Retrieved from H. W. Wilson.

Frost, D., & Harris, A. (2003). Teacher leadership: Towards a research agenda. *Cambridge Journal of Education, 33*(3), 479–498. Retrieved from Academic Search Complete.

Gilchrist, D. L. (2007). *Academic libraries at the center of instructional change: Faculty and librarian experience of library leadership in the transformation of teaching and learning.* Retrieved from ProQuest Research.

Grassian, E. S., & Kaplowitz, J. R. (2001). *Information literacy instruction: Theory and practice.* New York, NY: Neal-Schuman.

Grassian, E. S., & Kaplowitz, J. R. (2005). *Learning to lead and manage information literacy instruction.* New York, NY: Neal-Schuman.

Guskin, A. E., & Marcy, M. B. (2003). Dealing with the future NOW. *Change, 35* (4), 10–22. Retrieved from Ebsco.

Holmes, K. E. (2003). A kaleidoscope of learning styles: Instructional supports that meet the diverse needs of distant learners. *Journal of Library Administration, 37*(3–4), 367–378. Retrieved from Haworth Press Journals.

Jacobson, T. E., & Germain, C. A. (2006). A campus-wide role for an information literacy committee. *Resource Sharing and Information Networks, 17*(1–2), 111–121. Retrieved from H. W. Wilson.

Johnson, A. M. (2003). Library instruction and information literacy. *Reference Services Review, 31*(4), 385–418. Retrieved from H. W. Wilson.

Keyser, M. W. (1999). Active learning and cooperative learning: Understanding the difference and using both styles effectively. *Research Strategies, 17*(1), 35–44.

Krippendorff, K. (1980). *Content analysis: An introduction to its methodology.* Beverly Hills, CA: Sage Publications.

Lakos, A., & Phipps, S. (2004). Creating a culture of assessment: A catalyst for organizational change. *portal: Libraries and the Academy, 4*(3), 345–361. Retrieved from Project MUSE.

Lindauer, B. G. (2004). The three arenas of information literacy assessment. *Reference and User Services Quarterly, 44*(2), 122–129. Retrieved from H. W. Wilson.

Middle States Commission on Higher Education. (2003). *Developing research and communication skills: Guidelines for information literacy in the curriculum.* Philadelphia, PA: Author.

Neely, T. Y. (2006). *Information literacy assessment: Standards-based tools and assignments.* Chicago, IL: American Library Association.

New England Association of Schools and Colleges Institutes for Higher Education. (2005). *Standards for accreditation.* Bedford, MA: Author. Retrieved from http://www.neasc.org

Northwest Commission on Colleges and Universities. (2003). *Accreditation handbook.* Redmond, WA: Author. Retrieved from http://www.nwccu.org

Oakleaf, M. (2008). Dangers and opportunities: A conceptual map of information literacy assessment approaches. *portal: Libraries and the Academy, 8*(3), 233–253. Retrieved from Project MUSE.

O'Hanlon, N. (2007). Information literacy in the university curriculum: Challenges for outcomes assessment. *portal: Libraries and the Academy, 7*(2), 169–189. Retrieved from Project MUSE.

Radcliff, C. J. (2007). *A practical guide to information literacy assessment for academic librarians.* Westport, CT: Libraries Unlimited.

Rader, H. B. (2004). Building faculty-librarian partnerships to prepare students for information fluency: The time for sharing information expertise is now. *College and Research Libraries News, 65*(2), 74–76, 80, 83, 90. Retrieved from H. W. Wilson.

Ratteray, O. M. T. (2002). Information literacy in self-study and accreditation. *Journal of Academic Librarianship, 28*(6), 368–375. Retrieved from H. W. Wilson.

Ruediger, C., & Jung, D. (2007). When it all comes together: Integrating information literacy and discipline-based accreditation standards. *College and Undergraduate Libraries, 14*(1), 79–87. Retrieved from Ebsco.

Saunders, L. (2009). The future of information literacy: A Delphi study. *portal: Libraries and the Academy, 9*(1), 99–114. Retrieved from Project MUSE.

Saunders, V. (2007). *Does the accreditation process affect program quality? A qualitative study of perceptions of the higher education accountability system on learning.* Retrieved from Proquest Digital Research (AAT 3268202).

Scales, J., Matthews, G., & Johnson, C. M. (2005). Compliance, cooperation, collaboration, and information literacy. *Journal of Academic Librarianship, 31* (3), 229–235. Retrieved from H. W. Wilson.

Scott, G., & Marshall, G. (2005). Organizational culture. In *Dictionary of Sociology.* Retrieved from Oxford Reference.

Smith, G. A. (2009). Retooling the profession: Librarianship in an era of accountability and competition. *Christian Librarian, 52*(3), 76–84. Retrieved from Ebsco.

Smith, K. R. (2001). New roles and responsibilities for the university library: Advancing student learning through outcomes assessment. *Journal of Library Administration, 35*(4), 29–36. Retrieved from Informaworld.

Stamatoplos, A. (2009). The role of academic libraries in mentored undergraduate research: A model of engagement in the academic community. *College and Research Libraries, 70*(3), 235–249. Retrieved from H. W. Wilson.

Swanson, T. (2005). Teaching students about information: Information literacy and cognitive authority. *Research Strategies, 20*(4), 322–333.

Thompson, G. B. (2002). Information literacy accreditation mandates: What they mean for faculty and librarians. *Library Trends, 51*(2), 218–241. Retrieved from H. W. Wilson.

Trussell, A. (2004). Librarians and engineering faculty: Partnership opportunities in information literacy and ethics instruction. *IATUL Proceedings,* 1–8. Retrieved from H. W. Wilson.

Tunon, J. (2003). The impact of accreditation and distance education on information literacy. *Florida Libraries, 46*(2), 11–14. Retrieved from H. W. Wilson.

US Department of Education. (2008). *Glossary.* Retrieved from http://studentaid.ed.gov/PORTALSWebApp/students/english/Glossary.jsp

VanderPol, D., & Taranto, C. (2002). Information literacy: A new tune for library instruction to music students. *Music Reference Services Quarterly, 8*(2), 15–24. Retrieved from H. W. Wilson.

Walter, S. (2008). Librarians as teachers: A qualitative inquiry into professional identity. *College and Research Libraries, 69*(1), 51–71. Retrieved from H. W. Wilson.

York-Barr, J., & Duke, K. (2004). What do we know about teacher leadership? Findings from two decades of scholarship. *Review of Educational Research, 74*(3), 255–316. Retrieved from ProQuest.

CHAPTER 4

Quantitative Findings of Institutes Accredited by the Middle States Commission and Case Study Selection

As a study using mixed methods, this research combines the quantitative results of phase two with qualitative information from case study interviews and observations in phase three. This chapter reviews the quantitative findings garnered from the content analysis of self-studies. The results of the content analysis informed the choice of case study institutions, and the final part of the chapter details the reasons for each choice. Consistent with qualitative methods, the findings from the case studies, phase three, are intertwined in the discussion in Chapters 7 through 11.

The population for this study was composed of 264 of the academic institutions in the continental United States that are accredited by the Middle States Commission; these institutions are located in the states of Pennsylvania, New York, New Jersey, Delaware, and Maryland, and the District of Columbia. A search of institutional websites for the self-study reports submitted to the Middle States Commission uncovered 63 that were publicly available. For the remaining 201 institutions, the investigator contacted the provost, vice president, or academic dean, to request copies of the reports. A total of three requests were sent to each institution, one by post and two follow-up requests by e-mail.

RESPONSE RATES

In total, 111 of the 201 institutions replied to the requests, for a response rate of 55.2 percent. Of these, 46 (22.9%) agreed to provide documents, while 66 (32.8%) declined. In some cases, participating institutions provided incomplete or incorrect reports (such as periodic reviews and monitoring reports rather than decennial review self-studies). In the end, 34 of the 46 responses were usable. Combined with the 63 publicly available reports, this resulted in a total of 97 self-studies and an overall participation rate of 36.7 percent.

AGE OF REPORT

The self-studies examined ranged in publication date from 1999 to 2009 and came from both public and private institutions at all levels of the Carnegie classification (see http://classifications.carnegiefoundation.org). The documents reveal the number of institutions currently addressing information literacy within their curricula, who is involved in information literacy planning and instruction, the levels and types of collaboration between faculty and librarians, and the types of assessment for learning outcomes related to information literacy. Figures 4.1 and 4.2 show the level of response from each year and each level of Carnegie classification, respectively. As Figure 4.1 illustrates, the number of self-studies reviewed for each year ranged from a low of 4 to a high of 14. The fewest documents were available for 2000, while 14 self-studies were included for each of the years 2004, 2005, 2006, and 2008. It is worth noting that the current Middle States Commission (2002) standards went into effect in 2003.

Because institutions often begin collecting data for self-studies between 18 months and two years before the report is due, this study uses the year

Figure 4.1   Self-Studies Published by Year

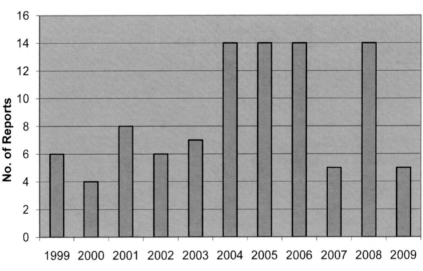

Figure 4.2   Self-Studies by Carnegie Classification*

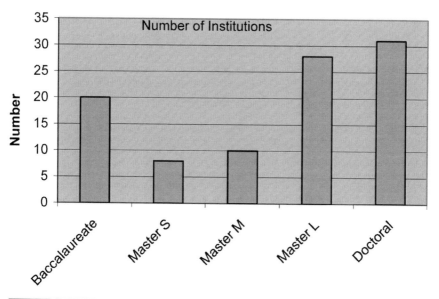

*Chapter 3 of this research defines the classification terms.

2004 as a dividing point, with the assumption that those self-studies completed after 2004 are most likely to comply with current standards. With that cutoff, 45 of the self-studies (46.4 %) included are from 2004 or before, leaving 52 documents (53.6%) completed after 2004. Figure 4.2 offers a breakdown of the number of self-studies included in each of the Carnegie classification bands (defined in Chapter 3). Master's smaller institutions proffered the fewest reports, while doctoral/research institutions produced the highest number.

Incidence of Information Literacy

The self-studies were analyzed and coded with respect to their coverage of information literacy as a student learning outcome. For each self-study, the investigator noted whether the phrase was used at all, how many times it was used, and within what context. In addition, she reviewed the documents for evidence of equivalent language or the use of words and phrases commonly associated with information literacy, such as locating and accessing information, critically evaluating information, or using information ethically. Finally, each document was reviewed for uses of the phrases "critical thinking," "liberal arts," "lifelong learning," and "technology literacy (or competency)." While these phrases are not synonymous with information literacy, the concepts form part of a coherent undergraduate education (see Chapter 2). In addition, by comparing the number of times these words and phrases are used in relation to the incidence of the phrase information literacy, one can estimate the relative importance of each concept to the institutions studied. These word counts give a breakdown of how many institutions address information literacy and offer a broad overview of the amount of attention, in terms of text, that is devoted to the topic. As such, these counts help to gain a perspective on the relative importance of information literacy within the population of institutions studied.

Evidence from the self-studies demonstrates that institutions address information literacy within accreditation documents, and that the concept is receiving relatively widespread attention. In all, 78 institutions (80.4%) used the phrase "information literacy" at least once in their self-study. On average, the self-studies included the phrase 8.9 times. That over three-quarters of institutions used the phrase information literacy demonstrates broad attention to the topic. While the Middle States Commission first included the term information literacy in its standards in 1994 (Middle States Commission, 2003), the standards that defined information literacy as a learning outcome went into effect in 2003. For this reason, one expects that self-studies published subsequent to 2003 would be most likely to address information literacy. However, 45 of the 97 documents (46.4%) reviewed were written in 2004 or earlier, before those standards took effect. Nevertheless, as Figure 4.3 shows, at least half of the self-studies reviewed covering each year from 1999 to 2003 mention information literacy.

Figure 4.3   Self-Studies Containing Information Literacy by Year of Publication

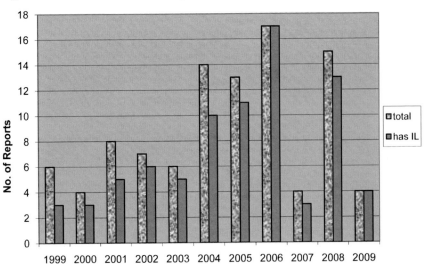

These numbers demonstrate that institutions of higher education recognize the importance of information literacy to their students, and address it on their campuses. In fact, they did so before implementation of the 2002 accreditation standards. However, basic counts show only that the self-studies included information literacy within the text. They do not reveal the context in which the topic was discussed, or offer any insight into how information literacy is integrated into the organizational culture and curriculum. While much of the evidence related to integration was culled through case study interviews, and is presented in the following chapters, placement and context of the phrase information literacy within self-study documents suggests how institutions address information literacy broadly on their campuses.

INFORMATION LITERACY: USES AND CONTEXTS

Simple counts do not account for the context in which the phrase is used, how it is interpreted in individual institutions, or how the standard of information literacy outcomes is applied within the institution. To study these questions, the documents were further analyzed with attention to how institutions address information literacy, rather than just whether they are discussing it. The fact that information literacy as a learning outcome has yet to permeate the larger culture of these institutions is evidenced by the fact that only two institutions (2.1%) included the term in their institutional mission statements. Each of these institutions lists information literacy as a learning goal in the mission statement; one institution places information literacy in its "life goals" for students, asserting its graduates "achieve a high degree of information literacy," while the other offers "comprehensive majors that integrate communications, math, science, art, ... and information literacy." Accreditation organizations emphasize the importance of individual mission statements in defining learning outcomes and interpreting accreditation standards. By including information literacy in their mission statements, these institutions clearly place a high value on it, and they consider it an integral part of their institution. Interestingly, both institutions with information literacy in their mission statements are schools of technology. Perhaps institutions with a strong technological focus realize the complexity and importance of locating and manipulating information in an increasingly technological world.

The institutions reviewed here are more likely to include terms such as critical thinking (12, 12.4%), lifelong learning (23, 23.7%), and liberal arts (40, 41.2%) in their mission statements. Two institutions include technology literacy, which is often conflated with information literacy. As with the institutions that included information literacy in their mission statements, one of these institutions listed educational goals, one of which is technology literacy, in its mission statement. The other states that it graduates students who are "technically and academically competent."

The evidence suggests that information literacy is beginning to be integrated in the curriculum, but it is not as strongly supported as other learning outcomes. However, the self-studies suggest that the relative importance of information literacy is growing. These reports often include a section for future plans, and 35 of the self-studies reviewed (36.1%) include specific plans related to information literacy. The content of these recommendations varies, but plans include addressing information literacy in general education programs, developing assessment plans for information literacy, and integrating information literacy into the curriculum beyond the general education level. These recommendations suggest that information literacy is in a relatively early stage as a learning outcome, and that institutions are only beginning to address the issue. If institutions act on the recommendations, future iterations of these self-studies might reveal higher levels of information literacy integration.

Integration at Various Levels

Instruction for information literacy can take place at various levels in the curriculum, depending on the mission and goals of the institution and programs. The Middle States Commission (2003) supports the integration of information literacy at the course, program, and institutional levels as well as at both the undergraduate and graduate levels, contending that information literacy applies across disciplines and that the competencies should be built on developmentally as students progress through their program of study. In order to clarify the results of the study, it is necessary to define what is meant by the terms course, program, and institutional levels of the curriculum. At the institutional level, those in charge of the curriculum set learning goals that extend to all students. In other words, these goals define the knowledge and abilities that all students, regardless of individual major or program, should be able to demonstrate upon graduation.

What is meant by program is often unclear, as the word is applied differently in different institutions. For instance, some self-studies use the word "program" to describe any instruction for information literacy, even if that instruction largely comprises one-shot sessions. Because these courses are not intellectually linked to each other, and individual sessions do not build on each other, the word program is misapplied in these cases. Many institutions also refer to their core curriculum, or the sequence of courses required of all students, as the general education program. These courses may be sequenced so that they build on each other. However, because they are required of all students, the learning outcomes addressed in these courses often represent broad-based skills and overlap with the institutional student learning outcomes. As such, the general education program could also be viewed as part of the institutional level of the curriculum. Ultimately, programs are made up of courses that are developmentally linked, meaning that skills build on each other in successive courses, and/or linked by discipline, meaning that they are parts of the same field. A program can exist in a larger department or division, and the words "program" and "major" are sometimes used interchangeably. For instance, a humanities department might offer programs in English literature and history, while a business department might have an accounting major. Ideally, each program has its own set of learning outcomes, which make explicit what students studying in that discipline or field should know and be able to do after completing all of the courses in the program. For the purposes of this study, program refers to sequences of courses that are linked to each other by field and/or by courses that build on each other. The definition of program includes general education if the institution under study uses that term.

Courses are the individual units that make up the curriculum. Traditionally, one faculty member teaches a course, although some courses feature team-teaching in which two or more instructors collaborate in instruction. Most courses exist in or are a part of a particular department or program, and as such, accreditation organizations expect courses to include program outcomes as part of their course outcomes. In addition, each course has its own objectives and sometimes learning outcomes, set by the faculty member teaching the course, but perhaps drawing on the program and institutional learning outcomes of the broader curriculum.

Course and Program Attention to Information Literacy

The majority of information literacy instruction takes place at the course level. In fact, 62 self-studies (63.9%) indicate that at least some of the information literacy instruction at their institutions is done through one-shot sessions, and 44 documents (45.4%) state that librarians run workshops for information literacy. Twenty institutions (20.6%) reveal that they offer credit-bearing information literacy courses, and at five of these institutions, the course is required. While they allow for more in-depth and sustained instruction, these courses are generally somewhat peripheral to the curriculum, and in each instance the course is a stand-alone. In other words, this course is not part of a sequence, nor does it serve as a prerequisite for any other courses, and thus it does not allow for instructors to build on competencies.

None of the institutions in this study appear to integrate information literacy at the program level, but some self-studies describe efforts in that direction. For instance, one document indicates that students in the college writing classes receive instruction from librarians based on the level of the course. Those in Writing I receive basic instruction, those in Writing II are introduced to advanced techniques, and those in the Analytical Writing course are taught "problem solving research techniques." This institution offers one of the few examples of sequentially integrated information literacy, where more advanced skills are taught through successive sessions. However, it is unclear from the report whether students are required to take any or all of these writing courses. If the courses are electives, or if large numbers of students test out of the course requirement, integrating information literacy into these courses may not be a useful approach. Another university indicates that subject specialists work closely with department faculty to integrate instruction into the program majors, and to build on skills sequentially. The self-study indicates that librarians focus their integration on research methods courses, or capstone experience projects, where they likely assist students with literature reviews.

Undergraduate- and Graduate-Level Information Literacy

The self-studies indicate that institutions largely associate information literacy with undergraduate education, and at the course level. Fifty of the self-studies (51.5%) include information literacy within the broader context of undergraduate education, as opposed to only 11 self-studies (11.3%) that explicitly incorporate information literacy into the graduate programs. As further evidence that these institutions largely associate information literacy with undergraduate education, 58 self-studies (59.8%) locate information literacy within the general education curriculum. Indeed, this number is even greater than the number of documents that place information literacy in the context of the library. Only 56 documents (57.7%) use the phrase information literacy in sections devoted to the library. It is important, however, to note that many of these documents use equivalent or related language in the library sections. For instance, many of the self-studies still use the phrases bibliographic instruction or library instruction, although they often refer to instruction in information literacy competencies such as locating, accessing, and evaluating information. As such, these institutions associate information literacy with the library, even though they do not explicitly use the term.

Attention to information literacy at the graduate level is low. Of the 97 institutions included, only 11 self-study documents mentioned learning outcomes or instruction for information literacy at the graduate-student level. When the 18 baccalaureate institutions (institutions that award bachelor's degrees as their highest degree) are removed from the total number of institutions, the result is that only 13.9 percent of institutions address information literacy at the graduate level.

Division of Responsibilities and Attention to Competency Areas

Developing Research and Communication Skills (Middle States Commission, 2003) and the ACRL (American Library Association, Association of

College and Research Libraries, 2000) identify the competency areas for information literacy, and call for faculty and librarians to work in collaboration on the delivery and assessment of information literacy instruction. The Middle States Commission (2003) does not intend for institutions to address learning outcomes for information literacy solely through library instruction. Figure 1.1 defines the Middle States Commission's vision of how responsibilities for instruction of information literacy might be divided between faculty and librarians. It suggests that faculty can best address information literacy competencies within the context of the disciplines, and they can reinforce concepts through assignments and class discussions. Librarians can use their expertise in searching and accessing information and evaluating sources to support and reinforce classroom instruction. ACRL (2000) supports a collaborative approach as well, stating "through lectures and by leading discussions faculty establish the context for learning ... academic librarians coordinate the evaluation and selection of intellectual resources for programs and services; organize and maintain collections and many points of access to information; and provide instruction to students and faculty who seek information" (section 3, para. 3).

Nineteen institutions (19.6%) referenced the ACRL standards within their self-studies, and two others (2.1%) referred to the Middle States Commission (2003). Further, institutions used the language contained in the ACRL and Middle States Commission frameworks when they discuss information literacy in self-studies. For instance, 32 institutions (33%) referred to a student's ability to locate and access information, while 29 (29.9%) mentioned the need for students to evaluate information. As such, it would appear that institutions grasp the importance of information literacy and understand the areas that need to be assessed. However, awareness of standards is not the same as addressing them. While some self-studies reference the ACRL and Middle States Commission standards, and discuss terms related to information literacy, only 29 (29.9%) actually identify information literacy as a separate student learning outcome.

In terms of dividing the responsibilities, the self-studies did not always clearly indicate who was responsible for teaching information literacy. Twenty-nine (29.9%) of the documents mention that faculty address information literacy in some way in their courses. Still, librarians are most heavily connected with information literacy, with 71 (73.2%) self-studies indicating that librarians have some responsibility for its instruction. In terms of how the competency areas are addressed, 49 self-studies (50.5%) list location and access of information as the focus of information literacy instruction, making that the most popular area of instruction. Evaluation of information sources is the second-most popular topic, highlighted in 27 (23.7%) of the self-studies, followed by use of information (11.3%). The ethical use of information and defining a topic receive the lowest amounts of attention, at 9.3 percent and 5.2 percent, respectively. One competency area, incorporating new information into the knowledge base, is not mentioned at all in the self-studies in relation to information literacy instruction.

INFORMATION LITERACY: THEMES

In analyzing the documents for uses and contexts of information literacy, certain themes emerge that appear to influence the implementation of information literacy on campuses. The issues cluster around five main themes:

1. Collaboration
2. Assessment
3. Accountability and transparency
4. Institutional culture
5. Leadership

These themes form the larger institutional context for the topic of information literacy, as they bring together accreditation expectations, library priorities, institutional goals, faculty priorities, and stakeholder concerns. These themes are discussed in greater detail in the following chapters through analysis of the case study data. The remainder of this chapter offers the breakdown of the findings from self-study analysis, and a brief discussion of the selection of the case study institutions, thus providing an overview of findings as a framework for subsequent chapters.

Collaboration

Of the 97 self-studies reviewed for this research, 39 institutions (40.2%) indicate that their librarians offered course-integrated instruction, which suggests collaboration between the librarian and the course instructor. Much of this instruction takes place within the first-year orientation or writing program. However, the term "course-integrated" was generally left undefined and, in some cases, could mean as little as offering a link to a library liaison from a course home page. Some institutions, for instance, consider any instruction in which librarians consult with faculty and tailor materials to a specific course or assignment to be integrated, even if it is only a one-shot session. Likewise, of the 58 (59.8%) institutions that mention information literacy in the context of their general education programs, most do not specify exactly how they address information literacy. For example, some self-studies state that rather than offer designated information literacy courses, the concept is integrated throughout the general education curriculum. However, the self-studies do not indicate which competencies listed in Figure 1.1 are included in which courses.

A slightly lower number of institutions (38.1%) provided evidence of more in-depth faculty-librarian collaboration in their documentation, still at the course level. For example, one institution indicates that the instruction librarian participates in the planning of a required seminar course, and "is developing curriculum with three progressive sessions on library research." The self-study for this institution recognizes that the decision to integrate information literacy into the core will have an impact on library staff time and budget, and will "require thoughtful and collaborative planning and preparation of lessons, reading lists, assignments ... with librarians being treated as equal partners integrated systematically into the classroom instruction." Another institutional self-study states that librarians, faculty, and members of the information technology department worked together to create rubrics for scoring outcomes for information literacy in its general education program. A third institution claims that it encourages co-teaching by faculty and librarians for information literacy "to deepen the level of engagement with the students."

Assessment

Assessment initiatives for learning outcomes related to information literacy vary across institutions. For institutions included in this study, the overall rate of using assessment for learning outcomes related to information literacy is 42.3 percent (41 institutions). This percentage is higher than that reported by the ACRL in 2001. At that time, a survey of 664 colleges and universities found that only 14.2 percent (94) had a formal plan for assessing information literacy. Still, according to the study data, more than half of institutions do not report any assessment of information literacy, despite the fact that the Middle States Commission (2009) requests such assessment.

As with collaboration, this assessment takes place largely at the course or class level, with 14 institutions (14.4%) assessing at the institutional level, and 5 (5.2%) assessing for information literacy within the general education program. Typically, program-level assessment is tied to general education programs, not major. Establishing learning outcomes is generally a precursor to assessment, as those outcomes describe the goal against which progress is measured. While more than half of the institutions included in this study mention information literacy in the context of general education, only 29 of them (29.9%) identify it as a separate student learning outcome. The others either include information literacy competencies as a subset of another competency area, such as critical thinking, or as a desirable but incidental area of knowledge. Thus, it stands to reason that institutions that do not define separate learning outcomes for information literacy are less likely to assess information literacy competencies.

Assessment methods can be either direct, meaning that they measure actual learning, or indirect, meaning that they measure perceptions of learning. Within the institutions reviewed, indirect methods are generally more popular. For instance, 18 institutions (18.6%) report using surveys, and

10 institutions (10.3%) rely on faculty feedback and debriefings with librarians. Nine institutions (9.3%) use course evaluations, while two (2.1%) institutions conduct exit interviews with graduating seniors, and one (1%) uses comment cards. While surveys and exit interviews are not without merit, they rely on students' subjective input of what they learned or how knowledgeable they are—in other words, they measure perceptions, but not actual learning. Course evaluations and comment cards are not assessment tools, as they do not measure impact or progress toward goals. When institutions use class or course evaluations, they are really engaged in evaluation, not assessment. That some institutions list these among assessment activities suggest a misunderstanding of either the tools themselves or the terms used to describe them.

While many institutions report engaging indirect methods such as self-reporting, focus-group interviews, and surveys, it is unclear from the documents reviewed here whether such use results from misunderstanding or misuse. These methods might be misapplied to reflect student learning because those who use them do not understand their proper use. On the other hand, perhaps institutions, faculty, and librarians rely on indirect measures even though they know them to be misapplied because they are generally easier to administer and score, and because they are familiar with them. In either case, if visiting teams and accreditation organizations accept these measurements as being indicative of student learning, they are propagating the misuse.

While indirect methods such as surveys are most popular, institutions do report use of direct measures as well. Tests, either standardized or locally produced, are also widely used (15 institutions, 15.5%). Four institutions (4.1%) assess information literacy as part of senior capstone projects, and two (2.1%) use portfolios. Seven institutions (7.2%) state that they use a rubric to assess information literacy, but they do not explain how the rubrics are applied. Rubrics themselves are scoring devices, in which graders determine novice, intermediate, and expert levels of learning and use that framework to grade or score performances, assignments, or other projects. Use of rubrics suggests a move toward direct, authentic assessment, but without knowing the context in which the rubrics are used, it is impossible to determine their actual usefulness in measuring learning.

Part of the purpose of assessment is to improve learning by identifying areas that need improvement. Evidence of changes in information literacy instruction resulting from assessment data in the studies included here is minimal. However, it is important to note that this lack of evidence may be more a function of the nature of accreditation documents than a sign of inaction on the part of institutions. It is possible that, in order to demonstrate compliance with standards, institutions focus more on the assessment measures and processes than on the handling of results when reporting to accreditation organizations. That said, only eight institutions (8.2%)

explicitly addressed the use of assessment data to implement changes for information literacy. Inevitably, the context of these claims is vague. For instance, one institution writes in its self-study that an information literacy steering committee gathers assessment data from all sections of the credit-bearing information literacy courses each year, and uses those data to "suggest revisions to course content and testing methods." Another report offered more detail, indicating that after assessing a core course for information literacy, the institution restructured a major assignment and gave clearer instructions for completing the assignment.

Accountability and Transparency

Assessment of student learning outcomes, including information literacy, offers an important way for institutions to provide evidence of progress toward meeting learning goals. In relation to assessment, various stakeholder groups demand increased accountability and transparency from institutions of higher education. Not only do stakeholders want institutions to be accountable for their learning goals by assessing student progress, they are calling on institutions to make that data publicly available. The response rates for this study, as well as the reasons offered for not participating, offer some insight into the level and culture of transparency at these institutions.

As noted above, this study included both institutions that post accreditation documents publicly on the web, and institutions that provide accreditation documents upon request. By sharing information, participating institutions are engaging in some level of transparency, with those institutions publicly posting documents offering a higher level of transparency. On the other hand, 67 institutions (59.8%) declined to participate for various reasons. These reasons are examined at length in Chapter 9, but for now, it is worth noting the wide variance of responses despite a climate of pressure for accountability and transparency.

Institutional Culture

Each institution has its own culture, or set of values, priorities, and attitudes that guide the behavior of individuals within the organization. How institutions respond to requests for information, the amount of data they make publicly available, and the levels and types of collaboration and assessment that take place on campus, all speak to the institutional culture of the college or university. Likewise, information literacy is related to institutional culture. Institutions demonstrate a strong commitment to information literacy in various ways. For example, institutions that integrate information literacy into the curriculum rather than just treating it as an add-on, instances of high levels of collaboration between librarians, faculty, and other staff, and assessment of learning for information literacy all suggest that information literacy has permeated the culture of an institution. Two institutions include information literacy in their mission statements, and the two institutions that devoted a selected topics self-study to information literacy likely have an institutional culture of information literacy. In addition, eight institutions (8.2%) indicate that they have committees dedicated to information literacy. Although the self-studies did not always document the membership or charge of these committees, some appear to include both faculty and staff and/or have some connection with curriculum committees. The interviews and observations at case study institutions provided greater campus context, and thus more insight into how well information literacy is integrated into the culture of those institutions.

Leadership

Ultimately, effective leadership underlies success in each of the other theme areas. In other words, whether faculty and librarians are encouraged to collaborate, how much assessment takes place, and how transparent an institution is depends on effective leadership. Campus leaders establish the institutional culture through their actions and attitudes, and through the priorities they establish. If they come to accept that information literacy is an important learning outcome, and establish infrastructures and incentives to support collaborative efforts among faculty and with librarians, these initiatives are more likely to succeed.

In nine of the self-studies, librarians show signs of leadership behavior, or are named as leaders on campus. For instance, one self-study states that "the library's leadership in issues related to instructional literacy has been demonstrated in a number of initiatives." The study mentions the publication of a learning framework for information literacy and the development of an online tutorial for undergraduates. Another self-study claims that one campus librarian is "a nationally recognized leader" for information literacy. As with accountability and transparency and institutional culture, examples of leadership are mostly inferred from self-study data, as the topic is not typically addressed as part of a self-study. However, it became evident during self-study analysis that an effective leader is an essential component of an information literacy program, and this theme is explored more extensively through case study evidence in Chapter 11.

CASE STUDY SELECTION

Review of the self-study documents uncovered certain patterns or themes central to developing and implementing information literacy initiatives on campus. In particular, because faculty control the curriculum and have direct, consistent contact with students, collaboration between faculty and librarians is essential for an information literacy program to be integrated into the curriculum. However, institutional, cultural, and practical barriers make undertaking such collaboration a challenge in many instances. Because stakeholders demand accountability and transparency, it is imperative that institutions engage in the assessment of student learning outcomes to demonstrate achievement and disseminate those assessment results for public consumption (Miller & Malandra, n.d.; Suskie, 2004; U.S. Department of Education, 2006). Despite demands for transparency, there is an uneven response to requests for self-study reports. Finally, as the findings indicate, information literacy has not extended much beyond the course level. The number of challenges and barriers to integrating information literacy suggests the need for greater leadership to guide information literacy at individual campuses, and in higher education in general, before institutions can fully integrate information literacy into the curriculum.

Several institutions have more highly developed information literacy initiatives than others. Essentially, the self-study documents of these institutions provided more in-depth discussions of information literacy, and more specific examples of how each campus currently addresses information literacy. Ultimately, the author in consultation with her research committee chose four case study institutions for on-site observations and interviews. Each institution, identified by a letter and not by a name, was selected for a different reason, and represents a different area or theme to be explored. In particular, the investigator looked for institutions that display strong collaborations between faculty and librarians; that address information literacy as a separate learning outcome, either integrated into the curriculum or through designated courses; and that engage in some form of assessment for learning outcomes related to information literacy.

Institution A, guided by a statewide mandate that prompts the inclusion of information literacy within the general education curriculum, identifies its instruction librarian as a "national leader" for information literacy. This is the only institution to include a librarian by name in its self-study. Both institutions A and B have a required information literacy class as a part of their general education curriculum. That the class is required highlights the value that the institution places on information literacy, and indicates a higher level of commitment than exhibited by most other institutions in the study. Institution B's self-study also suggests that the library actively assesses information literacy outcomes. Institution C is one of only two institutions to have focused its most recent decennial review on information literacy. The Middle States Commission allows institutions to choose a selected topics study in place of a comprehensive study, in which the institution examines one or two areas in depth. Institution C focused its 2002 self-study on information literacy, before the Middle States standards including information literacy went into effect. This institution is an early adopter of information literacy as a learning outcome, making it an appropriate site for a case study. Further, since seven years had passed since the submission of that self-study to the Middle States Commission, it was intriguing to see what progress had been made on the campus in integrating information literacy beyond what was described in the self-study. Finally, institution D exemplifies a high level of collaboration. In response to the request for the most recent self-study, the provost of the institution included the visiting team report and institutional response, suggesting a high level of transparency in the willingness to share such information.

CONCLUSION

As stakeholders demand more proof of achievement of student success from institutions of higher education, assessment becomes an important means for institutions to be accountable for achieving stated learning goals. As part of accountability, stakeholders want institutions to be more transparent in sharing information with the public. While self-study documents address institutional accountability in relation to accreditation standards, response rates to requests for those self-studies offer insight into institutional transparency. In fact, despite an assurance of confidentiality and privacy in relation to information contained in self-study documents, more than half of the institutions responding to the request refused to participate.

The documentation and case study data reviewed reveal major trends related to information literacy as a student learning outcome in higher education. First, faculty and librarians are expected to collaborate in delivering information literacy instruction, but the extent and level of collaboration remain relatively low. Second, in order to demonstrate achievement of learning outcomes for information literacy and to improve instruction, institutions need to engage in more direct forms of assessment. Leadership for information literacy is another essential theme. Case study interviews and the literature of library and information science point to various barriers that hinder collaboration. Effective leadership is necessary to achieve program-level collaboration and integration of information literacy, and to motivate more assessment of information literacy as a learning outcome. Finally, institutions must be accountable for learning outcomes related to information literacy and be transparent in how they measure those outcomes. As institutions increase their levels of assessment, they must share the data they collect with the public in order to be accountable for achieving the learning goals they set.

Beginning with Chapter 7, this book will examine the themes of collaboration, assessment, accountability and transparency, institutional culture, and leadership in depth, in light of case study observations and interviews. Information from the case study interviews and observations helps to develop the context for the data provided in the self-studies. Each of those chapters traces the current state of one of these themes through the lens of the data generated through the case studies. Before looking at the case studies, however, it is instructive to look at institutions nationwide in order to draw comparisons across the regions regarding learning outcomes for information literacy. Thus, the next two chapters will offer an overview of the remaining five regions, and then an update to institutions accredited by the Middle States Commission since 2009.

REFERENCES

American Library Association, Association of College and Research Libraries. (2000). *Information literacy competency standards for higher education.* Retrieved from http://www.ala.org/ala/mgrps/divs/acrl/standards/informationliteracy competency.cfm

American Library Association, Association of College and Research Libraries. (2001). *National information literacy survey.* Retrieved from http://www.ala.org/ala/mgrps/divs/acrl/issues/infolit/professactivity/survey/index.cfm

Middle States Commission on Higher Education. (2002). *Characteristics of excellence in higher education.* Philadelphia, PA: Author. Retrieved from http://www.msche.org/publications/CHX06_Aug08REVMarch09.pdf

Middle States Commission on Higher Education. (2003). *Developing research and communication skills: Guidelines for information literacy into the curriculum.* Philadelphia, PA: Author.

Middle States Commission on Higher Education. (2007). *Student learning assessment: Options and resources.* Philadelphia, PA: Author. Retrieved from http://www.msche.org/publications/SLA_Book_0808080728085320.pdf

Middle States Commission on Higher Education. (2009). *Characteristics of excellence in higher education: Requirements of affiliation and standards for accreditation.* Philadelphia, PA: Author.

Miller, C., & Malandra, G. (n.d.). *Accountability/assessment.* Retrieved from http://www.ed.gov/about/bdscomm/list/hiedfuture/reports/miller-malandra.pdf

Suskie, L. (2004). *Assessing student learning: A common sense guide.* Bolton, MA: Anker Publishing.

US Department of Education. (2006). *A test of leadership: Charting the future of U.S. higher education.* Washington, DC: Author. Retrieved from http://www.ed.gov/about/bdscomm/list/hiedfuture/reports/final-report.pdf

CHAPTER 5

Quantitative Findings for Phase Four: The Remaining Five Regions

As the previous chapter emphasizes, the bulk of this research centers on institutions accredited by the Middle States Commission. Because the commission explicitly includes information literacy as a learning outcome and offers its constituents support for developing information literacy programs, including its handbook *Developing Research and Communication Skills* (Middle States Commission, 2003), it makes sense to anticipate that institutions accredited by this commission would respond to these standards and address them within their self-studies. The review analysis in Chapter 4 demonstrates that many of them are. It is important to note, however, that the Middle States Commission is not alone in addressing information literacy within its standards. In fact, according to successive reviews of accreditation standards, all six accreditation organizations include verbiage related to information literacy in their standards, with three of them, including the Middle States Commission, using the phrase *information literacy* explicitly, and the others using equivalent language such as references to locating, evaluating, and using information (Gratch-Lindauer, 2002; Saunders, 2007). The attention to competencies associated with information literacy in the standards, in conjunction with the broader emphasis on accessing and evaluating information, such as is evinced by the Project on Assessment and Accreditation (2004) and the National Leadership Council for Liberal Education and America's Promise (2007), suggests that many institutions nationwide are addressing information literacy within their curricula.

Building on this assumption, phase four of this study takes a cursory look at decennial self-studies of colleges and universities from the remaining five regions to see how they are implementing student learning outcomes for information literacy and how their approaches compare to each other and to the institutions accredited by the Middle States Commission. This phase relies solely on self-studies publicly available from the institutional websites. In order to obtain these studies, the author visited the website of each regional accreditation organization and compiled a list of accredited institutions from the organizations' membership directories. The complete list included only institutions within the United States; excluded were institutions operating overseas or in US territories, and for-profit, online-only, and specialized institutions such as medical schools. In all, the final list numbered 1,256 colleges and universities.

As with the institutions accredited by the Middle States Commission, the author searched the websites of each institution for publicly available copies of the self-study documents. The search used keywords such as "self-study," "accreditation," and the name or acronym of the appropriate regional accreditation organization. If the site did not support searching, the author navigated to administrative pages such as the president's page or provost's page to see if documents were linked from those areas. In all, these searches resulted in a total of 229 decennial self-studies, which indicates that 18.2 percent of the institutions reviewed make their self-studies publicly accessible.

Figure 5.1 shows the breakdown of publicly available documents by region, in comparison to the total number of institutional sites searched in that region. As the figure depicts, the Western Association of Schools and Colleges (WASC) offers the highest percentage of documents online, with 24 self-studies or 34.3 percent of the total institutions in its jurisdiction. The Northwest Commission on Colleges and Universities (NWCCU) is a

Figure 5.1   Availability of Self-Studies by Region

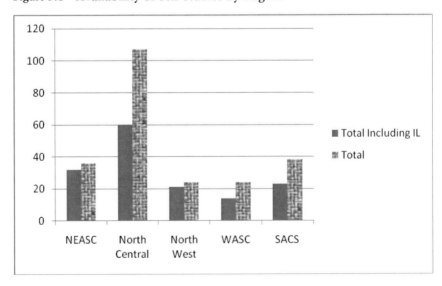

Figure 5.2   Availability of Self-Studies by Carnegie Classification

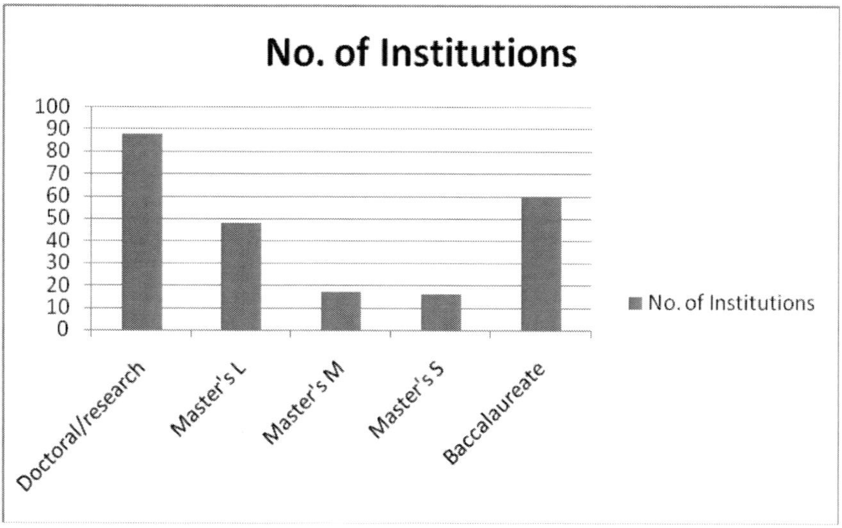

close second, also with 24 documents, representing 31.6 percent of its institutions. The New England Association of Schools and Colleges (NEASC)
and the North Central Association of Colleges and Schools (NCACS) follow
with 36 documents (22.8%) and 107 documents (19.9%), respectively. The
Southern Association of Colleges and Schools (SACS) has the lowest proportion, at 38 documents representing 9.2 percent of the total.

   Another way to look at the breakdown of institutions' publicly posted
documents is by Carnegie Classification. As was the case with the Middle
States Commission, institutions classified as either doctoral or research
have the highest representation, with 88 institutions (34.2%) providing
documents online. The next largest group, baccalaureate, is made up of 60
institutions (26.2%), followed by master's larger institutions at 48 (21%).
The remaining groups, master's medium and master's smaller, are nearly
equal, with 17 (7.4%) and 16 (7%) institutions, respectively (see Figure 5.2
for this breakdown).

DIFFERENCES IN REGIONAL ACCREDITATION

   The rest of this chapter analyzes these self-studies from the five regions as
a group. Before addressing the results of the content analysis, however, it is
important to examine some regional differences in accreditation standards
and reporting. Indeed, there are some major differences in accreditation
processes among the five regions examined here; at times, this makes direct

comparisons across the regions difficult. To begin with, although each of the accreditation organizations includes some language related to information literacy in its standards, emphasis on and treatment of the concept is not even across the organizations. As noted above, SACS, NWCCU, and NCACS do not actually use the phrase information literacy in their standards. Nevertheless, a 2007 analysis of the standards identified SACS and NWCCU as having "significant" treatment of information literacy through the use of equivalent language (Saunders, 2007, p. 321). On the other hand, NCACS is the only region classified as having "minimal" coverage of information literacy in its standards (Saunders, 2007). Further, NCACS does not include a separate standard for libraries in its accreditation handbook. Libraries are mentioned only in a parenthetical expression as an example of the resources an institution must provide to support student learning (NCACS, 2003, 3.1–3.4). While the previous chapter on the Middle States Commission reveals that information literacy need not be limited to library sections of a self-study, the concept is still most commonly associated with libraries, and is often discussed within that context. Thus, it is reasonable that an institution accredited by NCACS may engage in information literacy activities but might not report them in its self-study because such activities do not seem relevant to the standards.

Other differences in the accreditation standards and processes are not as directly related to information literacy, but still serve to limit comparisons across regions. For instance, institutions accredited by NEASC and NWCCU engage in narrative self-studies similar to those done by institutions accredited by the Middle States Commission, whereas SACS, NCACS, and WASC follow substantially different processes. SACS requires two sets of documents as part of the decennial accreditation. The first, termed the comprehensive certification, is similar to the self-studies done for NEASC, NWCCU, and the Middle States Commission. For this report, institutions address each standard and substandard individually, providing a brief narrative and supporting documentation to describe how it meets that standard. In addition, each institution submits a Quality Enhancement Plan (QEP), which identifies issues related to student learning outcomes or environments supporting such outcomes that emerged during the self-study process, and outlines a proposal for improving or enhancing that area by identifying goals, an implementation process, and an assessment plan (SACS, 2010, p. 7). Some institutions posted both the compliance report and the QEP, and some only made one document publicly available. Further, the topic of each QEP is unique to the institution, and examples varied widely. In two cases, institutions chose to focus their QEP on information literacy, and those two documents will be analyzed separately at the end of this chapter. For all other institutions, only compliance reports were included.

Like SACS, NCACS offers its constituents a portfolio-style report called the Academic Quality Improvement Program (AQIP). The QEP is a required element of the SACS accreditation process, while AQIP is actually "an alternative evaluation process for organizations already accredited by the Commission" (NCACS, 2010, para. 2). In other words, institutions applying for reaffirmation of accreditation may choose the AQIP format in place of the traditional narrative report. NCACS describes the AQIP process as one in which an institution "demonstrates how it meets accreditation standards and expectations through a sequence of events that align with the ongoing activities of an institution striving to improve its performance" (NCACS, 2010, para. 1), and the AQIP indicates the process "involves a structured set of goal-setting, networking and accountability activities" (NCACS, 2010, para. 2). Institutions often develop AQIP reports as online portfolios that bear little resemblance to the traditional self-studies or even the QEP reports generated for SACS accreditation. As such, it is difficult to draw comparisons between the AQIP reports and other self-studies reviewed for this book. As a result, only institutions posting traditional self-studies were included in this research.

Finally, WASC takes a more cyclical approach, with its accreditation process including three separate reports, usually submitted over a three- to five-year time period. The initial report, the institutional proposal, gives an overview of the institution and outlines the process it intends to take in addressing the accreditation standards. The second document, the Capacity and Preparatory Review, consists of a set of reflective essays and supporting documents to demonstrate how the institution meets the standards. Finally, the Educational Effectiveness Review requires institutions to "explore topics or themes that are related to the institution's own priorities and needs, with a special emphasis on the assessment and improvement of student learning" (WASC, 2008, p. 35). Because of the interrelated nature of the reports, only institutions that offer all three reports publicly are included in this study.

It is important to note that the varied nature of the accreditation processes and the decision to include only institutions that met certain criteria regarding the posting of their accreditation documents impact the number of institutions included in the study, and the number reflected in Figure 5.1. In particular, the numbers for institutions accredited by NCACS and WASC may be proportionally lower than those in the other regions not because institutions in those regions are less likely to make documents publicly available, but simply because they did not post the documents relevant to this study. For instance, institutions currently undergoing reaffirmation of accreditation by WASC may not have all three documents available because the accreditation is ongoing. As a result, that institution would not be included in this study. Likewise, those institutions in the NCACS region that chose to engage in an AQIP study rather than a traditional narrative self-study are not included here, even though many of those institutions make their AQIP portfolio available online. Ultimately, judgments about institutional transparency with regard to publicly posting accreditation documents should not be made based on the numbers reflected in Figure 5.1. Likewise, all discussion of information literacy included here is necessarily limited by these constraints. With that caveat, the rest of the chapter examines the results of the content analysis to see how institutions view information literacy.

INCIDENCE OF INFORMATION LITERACY

The process for analyzing these documents is the same as that described in Chapter 4, with attention to whether the phrase information literacy or equivalent language is evident in the documents, and the context in which it is used. Broadly, the use of and references to information literacy in these documents align with the findings outlined in the previous chapter. Of the 229 studies reviewed, 150 (65.5%) included the phrase information literacy, and an additional 29 institutions (12.7%) had equivalent language. In some cases, the equivalent language is an alternative word or phrase, such as information fluency or library research skills; and in other cases, it involves specific references to the skills and competencies generally associated with information literacy, such as locating, accessing, evaluating, and using information. If these two groups are combined, the total number of institutions addressing competencies related to information literacy is 179 (78.2%). The remaining 22.8 percent of institutions do not use either the phrase information literacy or equivalent language.

These numbers reflect the total for all five accreditation organizations, but as noted above, treatment of information literacy is not even within the various standards. Thus, it is revealing to examine the breakdown of institutions including information literacy within their self-studies by accreditation region. As depicted in Figure 5.3, NEASC and NWCCU have the highest proportion of documents that include information literacy. Within the NEASC region, 32 of 36 documents (88.9%) include the phrase information literacy at least once, while 21 of the 24 institutions (87.5%) in the NWCCU region do the same. These proportions are actually higher than those in the Middle States Commission's region, despite that accreditation organization's more extensive set of standards. The proportion of institutions from the remaining three regions are more than 20 percentage points lower than those of the Middle States Commission, NEASC, and NWCCU, but are all within 5 percentage points of each other. SACS has the highest proportion, with 23 of 30 (60.5%) institutions including the phrase, closely followed by WASC institutions, with 14 out of 24 (58.3%), and NCACS, with 60 out of 107 (56.1%). It is notable that, although the percentage of institutional documents including the phrase information literacy varies widely from one region to another, in all regions, more than half of the documents include the phrase, suggesting that information literacy is an important competency across all regions. Again, these documents suggest that information literacy has entered the lexicon of most American colleges and universities,

Figure 5.3   Number of Available Documents versus Number of Institutions by Region

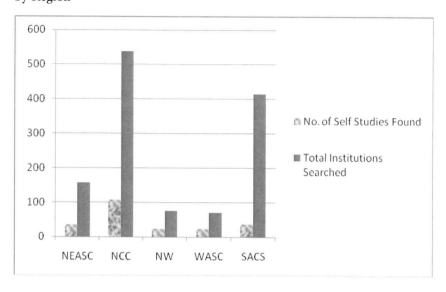

but these numbers do not reflect how the institutions are implementing student learning outcomes for information literacy. The context in which the phrase is used, described below, helps to illuminate this issue.

INFORMATION LITERACY IN CONTEXT

In many ways, the breakdown of information literacy within these self-study documents is similar to those from the Middle States Commission, with one important exception. While two institutions accredited by the Middle States Commission include information literacy in their institutional mission statements, there is no example of an institution in the other regions including the phrase information literacy in its mission statement. One institution, however, does include equivalent language, by stating that it will "teach our students how to obtain, evaluate, and use information." This is the only example of a reference within a mission statement to competencies associated with information literacy outside of the Middle States Commission. While this finding might suggest that information literacy holds a place of higher importance for institutions under the aegis of the Middle States Commission, other findings demonstrate that information literacy has made some inroads in the other accreditation regions. In fact, there is more evidence of integration for information literacy beyond the course level and moving toward the program level in this group as compared to those from the Middle States, as described below.

Integration at Various Levels

The previous chapter offers an overview of what is meant by course, program, and institutional levels of the curriculum, and describes the various uses of the word *program* within higher education. To reiterate, for this study, program refers to sequences of courses that are linked to each other by discipline, field, and/or by courses that build on each other. The definition of program includes general education if the institution under study uses that term.

Course- and Program-Level Information Literacy

Once again, the majority of instruction for information literacy takes place at the course or class level. One-shot sessions are still the most popular form of library instruction, with 176 institutions (76.9%) noting that librarians deliver instruction in this way, while 122 institutions (53.3%) state that librarians offer tours, orientations, and workshops within the library. Forty institutions (17.5%) offer credit-bearing courses for information literacy, and at 11 institutions, these courses are required.

Often, information literacy is embedded in a first-year seminar of some type, as is the case at 95 institutions (41.5%). Indeed, 64 institutions (27.9%) identify information literacy within the general education curriculum, and required first-year courses are an obvious way to address such competencies. Interestingly, 21 institutions (9.2%) in this group address information literacy within at least some discipline programs or majors. In some cases, this is a single department within the institution, while one institution indicates that eight departments have already developed a course related to information literacy, and plans are underway for other departments to do the same. These examples do not constitute information literacy programs because they are typically still single courses within a department, and not a sequence of developmentally linked courses as described in the previous chapter. Nevertheless, they might be described as program-integrated, in that the courses demonstrate an attempt by the department to address information literacy within the context of the discipline or field.

While still minimal, there is some evidence of program-level instruction in this group, as opposed to the institutions from the Middle States Commission. In fact, nine institutions (3.9%) offer examples of integration beyond the course level. For instance, one institution states that, because "staff identified the need to gradually increase the complexity of instructional content based on course level, instructor requirements, and subject areas," they created "a graduated program of workshops and class sessions for students and faculty." This approach includes three sessions over the student's education. The first two sessions take place in the first year, as part of the first-year course, while the third is subject-specific, typically taught by a library liaison to the department. The self-study also identifies the librarians as having taken a lead role for information literacy on campus. The report does not detail the specific actions librarians take to promote information literacy, but considering this is one of the few examples of the implementation of an information literacy program, it seems reasonable to assume that librarians at this institution may be engaging in some of the leadership behaviors discussed in Chapter 11.

Similarly, another institution takes a two-tier approach to information literacy. The first tier is integrated into the general education curriculum, while the second tier takes place within the disciplines. The self-study indicates that departments are "directed to establish the appropriate skill level for their discipline and to identify both a course sequence and a timeline whereby students obtain these skills." Clearly, these institutions are moving beyond a one-shot or ad hoc approach to information literacy in favor of a structured sequence of courses that allow instructors to build on skills and knowledge and address information literacy both as a core competency and within the context of the student's major. Further evidence suggests that other institutions may develop similar programs. Sixty-seven institutions (29.3%) included some mention of information literacy in their future goals or plans sections. In many cases, these institutions indicate that they plan to integrate information literacy further into the curriculum, which could mean at the program level.

Undergraduate- and Graduate-Level Information Literacy

The evidence from these self-studies supports the idea that institutions largely focus attention for information literacy at the undergraduate level. Sixty-four institutions (27.9%) place information literacy in the context of their general education program, while 41 (17.9%) address information literacy somewhat more broadly as part of the overall undergraduate education. While these numbers are proportionally smaller than institutions accredited by the Middle States Commission, they demonstrate an understanding that competencies for information literacy are broader than library research skills, and should be addressed within the curriculum by teaching faculty in addition to librarians.

Attention to information literacy at the graduate level is much lower, with only seven institutions, or 3.1 percent, mentioning it in this context. While these numbers are low, some of the examples demonstrate a high level of support for information literacy at the graduate level. For instance, one institution includes a required information literacy course for all master's and PhD students in a seminary program. This course is described as a research methods course, taught by a librarian and covering both research and information literacy skills. Another institution describes "problem-based learning groups" within the veterinary and medical schools, each of which are assigned to a specific librarian who assists them in developing information literacy competencies. Though rare, some institutions do integrate these competencies at the graduate level.

DIVISION OF RESPONSIBILITY AND ATTENTION
TO COMPETENCY AREAS

As with documents from phase two, the content analysis here considers whether librarians and teaching faculty collaborate and share responsibility for the instruction and assessment of information literacy as outlined in Figure 1.1. Further, it is noted whether the self-studies cite certain documents such as the Association of College and Research Libraries' (ACRL) *Information Literacy Competency Standards for Higher Education* (American Library Association, Association of College and Research Libraries, 2000), which defines information literacy and guides institutions in implementing an information literacy program. In fact, as was the case with institutions accredited by the Middle States Commission, institutions reference ACRL's competencies most frequently, with 39 institutions (17%) citing it within their self-studies. Two other institutions cite the American Library Association's (1989) *Final Report* on information literacy, which was the precursor to the ACRL standards. Not surprisingly, no institutions reference the Middle States Commission's handbook *Developing Research and Communication Skills* (2003), probably because institutions do not frequently consult documentation from regional accreditation organizations other than their own.

In terms of how responsibilities are divided, librarians seem to bear most of the burden for instruction and assessment of information literacy. Only 22 institutions (9.6%) indicate that faculty have responsibility for addressing information literacy in their courses, while librarians at 121 institutions (52.8%) actively engage in teaching information literacy. The numbers for assessment are similar, with only 8 documents (3.5%) stating that faculty assess learning outcomes for information literacy, while in 44 cases (19.2%), librarians assess. The fact that overall numbers for assessment are low compared to the numbers for instruction speaks to the fact that much instruction is not assessed, and that assessment may not be a priority. The breakdown of competencies addressed through instruction mirrors the findings of institutions accredited by the Middle States Commission. The most frequently addressed competency is location and access of information, mentioned 98 times (42.8% of institutions), followed by evaluation of information with 71 mentions (31% of institutions). The ethical use of information was the third-most common competency area addressed (22.3%), closely followed by use of information (20.1%). Defining an information need, or assisting in developing or refining a topic, is the most infrequently mentioned, at just 7 percent.

INFORMATION LITERACY: THEMES

The content analysis in Chapter 4 identified the five themes of collaboration, assessment, institutional culture, accountability and transparency, and leadership as providing the larger context for how campuses address information literacy. The remainder of this chapter examines the self-studies in light of each of these thematic areas.

Collaboration

The expectation that librarians and faculty should work together to instruct and assess for information literacy is not unique to the Middle States Commission. Indeed, NEASC and NWCCU in particular seem to support the idea that faculty and librarians should collaborate by emphasizing that information literacy should be integrated into the curriculum, with NWCCU specifically calling for a partnership between librarians and faculty (Saunders, 2007). The self-studies reviewed here support some collaboration between librarians and faculty, but it is almost exclusively at the course level. Seventy-one institutions (31%) indicate that information literacy is course-integrated, which suggests that there might be more collaboration between faculty and librarians. Few of the self-studies, however, elaborate on what is meant by "course-integrated," and the evidence suggests that this term could mean anything from an expectation that faculty implicitly or explicitly will address information literacy competencies to models that involve librarians and faculty in co-teaching and collaborating on assignment design and grading. In other words, the actual level of attention to information literacy under the label of "course-integrated" varies widely.

In some cases, the self-studies offer clear examples of how the collaborative efforts are carried out. Most often, these examples entail librarians and faculty working together to develop assignments with specific learning outcomes for information literacy. In such cases, librarians often work with faculty to integrate existing library resources into their assignments. Librarians might help faculty identify resources for students to use in assignments, or assist in developing explicit learning outcomes for information literacy for assignments. However, in some instances, faculty and librarians team-teach courses, as is the case in institutions in which librarians and faculty members codeveloped and co-teach courses such as humanities and the Internet, chemistry, and writing. Several of the institutions offering program-level instruction for information literacy note that faculty and librarians are discussing learning outcomes for information literacy at the department or program level. In these institutions, collaboration is beginning to extend beyond the course level. This is an important finding, as no such evidence surfaced in documents from institutions accredited by the Middle States Commission; however, further research, perhaps through case studies and campus visits, is needed to follow up on these findings. It might also be interesting to investigate whether librarians at institutions with higher levels of integration or collaboration for information literacy are accorded faculty status.

Assessment

While this group of institutions offers some more progressive examples of collaboration and instruction beyond the course level, findings related to assessment are not as encouraging. In fact, at 32.8 percent (75 institutions), overall assessment of student learning outcomes for information literacy at any level of the institution was lower with this group than for institutions accredited by the Middle States Commission. This difference perhaps is not surprising, considering that the proportion of institutions identifying information literacy as a separate student learning outcome is also smaller, with only 41 institutions (17.9%) doing so in this group as opposed to 29 (29.9%) in the Middle States Commission group. Once again, the majority of assessment takes place at the course or class level (23.6% and 12.2%, respectively), followed by institutional-level assessment at 17.9 percent (41 institutions). Program-level assessment is minimal, with only six institutions (2.6%) reporting any program-level assessment; but in contrast, for the institutions accredited by the Middle States Commission, the only evidence of program-level assessment is linked to general education programs and not the discipline majors. In two cases, institutions state that they are engaged in the assessment of student learning outcomes for information literacy at the program level, but they do not explain how such assessment takes place. Another institution indicates that students in the economics and psychology departments are assessed for information literacy through research papers. It remains unclear, however, whether or not these assignments are scored by a rubric. Two institutions state that capstone projects include assessment for information literacy, and one of these uses a rubric for such assessment.

Methods used to measure learning for information literacy are not always assessment measures. Chapter 4 offers an explanation of the difference between direct and indirect assessment, while Chapter 8 examines the difference between assessment and evaluation, and the application of these methods within institutions. For now, suffice it to say that many institutions confuse these terms, and most engage in indirect assessment if they are doing assessment at all. As was the case in the previous chapter, surveys (an indirect method that really measures perception of learning, rather than actual learning) are the most popular form for gathering feedback, with 59 institutions (25.8%) using this method. Tests closely follow surveys (55 institutions, 24.0%). Standardized tests are a subset of this group, with 12.2 percent of institutions reporting use of such tools. While tests are a direct measure of learning, they tend to focus more on the lower-level thinking skills of knowledge and understanding, rather than higher-order skills such as evaluation or synthesis. The next-most popular tool is course or class evaluations (39 institutions, 17%). Like surveys, course and class evaluations focus on perceptions and perhaps satisfaction with learning experiences, but do not directly measure learning. The use of portfolios, which is a direct method, falls at less than 1 percent, with only two institutions reporting use. Perhaps most surprising, 13 institutions (5.7%) claim to use LibQUAL+ as an assessment tool for information literacy. In fact, as addressed in Chapter 8, LibQUAL+ measures service quality, and is not an assessment tool, despite the fact that accreditation teams appear to accept it as such. Finally, 41 institutions (17.9%) engage in other direct and indirect activities, ranging from discussion with faculty, to course-embedded assignments (with or without scoring rubrics), to curriculum mapping.

Accountability and Transparency

The levels and types of assessment activities described in these self-studies offer some insight into how institutions hold themselves accountable for student learning outcomes related to information literacy. Assessment activities that directly measure student learning in the sense of how student knowledge and behaviors change as a result of their education are a necessary prerequisite to accountability. Only with such evidence can institutions offer proof of goal attainment. In relation to information literacy, however, most institutions do not gather such data. As noted above, the majority of institutions are engaged in indirect assessment, and in some cases, they are not measuring learning, but are actually investigating service quality, satisfaction, or student and faculty perceptions of whether learning has occurred. These institutions need to implement more direct methods of assessment if they truly want to be accountable and to improve learning in the area of information literacy. In terms of transparency, all of the institutions included in this section post accreditation documents publicly on their websites, which indicates a higher level of transparency than institutions that do not.

Institutional Culture

A number of indicators within self-studies hint at institutional culture within the organization. The amount of attention given to information literacy in the self-study, the level to which information literacy is integrated into the curriculum, types of collaboration, and levels and methods of assessment all speak to the extent to which the institution buys into information literacy as a student learning outcome. While it is unwise to extrapolate too much from the self-studies, several of them suggest a culture that is more supportive of information literacy, relative to the others. For instance, those institutions that have tiered levels of instruction for information literacy seem to have made information literacy part of their culture. In order to have a sequence of courses such as these institutions describe, there must be buy-in from faculty and administrators. To begin with, those in charge of the curriculum had to agree on the necessity of addressing information literacy beyond one-shot sessions. Moreover, on both of these campuses, the final tier of information literacy instruction takes place within the major; this implies support from faculty at the departmental level. Two institutions demonstrate an even higher level of commitment to information literacy, as they incorporate learning goals specific to information literacy into the students' senior capstone project. Again, for such activities to take place, there must be a high level of faculty buy-in. Finally, several institutions indicate that members of the community attended a conference sponsored by the Council for Independent Colleges on implementing information literacy programs. In most cases, conference attendance included administrators such as a provost or academic dean, as well as representatives from the faculty and the library. That such high-level administrators would commit time as well as resources to learn about information literacy suggests a strong commitment and support. In addition to these examples, two institutions accredited by SACS stand out as having focused their QEPs on information literacy, and thus offering the suggestion that their campuses embody a culture of information literacy. These two institutions are examined in greater depth at the end of the chapter.

Leadership

Leadership is necessary for information literacy to be integrated beyond the course level. Seven self-studies (3.1%) state that leadership for information literacy occurs on their campuses. Among these is the institution that assesses information literacy through senior capstone projects. The self-study for that institution also indicated that its information literacy activities had been recognized by ACRL as one of the top information literacy programs for undergraduates. A second institution also states that it has a nationally recognized information literacy program, although it does not specify whether the recognition comes from ACRL. This second institution is also unique in that it conducted a longitudinal study to evaluate the information literacy competencies of its students. Along the same lines, an institution from the WASC region indicates that the accreditation organization commended it for "outstanding collaboration." In addition to these examples, those institutions noted above that sent administrators, faculty, and librarians to the Council for Independent Colleges training sessions appear to have leadership for information literacy. What will be most telling, however, is if the strategies for integrating information literacy learned at these conferences translate into action on campus. These institutions indicate plans to implement some new strategies, but a follow-up through case studies would be necessary to see if they achieve these goals.

REGIONAL DIFFERENCES REVISITED

Most of the data reported above are in aggregate, showing the responses of all five regions grouped together. Because there is such variation in standards, however, it is instructive to look at some of the differences in findings by region. This section looks at some of the more notable differences.

Whether institutions place information literacy in the general education curriculum varies by accreditation region. Institutions accredited by NWCCU, WASC, and NEASC are most likely to include information literacy in general education programs, with 41.7 percent, 37.5 percent, and 36.1 percent, respectively, doing so. NCACS institutions are close behind, with 27.1 percent doing so. On the other hand, institutions accredited by SACS report placing information literacy in the general education curriculum only 7.9 percent of the time. Similarly, while at least one institution in each of the other regions indicates some attention to information literacy within the majors and at the graduate level, there is no evidence of either from SACS institutions.

Evidence of collaboration and assessment varies by region as well. Institutions from the NWCCU region show the highest level of collaboration between librarians and faculty, at 50 percent, followed by NEASC at 36.1 percent. Institutions from WASC and NCACS are nearly equal in collaborative efforts, at 12.5 percent and 10.3 percent, respectively. Here again, institutions accredited by SACS show the lowest levels of collaboration at only 7.9 percent. Interestingly, the regions rank in almost the same order for evidence of program integration of information literacy, with NWCCU having the highest proportion (29.2%), followed by NEASC (16.7%), WASC (12.5%), SACS (5.3%), and NCACS (2.8%).

Overall levels of assessment, on the other hand, deviate from the patterns of collaboration. Institutions accredited by SACS are actually the most likely to assess learning outcomes for information literacy, with 57.9 percent of them reporting such activity. WASC, NWCCU, and NEASC have equal levels of assessment, each at 41.7 percent, while institutions accredited by NCACS trail far behind at 16.8 percent. These assessment activities are interesting when viewed in light of the proportions of institutions listing information literacy as a separate learning outcome. It is reasonable to assume that institutions that include separate student learning outcomes for information literacy would be more likely to have higher levels of assessment as they try to measure learning for information literacy. In fact, this holds true for four of the regions. Once again, WASC, NWCCU, and NEASC are closely aligned. NWCCU has the most institutions with information literacy as a separate learning outcome (33.3 percent), followed by WASC at 25 percent and NEASC at 22.2 percent. Again, NCACS institutions are at lower rates, with only 15 percent reporting information literacy as a separate learning outcome. The SACS institutions do not follow this pattern, however. Even though these institutions report the highest levels of assessment for information literacy, they are the least likely to list information literacy as a separate learning outcome, with only 7.9 percent doing so.

These differences among the regions may reflect the differences in attention to information literacy in the regional accreditation standards, but they do not align exactly. According to Saunders (2007), NCACS standards devote the least amount of text to competencies related to information literacy, and do not use the phrase itself at all. Perhaps not surprisingly, then, the reports reviewed here show institutions accredited by NCACS to generally have the lowest rates of activity related to information literacy. While the SACS accreditation standards are categorized as having significant coverage of information literacy (Saunders, 2007), they do not use the phrase, either; and aside from having high rates of assessment, the overall levels of information literacy reported in its institutions' documentation is likewise low. On the other hand, NWCCU does not use the phrase information literacy, but its coverage is considered significant, and its institutional reports tend to demonstrate higher levels of engagement with information literacy. NEASC and WASC self-studies seem to align well with standards in that the standards have significant coverage of information literacy, and the institutions show proportionally high levels of activities. One surprising finding is that some of these institutions appear to be doing more in terms of integrating information literacy at the program level than institutions accredited by the Middle States Commission, despite that organization's extensive treatment of information literacy in its standards.

QUALITY ENHANCEMENT PLANS FOR INFORMATION LITERACY

Unique among the regional accreditation organizations, SACS requires its constituents to submit a supplemental report along with its decennial self-study. The QEP identifies a topic emerging from the self-study and campus discussions that the institution will target for improvement or enhancement. Two institutions, North Georgia College and State University (2007, http://www.northgeorgia.edu/) and North Carolina Wesleyan College (2009, http://www.ncwc.edu/), have QEPs devoted to information literacy. In addition to identifying a topic, these reports outline implementation and assessment plans as well as budgets to support them. From topic selection to implementation, these plans often take several years to develop, and require a significant amount of time from those involved as well as budgetary support. Further, according to SACS guidelines and the QEP reports themselves, choosing and developing a topic is a campus-wide effort involving constituents from across the institution, including students, faculty, staff, and administrators. As such, QEP reports represent a strong commitment on the part of the institution, and the fact that these two institutions chose information literacy as their topic suggests that they are at least in the process of developing a culture of information literacy, if one does not already exist.

Both QEP reports demonstrate a commitment to collaboration and integration of information literacy into the curriculum beyond the course level. In both cases, the selection of information literacy as a topic grew out of large-scale campus discussions that included participants from all areas of the institution. This organic process implies that there is widespread buy-in for the topic. Further, once a topic was identified, each campus developed a team to oversee and facilitate the implementation phases, again with team members drawn from across the institution, including faculty, administrators, librarians, staff, and students. Indeed, at North Carolina Wesleyan College, the Student Government Association has participated in each step of the process and has responsibility along with the design team for reviewing the program as it develops. At North Georgia College and State University, the Center for Teaching Excellence plays a strong role along with the director for institutional effectiveness. These teams suggest that the process is collaborative, and that collaboration may likely be supported within the information literacy program.

Assessment plans are an inherent part of the QEP, and SACS requires that institutions identify specific methods for measuring their progress toward QEP goals. Both institutions propose similar assessment approaches for learning goals for information literacy. Each chose a standardized test to serve as one method of assessment, with North Georgia College and State University planning to use both SAILS and ETS' Information and Communication Technology (ICT) Literacy Assessment; while North Carolina Wesleyan College chose Central Michigan University's Research Readiness Self Assessment (http://rrsa.cmich.edu/). In addition to testing, both institutions propose to use course-embedded assignments within designated courses, including research papers, quizzes, and other exercises. One important distinction is that North Carolina Wesleyan College specifies that these assignments will be scored using a rubric. This is especially important because in many cases, different faculty members will be assessing learning for the same outcomes, and the use of rubrics helps to ensure consistency. On the other hand, North Georgia College and State University intends to supplement its assessment efforts with the use of periodic surveys, including the National Survey of Student Engagement (NSSE) and LibQUAL+. Once again, it is important to highlight the fact that these tools are both indirect methods, and that NSSE measures student perceptions, while LibQUAL+ focuses on service quality rather than on learning. Nevertheless, the fact that these institutions are planning for assessment is a good sign. It is hoped that they intend to hold themselves accountable for student learning for information literacy. Whether accountability translates into transparency remains to be seen, but the fact that these institutions have made so much documentation available so far suggests that they will continue to be transparent going forward.

That these institutions are developing and promoting a culture of information literacy is borne out by the level of involvement of the institutional community and by other details in the QEP reports. One of the most important indicators of a culture of information literacy is that both institutions are planning to integrate student learning outcomes in this area beyond the course level. Both institutions underscore the importance of addressing information literacy in both the general education program and within the discipline majors. In fact, after researching different information literacy program models, each institution independently concluded that curriculum integration at the program level is the best approach. North Carolina Wesleyan College (2009) states that "a structured, college-wide approach that permanently embeds information literacy into the curriculum is needed to foster the development of higher order learning skills in upper-level courses in the major" (p. 18). Thus, both institutions propose a sequential program in which students develop basic information literacy skills as part of their general education courses, and at least one course within the major builds upon these competencies. Further, faculty, librarians, and other staff and administrators are planning student learning outcomes for information literacy, and they are identifying and developing courses in which to embed these outcomes. Such conversations and collaboration in order to integrate information literacy at the program level is indicative of a culture of information literacy.

Finally, these QEP reports suggest that leadership for information literacy is occurring at these institutions. Chapter 11 discusses the definition of leadership in an information literacy context, and highlights the need for high-level administrative and faculty buy-in and a shared vision in order for information literacy efforts to succeed. Both institutions offer evidence of these circumstances. A shared vision for information literacy is crucial because it presupposes a network of followers who share a common goal, have common language for communicating about that goal, and are willing to work toward achieving the goal. One indication of a shared vision on these two campuses is that both institutions facilitated discussions that resulted in a local definition of information literacy. Even though both definitions closely mirror the ACRL (2000) definition, the process of developing a definition itself is what is important. Different constituents have a chance to voice their opinions and thoughts, and through an organic process, a shared definition resulting in a common vocabulary emerged. As a result, all those involved understand what is meant by information literacy on that campus, and believe that they have a stake in developing and achieving learning goals related to information literacy. High-level support is evident from the commitment of time, staff, and resources at all levels of the institution. At North Carolina Wesleyan College, representatives including the library director, a dean, and some faculty attended the CIC program on information literacy, demonstrating even more commitment of resources to developing their information literacy program. Perhaps one of the most important points is that in both institutions, the process was organic and inclusive. Input was sought at all levels from a variety of constituents, and the process was iterative, involving multiple rounds of discussion and refinement, resulting in the shared vision. Nevertheless, while the process itself was organic, the impetus for these plans is external, namely the requirement of the accreditation organization that institutions develop such a plan. This is not to say that institutions cannot or would not create similar programs on their own, and indeed, the self-studies indicate that some have. These two documents, however, suggest that accreditation organizations can play an important role in motivating and facilitating the sort of planning and shifts in institutional culture that might be necessary to implementing an integrated information literacy program. Finally, while these two institutions offer exciting programs, both are only in the planning stages. The QEP documents are really proposals, and it is too soon to know whether the programs they outline will fulfill the expectations. A future study might use these two institutions as case studies to examine the implementation and outcomes of the proposals.

CONCLUSION

These findings mirror those of the previous chapter and indicate that in these five accreditation regions, as in that of the Middle States Commission, information literacy in most places is still discussed as a concept, but has not become part of the institutional culture. Some evidence, however, suggests that a few institutions have begun to move beyond the course level and are integrating information literacy into major programs. This finding is important because the Middle States Commission has the strongest set of standards in support of information literacy, and as such, one would expect their constituents to be further along in implementing information literacy programs. It is important to note, however, that nearly a year has passed since the documents from institutions accredited by the Middle States Commission were retrieved and analyzed, and some institutions were undergoing re-accreditation when the search was conducted. Thus, the next chapter provides an update to accreditation and information literacy activities by institutions accredited by the Middle States Commission since the last review was conducted.

REFERENCES

American Library Association. (1989). *Presidential committee on information literacy: Final report*. Chicago: American Library Association. Retrieved from http://www.ala.org/ala/mgrps/divs/acrl/publications/whitepapers/presidential.cfm

American Library Association, Association of College and Research Libraries. (2000). *Information literacy competency standards for higher education*.

Retrieved from http://www.ala.org/ala/mgrps/divs/acrl/standards/information literacycompetency.cfm

Gratch-Lindauer, B. (2002). Comparing the regional accreditation standards: Outcomes assessment and other trends. *Journal of Academic Librarianship, 28*(1–2), 14–25. Retrieved from H. W. Wilson.

Middle States Commission on Higher Education. (2003). *Developing research and communication skills: Guidelines for information literacy in the curriculum.* Philadelphia, PA: Author.

National Leadership Council for Liberal Education and America's Promise. (2007). *College learning for the new global century.* Washington, DC: Association of American Colleges and Universities.

North Carolina Wesleyan College. (2009). *GIST: Getting information skills today.* Retrieved from http://ncwc.libguides.com/data/files5/146960/QEP_Document _Aug_2009.pdf

North Central Association of Schools and Colleges, Higher Learning Commission. (2003). *Handbook of accreditation* (3rd ed.). Chicago, IL: Higher Learning Commission. Retrieved from http://www.ncahlc.org/download/Handbook03 .pdf

North Central Association of Schools and Colleges, Higher Learning Commission. (2010). *Academic quality improvement program (AQIP).* Retrieved from http://www.ncahlc.org/aqip-home/

North Georgia College and State University. (2007). *IL=IL: Information literacy = Informed leaders: North Georgia College and State University Quality Enhancement Plan.* Retrieved from http://www.northgeorgia.edu/sacs/ documents/

Project on Accreditation and Assessment. (2004). *Taking responsibility for the quality of the baccalaureate degree.* Washington, DC: Association of American Colleges and Universities.

Saunders, L. (2007). Regional accreditation organizations' treatment of information literacy: Definitions, collaboration, and assessment. *Journal of Academic Librarianship, 33*(3), 317–326. Retrieved from H. W. Wilson.

Southern Association of Colleges and Schools. (2010). *Principles of accreditation: Foundations for quality enhancement.* Decatur, GA: Author. Retrieved from http://www.sacscoc.org/pdf/2010principlesofacreditation.pdf

Western Association of Schools and Colleges Accrediting. (2008). *Handbook of accreditation.* Alameda, CA: Author. Retrieved from http://www.wascsenior .org/

CHAPTER 6

Updates to the Middle States Commission Region

Nearly two years passed between the initial search of websites of institutions accredited by the Middle States Commission and the completion of the nationwide portion of the study. In order to ensure the most updated information, the author revisited the sites of all institutions whose decennial accreditation took place between 2009 and 2011. This allows for the possibility of retrieving documents that have been completed and posted since the initial search. In addition, in some cases, institutions complete accreditation somewhat earlier than scheduled, or post draft copies of documents for an accreditation that is in progress, possibly allowing the researcher access to self-studies coming up in the next few months. This review is especially important because the previous re-accreditation for these institutions took place between 1999 and 2001, before the revised standards with the increased emphasis on information literacy went into effect. As such, it is reasonable to expect that a more current self-study would reflect the changes in the standards.

The follow-up search resulted in seven additional documents, two of which were in draft format. Six of these are from institutions that had not posted earlier studies. In one case, a previous self-study from 10 years ago had been discovered in the initial search and included in the original findings, while this chapter will examine the updated self-study. This institution represents a unique opportunity to compare successive decennial studies written in response to a changed set of accreditation standards side by side, to see how the difference in compliance to the standards is reflected in the self-study. The first part of this chapter will look at the seven new studies as a group, while the second part examines the two self-studies from the same institution in greater detail.

UPDATED FINDINGS

The new set of documents does not deviate much from the initial set. The incidence of the phrase "information literacy" is high in the group, with all seven including the term; the number of mentions ranges from as few as 2 to a high of 17. The context for information literacy continues to be mostly within the library and general education programs for these institutions. Three institutions place information literacy in the context of their general education program, while six of the seven mention the phrase in connection with the library. Only one document discusses instruction for information literacy at the graduate level. Thus, with these institutions as with those examined in Chapters 4 and 5, attention to information literacy continues to concentrate on the undergraduate level.

Further, most of the instruction for information literacy takes place at the course level. In keeping with the focus on the undergraduate level and general education programs in particular, four documents indicate that information literacy is in some way integrated into a first-year seminar or other type of first-year experience course. One-shot sessions are still the most popular format for delivering information literacy instruction, with six institutions including such sessions as one of their methods. Four institutions engage in some form of course-integrated instruction, but as Chapters 4 and 5 explain, it is unclear what the actual level of integration is in most of these courses.

There is little evidence of program-level information literacy. In its report, one institution states that information literacy is integrated at the program level, but does not elaborate. In other words, are student learning outcomes for information literacy mapped to particular courses? Is a dedicated information literacy course included within each major? Without an explanation, it is difficult to gauge whether information literacy is explicitly addressed in each program, or whether there is simply an assumption that programs include information literacy. A second institution offers an information studies area of concentration within its general education program. At this institution, general education is tiered. All students take a group of core courses, followed by a sequence of courses in an elective area, one of which is information studies, which this institution equates with information literacy. While this concentration does represent a program as defined in Chapter 4, in that it is comprised of a series of sequential and developmental courses, it is a stand-alone program. Students who choose this elective area are exposed to higher-order information literacy competencies, but there is no guarantee that students in other areas of concentration receive similar exposure within their chosen area. Finally, a third institution includes plans to develop and integrate student learning outcomes for information literacy at the program level within the self-study's section on future recommendations. The self-study describes a proposal that would "weave information literacy into the students' four year course of study." According to the self-study, a library advisory group composed of librarians, faculty from each department, and students has identified both core courses and courses within the majors that could address information literacy. This committee has invited broader faculty feedback on their proposal, which also includes a mission statement for the program, information literacy goals, and objectives. While this proposal outlines program-level integration, it is still in the early stages. The institution merits revisiting in the future to see if the program is actually implemented, and how many students it reaches. Output counts such as numbers of students enrolled in a course or program constitutes a student outcome, as opposed to a student learning outcome, and it would be interesting to examine both at this institution.

Collaboration

Current collaboration between librarians and teaching faculty is not emphasized in these documents, but since the majority of instruction for information literacy takes place at the course level, one can safely assume that collaboration occurs at the course level as well. When information literacy is described as "course-integrated," it may mean that librarians and faculty work together to define student learning outcomes and design assignments, and they may share teaching responsibilities. Indeed, several of the documents state that librarians tailor information literacy sessions to specific courses and assignments, which implies that they are talking with faculty to learn about the course. Finally, one institution indicates it is in the planning process for integrating information literacy at the program level. The advisory group that designed the proposal for this integration is made up of librarians and faculty, and in fact, the self-study states that the new program was developed in response to "a plan that did not sufficiently engage faculty participation." The new plan incorporates greater cooperation between librarians and faculty, suggesting that collaboration is important to this institution.

Assessment, Accountability, and Transparency

The assessment activities related to student learning outcomes for information literacy generally follow the same patterns as previous chapters, with little assessment taking place, and mostly at the course level. One difference in this group is that tests are the most used form of assessment, as opposed to surveys. In fact, six institutions (85.7%) report using tests including standardized tests such as SAILS and iSkills (now ICT). Conversely, indirect methods are much more infrequent among this group. One institution reports using surveys, and one relies on course evaluations, both of which constitute evaluation rather than assessment. Another institution describes the use of "clickers," or remote devices with which students answer in-class questions. The institution reports positive reactions from students and faculty, and states that the feedback from the clickers allows librarians to identify instructional areas that need improvement. Clickers, however, are problematic as an assessment tool because answers are reported in aggregate, which means instructors cannot offer individualized feedback or assistance to students who give incorrect answers. Information gained through clickers is at a superficial level. The one institution that reports having program-integrated information literacy includes information literacy when assessing senior capstone projects, the only example of program-level assessment in this group.

Overall, assessment activities are low, suggesting that assessing information literacy is not a priority at these institutions. Only two of the seven institutions (28.6%) identify information literacy as a separate student learning outcome, which perhaps, in part, explains the low levels of assessment. In general, institutions might be more likely to assess for student learning outcomes that they have explicitly identified. Equally important, most of the institutions that engage in assessment do not indicate that the data are used to make curricular or pedagogical changes in order to improve student learning. While answering stakeholder demands for accountability and transparency is one purpose of assessment, the ultimate reason to engage in assessment is to continuously improve teaching and learning (Middle States Commission, 2003, 2005, 2007; Suskie, 2010). Institutions that collect assessment data but do not use them for improvement are not fully meeting accreditation expectations.

Assessment is a prerequisite of accountability, just as explicit student learning outcomes are a precursor of implementing assessment. If institutions do not engage in direct assessment of learning outcomes for information literacy, they cannot be accountable for progress toward those learning goals. Yet, at this point, most institutions still rely on indirect methods of assessment, or substitute evaluation for assessment. The institution that claims program-level integration and that assesses information literacy as part of the students' capstone projects is one of a few examples of direct assessment. Capstone projects require students to integrate and synthesize knowledge and competencies gained throughout their program of study and to produce some work that demonstrates mastery in their area. As such, these projects demonstrate the growth and change in student knowledge and ability. One drawback in this example is that the institution does not mention whether rubrics are applied in assessing these capstone projects. As described in Chapter 8, rubrics define levels of competency for learning goals and help to ensure consistency in scoring. Without a rubric, the assessment might be subjective. In addition, the reports do not indicate how the assessment data are used to improve student learning.

Finally, institutional transparency is tied into assessment and accountability. Institutions may engage in assessment but not willingly share their methods and results with some stakeholders, as evidenced by the number of institutions that do not make their self-studies publicly available. It is possible that there are higher levels of integration of information literacy beyond the course level, and/or assessment of learning outcomes related to information literacy than are reported in this study, because institutions engaged in these activities do not post their self-studies. In such cases, assessment might lead to improved quality in teaching and learning, but without the transparency of sharing such information with the public, these institutions are not demonstrating full accountability to their stakeholders. Accreditation organizations might spur transparency by making more information on accreditation decisions public, and encouraging their institutions to share self-studies and other accreditation documents more readily (Gillen, Bennett, & Vedder, 2010; Higher Education Opportunity Act, 2008).

Institutional Culture and Leadership

At present, none of the institutions reviewed here appear to have developed a culture of information literacy, although the institution that claims program-level integration and the one that has proposed integration of information literacy at the program level may be moving in that direction. As the findings illustrate, for the most part, information literacy is addressed largely at the course level, and there is little evidence that teaching faculty are taking on responsibility for its instruction and assessment. Rather, librarians seem to shoulder most of the responsibility for instruction, which they do mostly through one-shot sessions.

Efforts to integrate information literacy beyond the course level suggest greater buy-in from faculty and high-level administrators, and may be evidence of an institutional culture of information literacy. For example, librarians at the institution with the new information literacy proposal are engaging in conversations with faculty beyond the course level, with a focus on greater collaboration between faculty and librarians. However, the extent to which faculty members were involved in developing the proposal is unclear. While the self-study indicates that a library advisory group including faculty worked on a plan for greater collaboration, other sections of the document that describe the development of a mission statement and goals for the program mention only librarians. If faculty and others such as senior administrators were directly involved in planning and identifying goals, this might be an example of creating a shared vision, a component of leadership as identified in Chapter 11. Further, such collaboration and shared vision could lead to a culture of information literacy; but at this point, it remains unclear if this campus will achieve such a culture.

COMPARISON OF SUCCESSIVE SELF-STUDY DOCUMENTS

This updated review uncovered a self-study from an institution whose previous self-study was included in the initial review. The discovery offers a unique opportunity to compare the two successive documents side by side. This review was particularly interesting given that the first self-study took place in 1999, before the publication of the current Middle States Commission standards with its emphasis on information literacy, and also before the Association of College and Research Libraries (ACRL) issued the *Information Literacy Competency Standards* (American Library Association, Association of College and Research Libraries, 2000). A comparison of the two documents suggests that the new standards had an impact on information literacy on this campus. In fact, the earlier self-study included no mention of information literacy. Further, there was essentially no equivalent language in the document, aside from a reference to enabling the "efficient and responsible use of information" in the library mission statement. The library section of the report does not even mention instruction as a service.

Conversely, the more recent self-study includes the phrase information literacy eight times. Attention to information literacy is still in the very early stages on this campus. The concept is discussed only in terms of library instruction, and the delivery of that instruction appears to take place only at the course level; indeed, mostly through one-shot sessions. Not surprisingly, there is little evidence of assessment or evaluation, with tests and course or class evaluations the only methods mentioned. Still, the institution includes future recommendations for information literacy in the report. Specifically, the self-study mentions plans to develop and incorporate student learning outcomes for information literacy into core courses, suggesting that the institution is beginning to view information literacy as broader than library research skills, and that it will continue to address it in the coming years.

While attention to information literacy on this campus is still relatively superficial, it does show progress. From having no mention, even tangentially, to information literacy, this institution has begun to address the concept and work it into its curriculum. The use of pre- and posttests demonstrates that the institution values the competencies associated with information literacy and is trying to measure student learning in this area. Including plans to develop student learning outcomes for information literacy in its future recommendations indicates that the institution intends to continue to grow its activities in this area. While a number of forces, both internal and external, could be responsible for promoting this change within the institution, the fact that the decennial self-studies show such a difference in approach suggests that the changing standards of the Middle States Commission has an impact on how institutions address learning outcomes such as information literacy. If the accreditation organization sets an expectation that such learning outcomes must be addressed, this example seems to support the idea that institutions will likely comply.

CONCLUSION

The updates to the Middle States Commission institutions do not show substantial differences from two years ago. This is perhaps not surprising, given that there were only a small number of new self-studies to review, and that the Middle States Commission has not issued new standards since the initial study. What is surprising is that, despite the Middle States Commission's strong emphasis on information literacy as a student learning outcome, the institutions reviewed here do not seem to have moved any further toward implementing and assessing information literacy programs than institutions from the other five accreditation regions. In fact, several institutions from the other five regions provide evidence of tiered or programmatic approaches to information literacy, suggesting they are more advanced than the institutions under the aegis of the Middle States Commission. With one exception of an institution that states it has program-integrated information but does not elaborate on how such integration is achieved, institutions accredited by the Middle States Commission appear, at most, to still be in the planning stages of program integration.

That said, some of these institutions are actively engaged in trying to promote information literacy on their campuses. Using results from phase two, the initial review of self-studies from institutions accredited by the Middle States Commission, four institutions with evidence of such activity were selected to serve as case studies. The following chapters present the findings of the case studies, and examine the themes that emerged from these visits.

REFERENCES

American Library Association, Association of College and Research Libraries. (2000). *Information literacy competency standards for higher education.* Retrieved from http://www.ala.org/ala/mgrps/divs/acrl/standards/informationliteracy competency.cfm

Gillen, A., Bennett, D. L., & Vedder, D. (2010). *The inmates running the asylum? An analysis of higher education accreditation.* Washington, DC: Center for College Affordability and Productivity. Retrieved from http://www.centerforcollege affordability.org/uploads/Accreditation.pdf

Higher Education Opportunity Act of 2008, P.L. 110-315. Retrieved from http://purl .access.gpo.gov/GPO/LPS103713

Middle States Commission on Higher Education. (2003). *Developing research and communication skills: Guidelines for information literacy in the curriculum.* Philadelphia, PA: Author.

Middle States Commission on Higher Education. (2005). *Assessing student learning and institutional effectiveness.* Philadelphia, PA: Author. Retrieved from http://www.msche.org/publications/Assessment_Expectations051222081842 .pdf

Middle States Commission on Higher Education. (2007). *Student learning assessment: Options and resources.* Philadelphia, PA: Author. Retrieved from http://www.msche.org/publications/SLA_Book_0808080728085320.pdf

Suskie, L. (2010, October 26). Why are we assessing? *Inside Higher Ed.* Retrieved from http://www.insidehighered.com/views/2010/10/26/suskie

CHAPTER 7

Collaboration

Collaboration between faculty and librarians is an important and recurring theme in information literacy. Information literacy is a metacognitive competency that is applicable across disciplines, and involves abilities traditionally associated with library skills (Middle States Commission, 2003). This breadth and depth of knowledge suggests that information literacy is best addressed by faculty and librarians working collaboratively to introduce students to the concepts of finding, evaluating, and using information both generally and in the context of the disciplines. Among the case study institutions, librarians place a heavy emphasis on the importance of collaboration with faculty, and express varying levels of satisfaction at the response to their outreach efforts.

FRAMEWORK FOR INFORMATION LITERACY COLLABORATION

The Middle States Commission (2003) emphasizes the importance of collaboration for information literacy by offering guidelines to librarians and faculty on the roles and responsibilities that each could take in instructing and assessing information literacy (see Figure 1.1). That figure depicts a framework for collaboration based on the ACRL standards (American Library Association, Association of College and Research Libraries, 2000). The figure suggests that faculty lead in subject content within their disciplines, in part by creating assignments requiring students to choose and refine a topic area for a project, evaluate the content of a resource, and use the information to accomplish a specific purpose. In addition, faculty assume the lead in the fourth competency, incorporation of new information into the knowledge base, in that they facilitate and reinforce learning through coursework, class discussions, and activities. Librarians can support faculty in each of the information literacy competencies depicted in the figure, and they might assume the lead in the search for, finding of, and evaluation of information sources. Further underscoring the importance of collaboration, the Middle States Commission (2003) warns against "relegating to the librarian what the faculty member perceives as information literacy" (p. 21).

A TYPOLOGY OF COLLABORATION

The Middle States Commission (2003) specifies that faculty and librarians should work together to deliver and assess information literacy instruction "within and across academic levels" (p. 21), indicating that institutions should address information literacy at the course, program, and institutional levels as well as at both the undergraduate and graduate levels. *Developing Research and Communication Skills* (Middle States Commission, 2003) proffers several models for addressing information literacy across the curriculum, including the compartmentalized model that involves stand-alone information literacy courses or one-shot instruction modules.

While refraining from a prescribed program, the Middle States Commission (2003) promotes a developmental and sequential approach, in which information literacy skills are introduced early and built upon throughout a student's education. With such an approach, faculty and librarians identify different skills and levels of competency expected of students at different points in the curriculum, with seniors demonstrating greater proficiency than first-year students, and graduate students attaining even more specialized skills. This progression reflects "the progressive development of their information literacy skills throughout their college experience" (Middle States Commission, 2003, p. 13). Finally, in its guidelines for integrating information literacy into the curriculum, the Middle States Commission (2003) encourages collaboration among cocurricular and extracurricular departments, including writing centers, student affairs, and even athletics. While Figure 1.1 centers on generic collaboration between faculty and librarians, opportunities exist for collaboration at the course, program, and institutional levels, across various departments, and at both the undergraduate and graduate levels. The rest of this chapter provides examples of collaboration across types from case study institutions.

Course-Level Collaboration

Course outcomes define the specific abilities students should demonstrate at the end of an individual course, and the vast majority of collaborations take place at this level. Institutions A, B, and C offer classes that are team-taught by faculty and librarians. For instance, at institution A, one librarian team-teaches a geography course with a departmental faculty member. The librarian attends all or most class sessions, participates in some lectures and discussions, and teaches two or three class sessions devoted to information literacy, covering topics such as finding, selecting, and evaluating resources. The faculty member and librarian together grade the assignment for the class, an annotated bibliography. Such collaborations provide a good opportunity to build toward program-level integration, if other faculty within the department become interested. However, if collaboration remains at the course level, it represents the low end of the Middle States Commission's (2003) expectations.

At institution B, a librarian and a chemistry faculty member received an institutional award for team teaching. At the same institution, librarians worked with an education faculty member to create an information literacy–related conceptual model, known as the relevance/credibility model. Consisting of 10 domains (e.g., authority, currency, and relevance), this model guides students in selecting appropriate materials for inclusion in their research papers. Students are introduced to the model in table format, and throughout the semester, they apply the criteria to different information sources. They develop the criteria from the table format into paragraph descriptions, which requires them to think more deeply about the content behind the criteria. Finally, the students develop PowerPoint presentations highlighting why they would or would not choose certain sources for research papers. In a similar fashion, librarians at institution C worked closely with faculty to develop assignments for the freshman writing class, which the librarian then grades.

In each of these instances, librarians are extensively involved in designing, delivering, and evaluating course content; but thus far, these examples have not been expanded into program-level collaboration. While these examples are often referred to by interviewees as "model" or "ideal," they remain isolated examples that depend on the involvement of one or two interested faculty members. That such courses would receive institutional awards and be so widely discussed by various interviewees demonstrates that these classes receive recognition on campus. However, they do not appear to arouse the interest or lead to the participation of other faculty or departments. Similarly, reports of collaboration in the literature of library and information science concentrate largely on the course level (see e.g., Bhavnagri & Bielat, 2005; Hearn, 2005; Kearns & Hybl, 2005; Mounce, 2009), and indicate that such instruction continues to be offered largely through one-shot sessions (Badke, 2005; Owusu-Ansah, 2007).

Program-Level Collaboration

Program outcomes, which are specific to the major or field of study, emphasize certain competency areas over others, and define more specifically the skills necessary to be mastered by students concentrating in that discipline. Among the case studies, the only explicit example of the movement toward program-level collaboration is at institution C, where all new or revised courses and programs have to include information literacy goals in their proposals to the curriculum committee. At this institution, the faculty realize that information literacy is a requirement, and they often consult with librarians to determine how to meet that requirement in their courses. For instance, concurrent with the on-site interviews at this institution, a librarian talks with the chair of the computer science department to discuss information literacy outcomes for an AutoCAD (computer-aided design software) course. Though the meeting focused on one course, it lays the groundwork for integrating information literacy throughout the program. The faculty member expressed interest in meeting with the librarian again to discuss other classes and further integration for the department. One senior administrator commented that faculty at this institution are aware of information literacy and understand that they need to integrate different skills at different levels, although they have not yet reached that level of campus-wide integration.

The Middle States Commission (2003) underscores the importance of a disciplinary approach, or program-level integration, that allows students to deepen their understanding of the production, dissemination, and uses of information particular to their chosen field, and provides opportunities to combine information literacy with other content. While acknowledging that a distributed model with information literacy integrated seamlessly into the curriculum takes time to achieve, the Middle States Commission (2003) discourages institutions from relying on separate, discipline-specific information literacy courses. It indicates that separate courses might be implemented early on, but should be "regarded as only a transition and not as a final goal" (p. 18).

Despite the Middle States Commission's (2003) emphasis on moving past segregated information literacy courses, in the majority of cases, librarians teach these courses outside of any distinct major or program of study. As a result, the courses tend to take a broad perspective on information and, although librarians interviewed for the case studies try to make the course content relevant to students, they suspect that students do not often see the connections between the information literacy course and their program of study. While these segregated courses are acceptable stop-gap measures while the institution prepares for further integration, most institutions appear to have stalled at this stage. Institutions A and B introduced their credit-bearing information literacy courses nearly a decade ago, and neither has expanded the initiative since then. Only institution C, with its policy of requiring learning goals for information literacy in the new and revised courses, actively integrates information literacy in the broader curriculum. With this exception, however, most institutions do not meet the Middle States

Commission's (2003) expectations for integrating information literacy into the curriculum.

Institutional-Level Collaboration

Librarians at case study institutions are involved in institutional-level collaboration mostly through committee work. At two case study institutions, librarians serve on institution-wide curriculum committees. All full-time librarians at institution C serve on at least one faculty governance committee, while librarians at institution B participate in both the faculty senate and the university-wide assessment committee. Serving on these committees allows librarians to work with faculty to set policy and learning goals at the institutional level.

In addition, some librarians cooperate with campus-wide departments to deliver various types of instruction. For instance, librarians at institution B work with the center for teaching excellence to offer a series of professional development workshops for faculty. The center director speaks highly of the librarians and the relevance of the sessions they offer. At institution D, librarians are involved in the writing across the curriculum (WaC) initiative, which supports institutional-level learning outcomes for writing. The librarians work with the WaC director to train student writing fellows in information literacy competencies. As a result, the writing fellows are able to assist their peers with issues such as proper citation as well as with literature searches. These collaborations also serve as examples of cross-campus collaborations, discussed further in the next section.

Cross-Campus Collaboration

While much discussion centers on collaboration between teaching faculty and librarians, it is important to note that collaboration in extracurricular and cocurricular activities can support information literacy learning outcomes as well. The Middle States Commission (2003) states that "any extra-curricular activity can promote information literacy and reinforce principles learned in classroom activities" (p. 18). Such integration is supported through collaboration and partnerships among academic departments and others involved in student learning, including student support services, student life, and athletics.

The case studies offer a number of examples of collaboration moving beyond the classroom faculty. As noted above, librarians at institution B extend their influence through collaborations with the center for teaching excellence. By partnering with the center's director, librarians offer a number of professional development sessions for faculty. They also get staff from other departments to teach the credit-bearing information literacy course.

For instance, one of the regular teachers of this course is not a librarian, but an academic advisor who is enthusiastic about the information literacy course and praises the librarians for the amount of training and orientation they provide.

Institution D is another example of a successful partnership. Librarians here work closely with the director of the writing across the curriculum (WaC) program to infuse information literacy into the writing-intensive courses. In particular, the WaC director brings librarians into a new writing fellows program. Modeled after a similar one at Brown University, this program recruits upper-class students to serve as writing fellows in composition classes. Unlike general writing tutors, however, these fellows are assigned to particular classes and meet with the same students throughout the semester, as they read successive drafts of papers. The fellows go through an intensive orientation program in which they are trained to assist their peers in thinking through and critiquing drafts of research papers.

The WaC director, with the assistance of a librarian, also teaches the fellows to assist students in their library research. In other words, if the fellows find errors in the mentee's citations or a lack of support for assertions, rather than simply pointing it out, the fellow instructs his/her peers in how to find the necessary information. The fellows also direct other students to the library for additional help. The WaC director is enthusiastic about the program, stating that by bringing together information literacy and writing, the institution lets "things heal that never should have been divided in the first place." In other words, the WaC director recognizes that, like writing, information literacy is applicable across the curriculum in all different subject areas, and in order to produce well-supported and accurately cited papers, students need both information literacy competencies and strong writing skills.

Similar examples exist throughout the literature of library and information science. Librarians describe fruitful partnerships with international student services, writing centers, and career services to promote information literacy (Hernon & Powell, 2008). Mounce (2009) identifies 18 articles that detail collaboration between librarians and composition instructors published from 1998 to 2007. Similarly, Swartz, Carlisle, and Uyeki (2007) describe a partnership at the University of California, Los Angeles, between librarians and the office of the dean of students that was undertaken to educate students about academic integrity, including the ethical and legal use of information. Scales, Matthews, and Johnson (2005) contend that the increased attention to information literacy in higher education has been accompanied by a shift from informal one-on-one collaborations between librarians and faculty to "a more formal sharing of information literacy goals with broader academic and nonacademic entities, organizations, and bodies" (p. 229). They define librarians, staff at the Center for Teaching, Learning and Technology, and those in charge of the distance-degree program as the key players for infusing information literacy into the general education curriculum at their campus.

Barratt, Nielsen, Desmet, and Balthazor (2009) argue that such collaborative approaches are more effective in achieving learning outcomes for information literacy.

While these examples demonstrate high levels of collaboration, overall, the examples are only intermittent and highly concentrated on course-level collaboration. There is a general lack of program-level collaboration, in which information literacy skills and competencies are addressed developmentally and sequentially throughout the student's education. As Badke (2005) asserts, "effective collaboration simply is not the norm" (p. 68). As such, institutions achieve only what the Middle States Commission (2003, p. 15) describes as a "baseline" level. While baseline offerings may be sufficient as colleges and universities transition, ultimately the expectation is that information literacy will be addressed throughout the curriculum at the program and institutional levels. Some interviewees at case study institutions realize that they have not reached that level of integration. Those librarians involved in team teaching, for instance, maintain that more classes should develop such partnerships. However, even increasing the number of high-level collaborations does not generate program-level integration if the courses are not sequentially connected. Librarians at institutions B and D, in particular, emphasize that they have not achieved the level of integration that they would like. They are trying to find additional ways to promote information literacy. However, they are aware of a variety of obstacles as they pursue the integration of information literacy into the curriculum.

Collaboration at Degree Levels

Collaboration for information literacy can occur at the undergraduate or graduate level, or at institutional, program, and course levels. Although graduate students should demonstrate greater depth and complexity of knowledge, the focus on information literacy occurs solely at the undergraduate level for the vast majority of the institutions included in this study. The four case study institutions do not address information literacy at the graduate level, but they focus mostly on the undergraduate and the general education curriculum.

The reason why most participating institutions do not view information literacy as necessary for graduate students remains unclear. Interviewees from some of the case study institutions suggest that faculty assume students at that level have already attained the competencies and mastered the skills they need. Rather, emphasis for information literacy is placed within the context of general education. These courses are typically among the first that entering students take, and as such tend to focus on introductory topics and skills. In order to comply with the Middle States Commission's (2003) suggestion of distributed integration of information literacy, institutions should not focus only on general education, but integrate information literacy through the rest of the institution over time. However, it is not clear that this is the intention of most institutions.

DIVISION OF RESPONSIBILITIES

Interviews and observations at the case study institutions reveal examples of collaboration across the different departments and divisions, broadly conforming to the framework in Figure 1.1. Likewise, the division of responsibilities between librarians and faculty generally align with the figure. As noted in Chapter 4, instruction in finding and accessing information is the most widely addressed information literacy topic, followed by evaluation of information. Librarians at case study institutions generally confirmed these findings. For instance, syllabi for stand-alone courses for information literacy at two of the case study institutions list accessing resources, finding information, and evaluating information as course objectives, and class topics emphasize search strategies. Librarians at institution D indicate that they focus on search techniques because pretests given to first-year students revealed that most did not understand the proper use of Boolean operators in searching for information.

One much-discussed area that was not well represented in the study data is instruction in the ethical and legal use of information. The Middle States Commission (2003) underscores the importance of this topic for students by indicating it should be addressed by both faculty and librarians "jointly and continuously" (p. 23). The dean of general education at institution A indicates that ethical use of information is one of the drivers for information literacy. She notes that the widespread access to information made possible by the Internet has led students into "bad habits," and that they need assistance in learning how to use information ethically. Happel and Jennings (2008) contend that student cheating and plagiarism are commonplace in colleges and universities, while a study of bioscience students at three different levels at the University of Leeds (Dawson & Overfield, 2006) confirms that students are often unclear about what constitutes plagiarism.

Although the Middle States Commission (2003) suggests that both faculty and librarians should be instructing students on proper use of information and citations, there actually appears to be a lack of ownership in this area. For instance, focus group interviews conducted with faculty at institution D reveal that the faculty are concerned with plagiarism and student's research abilities, but they believe that these topics are covered elsewhere in the curriculum. As one librarian states, the faculty's reaction seems to be, "isn't someone teaching this?"

Librarians participating in case study interviews acknowledge the importance of ethical use of information, but they have difficulty in finding effective ways to address the issue. The syllabi of stand-alone information literacy courses at institutions A and B address ethical use of information, including issues of copyright, proper citations, and plagiarism. In both cases, librarians spend between two and three class sessions discussing these topics. Outside of these courses, however, librarians focus the majority of their one-shot sessions on searching, access, and evaluation, and they often only superficially touch on ethical use. Indeed, several librarians indicate that they point students to citation software such as RefWorks or EndNotes. While these tools may assist students in properly formatting citations, they cannot help students to understand when and what to cite, or even why proper citation is important. As a result, ethical use of information receives little attention, despite an apparent need on the students' part for it to be addressed.

BARRIERS TO COLLABORATION

A host of barriers often deter collaboration and may help to explain why many information literacy initiatives stall at the course level. The formal position that the library and librarians hold within the larger organization may constitute a barrier. Further evidence from the case studies suggests that barriers derive from limited time and resources to address additional content, lack of understanding of the role of information literacy within the larger curriculum, and segregation of information literacy courses from the rest of the curriculum.

Status of the Library and Librarian

An initial barrier in some places is the status and placement of the library and librarians within the organizational structure of the institution. The library director may report to an academic provost, vice president, or dean. Lacking the status of an academic department, some libraries find it difficult to offer a credit course. For instance, at institution B of the case studies, the central administration supports the development of an information literacy course, but the course cannot be offered through the library since it is not an academic department. Rather, the librarians had to find a department willing to house the course, even though they develop and provide most of the content. The librarians believe the institution does not recognize or value their contribution as educators, and they resent that budget money to support the course goes to the academic department rather than to the library.

Likewise, while library positions are most likely considered professional, many librarians believe that faculty members do not consider them as peers, even at institutions where librarians hold faculty status. As such, the faculty may turn to librarians for search assistance or send students for help, but may not think of them as potential partners in curriculum planning and instruction. One of the interviewees strongly asserts that status is important for implementing an information literacy program. This librarian had moved from a library position with faculty status to her current position without faculty status. She believes that not having the status creates a barrier to approaching and working with faculty. She states that faculty "do not always start off looking at you as a colleague," implying that these faculty view librarians as of a lower status.

Her view may oversimplify the matter, however. While Welch (2006) argues that faculty status is crucial for librarians to be fully integrated into the institution's governance and academic structures, it is important to consider that institutions have different cultures (discussed further in Chapter 10). The interviewee librarian's experience of receiving a different reception by faculty upon changing jobs may have had more to do with a different institutional culture than with not having faculty status. Further, faculty status often entails requirements for publication and service within or outside of the institution. These additional responsibilities impinge on the librarian's time and might detract from offering information literacy services. Finally, as Leonhardt (2004) argues, the quality of the librarian's work and not a faculty position is what leads to respect. The idea that simply giving librarians faculty status would change other faculty members' perceptions of the librarians is doubtful and simplistic.

Faculty Reticence

Regardless of the librarians' status, faculty reticence is frequently mentioned as a barrier to collaboration on information literacy programs (Badke, 2005; Farber, 2004; Given & Julien, 2005; Hardesty, 1995; Manuel, Beck, & Molloy, 2005). While the institutions included in the case studies were chosen for their relatively robust programs, several librarians express concern and frustration over perceived rebuffs from faculty. At each institution, collaborative efforts still largely depend on faculty willingness to share class time, and such willingness is not always apparent. An academic dean at institution A suggests that faculty tend to concentrate on their own academic areas, and do not view information literacy as their "turf." Some interviewees believe that some faculty are interested in incorporating information literacy topics into their courses and working with librarians, but they are overwhelmed with content already. As an extreme example, a business librarian at institution D comments that she is regularly given 10 minutes in introduction to accounting classes to offer an overview of the library and its resources. In some cases, faculty recognize a need for students to be exposed to information literacy and to be aware of the role librarians can play. Nevertheless, they are unwilling to devote class time to address the issue. As long as faculty and librarians approach teaching from the point of view of covering content, as opposed to creating learning opportunities, a lack of time will continue to be a barrier (Ironside, 2004).

Pedagogical trends in higher education support a move from content-focused teaching to more student-centered learning. Current theories emphasize the importance of engaging students in the learning process through active participation in class discussions, hands-on practice, and problem solving. Active learning often involves group work or other collaborative projects that require social interaction among students. Such approaches to learning are thought to be more engaging for students and to result in deeper learning (see, e.g., Remler, 2002; Schroeder & Spannagel, 2006; Zmuda, 2008). If lack of time and coverage of content are barriers to integrating information literacy, then the shift to active learning may facilitate greater integration.

Librarians find it difficult to meet demands for information literacy with current resources of staff and budget. At institutions A and B, where librarians teach credit-bearing information literacy courses, little staff time remains to attend to faculty requests for in-class instruction. Yet, when they teach stand-alone courses, librarians work alone, whereas other course-related instruction allows them to work with faculty and perhaps cultivate deeper relationships. The librarians at institution D also mention a shortage of staff as a barrier to implementing a campus-wide information literacy program. Indeed, the arts and sciences librarian at this institution said that the information literacy program could not really be described as integrated, but indicates that the library had to develop a program that it "could live with and was sustainable."

Online access and instruction may offer librarians an opportunity to stretch their resources, as it offers them the possibility to deliver instruction remotely and asynchronously. The case study institutions use online tutorials, web guides, and links within course pages to reach a greater audience. Librarians at institution C collaborate with faculty on a distance learning course, where they offer "in-class" instruction virtually. Nevertheless, librarians encounter some of the same barriers in the online world as they do in traditional instruction. For instance, librarians at institution D find it hard to convince faculty to give them a presence on their course pages. When they do, that presence is often limited to a link to the library page buried somewhere on the larger site, and not easily found by students. As with traditional in-class instruction, librarians depend on faculty invitations for such access to students.

Segregation of Information Literacy

One option available to institutions is to address information literacy through separate, credit-bearing courses. Case study librarians tend to view the creation of such courses as a coup, signaling institutional commitment to information literacy as a learning outcome. Ironically, however, such courses seem to discourage, rather than facilitate, collaboration. The majority of these courses are taught by librarians without input from faculty, and without direct connection to the rest of the curriculum. While librarians try to make course content relevant and engaging for students, they admit that the students often do not appreciate the relevance or readily understand how the concepts apply to other courses. On the other hand, when discipline faculty teach the information literacy courses, they do not necessarily look to librarians for support.

Institution A established its information literacy program in 2000, with the momentum of a system-wide mandate. At the time, the institution decided to have the library offer sections of a one-credit course to fulfill that mandate, but also gave academic departments the option of developing a designated information literacy course within their major. Nine years later, six departments offer their own information literacy course, while the library runs 30 sections of its class. Moreover, virtually all of the departmental courses were developed in the first couple of years of the new mandate, with little interest being shown since that time; and some departments have even dropped their information literacy course within the last few years. Thus, the faculty appear to have little interest in adopting and integrating information literacy into their departments if requirements can be met by stand-alone library courses.

Institution B faced a similar situation. When administrators decided, with the prompting of an accreditation review by the Middle States Commission, that information literacy needed to be more widely addressed, they asked the librarians to develop a plan. The librarians suggested a number of options for integrating the information literacy component into the curriculum. They contend that they advocated for having departments develop their own information literacy–designated course, with support from the library. Ultimately, however, those in charge of curriculum development chose to have the library teach its own course. Only two departments developed discipline-specific courses, suggesting that faculty have little interest in developing such courses, with or without the help and support of librarians, let alone move to program-level integration.

Those departments that develop their own information literacy course do not always integrate the library into that course. One faculty member teaching a departmental information literacy course at institution A indicates that she encourages her students to use the library and ask librarians for assistance, but she does not invite the librarians to help with the course. In fact, she maintains that the librarians could not answer the types of questions she asks of her students, because they lack the content knowledge. Likewise, the librarians at institution B are not involved in the two departmental information literacy courses.

The focus on faculty barriers to collaboration derives mainly from the fact that librarians depend on faculty willingness or invitations to collaborate. It is worth noting, however, that librarians do not always successfully achieve collaboration themselves. For instance, at institution A, six librarians teach about 30 sections of the credit-bearing information literacy class. However, the librarian who teaches the course-integrated geography information literacy class is not one of those six. When asked if she meets with those teaching the general information literacy classes to share ideas, her immediate response was "no," because she "is not part of the instruction team." Despite the fact that her class was pointed to as an "ideal" by others, and she finds other instruction librarians "supportive" of her work, she indicates that overall, not much centralized discussion or cross-fertilization takes place among the teaching librarians. This lack of collaboration among the librarians offering instruction seems like a missed opportunity. Not only could the librarians benefit from sharing ideas and experiences, but such collaboration would allow them to model the type of partnerships they hope to have with faculty.

Understanding Information Literacy

The lack of interest on the part of faculty may be less about librarians' status or abilities as teachers and more about the faculty's understanding of information literacy and its place within the curriculum. Some of the interviewees at case study institutions believe that faculty do not have a strong understanding of the concept of information literacy, and that lack of understanding was a barrier. For instance, the dean of general education at institution A acknowledges that many faculty are primarily interested in their own areas and reluctant to address information literacy. The Middle States Commission's (2003) view is that information literacy is relevant in all disciplines and that faculty are central to its instruction, although it does not regard this position as a mandate for all institutions to adopt.

Some librarians suggest that the phrase "information literacy" contributes to faculty resistance and express discontent with the term for this reason. They believe it alienates faculty because it is overly associated with library research skills. As one librarian puts it, "faculty just don't get it." Indeed, evidence of such misunderstanding surfaced during an interview with a non-librarian who teaches an information literacy course at institution B. In describing her teaching responsibilities for the course, this instructor focused almost exclusively on the technology aspects, such as Word, Excel, and PowerPoint. When pressed to talk about the areas more specific to information literacy, she was unable to name any. Such conflation of technology literacy with information literacy is not uncommon, but it highlights the fact that many people do not recognize the broader applicability of information literacy, and raises particular concern for someone who actually is responsible for teaching an information literacy course.

In general, however, perhaps it is more accurate to say that faculty consider information literacy as it is popularly defined to be of lesser importance to their courses and programs than other competency areas, even though the current Middle States Commission emphasizes the cross-disciplinary applicability of information literacy. Ultimately, the fact that the concept is rooted in traditional bibliographic instruction may lead faculty to believe that it is "primarily a librarian's responsibility" (Ratteray, 2002, p. 369). Moreover, librarians, like faculty, are sometimes territorial and protective of what they see as their domains (Julien & Given, 2002–2003). A librarian at institution D suggests that librarians have to "share ownership" of information literacy.

If faculty do not fully understand the concept of information literacy, the problem is compounded by debate within the library community. The literature of library and information science demonstrates that librarians themselves do not agree on the exact definition of information literacy (Lloyd, 2005; Owusu-Ansah, 2005; Saunders, 2009). Ratteray (2005, 2008) laments the library-centric use of the term, stating "I agonize every time I hear someone define information literacy (the big picture) by a subset of its components (effectively Standards 1, 2, and part of 5, from a librarian's perspective)" (2005, para. 1). In other words, librarians may be damaging their own cause by being too narrow in their focus when they discuss information literacy. By focusing on the aspects of information literacy most closely related to library skills, librarians reinforce the notion that information literacy is synonymous with library skills. Ratteray (2005) further suggests that, by not including faculty on the task force that developed the definition of information literacy, ACRL "dropped the ball" and alienated faculty from further involvement. Librarians have to broaden the discussion to engage faculty and work toward consensus on learning goals for information literacy, a theme discussed further in Chapter 11.

Understanding Roles

The interactions between librarians and faculty discussed here suggest that faculty and librarians may not fully understand and appreciate each others' roles with regard to students and learning outcomes. Studies of faculty perceptions of collaboration with librarians reveal that most faculty neither view librarians as partners in instruction nor tend to go to them for search assistance. Rather, faculty focus on the librarian's role in offering reference assistance and publicizing resources, and in providing services to them such as checking numbers of citations for their promotion and tenure dossiers (Ivey, 1994; Schulte & Sherwill-Navarro, 2009). When asked to respond to specific descriptions of collaboration, nursing educators are more likely to agree with having librarians involved in program/curricular development and its evaluation, and they are more neutral in their responses to having librarians involved in instruction (Schulte & Sherwill-Navarro, 2009). In a survey of science and engineering faculty, Leckie and Fullerton (1999) find that the vast majority have never made use of library instruction. Although they profess interest in collaboration, only about a third of those faculty express interest in collaboratively designing assignments with librarians, and even fewer want to team-teach or share grading (Leckie & Fullerton, 1999).

Faculty and librarians may not completely understand or appreciate the others' work roles, motivations, and responsibilities (Given & Julien, 2005). Some librarians (Farber, 2004; Hardesty, 1995) suggest that faculty value the autonomy and independence they have within the classroom, and they are reluctant to share that sphere of influence with anyone else. In an analysis of librarians' posting to a listserv, Julien and Given (2002–2003) find that librarians consistently characterize faculty negatively as "rude, 'touchy,' rarely cooperative, recalcitrant about change, and out of touch with their students' skill levels" (p. 77). Further, some librarians express "feelings of competition with faculty for students' attention" (p. 75). While faculty and librarians ultimately work to enhance student learning, their spheres of responsibility differ. Some faculty may have a limited understanding of the librarians' expertise and skill in the areas of information literacy and how they can relate to course content. Librarians, meanwhile, may not appreciate the time constraints and competing priorities with which faculty must contend.

Culture and Collaboration

In the end, however, the underlying problem may be inherent in a higher-education culture that does not always value or reward collaboration. Kezar (2006) maintains that colleges and universities are not structured to support collaboration, because "higher education institutions work in departmental silos and within bureaucratic/hierarchical administrative structures" (p. 805). Indeed, the writing-across-the-curriculum director at institution D questioned whether "institutions reward individual achievement too much" and if this might be a barrier to collaboration. He maintains that individuals, perhaps especially those who have not yet achieved tenure, are often concerned about "who's getting the credit" for a project. Kezar (2006) also mentions promotion and tenure requirements, which typically do not favor, and indeed sometimes discourage, collaborative work as a barrier. She notes that "one cannot impose collaboration within a context designed to support individualistic work" (Kezar, 2006, p. 809). The idea of institutional and organizational culture is explored in more depth in Chapter 10.

While such attitudes toward collaboration might have been the norm historically, trends toward interdisciplinary study and teaching that supports cross-departmental collaboration are gaining in popularity. For instance, Taylor (2009) argues that higher education should "abolish permanent departments, even for undergraduate education, and create problem-focused programs" (section 12, sentence 1), which would be organized around common problems or issues, rather than the traditional disciplines.

In his view, such programs would bring together faculty and researchers from many disciplines to "engage in comparative analysis" (section 11, sentence 1). While Taylor's view is extreme, some institutions are moving toward more interdisciplinary education. Ten research universities created the Consortium on Fostering Interdisciplinary Inquiry, which has as its mission to "transform the capacity of the participating universities to successfully engage in interdisciplinary research, education and training, and creative activity" (University of Minnesota, 2007). Government agencies such as the National Science Foundation and the National Institutes of Health offer grants specifically to promote interdisciplinary projects (Jacobs & Frickel, 2009).

In addition to having an interest in the educational benefits it offers, some institutions turn to collaboration as a cost-cutting measure, especially during the 2008–2009 economic recession. Peterson (2007) notes that collaboration can help institutions to save money and stretch resources, and she views collaboration as necessary to the future of higher education. Thomas (2009) likewise calls on institutions to "expand cost-saving collaboratives in administrative and academic realms" (p. 11). These trends suggest that colleges and universities are increasingly considering collaboration, if they have not yet fully embraced it.

As one of the core areas for facilitating collaboration, Kezar (2005, 2006) suggests that, for collaboration to succeed, reward systems must be designed to support such work. The notion that institutional cultures are a barrier to collaboration was borne out by other examples. Eisen, Hall, Lee, and Zupko (2009) contend that at most institutions, there is "little incentive or support for innovative teaching and virtually no facilitating infrastructure to teach across departments" (para. 3). At institution B, a faculty member and librarian won an institutional award for co-teaching a chemistry class. However, the director of the center for teaching excellence indicates that the review panel was initially unimpressed by the report, stating librarians and faculty collaborate "all the time." Likewise, the faculty member at institution A who teaches an information literacy course in East Asian Studies indicates that the course was originally team-taught by three faculty members, one from each of the areas of Japanese, Korean, and Chinese studies. She speculates that the team-taught class is richer because each faculty member draws on distinct knowledge of specific resources in her subfield, but that the department decided it was not worthwhile to pay three salaries for one class. If these examples are indicative of a widespread culture, institutions may have to reexamine their systems of rewards and incentives before achieving deeper levels of collaboration. On the other hand, however, the economic recession may deter institutions from collaboration, but encourage greater innovation and entrepreneurial activity. Glenn and Fischer (2009) quote a humanities professor's opinion that, "when times get tight, people don't always think imaginatively" (para. 24). If that is true, retrenchment from deep budget cuts during the present recession will take years to offset. Still, librarians will have to identify core areas and deliver exceptional service. With its alignment to institutional missions and goals, information literacy should be one of those core services.

BENEFITS OF COLLABORATION

A number of considerations underlie the imperative for faculty and librarians to collaborate on information literacy. Perhaps most importantly, as the Middle States Commission (2003) notes, although information literacy has its foundations in bibliographic instruction, the concept "now goes much further than accessing and evaluating bibliographic sources" (p. 51). Indeed, information literacy is a metacognitive process that "applies to anyone learning anything, anywhere, and at any time" (Middle States Commission, 2003, p. 2). When it is so broadly defined, information literacy cannot be addressed solely by librarians. First, most librarians have neither the highly specialized discipline knowledge to engage in deep evaluation of content, nor the prolonged and ongoing involvement with students that comes with teaching courses and advising activities. Yet, such involvement is necessary to assist students with a process such as incorporating new information into the knowledge base, which is the fourth competency listed in Figure 1.1.

Faculty, on the other hand, have the specialized content knowledge and engage with students. However, they may not be fully aware of the range of resources available to them and their students, or how best to design assignments that make use of those resources. They may also need to update their technology skills or refresh their knowledge of information organization and access outside of their field of study. Thus, a partnership between librarians and faculty can address the full complement of ACRL information literacy competencies.

Participants from case study institutions attest to the importance of collaboration for increasing the relevancy of content and for student learning. While some librarians are satisfied and even feel "lucky" to be able to offer credit-bearing information literacy courses, others believe stand-alone courses have limited value because they are segregated from the rest of the curriculum. While a required credit-bearing course ensures that students receive exposure to information literacy, the instruction is largely separate from students' other courses. As such, many librarians, including those at institutions B and D, indicate that students often do not realize the connection between the competencies they are learning in information literacy classes and the coursework they are required to do within their major. Indeed, librarians at institution A find that most students wait until their junior or senior year to take the required information literacy course, mainly because they see it as a burden and do not recognize the relevance of the information to their other classes. When librarians set aside one section of the course for first-year students, they find that they cannot fill the section due to lack of interest, and they are forced to open the section to upper-division students.

The librarian who teaches the information literacy geography course at institution A maintains that she was first spurred to pursue subject-oriented, team-taught information literacy when she overheard students that she advised in an extracurricular club complaining about the new information literacy mandate, requiring them to take an information literacy–designated course. She believes, as did the students, that a stand-alone library course is not the most effective way to deliver information literacy instruction, because it divorces the competencies from the content. As such, the students may have difficulty transferring the skills and knowledge from the stand-alone information literacy course to other courses. Further, stand-alone courses may obstruct a more distributed approach, as institutions seem to consider stand-alone courses as sufficient to meet the Middle States Commission's (2003) expectations for information literacy, rather than as a transitional stage as they move toward curriculum-wide integration. Librarians at institution D indicate a similar disinclination to stand-alone courses, stating that they are not as relevant for students and that information literacy is best delivered at the point of need, such as at the reference desk. Such an approach, however, neither addresses program outcomes nor delivers instruction in a systematic and sequenced manner.

The literature of library and information science supports the benefits of collaboration. For librarians, it can help to raise their profile on campus, while the faculty endorsement implicit in the partnership may encourage students to seek librarians out for assistance on projects (Bowers et al., 2009; Hearn, 2005). With input from librarians, faculty can increase their own knowledge of library resources (Hearn, 2005) in order to design assignments that make better use of those resources (Bowers et al., 2009). Birmingham et al. (2008) suggest that such collaboration can assist faculty in "avoiding teaching rote, arhetorical, and decontextualized research assignments that merely dictate limitations to students (such as number and type of resources, page length, etc.)" (p. 9).

The most compelling reason for increased collaboration, however, is that it may lead to better learning (Kanter, 1994; Kezar, 2005; Senge, 1990). Hearn (2005) describes the effect of having a librarian embedded in a writing course, with the librarian teaching 3.5 class sessions. Students completed pre- and posttests and submitted three papers. After reviewing test results and the bibliographies of randomly selected papers, Hearn claims that students exposed to library instruction are more likely to choose scholarly articles over Internet resources. He also states that by the end of the course, students perform more targeted searches and are more likely to search resources introduced in class than to use Internet search engines. Other studies find similar results.

Ferrer-Vinent and Carello (2008) discovered that biology students who receive information literacy instruction are more adept at identifying relevant resources, perform better searches, and use library resources more often. Flaspohler (2003) describes a pilot project in which librarians offered a series of instruction sessions to several sections of a required first-year course, while other sections received the traditional one-shot session. Again, students in the pilot study use more reliable sources, refer to the Internet less often, and they score higher on an information literacy test. Faculty surveys conducted after in-class instruction sessions indicate that faculty agree that students choose better resources after course-integrated instruction (Ferrer-Vinent & Carello, 2008).

Barratt et al. (2009) support these findings through a citation study of student papers from classes cotaught by writing faculty and librarians. They conclude that collaboration between writing instructors and librarians has "a positive influence on the quality of research that students perform" (p. 54) because alone each instructor focuses on isolated elements. Writing instructors tend to focus on style and persuasive arguments over the use of scholarly resources, while librarians emphasize authority and credibility of resources. By working together, the two partners reinforce each other and introduce what the other is lacking. This type of collaboration mirrors Figure 1.1, which suggests that faculty take the lead on evaluating content, while librarians lead on evaluating sources. In addition to improved performance, Flaspohler (2003) finds that students are more excited about their work and more engaged with the assignments following library instruction sessions.

BUILDING BRIDGES

Collaboration is necessary for a fully integrated information literacy program. If, however, institutional cultures do not currently offer incentives for collaboration, it is incumbent on administrators to cultivate an environment that supports and encourages collaboration. Writing from a faculty perspective, Smith (2001) acknowledges that the focus on student learning, rather than faculty teaching, creates new opportunities for librarians to complement course content with library-specific learning outcomes. He advocates for librarians to partner with academic departments in achieving student learning outcomes. He also insists, however, that "the library must take the initiative in determining what the library has to offer," since it is "unlikely that the department on its own will identify the library as a place to turn for help" (p. 35).

The librarians interviewed for the case studies are cognizant of the need to identify instructional roles for themselves and to reach out to faculty and administrators for opportunities to fill those roles. Throughout the interviews, the librarians repeatedly used words such as "relationship building," "boundary-spanning," and "personal diplomacy" to characterize their outreach efforts. One librarian in particular, at institution B, emphasizes the importance of getting to know "key allies" on campus, understanding and anticipating their needs, and finding ways to support them so that they will view the library as a potential partner. Kezar (2005) describes such efforts as building campus networks, which she identifies as one of the most crucial elements for collaboration. She contends that "relationships were much more important in the higher education setting than learning or formal assessments to the development of a context for collaboration." She describes such relationship development and campus network building as "the key element" (p. 846) for creating a context for collaboration.

Librarians use a variety of methods to reach out to other departments, running focus group interviews, offering professional development opportunities for faculty, partnering with centers for teaching excellence and writing programs, and serving on campus-wide committees. These efforts have been somewhat effective in catalyzing some collaboration at the course level. Nevertheless, librarians also acknowledge the need for support from high-level administrators and accreditation organizations to effect change. Nearly all the librarians, and even some administrators, point to the Middle States Commission standards as a driving force for implementing information literacy programs. Additionally, each campus identifies certain individuals, usually academic deans or library directors, whose support for such programs provides the momentum to implement them.

Figure 7.1 illustrates how bridging the barriers to collaboration can result in integrating information literacy across the curriculum. As the figure suggests, with the support of institutional administrators and accreditation mandates, faculty and librarians can build on the foundations they have made through cultivating relationships to implement an information literacy program that is integrated developmentally and sequentially through the curriculum.

A mission supportive of collaboration is crucial for creating an environment that facilitates collaboration. In addition, external pressures such as accreditation standards or state mandates act as a catalyst for collaboration if faculty are aware of and responsive to them. The external pressures might also influence administrators—for instance, as they prepare for accreditation—encouraging them to adopt policies or behaviors that better support collaboration and help to overcome those barriers. Senior administrators can further encourage collaboration by creating policies that reward collaborative efforts. They can also realign infrastructures and budgets to make cross-campus collaborations easier. With the buy-in and encouragement of senior administrators, librarians and teaching faculty can create a campus network that further supports and sustains collaboration. In the figure, the dotted line around the "barriers" section represents the breaking down of those barriers from the various pressures and influences. Finally, as the barriers are overcome, information literacy can be integrated into all levels of the curriculum, as depicted by the concentric circles.

Figure 7.1   Overcoming Barriers to Collaboration

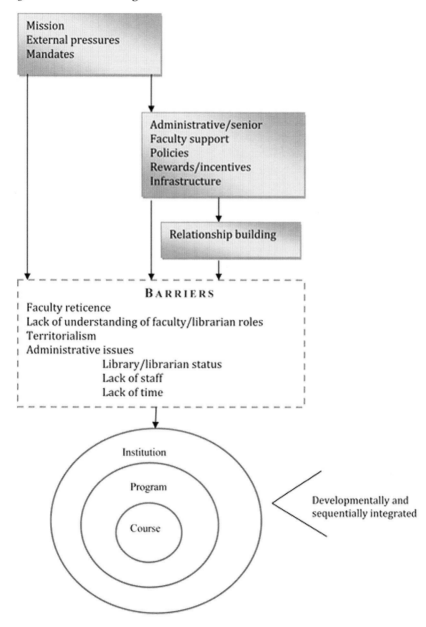

CONCLUSION

Collaboration is essential to the successful integration of information literacy into the curriculum. Without the support and buy-in of faculty who have sustained and ongoing interactions with students and control of the curriculum, information literacy will remain at the course level. Whatever the reasons underlying the faculty's lack of interest or involvement, currently the onus lies with librarians continually to reach out to faculty, build relationships, and extend their interactions with students through involvement in the classroom (Badke, 2005; Given & Julien, 2005; Smith, 2001).

Another important theme closely related to instruction for information literacy is its assessment. As noted in Chapter 2, stakeholders call on institutions to hold themselves accountable for learning goals like information literacy by measuring progress toward those goals, and sharing that information with the public. Only through assessment can instructors gauge how much students are learning and how effective instructional programs are, and then isolate areas for improvement, and implement changes for improvement. The next chapter explores the levels and methods of assessment for learning outcomes related to information literacy at case study institutions.

REFERENCES

American Library Association, Association of College and Research Libraries. (2000). *Information literacy competency standards for higher education.* Retrieved from http://www.ala.org/ala/mgrps/divs/acrl/standards/information literacycompetency.cfm

Badke, W. B. (2005). Can't get no respect: Helping faculty to understand the power of information literacy. *Reference Librarian, 43*(89), 63–80. Retrieved from Haworth Press Journals.

Barratt, C. C., Nielsen, K., Desmet, C., & Balthazor, R. (2009). Collaboration is key: Librarians and composition instructors analyze student research and writing. *portal: Libraries and the Academy, 9*(1), 37–56. Retrieved from ProjectMUSE.

Bhavnagri, N. P., & Bielat, V. (2005). Faculty-librarian collaboration to teach research skills: Electronic symbiosis. *Reference Librarian, 43*(89), 121–138. Retrieved from Haworth Press Journals.

Birmingham, E., Chinwongs, L., Flaspohler, M. R., Hearn, C., Kvanvig, D., & Portmann, R. (2008). First-year writing teachers, perceptions of students' information literacy competencies, and a call for a collaborative approach. *Communications in Information Literacy, 2*(1), 6–24. Retrieved from H. W. Wilson.

Bowers, C. V. M., Chew, B., Bowers, M. R., Ford, C. E., Smith, C., & Herrington, C. (2009). Interdisciplinary synergy: A partnership between business and library faculty and its effects on students' information literacy. *Journal of Business and Finance Librarianship, 14*(2), 110–127. Retrieved from InformaWorld.

Dawson, M. M., & Overfield, J. A. (2006). Plagiarism: Do students know what it is? *Bioscience Education e-Journal, 8*(1). Retrieved from http://www.bioscience.heacademy.ac.uk/journal/vol8/beej-8-1.aspx

Eisen, A., Hall, A., Lee, T. S., & Zupko, J. (2009). Teaching water: Connecting across disciplines and into daily life to address complex societal issues. *College Teaching, 57*(2), 99–105. Retrieved from Gale.

Farber, E. I. (2004). Working with faculty: Some reflections. *College and Undergraduate Libraries, 11*(2), 129–135. Retrieved from InformaWorld.

Ferrer-Vinent, I. J., & Carello, C. (2008). Embedded library instruction in a first-year biology laboratory class. *Science and Technology Libraries, 28*(4), 325–351. Retrieved from Informaworld.

Flaspohler, M. (2003). Information literacy program assessment: One small college takes the big plunge. *Reference Services Review, 31*(2), 129–140. Retrieved from Emerald.

Given, L. M., & Julien, H. (2005). Finding common ground: An analysis of librarians' expressed attitudes toward faculty. *Reference Librarian, 89*(90), 65–87. Retrieved from Haworth Press Journals.

Glenn, D., & Fischer, K. (2009, August 31). The canon of college majors persists amid calls for change. *Chronicle of Higher Education*. Retrieved from ProQuest.

Happel, S. K., & Jennings, M. M. (2008). An economic analysis of academic dishonesty and its deterrence in higher education. *Journal of Legal Studies Education, 25*(2), 183–214. Retrieved from Ebsco.

Hardesty, L. (1995). Faculty culture and bibliographic instruction: An exploratory analysis. *Library Trends, 44*(2), 339–368. Retrieved from Gale.

Hearn, M. R. (2005). Embedding a librarian in the classroom: An intensive information literacy model. *Reference Services Review, 33*(2), 219–227. Retrieved from Emerald.

Hernon, P., & Powell, R. R. (2008). Introduction. In P. Hernon & R. R. Powell (Eds.), *Convergence and collaboration of campus information services* (pp. 1–31). Westport, CT: Libraries Unlimited.

Ironside, P. M. (2004). "Covering content" and teaching thinking: Deconstructing the additive curriculum. *Journal of Nursing Education, 43*(1), 5–12.

Ivey, R. T. (1994). Teaching faculty perceptions of academic librarians at Memphis State University. *College and Research Libraries, 55*(1), 69–82. Retrieved from H. W. Wilson.

Jacobs, J. A., & Frickel, S. (2009). Interdisciplinarity: A critical assessment. *Annual Review of Sociology, 35*, 43–65. Retrieved from Annual Reviews.

Julien, H., & Given, L. M. (2002–2003). Faculty-librarian relationships in the information literacy context: A content analysis of librarians' expressed attitudes and experiences. *Canadian Journal of Information and Library Sciences, 27*(3), 65–87. Retrieved from Ebsco.

Kanter, R. M. (1994). Collaborative advantage: The art of alliances. *Harvard Business Review, 4*, 96–108. Retrieved from Ebsco.

Kearns, K., & Hybl, T. T. (2005). A collaboration between faculty and librarians to develop and assess a science literacy laboratory module. *Science and Technology Libraries, 25*(4), 39–56. Retrieved from Haworth Press Journals.

Kezar, A. (2005). Redesigning for collaboration within higher education institutions: An exploration into the developmental process. *Research in Higher Education, 46*(7), 831–860. Retrieved from Ebsco.

Kezar, A. (2006). Redesigning for collaboration and learning initiatives: An examination of four highly collaborative campuses. *Journal of Higher Education, 77*(5), 804–838. Retrieved from ProQuest.

Leckie, G. J., & Fullerton, A. (1999). Information literacy in science and engineering undergraduate education: Faculty attitudes and pedagogical practices. *College and Research Libraries, 60*(1), 9–29. Retrieved from H. W. Wilson.

Leonhardt, T. W. (2004). Faculty status. *Technicalities, 24*(4), 3–5. Retrieved from H. W. Wilson.

Lloyd, A. (2005). Information literacy: Different contexts, different concepts, different truths? *Journal of Librarianship and Information Science, 37*(2), 82–88. Retrieved from Emerald.

Manuel, K., Beck, S. E., & Molloy, M. (2005). An ethnographic study of attitudes influencing faculty collaboration in library instruction. *Reference Librarian, 43*(89), 139–161. Retrieved from Haworth Press Journals.

Middle States Commission on Higher Education. (2003). *Developing research and communication skills: Guidelines for information literacy into the curriculum*. Philadelphia, PA: Author.

Middle States Commission on Higher Education. (2009). *Characteristics of excellence in higher education: Requirements of affiliation and standards for accreditation*. Philadelphia, PA: Author.

Mounce, M. (2009). Academic librarian and English composition instructor collaboration: A selected annotated bibliography 1998–2007. *Reference Services Review, 37*(1), 44–53. Retrieved from Emerald.

Owusu-Ansah, E. K. (2005). Debating definitions of information literacy: Enough is enough! *Library Review, 54*(6), 366–374. Retrieved from Emerald.

Owusu-Ansah, E. K. (2007). Beyond collaboration: Seeking greater scope and centrality for library instruction. *portal: Libraries and the Academy, 7*(4), 415–429. Retrieved from Project MUSE.

Peterson, L. M. (2007). Articulating the future through collaboration. *New Directions for Higher Education, 138*, 95–102. Retrieved from Ebsco.

Ratteray, O. M. T. (2002). Information literacy in self-study and accreditation. *Journal of Academic Librarianship, 28*(6), 368–375. Retrieved from Ebsco.

Ratteray, O. M. T. (2005, November 20). Re: What to call what we do: Information literacy vs. research fluency (electronic mailing list message). Retrieved from Information Literacy Listserv, http://lists.ala.org/wws/arc/ili-l

Ratteray, O. M. T. (2008, July 17). Information literacy and faculty: Summary of responses (Electronic mailing list message). Retrieved from http://lists.ala.org/sympa/arc/ili-l

Remler, N. L. (2002). The more active the better: Engaging college English students with active learning strategies. *Teaching English in the Two Year College, 30*(1), 76–81. Retrieved from ProQuest.

Saunders, L. (2009). The future of information literacy in academic libraries: A Delphi study. *portal: Libraries and the Academy, 9*(1), 99–114. Retrieved from Project MUSE.

Scales, J., Matthews, G., & Johnson, C. M. (2005). Compliance, cooperation, collaboration, and information literacy. *Journal of Academic Librarianship, 31* (3), 229–235. Retrieved from H. W. Wilson.

Schroeder, U., & Spannagel, C. (2006). Supporting the active learning process. *International Journal on E-Learning, 5*(2), 245–265. Retrieved from Gale.

Schulte, S. J., & Sherwill-Navarro, P. J. (2009). Nursing educators perceptions of collaboration with librarians. *Journal of the Medical Library Association, 97*(1), 57–60. Retrieved from Ebsco.

Senge, P. (1990). *The fifth discipline: The art and practice of the learning organization.* New York, NY: Doubleday.

Smith, K. R. (2001). New roles and responsibilities for the university library: Advancing student learning through outcomes assessment. *Journal of Library Administration, 35*(4), 29–36. Retrieved from InformaWorld.

Swartz, P. S., Carlisle, B. A., & Uyeki, E. C. (2007). Libraries and student affairs: Partners for student success. *Reference Services Review, 35*(1), 109–122. Retrieved from Emerald.

Taylor, M. C. (2009, April 27). End the university as we know it. *New York Times.* Retrieved from Lexis-Nexis.

Thomas, M. K. (2009). Time for higher ed to survive crisis and thrive. *New England Journal of Higher Education, 23*(3), 11.

University of Minnesota. (2007). Consortium on fostering interdisciplinary inquiry. Retrieved from https://www.myu.umn.edu/metadot/index.pl?id=1562406

Welch, J. M. (2006). Loosening the ties that bind: Academic librarians and tenure. *College and Research Libraries, 67*(2), 164–176. Retrieved from H. W. Wilson.

Zmuda, A. (2008). Springing into active learning. *Educational Leadership, 66*(3), 38–42. Retrieved from Ebsco.

CHAPTER 8

Assessment of Learning Outcomes for Information Literacy

Assessment lets institutions determine how well they are accomplishing their missions and learning goals. The terms *assessment* and *evaluation* are often used interchangeably, but they are not synonymous. Assessment, which is process-oriented, involves the systematic gathering, analyzing, and interpreting of evidence to gauge progress toward meeting a specific, measurable standard set by accreditation organizations. Evaluation, which is product-oriented, occurs after assessment data have been gathered, when data are interpreted, and decisions made about whether goals have been met and determinations made about overall worth, value, and effectiveness of programs (Dugan, personal communication, September 3, 2008). Evaluation can also occur without assessment, as a "political and managerial activity, which provides insights for making policy decisions and resource allocations" (Hernon & Dugan, 2009, p. 148).

Institutional missions and goals lead to a variety of student outcomes, (e.g., graduation rates, persistence, retention, and job placement upon graduation), and student learning outcomes. Institutions engage in assessing both student outcomes and student learning outcomes in a systematic and ongoing way to obtain a picture of student success. The assessment of learning outcomes is a crucial element of teaching and learning in that it provides the type of evidence that stakeholders demand, namely how well institutions are achieving learning goals and using the evidence gathered for educational improvement (Middle States Commission, 2005). Assessing student learning requires setting clear and specific goals, possibly through rubrics, that define what a student should know or be able to do at the end of a course, program, or other interaction, and then collecting data to measure progress toward those learning goals.

Figure 8.1   Assessment Process for Information Literacy

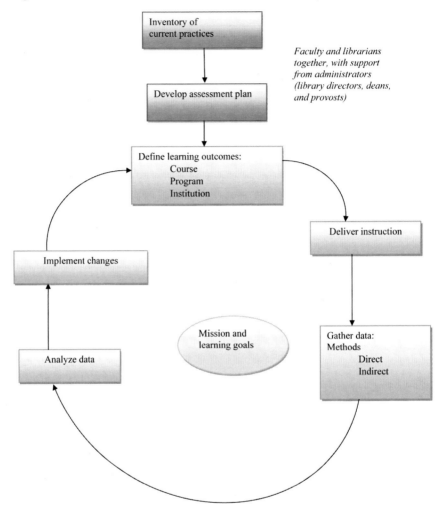

Figure 8.1 describes the assessment process. Faculty and librarians review the current curriculum to identify areas where information literacy is addressed, and ensure that learning goals are explicitly defined at course, program, and institutional levels. Once they have identified the goals, faculty and librarians should engage in the iterative process of delivering instruction and gathering and analyzing evidence to determine where changes should be made. As the figure suggests, the mission and learning goals should be at the center of the assessment process and should guide all

decisions. The rest of this chapter examines current assessment practices for information literacy as described in the case study visits.

INFORMATION LITERACY ASSESSMENT: ITS CONTEXT

As is the case with collaboration and instruction, assessment for information literacy can take place at the course, program, and institutional levels, and while the Middle States Commission (2003) allows institutions to choose the level for outcomes assessment, it acknowledges that engaging in assessment at multiple levels and involving faculty and librarians, generally leads to better comprehension of student learning. Nevertheless, as with collaboration, the majority of assessments observed at case study institutions and described in the literature take place at the course level or even at the individual class level for one-shot sessions. Program-level assessment occurs at the lowest rates, and most institutions that undertake program-level assessment do so within the context of the general education program rather than within the majors and disciplines. Although assessment beyond the course level is rare, the fact that some institutions are engaged in assessment at a higher level indicates that there is some broad-based support for information literacy at these institutions.

Course-Level Assessment

That assessment for information literacy remains largely at the course level is not surprising, since librarians traditionally have been involved at the session or course level. Both institutions A and B offer required, credit-bearing courses for information literacy, largely led by librarians. A credit-bearing course carries a grade, and it is natural that instructors would engage in course-embedded assessment such as assignments and tests to gauge student learning. Syllabi for these courses describe a mix of quizzes and assignments, including a term assignment of an annotated bibliography, as part of the course. However, unless such quizzes and assignments are measured against predetermined goals, such as rubrics, they do not count as assessments. Broadly, tools that ask for students' opinions or perceptions, and assignments graded without rubrics, are evaluations. Tools that measure progress in learning, such as assignments that use rubrics, pre- and posttests, and minute papers, constitute assessment. Without preset goals, the instructor has no benchmark against which to measure learning, and so such measures actually comprise evaluations. Librarians at institution B have developed rubrics for several of their assignments, while those at institution A did not mention any. Whether intentional or not, many institutions substitute evaluation for assessment, and such substitutions appear to pass review. The majority of activity reported in self-studies and observed in case studies centers on evaluations, including course evaluations and surveys. However, neither visiting teams nor the accreditation organizations they represent appear to question institutions for these practices, or demand changes.

Outside of teaching information literacy courses, most of the instruction by librarians occurs at the request of faculty. As Chapter 7 notes, most collaboration between faculty and librarians takes place at the course level, so it follows that assessment resulting from these collaborative efforts also focuses on course outcomes. In order for assessment to progress to the program level, learning outcomes for information literacy must be clearly and explicitly defined at that level. The literature of library and information science (LIS) describes levels of assessment that mirror those at the institutions included in this study. For instance, Bowers et al. (2009) outline an introductory business course team taught by business faculty and librarians, who also work together to review assignments (i.e., a workbook and a term paper). They indicate plans to move from evaluation to assessment by including a senior capstone project in order to determine how well students retain the information learned at the beginning of the program, and whether students who attended the introductory class perform better on the capstone. Currently, however, the assessment remains at the course level. Indeed, Furno and Flanagan (2008) describe assessment tools for one-shot instruction sessions, reflecting the reality that much information literacy instruction still occurs through this method.

Program-Level Assessment

Some limited program-level assessment is taking place, although again, there is confusion between assessment and evaluation. For instance, the academic dean at institution A states that her institution uses curriculum mapping, which consists of asking faculty who teach general education courses to indicate where and how they address information literacy in their courses, to assess information literacy. Since this method indicates only where the concept is taught, and not whether students are learning, it is really more of an evaluation than an assessment. Although institution C has not yet undertaken a campus-wide assessment of information literacy, an academic dean notes that plans are in place to begin such assessment within the next year. Over the spring of 2009, the college identified core competencies for information literacy in the general education curriculum, and it plans to begin assessing those goals over the next year, although they do not yet appear to have identified the tools they will use to approach assessment. At case study institutions, all program-level assessment is connected to the general education program, and does not extend to the majors. The Middle States Commission (2009) notes that, while skills such as information literacy and technical competency are often included in general education courses, "they must be further addressed within degree or certificate programs so that students may become proficient in these skills as they are applied within a particular field of study" (p. 42). Institutions that do not extend information literacy initiatives beyond the general education level are not complying fully with the intent of the standards. Rather, information literacy in the general education program should form the basis for further development within the majors.

Part of the reason why assessment for information literacy learning outcomes is not taking place at the program level may be that many programs simply do not engage in assessment of learning, and those that do often confuse assessment with evaluation. Program-level assessment "does not focus on the individual student. Rather, the emphasis is on what and how an educational program is contributing to the learning, growth, and development of students as a group" (University of Central Florida, 2008, p. 2). The National Research Council (2001) further clarifies the distinction. Classroom assessment is closely tied to the work students do throughout the course, and such assessment informs instructors about the effect and effectiveness of student learning in their courses. However, because classroom assessment measures are "individualized and highly contextualized, neither the rationale nor the results of typical classroom assessments are easily communicated beyond the classroom" (National Research Council, 2001, p. 222). In other words, classroom assessment focuses on the progress of each student and cannot be generalized beyond the course in which it takes place. Program-level assessment often focuses on a group of students, perhaps a sample, and provides instructors, department heads, and administrators with trends and patterns of performance.

Indeed, some programs incorporate senior capstone projects or portfolios (explored in more depth in the next section) that allow for program-level assessment. Capstone projects require students to use skills and demonstrate knowledge and abilities gained throughout their course of study, while portfolios document the student's progress throughout the program. As such, these indicators allow departmental faculty to see how well students meet program-level outcomes. In many places, however, "the information that best reflects learning objectives is kept at the course level—departmental level analyses/synthesis of student learning is rarely done" (Stassen, Doherty, & Poe, 2001, p. 23). Learning objectives focus on student performance and state what a student should be able to do by the end of a course or program (Florida State University, n.d.).

Interestingly, a number of self-studies boasted of program-level assessment taking place within certain departments on campus, and they often tied the development and implementation of assessment plans to program accreditation. For instance, engineering and nursing departments on several campuses were singled out as *ideal* or *model* programs because they engaged in program-level assessment in order to meet standards set by the accreditation organization for that discipline. For instance, to achieve or maintain accreditation from the Accreditation Board for Engineering and Technology (ABET), engineering programs must indicate which courses address each of the learning outcomes outlined within the standards, and document how learning is assessed within those courses. If program accreditation organizations influence departments within an institution to develop and implement program-level assessment plans, perhaps the regional accreditation organizations can motivate similar assessment for learning outcomes related to information literacy.

Institutional-Level Assessment

Some institutions broadly assess student learning for information literacy at the institutional level. As with program-level assessment, institutional-level assessment also looks at students as a group and attempts to ascertain how the entire educational experience of the institution has contributed to the learning of students across campus and across disciplines. Typically, institutions assessing at the institutional level use either a standardized test, such as Project SAILS (2009) or iCritical Thinking (Educational Testing Service, 2009), or a locally produced test, which is administered to students across the institution to form a baseline of student knowledge for information literacy. For instance, institution D of the case studies uses a locally produced test. Beginning four years ago, the institution administered the test to incoming freshmen to determine their information literacy abilities. This past year, those same students, now graduating seniors, were tested again. During the interview, the librarian hesitated to offer details of the assessment, stating only that the results were disappointing, and that the response rate, at about 27 percent, was low. She suggests that, unlike the freshmen, seniors know that this test is not mandatory and does not count toward their grades. She believes they did not take it seriously. Next year, the institution hopes to increase participation and to motivate students to do well on the test by offering a prize to those who participate and receive a certain score. However, such incentives present a validity problem in that the scores for that test cannot validly be compared to the scores from the previous year because the incentives might change students' approach to the test.

While the results of the assessment may have disappointed the librarians, it is important that poor results do not lead to abandoning assessment measures altogether. One problem that often arises when institutions plan to implement assessment is pushback from faculty and staff who fear that the assessment results will be used to judge their performance and possibly to make program or budget cuts. Such fears dissuade faculty and staff from engaging in assessment, or from reporting unflattering results (University of Central Florida, 2008). As a result, it is important to emphasize the role of assessment in accountability and to make changes that improve the quality of programs.

Disappointing results therefore provide a good opportunity to pinpoint problem areas and to make positive changes.

DEFINING LEARNING OUTCOMES FOR INFORMATION LITERACY

As Figure 8.1 notes, once institutions have reviewed current practices, the next step in implementing an assessment plan is to define learning outcomes for information literacy at all levels. Although each institution may develop its own learning outcomes, several frameworks exist that might be adapted to form such learning outcomes. For example, Figure 1.1 offers a framework of competency areas that comprise the learning outcomes for information literacy. The Middle States Commission adapted the particular areas from the ACRL (Association of College and Research Libraries, 2000) standards. These areas, comprising the broad learning outcomes that colleges and universities might address, define an information-literate person as one who can:

- Determine the nature and extent of information needed
- Access information efficiently and effectively
- Critically evaluate information and its sources
- Incorporate new information into his or her knowledge base
- Use information to accomplish a specific purpose
- Understand the ethical, social, and legal implications of information and its use

It is important to note that the ACRL (2000) information literacy standards are defined in broad terms and, as with accreditation standards, institutions and individual departments within the institution may refine these competencies within the context of their missions and goals. ACRL recognizes and attempts to assist with this process by offering several discipline-specific sets of information literacy guidelines. These include guidelines for:

- Anthropology and sociology (American Library Association, Association of College and Research Libraries, 2008a)
- Political science (American Library Association, Association of College and Research Libraries, 2008b)
- English literature (American Library Association, Association of College and Research Libraries, 2007)
- Science and technology (American Library Association, Association of College and Research Libraries, 2006)

In each instance, ACRL gives objectives and performance indicators specific to the disciplines to aid faculty and librarians in identifying and assessing learning outcomes for their students. For instance, ACRL suggests that literature majors "differentiate between reviews of literary works and literary criticism" (American Library Association, Association of College and Research Libraries, 2007, section I.4), an ability not listed in any of the other versions of the standards.

Of importance with each of these versions of the ACRL standards is that institutions and programs do not have to accept or use the entire framework as it is presented. On the contrary, ACRL encourages those involved in information literacy instruction and assessment to adapt the standards to reflect the unique missions and goals within which their institution or program functions. In this sense, librarians and faculty might work together to develop a plan that would highlight the particular competencies important to students within a major program or field of study, and break down each competency into a rubric showing progressive levels of understanding (e.g., novice, intermediate, and proficient). The librarian at institution C emphasizes this adaptability for the disciplines when working with faculty. For instance, she mentioned that students studying masonry might need to be able to find and interpret building codes, rather than the literary criticism important to students in a literature program.

Despite encouragement and support from ACRL, there are only a few examples of individual programs setting their own learning goals for assessment of information literacy in the literature. Some institutions have incorporated learning goals for information literacy into the general education program (Sonntag, 2008), and some articles in the literature describe learning outcomes related to information literacy for specific courses or projects (see, e.g., Bennet & Gilbert, 2009; Edzan, 2008; Rossin, Ro, Klein, & Yi, 2009), but very little at the program level within academic departments.

One example of program-level assessment comes from Kennesaw State University, where faculty and librarians set learning goals, some of which are specific to information literacy for the information systems program. One goal states that "the graduate is able to recognize, define, and analyze real-world business problems and develop, evaluate and implement information technology solutions to address them" (Murray, Perez, & Guimaraes, 2008, p. 199). To assess student learning, the faculty and librarians developed a rubric for each of the student learning outcomes that is applied to a capstone project. Few such examples exist, however. Harrod (2008), who studied 30 biology departments in colleges and universities across the country, concludes that "the inclusion of objectives which explicitly address information literacy in biology department assessment plans is rare" (Conclusions, point 1). He notes that some information literacy learning outcomes are implicit in other learning goals, but he still maintains that most biology department assessment plans "identify few, if any, information literacy skills among their desired outcomes" (Recommendations, point 1).

TYPES OF ASSESSMENT ACTIVITIES

Where assessment for information literacy occurs, those involved have a variety of methods from which to choose to gather data at the course, program, and institutional levels. Broadly speaking, approaches to assessment are generally characterized as formative or summative, direct or indirect, and quantitative or qualitative. Formative assessment is "ongoing assessment that is intended to improve a student's performance, student learning outcomes, or overall institutional effectiveness," while summative assessment "occurs at the end of a unit, course, or program … to determine whether or not overall goals have been achieved" (Middle States Commission, 2007, p. 27). Formative assessment focuses on improvement, whereas summative assessment helps in changing or eliminating services or programs.

The Middle States Commission (2007) describes direct assessment as "providing [actual] evidence in the form of student products or performances" (p. 28). Such assessment "demonstrates that *actual learning* [emphasis original] has occurred" (p. 28). Indirect methods, on the other hand, measure characteristics related to learning, such as student confidence in or perceptions of their abilities, but these indicators only imply that learning has occurred.

Both direct and indirect measures of assessment have advantages and drawbacks to consider. Direct methods of assessment indicate what a student has learned, but they do not answer the question of why the student has or has not learned (Middle States Commission, 2007). In other words, what contextual factors and particular learning experiences facilitated or hindered learning for the student? Indirect measures, on the other hand, do not measure learning per se, but can sometimes elicit from students which experiences they believe contributed most to their learning. Some indirect measures (e.g., focus group interviews and surveys), rely on self-reporting and are subjective in nature.

The Middle States Commission (2003, 2007) encourages institutions to use both direct and indirect measures at all levels to get the fullest picture of student learning. Figure 8.2, adapted from the Middle States Commission, outlines examples of direct and indirect measures of student learning at the course, program, and institutional levels. The Middle States Commission's original figure mixes evaluation and assessment methods together and can mislead readers interested only in conducting assessment. The figure was therefore adapted to reflect only assessment measures related to learning outcomes.

Assessment at Case Study Institutions

Assessment at case study institutions follows patterns similar to those reported in self-study documents (see Chapter 4), again with some confusion between assessment and evaluation methods. Tests remain one of the most

Figure 8.2   Examples of Direct and Indirect Measures for Assessment*

	Direct	Indirect
Course	• Course and homework assignments** • Examinations and quizzes** • Standardized tests** • Term papers and reports** • Observations of field work, internship performance, service learning, or clinical experiences • Research projects • Case study analysis • Rubric (a criterion-based rating scale) scores for writing, oral presentations, and performances • Artistic performances and products • Scenarios • Portfolios	• Test blueprints (outlines of the concepts and skills covered on tests)
Program	• Capstone projects, senior theses, exhibits, or performances • Pass rates or scores on licensure, certification, or subject area tests • Student publications or conference presentations • Employer and internship supervisor ratings of students' performance • Scenarios • Portfolios	• Focus group interviews with students, faculty members, or employers • Department or program review data • Job placement • Employer or alumni surveys • Student perception surveys • Graduate school placement rates • Curriculum mapping • Proportion of upper level courses compared to program at other institutions
Institution	• Performance on tests of writing, critical thinking, or general knowledge • Rubric (criterion-based rating scale) scores for class assignments in General Education, interdisciplinary core courses, or other courses required of all students • Performance on achievement tests	• Locally developed, commercial, or national surveys of student perceptions or self-report of activities (e.g., National Survey of Student Engagement) • Transcript studies that examine patterns and trends of course selection and grading • Annual reports including institutional benchmarks, such as graduation and retention rates, grade point averages of graduates. • Explicit self-reflections on what students have learned related to institutional programs such as service learning (e.g., asking students to name the three most important things they have learned in a program). • Curriculum mapping

* Adapted from Middle States Commission (2007, p. 29). Reprinted with permission granted by Richard Pokrass on April 6, 2010.
**May qualify as assessment if assignments are returned with comments so students can improve on their next assignment, is formative rather than summative, or if a rubric is used and related to ongoing improvement.

From *Information Literacy as a Student Learning Outcome: The Perspective of Institutional Accreditation* by Laura Saunders. Santa Barbara, CA: Libraries Unlimited. Copyright © 2011.

popular measures. As noted above, institution D administers tests to incoming freshmen and graduating seniors to assess information literacy at the institutional level. Similarly, librarians at institution A administer a pre- and posttest for their information literacy courses to measure changes in student knowledge and understanding at the end of the course. A syllabus for the required information literacy course at institution B indicates four quizzes over 12 class sessions, including a cumulative final examination. Librarians who teach the information literacy courses use assignments as well as tests. Both of the required courses use an annotated bibliography as a major part of the course grade, which requires students to demonstrate their ability to locate and evaluate various resources on a specific topic. Librarians at institution B developed a rubric with which to score the final assignment. Although librarians at institution C do not teach a stand-alone information literacy course, they work closely with faculty in the general education program, including the first-year composition course. As part of this course, students complete an online library tutorial, which includes a quiz, and an information literacy assignment designed by the librarians. This assignment requires students to define a topic, locate relevant information sources, and evaluate those sources, and the librarian grades this assignment against a rubric. Thus far, none of the case study institutions report program-level assessment.

Similar to what is reported in self-study documents, case study institutions also use a mixture of indirect assessment and evaluation methods for information literacy. For instance, as noted earlier, the academic dean at institution A indicates that general education faculty are engaged in curriculum mapping, in which they indicate which courses address which aspects of information literacy. This method only identifies where instruction happens; it does not assess learning. Similarly, institutions A and B include student surveys and course evaluations as part of their information literacy courses. Tools such as surveys and course evaluations rely on students' perceptions of what they have learned and liked. Such self-reporting is subjective, and actually comprises evaluation, not assessment. Indeed, an interviewee at institution B notes that in focus group interviews, faculty acknowledge that there is often a "disconnect between what students said they learned and what faculty found" when reviewing assignments and test results. Despite the unreliable nature of self-reporting, and the fact that it is evaluation rather than assessment, librarians rely heavily on it for gathering data about student learning.

In addition to surveying students, most of the librarians at the case study institutions also include feedback from faculty to gauge student learning. In some instances, the feedback is informal and anecdotal; at other times, librarians survey faculty or hold focus group interviews to gather more formal feedback. Like student surveys, however, such feedback reflects only the faculty member's perceptions of how well students are learning, and does not directly measure the learning itself. In addition, it is not clear whether some of these course evaluations and surveys ask about learning, or try to focus more on satisfaction.

Measuring satisfaction does not provide insight into student learning. Similarly, instruments such as LibQUAL+ measure service quality, or customer perceptions of levels of service, by a gap analysis between expectations and services experienced. Broadly, these instruments ask participants to use Likert scales to indicate what level of service they desire from the library, and what level they actually receive. From responses, librarians can determine where they meet, exceed, or fall short of patron expectations. While these instruments may include questions regarding patron perceptions with instruction, they do not measure learning. Institutions that rely on such tools as a means of assessment for information literacy are essentially using a method that does not reflect learning, and they are confusing evaluation and assessment. Satisfaction and service quality may indirectly contribute to student receptivity to learning, "especially as it is related to persistence and therefore continued opportunities to learn" (Ewell, 2001, p. 6). However, stakeholders have not shown interest in such a connection when they ask for evidence of learning.

Ewell (2001) argues that "to count as evidence of student learning outcomes, the information collected should go beyond such things as surveys, interviews, and job placements to include the actual examination of student work or performance" (p. 7). Arguably much of what is called "assessment" at these institutions is really not a measurement of learning, but a general indicator of satisfaction or subjective self-reporting of one's perceptions. Surveys and course or class evaluations only reveal what a student or faculty member believes about what students learned. Tests and graded assignments that are not linked to rubrics may demonstrate what students know, but they do not measure progress toward goals because they lack baselines against which they can be compared. Nevertheless, institutions rely heavily on such methods, and sometimes label them as assessment when they really constitute evaluation.

The use of various tools and the confusion between assessment and evaluation that are observed at case study institutions is consistent with what is reported in the literature of library and information science. In an analysis of published literature, Walsh (2009) finds multiple-choice questionnaires the most popular tool, accounting for 34.1 percent of all assessment or evaluation, followed by bibliography analysis (18.7%) and tests (15.4%). Once again, although Walsh describes these tools as assessment, they appear to be evaluation, since the bibliography analyses do not seem to be linked to rubrics, and the tests appear to be all posttests, without pretests for comparison. In Walsh's (2009) review, self-assessment, or indirect methods, comprises 11 percent of the total. Portfolios have one of the lower rates of usage at 8.8 percent.

ACRL's *National Information Literacy Survey* (American Library Association, Association of College and Research Libraries, 2001) reveals similar findings. According to the survey, pre- and/or posttests are the most widely used form of assessment for information literacy, with 40 of 664 institutions using pretests and 49 using posttests. Again, those institutions relying solely on posttests, without a baseline for comparison, are really using evaluation rather than assessment. In addition to tests, institutions use portfolios (10), workbooks (8), and other assignments (12). Participants in this survey did not provide details about the tools used, but workbooks and assignments almost certainly comprise evaluation, while portfolios are a form of assessment in which progress in learning can be demonstrated over time.

Oakleaf (2008) subdivides direct assessment tools into authentic and inauthentic measures. Reviewing three commonly used assessment techniques (fixed-choice tests, performance assessment, and rubrics used as scoring devices), she describes the theoretical background, benefits, and limitations of each. Oakleaf warns that, while fixed-choice tests have been popular in the past because they are easy to score and highly reliable, they generally measure low-level thinking and recall, rather than the higher-order abilities of evaluation, synthesis, and analysis. As such, she suggests they are inadequate measures of learning. Rather, she champions performance assessments that require students to demonstrate learning and knowledge, and thereby allow educators to assess higher-level thinking abilities. By requiring "students to perform real-life applications of knowledge and skills" (Oakleaf, 2008, p. 239), performance assessments reinforce classroom learning and support the idea that learning is an active process in which students construct meaning through their interaction with information and resources. Oakleaf (2008) argues that such measures have increased validity, and allow for more opportunities to improve instruction based on assessment. Other librarians have also supported the use of performance assessment including portfolios (e.g., Scharf, Elliot, Huey, Briller, & Joshi, 2007; Sharma, 2006; Sonley, Turner, Myer, & Cotton, 2007), reflective journals (e.g., McGuinness & Brien, 2007), and rubrics (e.g., Diller & Phelps, 2008; Knight, 2006; Oakleaf, 2009a, 2009b). Despite the attention paid to portfolios, capstone projects, and rubrics in the LIS literature, however, tests remain one of the most popular forms of direct assessment.

ASSESSMENT FOR STUDENT OUTCOMES

In addition to assessment of student learning outcomes or changes in student knowledge and behavior, stakeholders in higher education (e.g., federal and state governments, accreditation organizations, students, and parents) are also interested in student outcomes that cover engagement, persistence, retention, and graduation rates. Among the self-studies examined and site visits, student outcomes were not discussed in relation to information literacy. Within the LIS literature, little research has connected library services, particularly information literacy services, with student outcomes. In a study of more than 300,000 student responses to the National Survey of Student Engagement (NSSE), Kuh and Gonyea (2003) note positive correlations between student use of the library and other educational activities, such as participating in outside research with faculty or engaging in discussions with faculty outside of the classroom. They also find that students who use more library resources report working harder to meet faculty expectations. As a result, they conclude that the library plays "an important role in helping the institution achieve its academic mission" (p. 267).

Gratch-Lindauer (2007) reached similar conclusions after reviewing NSSE data related to information literacy. She notes a positive correlation between information literacy and NSSE questions related to practical competence and general education, which means that "as scores increase in the information literacy scales they also increase in benchmarks and gains" (p. 434). Selegean, Thomas, and Richman (1983) report increased rates of persistence in students who received information literacy instruction. In fact, students who completed an elective library course average 2.9 quarters (as opposed to semesters) greater overall attendance than students who did not take the course. Other studies have found that students who receive library instruction perceive less anxiety when conducting research (Brown, Weingart, Johnson, & Dance, 2004; Kwon, 2008; Kwon, Onwuegbuzie, & Alexander, 2007). Because library anxiety inhibits problem solving and other critical thinking processes, a reduction in anxiety might result in better overall performance for students. While results are promising, these studies are mostly exploratory and reinforce the need for further research into the area of student outcomes related to information literacy.

USES OF ASSESSMENT DATA

As Figure 8.1 depicts, an integral part of the assessment cycle is to use assessment data to make decisions and enact change to improve learning. It is important for institutions to remember that "assessment is not the goal—it is the means to the goal . . . student learning" (Linville, 2009, p. 396). Arguably, assessment practices themselves are useful only to the "extent to which they promote student learning" (National Research Council, 2001, p. 221). To improve student learning, assessment must be tied to the curriculum and instruction in that learning goals are derived from the curriculum. The presence of assessment in the curriculum does not ensure better learning. Rather, it is the interpretation of assessment data, and the decisions and actions taken based on that interpretation, that should lead to improvement (National Research Council, 2001). Once learning goals are set at all levels of the curriculum, assessment data reveal student progress toward reaching those goals. Where gaps exist or progress is not sufficient, instructors can make changes to improve learning and advance progress toward goals. When instructors use assessment data to take action and close the gap, the circle of assessment is closed. This is not to say that the process ends when the circle is closed. Assessment is an ongoing cycle of data collection, interpretation, and revision to the curriculum.

A librarian from institution D explains that a test of incoming freshmen reveals that students had trouble with appropriately using Boolean operators and identifying discrete components of citations. Using these data, the librarians redesigned instruction sessions to focus more closely on those areas. However, the librarians did not indicate that they shared results of the test with faculty or involved faculty in the changes to instruction sessions. As such, these librarians are working to close the assessment feedback loop, but are not meeting the Middle States Commission expectations for partnering with faculty for information literacy. Nevertheless, this was one of the clearest examples of using data to change instructional approach. Though less detailed about their approach, librarians at institutions A and B who teach credit courses give examples of changing assignments or instructional approaches to improve learning.

While the actions described above are not large-scale changes, they are examples of instructors making decisions and enacting changes based on data gathered through evaluation or assessment. In each case, the changes are focused on improving student learning, in areas identified as weak. For instance, the decision to revise an assignment is ostensibly made because student work indicates that the original assignment is not contributing to learning in the way it is intended. Once again, however, the focus is at the course level. Even the example from institution A, although it used an institution-wide test to gather data, involves changes at the course level. The next step is to expand assessment and its attendant analysis and action for improvement to the program and institutional levels.

ESTABLISHING A PROGRAM

The Middle States Commission (2007) states that assessment methods "involve the systematic and thorough collection of direct and indirect evidence of student learning, at multiple points in time and in various situations, using a variety of qualitative and quantitative evaluation methods that are embedded in courses, programs, and overall institutional processes" (p. 3). The assessment efforts described at case study institutions, though a good start, do not amount to a systematic plan. Further, little evidence suggests that librarians and faculty collaborate for assessment. While some librarians at institutions A, B, and C work with faculty to create rubrics for scoring assignments, most efforts at assessment and evaluation are done by individuals within courses or one-shot sessions. In order to attain the sort of comprehensive assessment described by the Middle States Commission, institutions must develop a campus-wide program or plan for assessment, and make clear distinctions between assessment and evaluation.

Maki (2004) provides a framework for implementing an assessment program. The first step is to determine expectations, which involves establishing the expected learning outcomes. Acknowledging that students engage in various kinds of educational activities, she suggests that everyone who provides those educational opportunities should participate in the process. For information literacy, both faculty and librarians should work together to define learning goals at the course, program, and institutional levels. To identify curricular areas addressing information literacy, Maki (2004) suggests curriculum mapping, in which institutions locate "opportunities inside and outside of the classroom that intentionally address the development of desired outcomes" (p. 93). Basically, curriculum mapping requires that faculty and/or librarians identify learning outcomes and pinpoint the courses, programs, and activities on campus that support each of those outcomes, thereby creating a map or chart that visually depicts how the curriculum addresses each outcome. Following the identification of learning outcomes, faculty and librarians must decide on appropriate methods to assess student learning, and determine when and how to administer the assessment. Figure 1.1 proposes that faculty and librarians should share responsibility for the assessment of information literacy. The final step is to examine the evidence and make "decisions based on the interpretations of assessment results and then establishing communication channels to share those interpretations to improve student learning" (Maki, 2004, p. 98), thus creating a feedback loop. Bloomberg and MacDonald (2004) describe a similar process for creating a culture of assessment. They note the importance of involving faculty and staff at the planning stages and providing training and support for faculty and staff as they implement a meaningful assessment process.

CONCLUSION

The Middle States Commission (2003) indicates that "assessment of information literacy is an essential element of overall curricular evaluation" (p. 39), and asserts "it is the institution's responsibility to ensure the information literacy goals are defined and that the various elements [which comprise information literacy] scattered across the curriculum are identified as part of a coherent whole" (Middle States Commission, 2003, p. 40). In other words, faculty and librarians must develop a holistic approach to information literacy within the curriculum, rather than treat it as an add-on addressed mainly by one-shot sessions. Thus far, the assessment of learning outcomes for information literacy is minimal. Further, many of the methods used by institutions as assessment actually comprise evaluation, in that they focus on perceptions and self-reporting rather than progress in learning. In all, levels of assessment fall well below the expectations that the Middle

States Commission (2003) sets forth. However, the importance of assessment for information literacy goes beyond compliance with accreditation standards. Faculty and librarians must engage in assessment not because it is an obligation to retain accreditation, but because it is an essential step toward improving student learning.

For librarians, assessment related to learning outcomes for information literacy is especially crucial. Unlike inputs and outputs, outcomes demonstrate the impact that the library has on those using its services, and how the library contributes to the educational mission of the institution. Input and output measures, such as funding, staff, library visits, and reference transactions, offer a picture of library resources and use, but the "quantity of use and quality of performance do not yet prove that users benefited from their interaction with a library" (Poll & Payne, 2006, p. 548). Oakleaf (2008, 2009a) notes that if libraries want to be integral to the teaching and learning missions of their institutions, they must "prove that they contribute to the production of quality graduates" (2008, p. 233). In other words, librarians must demonstrate that the information literacy services they provide contribute to the advancement of student learning on campus. To do so, librarians must show what students have learned or are able to do as a result of their interactions with the library, or how support to and collaboration with faculty within departments furthers student learning, by applying direct and authentic assessment measures.

Finally, institutions must assess learning outcomes, including those for information literacy, in order to answer calls for accountability and transparency. Not only is assessment an important part of the cycle to improve student learning, but stakeholders demand proof that students are graduating with the knowledge and skills they need to succeed beyond college. In order to be accountable and demonstrate learning to stakeholders, institutions must gather data through assessment and be willingly transparent in sharing that information with the public. The next chapter explores these issues of accountability and transparency in higher education, especially in relation to information literacy learning outcomes. In particular, the chapter explores the responses to requests for documents and interviews for this study, and what those responses might reveal about institutional levels of transparency. It also offers a broad view of accountability for student learning outcomes in higher education generally, and learning outcomes for information literacy specifically.

REFERENCES

American Library Association, Association of College and Research Libraries. (2000). *Information literacy competency standards for higher education.* Retrieved from http://www.ala.org/ala/mgrps/divs/acrl/standards/information literacycompetency.cfm

American Library Association, Association of College and Research Libraries. (2001). *National information literacy survey*. Retrieved from http://www.ala.org/ala/mgrps/divs/acrl/issues/infolit/professactivity/survey/index.cfm

American Library Association, Association of College and Research Libraries. (2006). *Science and technology information literacy guidelines*. Retrieved from http://www.ala.org/ala/mgrps/divs/acrl/standards/infolitscitech.cfm

American Library Association, Association of College and Research Libraries. (2007). *Research competency guidelines for research in English literature*. Retrieved from http://www.ala.org/ala/mgrps/divs/acrl/standards/research competenciesles.cfm

American Library Association, Association of College and Research Libraries. (2008a). *Information literacy standards for anthropology and sociology students*. Retrieved from http://www.ala.org/ala/mgrps/divs/acrl/standards/anthro_soc_standards.cfm

American Library Association, Association of College and Research Libraries. (2008b). *Political science research competency guidelines*. Retrieved from http://www.ala.org/ala/mgrps/divs/acrl/standards/PoliSciGuide.pdf

Bennet, O., & Gilbert, K. (2009). Extending liaison collaboration: Partnering with faculty in support of a student learning community. *Reference Services Review, 37*(2), 131–142. Retrieved from Ebsco.

Bloomberg, S., & McDonald, M. (2004). Assessment: A case study in synergy. In P. Hernon & R. E. Dugan (Eds.), *Outcomes assessment in higher education: Views and perspectives* (pp. 259–289). Westport, CT: Libraries Unlimited.

Bowers, C. V. M., Chew, B., Bowers, M. R., Ford, C. E., Smith, C., & Herrington, C. (2009). Interdisciplinary synergy: A partnership between business and library faculty and its effects on students' information literacy. *Journal of Business and Finance Librarianship, 14*(2), 110–127. Retrieved from InformaWorld.

Brown, A. G., Weingart, S., Johnson, J. A. J., & Dance, B. (2004). Librarians don't bite: Assessing library orientation for freshmen. *Reference Services Review, 32*(4), 394–403. Retrieved from Emerald.

Diller, K. R., & Phelps, S. F. (2008). Learning outcomes, portfolios, and rubrics, oh my! Authentic assessment of an information literacy program. *portal: Libraries and the Academy, 8*(1), 75–89. Retrieved from Project MUSE.

Educational Testing Service. (2009). *iCritical thinking powered by ETS*. Retrieved from http://www.ets.org/

Edzan, N. N. (2008). Analysing the references of final year project reports. *Journal of Educational Media and Library Sciences, 46*(2), 211–231. Retrieved from Ebsco.

Ewell, P. T. (2001). *Accreditation and student learning outcomes: A proposed point of departure*. Washington, DC: Council for Higher Education Accreditation. Retrieved from http://www.chea.org/award/StudentLearningOutcomes 2001.pdf

Florida State University. (n.d.). *Instruction at FSU*. Retrieved from http://learningforlife.fsu.edu/ctl/explore/onlineresources/i@fsu.cfm

Furno, C., & Flanagan, D. (2008). Information literacy: Getting the most from your 60 minutes. *Reference Services Review, 36*(3), 264–271. Retrieved from Emerald.

Gratch-Lindauer, B. (2007). Information literacy-related student behaviors: Results from the NSSE items. *College and Research Libraries News, 68*(7), 432–436, 441. Retrieved from H. W. Wilson.

Harrod, T. (2008). *Where is information literacy in life sciences outcomes assessment?* Retrieved from http://www.aacu.org/meetings/engaging_science/Poster3 parta.pdf.pdf

Hernon, P., & Dugan, R. (2009). Assessment and evaluation: What do the terms really mean? *College & Research Libraries News, 70*(3), 146–149. Retrieved from H. W. Wilson.

Knight, L. A. (2006). Using rubrics to assess information literacy. *Reference Services Review, 34*(1), 43–55. Retrieved from Emerald.

Kuh, G. D., & Gonyea, R. M. (2003). The role of an academic library in promoting student engagement and learning. *Journal of Academic Librarianship, 64*(4), 256–282. Retrieved from H. W. Wilson.

Kwon, N. (2008). A mixed methods investigation of the relationship between critical thinking and library anxiety among undergraduate students in their information search process. *College and Research Libraries, 69*(2), 117–131. Retrieved from H. W. Wilson.

Kwon, N., Onwuegbuzie, A. J., & Alexander, L. (2007). Critical thinking disposition and library anxiety: Affective domains on the space of information seeking and use in academic libraries. *College and Research Libraries, 68*(3), 268–278. Retrieved from H. W. Wilson.

Linville, D. J. (2009). Assessing assessment. *Language Arts, 86*(5), 396. Retrieved from ProQuest.

Maki, P. (2004). *Assessing for learning: Building a sustainable commitment across the institution.* Sterling, VA: Stylus.

McGuinness, C., & Brien, M. (2007). Using reflective journals to assess the research process. *Reference Services Review, 35*(1), 21–40. Retrieved from Emerald.

Middle States Commission on Higher Education. (2003) *Developing research and communication skills: Guidelines for information literacy in the curriculum.* Philadelphia, PA: Author.

Middle States Commission on Higher Education. (2005). *Assessing student learning and institutional effectiveness.* Philadelphia, PA: Author. Retrieved from http://www.msche.org/publications/Assessment_Expectations051222081842 .pdf

Middle States Commission on Higher Education. (2007). *Student learning assessment: Options and resources.* Philadelphia, PA: Author. Retrieved from http://www.msche.org/publications/SLA_Book_0808080728085320.pdf

Middle States Commission on Higher Education. (2009). *Characteristics of excellence in higher education: Requirements of affiliation and standards for accreditation.* Philadelphia, PA: Author. Retrieved from http://www.msche .org/publications/CHX06_Aug08REVMarch09.pdf

Murray, M., Perez, J., & Guimaraes, M. (2008). A model for using a capstone experience as one method of assessment of an information systems degree program. *Journal of Information Systems Education, 19*(2), 192–208. Retrieved from Ebsco.

National Research Council. (2001). *Knowing what students know: The science and design of educational assessment.* J. Pellegrino, N. Chudowsky, & R. Glaser (Eds.). Washington, DC: National Academy Press. Retrieved from ebrary.

Oakleaf, M. (2008). Dangers and opportunities: A conceptual map of information literacy assessment approaches. *portal: Libraries and the Academy, 8*(3), 233–253. Retrieved from Project MUSE.

Oakleaf, M. (2009a). The information literacy instruction assessment cycle: A guide for increasing student learning and improving librarian instructional skills. *Journal of Documentation, 65*(4), 539–560. Retrieved from Emerald.

Oakleaf, M. (2009b). Using rubrics to assess information literacy: An examination of methodology and interrater reliability. *Journal of the American Society for Information Science & Technology, 60*(5), 969–983.

Poll, R., & Payne, P. (2006). Impact measures for libraries and information services. *Library Hi Tech, 24*(4), 547–562. Retrieved from Emerald.

Project SAILS. (2009). *Project SAILS.* Retrieved from https://www.projectsails.org/

Rossin, D., Ro, Y. K., Klein, B. D., & Yi, M. G. (2009). The effects of flow on learning outcomes in an online information management course. *Journal of Information Systems Education, 20*(1), 87–98. Retrieved from Ebsco.

Scharf, D., Elliot, N., Huey, H. A., Briller, V., & Joshi, K. (2007). Direct assessment of information literacy using writing portfolios. *Journal of Academic Librarianship, 33*(4), 462–477. Retrieved from H. W. Wilson.

Selegean, J. C., Thomas, M. L., & Richman, M. L. (1983). Long-range effectiveness of library use instruction. *College and Research Libraries, 44*(6), 476–480.

Sharma, S. (2006). From chaos to clarity: Using the research portfolio to teach and assess information literacy skills. *Journal of Academic Librarianship, 33*(1), 127–135. Retrieved from H. W. Wilson.

Sonley, V., Turner, D., Myer, S., & Cotton, Y. (2007). Information literacy assessment by portfolio: A case study. *Reference Services Review, 35*(1), 41–70. Retrieved from Emerald.

Sonntag, G. (2008). We have evidence, they are learning: Using multiple assessments to measure information literacy learning outcomes. *IFLA Conference Proceedings*, pp. 1–14. Retrieved from Ebsco.

Stassen, M. L. A., Doherty, K., & Poe, M. (2001). *Program-based review and assessment.* Amherst, MA: University of Massachusetts, Amherst. Retrieved from http://www.umass.edu/oapa/oapa/publications/online_handbooks/program_based.pdf

University of Central Florida. (2008). *Program assessment handbook.* Orlando, FL: University of Central Florida. Retrieved from http://oeas.ucf.edu/doc/acad_assess_handbook.pdf

Walsh, A. (2009). Information literacy assessment: Where do we start? *Journal of Librarianship and Information Science, 41*(1), 19–28. Retrieved from SAGE.

CHAPTER 9

Accountability and Transparency

Accountability and transparency, which are closely tied to assessment, are ubiquitous for institutions of higher education both in the United States and elsewhere, as stakeholders increasingly demand evidence that institutions are achieving their missions and meeting their learning goals. Accountability and transparency are largely connected with institutional quality, with the former relating to how institutions document their achievements, and the latter referring to the availability and accessibility of the supportive evidence to outside stakeholders. In order to satisfy demands for accountability and transparency, institutions must assess progress toward meeting learning outcomes and share the data they have gathered and the actions taken to make improvements with their stakeholders.

Kuh (2007) states that accountability involves providing "policymakers with assessment findings of students' learning and experiences. ... For instance, are students well prepared for 21st century challenges" (p. 32)? In other words, accountability begins with articulating the mission and goals of an institution, and then collecting data to document progress toward achieving that mission and those goals (Carey, 2007; Maki, 2004). Transparency, on the other hand, refers to making institutional data, including assessment data, available for public consumption. Transparency is the public reporting of "timely, accurate, institution-specific information about costs, learning, and other educational outcomes" (Kuh, 2007, p. 32). While public demands for transparency typically emphasize the availability of data, Carey (2007) also stresses that "simply disclosing the truth isn't enough" (p. 29). He maintains that sharing accountability information with the public should spur institutions to keep making improvements in meeting their stated outcomes, which again emphasizes the link between accountability and transparency.

For this study, questions of accountability and transparency center on the amount and type of data that institutions gather about information literacy, and whether institutions are willing to share that information publicly. At a broader level, however, institutional responses to this investigator's requests for information offer insight into individual levels of transparency and accountability. One question raised by the investigator and her research committee is, "Given the current climate of stakeholder pressure on institutions to provide evidence of achievement, are institutions likely to share accreditation documents or take part in interviews and campus visits?" The rest of this chapter examines the current context of accountability and transparency using the definitions set forth by Kuh (2007) and Carey (2007). The first part of the chapter examines data provided by individual institutions, with attention to institutional response levels, the amount of detail provided, and reasons given for declining to participate. The final section offers an overview of public demands for accountability and the broad institutional responses represented in the literature and through initiatives such as College Portrait and other web portals offering institutional data.

INDIVIDUAL RESPONSES AND LEVELS OF TRANSPARENCY

Levels of transparency and institutional responses to requests for documents varied greatly. Although the numbers are discussed in Chapter 4 with regard to response rates, this chapter reexamines the number in light of what they reveal about institutional transparency. Of the 264 institutions included in the study, 63 (24%) placed their self-studies publicly online. Of those, 32 institutions (12.2%) included the visiting team report, and 9 (3.4%) published the institutional response as well. The institutions providing all three documents constituted the highest level of transparency; any member of the public could gain access to the institution's accreditation documents without restriction. The 201 remaining institutions were contacted three times over several months to request access to their documents. In total, 111 (55.4%) of them responded to the request, with 45 institutions (22.3%) sharing documents. Overall, participating institutions provided documents without question, although several institutions did have concerns or requests prior to agreeing to share information. For instance, two institutions asked why they needed to provide the entire self-study, rather than just the portions referring specifically to information literacy, and several institutions expressed an interest in receiving a summary of the study results. In some cases, institutions provided documents that were not usable (e.g., a periodic review or a monitoring report instead of the decennial review self-study), or offered only excerpts of the reports. When institutions sent excerpts of their reports, a follow-up e-mail was sent requesting the entire document, and explaining that because the analysis looked for equivalent language as well as explicit mentions of information literacy, the entire document was necessary to draw valid comparisons. If an institution did not provide the full document, it was not included in findings or counted as a participating institution. Ultimately, only 34 of those institutions were included in the total. However, these numbers demonstrate that transparency in accreditation is uneven across institutions. While some offered complete and unrestricted access to documents, and nearly one-quarter provided access upon request, more than half of institutions refused to provide access, even with an assurance of privacy and confidentiality.

REASONS FOR DECLINING TO PARTICIPATE

Those institutions that declined to participate occasionally provided reasons for their refusal. Often, they indicated that they were preparing to undertake a new self-study, or were in the midst of a decennial review at the time of request. These institutions assumed that their reports would not be ready in time to be shared for this study, even though the letter of request did not specify a time frame for responding. In addition, these same institutions often stated that their previous reports were too old to be of value for this study.

While such assumptions seem valid, content analysis of available reports revealed that the date does not greatly affect the document's relevance to the study. In fact, as Figure 9.1 shows, between 1999 and 2009, at least half of the reports published each year include the phrase information literacy, with

Figure 9.1 Total Number of Self-Studies/Number Containing Information Literacy per Year

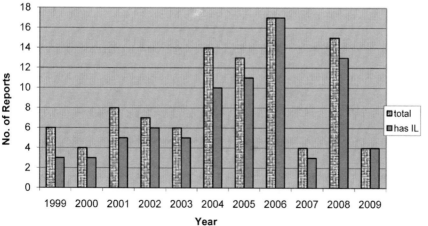

all of the documents from 2006 having the phrase. On average, 87 percent of the self-studies each year included some coverage of information literacy. The oldest reports, dated from 1999, have the lowest percentage of documents that addressed information literacy. Even for that year, however, 50 percent of the documents included the phrase information literacy. Indeed, the two selected topics studies that focused on information literacy were both written before the current Middle States Commission standards emphasizing information literacy took effect. In fact, one of those was actually written before the ACRL standards were published. The age of the report alone does not necessarily mean the document is irrelevant for this study.

Some institutions offer further explanations or reasons for not participating, and in some cases, these reasons give insight into the institution's level of transparency. One provost, for instance, characterized the request for accreditation documents as "odd." He indicated that the reports represent "some of the most important and sensitive information to any college," and expressed his disbelief that many institutions would be willing to share such information. From another institution, an academic vice president deemed it "inappropriate" to share the studies because they are not "created with the 'outside' reader in mind." In fact, such attitudes contradict the opinion of the stakeholders asking for increased transparency from accreditation organizations and institutions of higher education (see, e.g., Carey, 2007; US Department of Education, 2006). These responses suggest a concern that data in the reports might be misconstrued or interpreted in an unflattering way. While the concern might be legitimate in that an outside reader neither knows the campus context nor has access to the supplementary documentation provided to a visiting team, all institutions were assured of privacy and confidentiality. The request for documentation, which had been approved by the Simmons College Institutional Review Board, guaranteed that no information would be connected to an individual or an institution, and all data would be reported in aggregate.

Despite such assurances of privacy and confidentiality, two institutions declined to participate on the grounds that the information contained in the reports is not only sensitive, but represents intellectual property. One provost responded that, although he found the research to be "meritorious," his institution considered the reports to be "proprietary and thus confidential," and therefore would not share them. In another response, a director of institutional research also claimed the "detailed, proprietary" nature of the information as a reason for declining. In fact, although the Middle States Commission encourages institutions to share accreditation reports, it also states that the reports are the property of the institution, and thus each institution can decide whether to disseminate them (Middle States Commission, n.d.). However, it is surprising that with the current climate of public demand for accountability and transparency, coupled with the assurance of confidentiality, institutions would refuse to participate on these grounds.

Higher Levels of Transparency

While the refusals or reluctance to share information suggest a lesser degree of transparency, some were more forthcoming. For instance, in addition to providing a full copy of its self-study, one institution also forwarded the original request to the director of libraries, who provided additional information specific to the information literacy program on campus. Other institutions similarly offered to provide additional information such as periodic reports, appendices to self-studies, or documents specific to the information literacy initiatives.

The four case study institutions were likewise forthcoming with information. First, it is important to note that all four institutions initially chosen as prospective case study institutions agreed to participate. During campus visits, interviewees provided copies of various relevant documents, such as class syllabi and internal reports, in support of the overall research. Further, various people at all levels of the institution were willing to meet and discuss information literacy initiatives. Interviewees included staff librarians, library directors and assistant library directors, faculty, directors of writing centers, directors of teaching and learning centers, academic deans, and vice presidents. That such people would willingly participate speaks to a high level of transparency within the institutions.

It is perhaps worth noting that one of the case study librarians asked the author to sign an itemized list of the documents given to her, with an assurance not to publish or reproduce them without consent. While this was not a burdensome request, it was the only one of its kind, and it hearkens somewhat to those institutions that refused to share documents because they considered them proprietary. In such cases, it appears that the institutions are more concerned about the possibility of losing material or products produced by employees than of being misinterpreted. If that is indeed the concern, perhaps accreditation organizations could create guidelines for the copyrighting or otherwise marking of documents so that they could be more readily shared without such concerns, and thereby increase transparency.

ACCOUNTABILITY, TRANSPARENCY, AND INFORMATION LITERACY

While some of the institutions contacted are reluctant to share accreditation documents, they are more willing to share materials related specifically to information literacy. For instance, some institutions refused to share their entire self-study but did offer to share selected portions of the documents that reference information literacy. In those cases, the institutions were informed that such excerpts are not helpful, because the study looks for equivalent language, and because it is hard to draw valid conclusions without the same documents from each institution. In those cases, one institution followed up with the entire report, while another responded that it is not comfortable sharing the whole of the documents. Other institutions that declined to share accreditation documents redirected the researcher to contact library staff or to review other institutional web pages that contain information specific to information literacy, such as library pages with overviews of instruction initiatives and intended outcomes.

While institutions are more willing to share data and documents related to information literacy, such information is still difficult to gather and access. As noted in Chapter 8, few institutions engage in assessment of learning outcomes for information literacy, and some confuse assessment with evaluation. Thus, little data are produced to demonstrate achievement of these learning outcomes. The data that are available are uneven and not aggregated. For instance, while institutions largely acknowledge the Middle States Commission's focus on information literacy, how they address it in self-studies varies widely. Some institutions discuss the topic only briefly, with perhaps one or two mentions, while one report uses the phrase 134 times. Again, the age of the report does not necessarily determine how often information literacy appears, as the report with the most mentions was completed in 2002, before the current standards went into effect.

Similarly, the context in which information literacy is mentioned is not standardized. In some self-study reports, information literacy is presented entirely in the context of general education, while sections on the library used the older term "bibliographic instruction." In other documents, the phrase was scattered throughout, with mentions appearing in the context of general education, academic integrity, and the library. Such disaggregation makes it cumbersome to form a holistic view of the institutional approach to information literacy. Likewise, although some institutions are willing to share materials on information literacy, these materials seldom amount to more than lists of goals and objectives, class pages, or input and output measures. As with information on student learning outcomes in general, it is difficult, if not impossible, to find specific data about changes in student knowledge for information literacy due to the general lack of assessment being carried out. As noted in Chapter 8, very few institutions engage in direct assessment of learning related to information literacy. Too often, what passes for assessment is actually evaluation relying on student and faculty perceptions and opinions. As a result, little information regarding student learning for information literacy exists.

ACCOUNTABILITY AND TRANSPARENCY: A BROADER PERSPECTIVE

Figure 2.2 depicts the various stakeholders with an interest in student learning outcomes, and many of these stakeholders are among those calling for increased accountability and transparency from institutions of higher education. The data from this study offer a cross-sectional view of institutional accountability and transparency. The array of responses to requests for information and the type of data being collected speaks to varying levels of transparency and accountability across institutions, and suggests that, on the whole, many institutions may not be fully meeting stakeholder demands for evidence of student learning. While concerns and priorities vary according to stakeholders' interests, those who financially support these institutions, either directly or indirectly, want institutions to demonstrate that graduates have obtained the knowledge and abilities they need for success. The rest of this chapter outlines the concerns of individual stakeholder groups, and examines the broad response of the higher-education community to those stakeholders.

STAKEHOLDER DEMANDS

Stakeholders demand accountability and transparency across a range of institutional functions, from accounting and budgeting, to student outcomes such as graduation rates and job placement, to student learning outcomes. In terms of student learning outcomes, institutions should demonstrate that graduates actually learned—acquired the knowledge, "abilities, habits of mind, ways of knowing, attitudes, values, and other dispositions" (Maki, 2004, p. 3) necessary to succeed in work, graduate studies, and personal life. Stakeholders are particularly concerned that, while the cost of postsecondary education rises exponentially, reports contend that students are not learning what they need to learn in order to succeed after graduation. In addition, critics worry that the public does not have access to the information it needs to determine how well institutions of higher education are achieving learning goals, and how well one institution compares with another. Indeed, another important aspect of transparency is the use of common performance indicators to make comparisons among institutions possible and meaningful. Carey (2007) notes that institutions tend to emphasize differences as a form of uniqueness instead of focusing on their common educational goals. Recent calls for transparency stress the need for students and policymakers to be able to draw direct comparisons among institutions.

In its final report, the Spellings Commission (US Department of Education, 2006), a panel convened by then secretary of education Margaret Spellings to investigate higher education, notes "a lack of clear, reliable information about the cost and quality of postsecondary institutions, along with a remarkable absence of accountability mechanisms to ensure that colleges succeed in educating students" (p. x). Such indictments have led stakeholders from state and federal governments to research organizations to the public to demand that colleges and universities be more accountable in how they achieve learning goals and meet their missions. To this end, Carey and Alderman (2008)

Figure 9.2   Accountability and Transparency

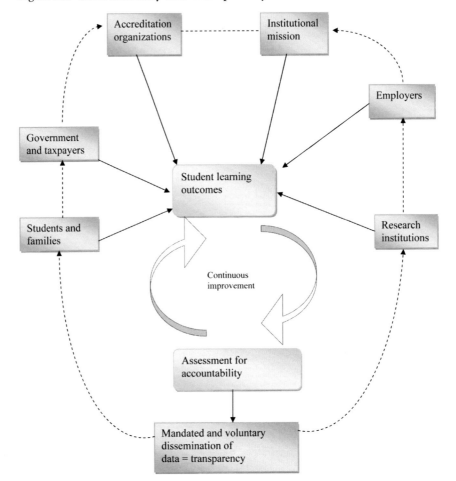

suggest that policy makers "gather much more information about college student outcomes, release the results to consumers and the general public, create explicit, mission-driven performance goals for institutions, and financially reward colleges and universities that excel" (p. 1).

Figure 9.2 depicts the relationship between stakeholder demands for student learning outcomes and accountability and transparency. The institutional mission is the primary influence on student learning outcomes, illustrated by its central placement. As the figure demonstrates, student learning outcomes are also subject to pressures from accreditation organizations, the government, students, parents, and employers. The lower half of the figure depicts the processes related to accountability and transparency. By assessing their progress toward meeting student learning goals, institutions document achievements and identify and act on areas for improvement. Thus, assessment is a crucial element in the figure, because the data gathered through assessment become the evidence for accountability, and the reporting of that evidence results in transparency. The dissemination of data, represented by the dashed lines in the figure, can take place through mandated reporting, voluntary sharing of information, or a combination of both. In other words, all institutions are required to report certain information to the government and to accreditation organizations. However, some institutions also make available additional information that may include information about assessment activities. Through this dissemination of information, institutions achieve accountability and transparency.

ACCOUNTABILITY: MEASURING ACHIEVEMENT

Driving demands for accountability and transparency is a concern that the national and international standing of American higher education has long rested on factors not directly connected to educational or learning outcomes. Carey and Alderman (2008) point out that inputs, outputs, and factors such as reputation, "[f]ame, wealth, and research prowess contribute far more to institutional status than student learning" (para. 3). Further, they contend that an institution's prestige is tied more closely to achievement scores of students enrolling as freshmen than to how much those students learn during their course of study at the institution. Current demands for accountability, however, require institutions to focus on key areas of importance to stakeholders, including cost, graduation rates, and measures of actual student learning.

Costs and Outcomes

Students and their parents are particularly concerned with the cost of education, especially since government funding has not kept pace with the rising cost of tuition, shifting a greater amount of the cost burden onto students. Miller (n.d.) suggests that students should have accurate information about the cost of attendance. This cost often varies greatly from the base tuition that institutions might advertise. Similarly, they need more straightforward information about assistance in paying for their education. Currently, there are more than 60 different websites and a dozen phone numbers for students seeking federal financial aid (Miller & Malandra, n.d.), making the process of finding and applying for assistance overwhelming for many students.

Cost of tuition is an important issue for federal and state governments as well. Because both government and, by extension, the taxpayers fund significant portions of higher education through financial aid, tax breaks to institutions, and direct funding to state universities, "government and the public point to the ever-growing taxpayer investment in higher education and demand more and more accountability from accreditation" (Eaton, 2010, para. 11). The Spellings Commission (US Department of Education, 2006) notes that "affordability is also a crucial policy dilemma for those who are asked to fund higher education, notably federal and state taxpayers" (p. 2). In fact, tuition costs may be more closely linked to institutional spending to increase rankings in lists such as that in *U.S. News and World Report*, than to efforts to improve instruction and learning or maintain accreditation (Kelderman, 2009; US Government Accountability Office, 2009). A survey of law schools finds that schools are implementing more hands-on and resource-based learning with the intention of increasing their rankings; this has led to increased costs and, in turn, driven up the cost of tuition (US Government Accountability Office, 2009). Without institutional demonstrations of achievement, public confidence in the higher-education system may waver if costs continue to rise (US Department of Education, 2006). In fact, the Commonwealth Foundation of Pennsylvania (2008) suggested "immediately halting all state higher education subsidies and making any increase contingent upon freezes in tuition costs and greater spending transparency for taxpayers" (p. 1).

The cost of higher education not only poses a barrier to entering postsecondary education for some students, but it also affects retention and graduation rates, as low-income students are significantly less likely than their high-income counterparts to persist in their degree (Leonhardt, 2009). Once students matriculate, stakeholders want more information about student outcomes such as persistence, graduation rates, and job placement upon graduation. Indeed, only half of the high school graduates who enter college actually earn a bachelor's degree (Leonhardt, 2009). A recent study of public colleges and universities in the United States revealed that the majority of students take more than four years to graduate, and in fact, a large percentage take up to eight years. In some state flagship universities, only one-third of students graduate in four years, and barely more than half graduate in six years (Jaschik, 2009). Moreover, since African Americans and Hispanics represent the fastest-growing student population and generally take the most time to completion, some critics (e.g., Nealy, 2009) warn that graduation rates will decline even further in coming years. The low graduation rates and the persistent gaps in graduation for minority students could perpetuate economic inequality in the United States, and this presents a challenge for higher education and many stakeholders (Dickson, 2008).

In response to concerns over cost, access, and persistence to graduation, President Barack Obama plans to issue "the largest increase in federal financial aid since the GI Bill" (Duncan, 2009, para. 3) by providing increases in financial aid such as Pell Grants by 30 percent as well as an additional $12 billion to build up community colleges over the next 10 years. The aim of this proposal is to enable more students, especially minorities and the economically disadvantaged, to attend and graduate from college or university.

Ultimately, the Obama administration hopes to see five million more students enroll in postsecondary education by 2020, thereby giving the United States the largest proportion of college graduates worldwide (Duncan, 2009). While the increased funding is substantial, the focus of the initiative seems to be quantity over quality. In other words, the proposed changes may make it financially easier for some students to attend college, but "the biggest problem with American higher education is not that too many students can't afford to enroll. It's that too many of the students who do enroll aren't learning very much and aren't earning degrees" (Carey, 2010, para. 3). As such, some critics believe that the Obama administration should require information on student learning before institutions can receive the proposed funding (Carey, 2010).

Concerns about Student Learning

Many stakeholders express concern over what students are learning in colleges and universities, and how well prepared they are for work or advanced study upon graduation. The Spellings Commission (US Department of Education, 2006) lamented declines in student learning. For instance, results of the *National Assessment of Adult Literacy* administered by the NCES (Kuntner et al., 2007) reported that, while overall literacy levels rose from 1992 to 2003, prose and document literacy significantly decreased for those with a bachelor's degree or higher. Bok (2005) argues that students make gains in learning, but too many of them graduate from college without learning as much as they should in critical areas. While Bok does not use the phrase information literacy, he does underscore the importance of competencies related to information literacy, such as the ability to find, obtain, and use information for problem solving.

Employers and business leaders indicate similar concerns. In a report prepared for the World Bank, Johnstone (1998) notes the "increasing level of skills and competencies required in a modern, globally-competitive economy" (p. 3), and contends that for employers, the problem of higher education is not so much the high costs as the "insufficient learning" (p. 6). The Business Higher Education Forum (1997) interviewed leaders from 10 corporations and 12 institutes of higher education to determine their opinion of how well new graduates were prepared for work. Interviewees largely believe that the transition from school to work could be greatly improved, and business leaders indicate that new graduates are generally weak in communication skills, the ability to work in teams, and dealing with ambiguity. The report concludes that "a gap exists between the skills mastered by students in college and those deemed most important by their future employers" (p. 22).

Recognizing that "complex tasks in information seeking are a characteristic of the workplace" (Crawford & Irving, 2009, p. 29), employers include information literacy among the skills and abilities they seek in new hires.

However, employers often do not use the term information literacy explicitly, but they "implicitly expect employees to have preexisting information skills" (Crawford & Irving, 2009, p. 34). For instance, employers in the physical sciences, such as biology and chemistry, want employees who can find, evaluate, and synthesize information (Macklin & Culp, 2008). Klusek and Bornstein (2006) contend that, although business and financial corporations do not typically use the phrase information literacy, they too value the skills and competencies associated with the concept.

The American Council of Trustees and Alumni (ACTA, 2009) voices concerns over gaps in student learning, especially in the liberal arts. In a report of core learning requirements for undergraduates, the council argues that too many institutions have abandoned a core curriculum in favor of a distributed learning approach, in which students choose which classes they will take to fulfill requirements. ACTA insists that as a result, students are not learning what they need to succeed after college, and that "colleges aren't delivering on their promises" (p. 12).

TRANSPARENCY: QUALITY AND ACCESSIBILITY OF INFORMATION

Miller and Malandra (n.d.) are critical of both the amount and the quality of the information currently available on higher education in the United States. Federal and state governments and accreditation organizations collect a lot of data on colleges and universities. Carey and Alderman (2008) maintain that state governments have to carry the greatest part of the burden to make colleges and universities accountable, because "states have most of the money and most of the power" (p. 1), although the economic recession has decreased the amount of money states have to devote to higher education. Currently, however, much of the data focuses on inputs, outputs, and processes, which are not helpful to consumers and policy makers looking to make informed decisions about quality of learning. In addition, the information that is publicly available is often "highly scattered and disaggregated" (Miller & Malandra, n.d., p. 6), making it difficult to locate. Some states are beginning to increase the amount of data they collect on their institutions, but that information is still uneven from state to state. In addition, the information is often designed to be used by specialists, not the public, making it difficult for lay consumers to interpret it (Miller & Malandra, n.d.).

For researchers and policy makers, concerns center on the ability to access the necessary information to make decisions. Carey and Alderman (2008) note that, if policymakers intend to fix the problems faced by higher education, they need much more information about student outcomes, including learning outcomes. Young (2009) agrees that, "by improving transparency, policymakers will be better able to discover problems and enact solutions to make the system of higher education more cost-efficient while providing greater value to higher education customers" (p. 2). She notes that the public cannot demand action and change if it does not realize that problems exist and insists that more information be shared. Likewise, a research report from the Education Sector (Wang, 2009) suggests that greater transparency will lead to greater market efficiency in higher education. If institutions compete with each other to deliver better value, the report contends, it could drive the cost of tuition down.

Employers may want to compare learning outcomes and achievement across campuses and programs in order to determine which graduates might be best suited for employment. Van der Wende (2000) contends that the current lack of transparency in higher education does not allow employers to make such comparisons, and as such, the system fails to make appropriate links between "intellectual power and employability" (p. 309). In the absence of reliable information on learning outcomes, employers, students, and parents rely on rankings lists generated by private companies, or on institutional reputation that is often based on personal knowledge, "grapevine" knowledge, and ranking systems (Morley & Aynsley, 2007). The Business Higher Education Forum (1999) suggests that, along with students, "corporations are the 'customers' of colleges and universities," and that open dialogue and communication between higher education and industry is necessary to ensure that students are prepared to enter the workforce upon graduation.

Miller (n.d.) also stresses the need for more data to be made available in order for students to compare institutions or programs. The Spellings Commission (US Department of Education, 2006) asserts that with regard to learning outcomes, "information should be made available to students, and reported to the public in aggregate form to provide consumers and policymakers an accessible, understandable way to measure the relative effectiveness of different colleges and universities" (p. 4). Currently, consumers have access to information such as size, location, and degree programs offered. Vedder (2008) contends that institutions should also provide actual data on learning, such as scores on standardized tests, acceptance rates to graduate and professional schools, and career information on alumni five years after graduation. He acknowledges that some issues should not have to be disclosed, such as personnel discussions and medical information, and he agrees that donors should remain anonymous if they so choose. Nevertheless, he suggests that in deciding what to disclose or not, "colleges should err on the side of openness" (para. 17).

Another concern is that the data that are collected and made available at the state and federal levels are limited to traditional students. For instance, Stokes (n.d.) notes that much of the data collected by the NCES under the Integrated Postsecondary Education System (IPEDS) focus only on full-time, first-degree-earning students, thereby excluding many adult and nontraditional students. He points out that "traditional" college students make up only 16 percent of the total enrollment, while the vast majority of students are studying part time, enrolled in two-year colleges, or are over the age of 22, with 40 percent being 25 or older. Because they represent such a large sector of the community, and because their success is vital to the overall economic success of the country, Stokes (n.d.) insists that collecting and disseminating data on this group "is an absolutely critical activity" (p. 2).

The lack of concrete data on learning outcomes means that students and their parents rely largely on institution or program reputation and rankings when they make a decision about which institution or program to attend. Miller and Malandra (n.d.) reiterate the common concern that private ranking systems, such as the *U.S. News and World Report* lists of best schools, rely on limited datasets that are not necessarily relevant to the decisions that students and policy makers make. As a result of the overwhelming lack of useful and accessible information, the authors lament that "most people must 'take on faith' what college quality might be because there is a lack of reliable ways of documenting and assessing what students learn" (p. 4), and they insist that "policymakers [*sic*] and consumers need better information" (p. 1).

Miller (n.d.) criticizes current ranking systems for being inflexible in their measurements and lacking transparency in their methods. Specifically, she objects to the fact that private rankings determine institutional rank based on a set of indicators, with each indicator weighted based on its importance to the overall score. Essentially, the private rankings use these indicators to define institutional quality. However, Miller points out that the companies providing these rankings lack transparency in that they often do not disclose the indicators and weighting systems they use, claiming they are "trade secrets." Further, there is "no agreement across reports as to what should be included in the rankings and how the indicators should be weighted" (p. 2). Finally, even if consumers knew what specific indicators are used and how they are weighted, consumers have no way to manipulate the system to address their needs and priorities. As Miller (n.d.) puts it, "the fact that there may be other legitimate indicators or combinations of indicators is usually ignored" (p. 2). For instance, in the *U.S. News and World Report* rankings, "graduation and retention rates, faculty resources, faculty financial resources, student selectivity, and alumni [donations] account for 75 percent of a college's score. The other 25 percent is based on a peer assessment" (Terrell, 2009, para. 4). While each of these measures gives some indication of achievement, none of them addresses what students learn during their tenure at the college.

ACCREDITATION CONCERNS AND RESPONSES

While most of the discussion of accountability and transparency has focused on institutions, accreditation organizations have been criticized as well. The Spellings Commission (US Department of Education, 2006) maintains that the system of accreditation has "significant shortcomings" (p. 15). The commission notes that, although accreditation organizations pay more attention to learning outcomes, they do not share most of their data or make them publicly accessible. As a result, "the conversations that happen between campuses and accreditors have zero visibility in the larger national and public conversation over higher education" (Lederman, 2009a, section 5, para. 1). In a commentary on *Inside Higher Ed*, Lederman (2009a) acknowledges that accreditation organizations raise important issues on campuses, but that the lack of transparency makes them seem unaccountable and mysterious to the public. He suggests that accreditation should be "less of an auditing process and more an iterative conversation about educational quality" (Lederman, 2009a, section 5, para. 3), and that the discussion should be public.

While in its early days, the Obama administration did not seem to engage issues of higher education as strongly as had the Spellings Commission, recent activity suggests concerns remain the same (Lederman, 2010a). The US Department of Education's Office of the Inspector General harshly criticized the North Central Association of Colleges and Schools for granting accreditation to a for-profit university despite concerns over how the school assigns credit hours (Lederman, 2009c; US Department of Education, Office of the Inspector General, 2009a), and subsequently Congress convened a hearing to look into how accreditation organizations set standards for and oversee assigning of credit hours by institutions (Epstein, 2010). The Office of the Inspector General (2009a) asserts that the accreditation organization's decision to grant full initial accreditation to the institution in question "is not in the best interest of students and calls into question whether the accrediting decisions made by the [North Central Association] should be relied on by the Department of Education when assisting students to obtain quality education" (p. 1). The Inspector General (2009b) similarly criticized the Middle States Commission, stating that despite the accreditation organization's claim that it focuses on student learning outcomes in accreditation decisions, the Inspector General's office "did not find that the Middle States provided any guidance to institutions and peer reviewers on minimum outcome measures to ensure that courses and programs are of sufficient content and rigor" (p. 2). In fact, rather than easing their scrutiny of higher education and accreditation, "the federal government is dead serious about holding colleges and universities accountable for their performance" (Lederman, 2010a).

Such rebukes suggest that the current administration "is continuing to expand its reach and authority into accreditation matters" (Lederman, 2009c, para. 7), and has provoked a backlash from accreditation organization leaders who describe the criticisms as "an unwarranted overreaction," and "wrongheaded and overreaching" (Lederman, 2009c, para. 3). The accreditation organizations claim the Department of Education appears "to have put themselves in the place of the evaluators" (Lederman, 2009c, para. 5), and complain that the department's new set of guidelines on recognition for accreditation organizations is too prescriptive and could be seen as "a backdoor way to avoid Congressional limitations on the government's ability to regulate accreditors" (Lederman, 2010b, para 4). Indeed, Eaton (2010) fears that the focus by stakeholders is on "consumer protection and compliance with law and regulation" (para. 4) rather than on the quality of the education.

Wheelan (2009) of the Southern Association of Colleges and Schools contends that accreditation organizations help to ensure quality in higher education, but admits that "there are major challenges to our accreditation processes that must be addressed" (p. 66). In particular, she notes that accreditation organizations have not done enough to keep the public informed of the results of accreditation and assessment processes, including the achievements of graduates. Eaton (2007, 2010), of the Council for Higher Education Accreditation, emphasizes that institutional mission must be kept central to the quality measurements. In other words, any accountability measures must accommodate the individual missions and goals of each institution, thus precluding a single set of nationalized standards. However, she agrees that accreditation organizations "need to be public with the results of our efforts" (para. 11), and she suggests that marketing tools such as institutional and accreditation websites should be transparent about performance.

Along these lines, the Spellings Commission (US Department of Education, 2006) recommends that sharing information on student learning should be made a condition of accreditation, and the commission encourages accreditation organizations to make their reports more easily accessible. More recently, the Department of Education has established new regulations that require accreditation organizations to disclose certain information regarding their actions and decisions. For instance, when these organizations decide to place an institution on probation or deny, withdraw, suspend, or revoke its accreditation status, they must inform the secretary of education and the public. In addition, within 60 days of the decision, the accreditation organization must issue a "brief statement summarizing the reasons for the agency's decision" (Institutional Eligibility under the Higher Education Act, 2009, sec. 602.26 [d]).

While the accreditation organizations generally support transparency, they must also respect institutional privacy and confidentiality. For instance, the Middle States Commission (2009) views "transparency about the accreditation process and the status held by each member institution" as one if its core values (section 3, line 6). As such, the Middle States Commission publishes an accreditation document that describes the status of each member institution, and it makes publicly available accreditation standards and all guidelines and supporting documents. The documents produced as part of the accreditation process, however, including the institutional self-study and visiting team reports, are the property of the institution. The Middle States Commission does not release copies of those documents without expressed consent from the institution (Middle States Commission, n.d.). While the Middle States Commission (n.d.) does not explicitly endorse disseminating institutional accreditation reports to the public, it does warn that institutions "must hold themselves accountable for honest communication with the public" (p. 1). Suskie (2004), vice president of the Middle States Commission, reminds institutions that the audience interested in assessment may be external as well as internal, and urges "when in doubt, plan to share your results widely rather than narrowly" (p. 276). Levels of response for documentation for this study varied, and they are discussed below.

INTERNATIONAL CONTEXT AND COMPETITION

Demands for greater accountability and transparency in higher education stem from concerns not only about individual student achievement, but also over the competitiveness of the American system of higher education on a global scale. The Spellings Commission (US Department of Education, 2006) warns that higher education in the United States has taken its position of superiority for granted, and is currently ranked 12th among industrialized nations for higher-education attainment. In other words, other countries are educating more people to higher grade levels than is the United States. The United States particularly lacks graduates in the areas of math, science, and engineering. As a result, employers in these fields are filling key positions with employees from other countries. The Spellings Commission notes that over 30 percent of science and engineering doctorate holders actively employed in the United States are foreign-born. In all, the Spellings Commission (2006) charges that the American higher-education system "has yet to address the fundamental issues of how academic programs and institutions must be transformed to serve the changing educational needs of a knowledge economy" (p. ix).

According to some critics, the American higher-education system lags behind other countries in its overall approach to accountability and transparency. Adelman (2008) asserts that "none of the major pronouncements on accountability that we have heard in the recent past—from [the Spellings Commission] to platitude pronouncements and wish lists for student learning from the higher education community—even begin to understand what accountability means" (p. 1). Instead, Adelman points to the Bologna Process, in which 46 European countries representing 4,000 higher-education institutions have agreed on and publicly defined performance standards for degrees and programs across institutions, as a model for the United States to consider. Within Europe, the Bologna Process has developed qualification frameworks, or "sets of learning outcomes and competencies that a student must demonstrate in order to receive a degree at a specific level," with common reference points at the disciplinary level (Redden, 2008). Adelman (2008) calls this framework "extraordinarily relevant to accountability challenges in the United States" (p. 2) and would like it to influence change in the Unites States.

THE HIGHER EDUCATION ACT

In 2008, the Higher Education Opportunity Act (P.L. 110-315) was enacted. Although it does not have the broad range of the Bologna Process, it does include a number of new requirements for consumer disclosure of higher education information that are meant to increase transparency. For instance, beginning in July 2011, the US Department of Education is required to publish a list in each of nine categories, "naming the top 5 percent of institutions with (1) the highest tuition and fees; (2) the highest 'net price'; (3) the largest percentage increase in tuition and fees; and (4) the largest percentage increase in net price" (American Council on Education, 2008, p. 1). The act also established an initiative to disseminate information on institutions in 27 categories, including applications, admissions, SAT scores, time to completion of degrees, cost of attendance, and financial aid. In addition, new proposals would require colleges and universities to publish information on the placement and types of employment their students obtain upon graduation (Lederman, 2009b).

With respect to accreditation organizations, the act reiterates the centrality of institutional mission in setting learning outcomes for students. Accreditation organizations must acknowledge and take into consideration individual institutional missions when conducting accreditation reviews. In addition, the act bars the Department of Education from setting specific criteria that "specify, define, or prescribe the standards accreditors use in assessing an institution's success" (American Council on Education, 2008, p. 3). It also requires accreditation organizations to respect individual institutional missions in their assessments. However, the act also encourages greater transparency on the part of accreditation organizations by requiring them to publicly disclose any adverse actions against institutions, including putting institutions on probation, or denying or withdrawing accredited status (American Council on Education, 2008).

INSTITUTIONAL CONCERNS AND RESPONSES

Despite the fact that the Higher Education Opportunity Act "reflects the historic distinction and collaborative relationship between institutional standards and accreditation standards" (American Council on Education, 2008, p. 2) by safeguarding the role of individual missions, institutions of higher education have given mixed responses to stakeholder demands for accountability and transparency. Benjamin (2008) argues that for a long time, "higher education leaders resisted the idea that comparative information about student learning should be collected for public consumption" (p. 52). Lombardi (2006) opines that measurements that focus on student improvement instead of overall student performance are invalid, stating they have "the perverse effect of devaluing accomplishment in favor of improvement" (para. 8). Further, he contends that employers are not interested in knowing which students improved the most, but which students are the highest performers. Others worry that any national measures of student learning outcomes produces oversimplified comparisons, akin to the *U.S. News and World Report* rankings (Lederman, 2008).

In the three years since the Spellings Commission report was published, institutions of higher education have undertaken a number of initiatives that provide the kind of information that the Commission wanted. Among these are:

- College Portrait, produced by the National Association of State Universities and Land-Grant Colleges and the American Association of State Colleges and Universities, http://www.collegeportraits.org
- University and College Accountability Network (U-CAN), started by the National Association of Independent Colleges and Universities, http://www.ucan-network.org/
- College Navigator, which the federal government operates, http://www.nces.ed.gov/collegenavigator/
- College Choices for Adults, maintained by the Western Cooperative for Educational Telecommunications, http://www.collegechoicesforadults.org/

Each of these sources offers institutional profiles and aggregate statistics for cross-institutional comparisons and guiding consumers in choosing an institution. These resources supplement commercially published directories, such as the College Board (http://www.collegeboard.com), and Peterson's (http://www.petersons.com), that allow prospective students to find and compare institutions based on publicly available information such as tuition, programs offered, and size.

Some institutions have also opted to publish particular data through a system of online indicators known as dashboards, or graphical interfaces that track performance indicators. For instance, the Minnesota State Colleges and Universities System has also launched a system-wide accountability dashboard (available at http://www.mnscu.edu/board/accountability/index.html) for sharing data on 10 indicators, including accessibility, licensure exam pass rates, and student engagement scores. Each indicator is scored through a dial-like graphic that rates performance in terms of "needs attention," "meets expectations," or "exceeds expectations." Visitors to the site can view aggregate data for the entire system or scores for individual institutions.

In response to criticisms that the vast majority of measures in higher education are heavily skewed toward traditional undergraduates, the Western Cooperative for Educational Telecommunications (WCET) launched College Choices for Adults (available at http://www.collegechoicesforadults.org/), which collects and disseminates data of particular importance to adult learners. This website includes scores from the *National Survey of Student Engagement* (NSSE) along with student performance in general education courses, but it also offers program-level specific data of interest to career-focused adult learners (Lederman, 2007). According to College Choices, the data help students answer the questions "What will I learn (what are the program outcomes) in each certificate or degree program?" and "How have recent students performed on those measures of what was learned?" (Western Cooperative for Educational Telecommunications, 2009).

The issue of mandated versus voluntary reporting relates to transparency. Virtually all institutions gather and report certain data to the federal and state governments, accreditation organizations, and other stakeholders. However, the data need not be made public. On the other hand, some institutions share information with the public voluntarily. For example, institutions wishing to gain or retain accredited status must collect information on various aspects of the institution and its functioning. Similarly, the NCES gathers data annually on topics such as tuition, enrollment, student persistence, and graduation rates. NCES data are publicly available through the agency's website (http://www.nces.ed.gov/). Accreditation organizations encourage institutions to share their accreditation documents, but they do not require it.

Table 9.1 shows reporting mechanisms for higher education, noting which are voluntary, which are mandatory, and which are publicly available. The third column, which indicates whether reports are publicly available, only states whether individual institutions have a choice in making the data available. In other words, accreditation reports are listed as "not publicly available" because it is up to the individual institution to release. Some may post the reports publicly or supply them on request, but they are not required to do so.

Many of these initiatives offer greater access to institutional data than was previously available, and suggest that some institutions of higher education heed the call for accountability and transparency. Nevertheless, some question the value of these systems. For instance, some critics contend that the sample of 100 students' aggregate test scores provided in College Portrait is not large enough to be meaningful and that a sample is not a sufficient indicator of student learning. Moreover, while providing scores is mandatory for participants, participation in College Portrait itself is voluntary, meaning that institutional comparisons are limited. For instance, the California state college system opted not to participate because it viewed the standardized test as interfering with institutional and faculty authority (Jaschik, 2008). For those institutions that participate, Bennett (2008) worries that students will not know which differences are most meaningful and important when

Table 9.1 Voluntary and Mandated Reporting for Higher Education

Reporting Mechanism	Responsible Entity	Mandatory or Voluntary?	Publicly Available?
Accreditation reports	Regional and program accreditation organizations	Mandatory (to gain or keep accreditation)	No
Integrated Postsecondary Education Data System (IPEDS)	NCES	Mandatory	Yes, in aggregate
College Navigator	NCES	Mandatory	Yes
U-CAN	National Association of Independent Colleges and Universities	Voluntary	Yes
Dashboards (or other graphic displays)	Individual institutions	Voluntary	Yes
College Portraits	American Association of State Colleges and Universities, Association of Public and Land-Grant Universities	Voluntary	Yes
College Choices for Adults (Transparency by Design)	Western Interstate Commission for Higher Education, Lumina Foundation	Voluntary	Yes
Tax returns (Form 990)	IRS	Mandatory	Yes

comparing institutions. In addition, he warns that reporting average scores of standardized tests can mask important differences in student experience.

Consumers face similar challenges when searching for data on accountability and transparency related to learning outcomes for information literacy. To begin with, there is no aggregate source of data on learning outcomes for information literacy. While the NCES collects data related to academic libraries, the data focus almost exclusively on inputs and outputs such as numbers of instruction sessions and numbers of students receiving instruction. Further, while some national standardized tests have been developed for information literacy, the testing sites do not publish aggregate results.

The Association of College and Research Libraries (ACRL) might be a logical organization to collect and disseminate data related to information literacy. While ACRL provides extensive information on information literacy, including general and discipline-specific standards, a database of exemplary instructional templates, and guidelines for planning, developing, and implementing an information literacy program, it has not collected statistics on information literacy since its 2001 *National Information Literacy Survey* (American Library Association, Association of College and Research Libraries, 2001). As a result, there is no centralized source of data on current information literacy practices and outcomes, and individual institutional treatment of the topic is uneven at best.

CONCLUSION

Despite some efforts to collect and disseminate institutional data related to student outcomes and student learning outcomes, thus far, responses to demands for accountability and transparency across institutions are uneven. The request for accreditation documents for this study was met with a wide range of responses, from full disclosure of reports to partial answers and outright refusals, and the reasons for refusing to participate are likewise varied. Because much of the reporting for accountability and transparency is voluntary, how an institution chooses to respond to requests for information and the amount and type of data it makes publicly available says a lot about the culture of that institution. An institution that willingly shares information probably has an institutional culture that supports transparency.

The requests for accreditation documents sent out for this study went to provosts and academic deans. Through their actions, language, and behaviors, individuals in these high-level positions help to set the tone and culture of their institution, and by being willing or unwilling to share information, especially when they are assured of confidentiality, such individuals might be giving insight into the culture of their institutions. While the accreditation organizations, cognizant of the widespread demands for transparency, encourage institutions to share information, they do not mandate it. Institutions appear to be more willing to share data on information literacy, but this information is scattered and disaggregated, making it difficult to construct a holistic overview. As with collaboration and assessment, there is a need for some agency or organization to collect, organize, and disseminate data related to information literacy (e.g., types and levels of instruction, types of assessment, and instances of collaboration), and to create an environment that encourages institutions to share such information.

Because it underlies the values, priorities, and behaviors of the institution, institutional culture affects all of the areas considered thus far in this study—collaboration, assessment, and transparency and accountability. Whether high-level and influential faculty and administrators within the organization give priority to these topics will determine how successful efforts on campus are. The next chapter examines institutional culture and its relation to information literacy.

REFERENCES

Adelman, C. (2008). *Learning accountability from Bologna: A higher education policy primer*. Washington, DC: Institute for Higher Education Policy. Retrieved from http://www.ihep.org/assets/files/publications/g-l/Learning_Accountability _from_Bologna.pdf

American Council of Trustees and Alumni. (2009). *What will they learn?* Washington DC: Author. Retrieved from https://www.goacta.org/publications/downloads/ WhatWillTheyLearnFinal.pdf

American Council on Education. (2008). *ACE analysis of higher education act reauthorization*. Retrieved from http://www.acenet.edu/AM/Template.cfm?Section =Home&TEMPLATE=/CM/ContentDisplay.cfm&CONTENTID=29218

American Library Association, Association of College and Research Libraries. (2001). *National information literacy survey*. Retrieved from http://www .ala.org/ala/mgrps/divs/acrl/issues/infolit/professactivity/survey/index.cfm

Benjamin, R. (2008). The case for comparative institutional assessment of higher-order thinking skills. *Change, 40*(6), 50–56. Retrieved from ProQuest.

Bennett, D. C. (2008). Templates galore: New approaches to public disclosure. *Change, 40*(6), 36–42. Retrieved from ProQuest.

Bok, D. (2005). *Our underachieving colleges: A candid look at how much students learn and why they should be learning more*. Princeton, NJ: Princeton University Press.

Business Higher Education Forum. (1997). *Spanning the chasm: Corporate and academic cooperation to improve work-force preparation*. Washington, DC: Author.

Business Higher Education Forum. (1999). *Spanning the chasm: A blueprint for action. Academic and corporate collaboration: Key to preparing tomorrow's high-performance workforce*. Washington, DC: Author.

Carey, K. (2007). Truth without action: The myth of higher-education accountability. *Change, 39*(5), 24–29. Retrieved from Ebsco.

Carey, K. (2010). That old college lie. *Democracy: A Journal of Ideas, 15*, online. Retrieved from http://www.democracyjournal.org/15/6722.php

Carey, K., & Alderman, C. (2008). *Ready to assemble: A model state higher education accountability system*. Washington, DC: Education Sector. Retrieved from http://www.educationsector.org/usr_doc/HigherEdAccountability.pdf

Commonwealth Foundation. (2008). High costs of higher education: Reforming how Pennsylvania taxpayers finance colleges and universities. *Commonwealth Policy Brief, 20*(6), 1–14. Retrieved from http://www.commonwealth foundation.org/docLib/20090904_HigherEdPB.pdf

Crawford, J., & Irving, C. (2009). Information literacy in the workplace: A qualitative exploratory study. *Journal of Librarianship and Information Science, 41*(1), 29–38. Retrieved from SAGE.

Dickson, L. (2008). Economic inequality and higher education: Access, persistence, and success. *Industrial and Labor Relations Review, 61*(3), 427–429. Retrieved from Ebsco.

Duncan, A. (2009). *What I really want to say . . . : Education secretary Arne Duncan's 21st century vision*. Retrieved from http://www.plotkin.com/ blog-archives/2009/10/education_secre.html

Eaton, J. (2007). Nationalization and transparency: On our own terms. *Inside Accreditation, 3*(1). Retrieved from http://www.chea.org/ia/IA_10807.htm

Eaton, J. (2010, July 20). Accreditation's accidental transformation. *Inside Higher Ed.* Retrieved from http://www.insidehighered.com/views/2010/07/20/eaton

Epstein, J. (2010, June 18). Method to Miller's madness. *Inside Higher Ed.* Retrieved from http://www.insidehighered.com/news/2010/06/18/credithour

Higher Education Opportunity Act of 2008, P.L.110-315. Retrieved from http://purl.access.gpo.gov/GPO/LPS103713

Institutional eligibility under the Higher Education Act, as amended, and the secretary's recognition of accreditation agencies: Final rule. 34 C.F.R. § 602 (2009).

Jaschik, S. (2008, November 17). Accountability system launched. *Inside Higher Ed.* Retrieved from http://www.insidehighered.com/news/2007/11/12/nasulgc

Jaschik, S. (2009, September 9). (Not) crossing the finish line. *Inside Higher Ed.* Retrieved from http://www.insidehighered.com/news/2009/09/09/finish

Johnstone, D. B. (1998). *The financing and management of higher education: A status report on worldwide reforms.* Retrieved from http://www.fel-web.org/fel/bolonia/noabolonia.es/bancomundial.pdf

Kelderman, E. (2009, October 26). Competition, not accreditation, pushes up law school cost, GAO survey says. *Chronicle of Higher Education.* Retrieved from ProQuest.

Klusek, L., & Bornstein, J. (2006). Information literacy skills for business careers: Matching skills to the workplace. *Journal of Business and Finance Librarianship, 11*(4), 3–21. Retrieved from InformaWorld.

Kuh, G. D. (2007). Risky business: Promises and pitfalls of institutional transparency. *Change, 39*(5), 30–35. Retrieved from ProQuest.

Kuntner, M., Greenberg, E., Jin, Y., Boyle, B., Hsu, Y., & Dunleavy, E. (2007). *Literacy in everyday life: Results from the 2003 National Assessment of Adult Literacy.* Washington, DC: National Center for Education Statistics.

Lederman, D. (2007, September 17). College accountability movement moves online. *Inside Higher Ed.* Retrieved from http://www.insidehighered.com/news/2007/09/17/adult

Lederman, D. (2008, August 18). Let the assessment PR wars begin. *Inside Higher Ed.* Retrieved from http://www.insidehighered.com/news/2008/08/18/cla

Lederman, D. (2009a, June 24). Advice for U.S. on accreditation. *Inside Higher Ed.* Retrieved from http://www.insidehighered.com/news/2009/06/24/naciqi

Lederman, D. (2009b, August 24). Carrying out the Higher Ed Act. *Inside Higher Ed.* Retrieved from http://www.insidehighered.com/news/2009/08/24/rules

Lederman, D. (2009c, December 18). Scrutiny for an accreditor. *Inside Higher Ed.* Retrieved from http://www.insidehighered.com/news/2009/12/18/hlc

Lederman, D. (2010a, April 13). No letup from Washington. *Inside Higher Ed.* Retrieved from http://www.insidehighered.com/news/2010/04/13/hlc

Lederman, D. (2010b, March 9). Unwelcome "help" from the Feds. *Inside Higher Ed.* Retrieved from http://www.insidehighered.com/news/2010/03/09/accredit

Leonhardt, D. (2009, September 8). Colleges are failing in graduation rates. *New York Times.* Retrieved from http://www.nytimes.com/2009/09/09/business/economy/09leonhardt.html

Lombardi, J. V. (2006, August 10). Virtues and vices of "value added." *Inside Higher Ed*. Retrieved from http://www.insidehighered.com/views/2006/08/10/lombardi

Macklin, A. S., & Culp, F. B. (2008). Information literacy instruction: Competencies, caveats, and a call to action. *Science and Technology Libraries, 28*(1), 45–61. Retrieved from InformaWorld.

Maki, P. (2004). *Assessing for learning: Building a sustainable commitment across the institution.* Sterling, VA: Stylus.

Middle States Commission on Higher Education. (2009). *Mission, vision, and core values.* Philadelphia, PA: Author. Retrieved from http://www.msche.org/?Nav1=ABOUT&Nav2=MISSION

Middle States Commission on Higher Education. (n.d.). *Public communication in the accrediting process.* Philadelphia, PA: Author. Retrieved from http://www.msche.org/?Nav1=POLICIES&Nav2=INDEX

Miller, C. (n.d.) *Accountability/consumer information.* Retrieved from http://www.ed.gov/about/bdscomm/list/hiedfuture/reports/miller.pdf

Miller, C., & Malandra, G. (n.d.). *Accountability/assessment.* Retrieved from http://www.ed.gov/about/bdscomm/list/hiedfuture/reports/miller-malandra.pdf

Morley, L., & Aynsley, S. (2007). Employers, quality, and standards in higher education: Shared values and vocabularies or elitism and inequalities? *Higher Education Quarterly, 61*(3), 229–249. Retrieved from Ebsco.

Nealy, M. J. (2009). Report: College graduation rates could dramatically decline. *Diverse Issues in Higher Education, 26*(11), 8. Retrieved from ProQuest.

Redden, E. (2008, July 28). On accountability, consider Bologna. *Inside Higher Ed*. Retrieved from http://www.insidehighered.com/news/2008/07/28/bologna

Stokes, P. J. (n.d.). Hidden in plain sight: Adult learners forge a new tradition in higher education. Retrieved from http://www.ed.gov/about/bdscomm/list/hiedfuture/reports/stokes.pdf

Suskie, L. (2004). *Assessing student learning: A common sense guide.* Bolton, MA: Anker Publishing Co.

Terrell, K. (2009, August 18). Harvard and Princeton top the *U.S. News* college rankings. *U.S. News and World Report.* Retrieved from http://www.usnews.com/articles/education/best-colleges/2009/08/19/harvard-and-princeton-top-the-us-news-college-rankings.html

US Department of Education. (2006). *A test of leadership: Charting the future of U.S. higher education.* Washington, DC: Author. Retrieved from http://www.ed.gov/about/bdscomm/list/hiedfuture/reports/final-report.pdf

US Department of Education, Accreditation Team. (2009). *Negotiated rulemaking for higher education. Session III, issues and draft regulatory language.* Retrieved from http://www.ed.gov/policy/highered/reg/hearulemaking/2009/accreditation.html

US Department of Education, Office of the Inspector General. (2009a, December 14). *Review of the Middle States Commission on Higher Education's standards for program length.* Retrieved from http://www.ed.gov/about/offices/list/oig/aireports/i13j0005.pdf

US Department of Education, Office of the Inspector General. (2009b, December 17). *Alert memorandum.* Retrieved from http://www.ed.gov/about/offices/list/oig/auditreports/AlertMemorandums/l13j0006.pdf

US Government Accountability Office. (2009). Higher education: Issues related to law school cost and access. Retrieved from http://www.gao.gov/new.items/d1020.pdf

Van der Wende, M. (2000). The Bologna declaration: Enhancing the transparency and competitiveness of European higher education. *Higher Education in Europe, 25*(3), 305–310. Retrieved from Ebsco.

Vedder, R. K. (2008). Colleges should go beyond the rhetoric of accountability. *Chronicle of Higher Education, 54*(42), A64. Retrieved from ProQuest.

Wang, P. (2009). Rein in the cost of higher ed. *Money, 38*(8), 18. Retrieved from Ebsco.

Western Cooperative for Educational Telecommunications. (2009). *College choices for adults.* Retrieved from http://www.collegechoicesforadults.org/

Wheelan, B. S. (2009). Colleges and universities must not rest on their laurels. *Diverse Issues in Higher Education, 26*(9), 66. Retrieved from ProQuest.

Young, E. (2009). *Policy briefs: Are Texas universities making the grade in accountability?* Retrieved from http://www.texaspolicy.com/pdf/2009-06-PB17-HE-transparency-ey.pdf

CHAPTER 10

Institutional Culture

In *Developing Research and Communication Skills* (Middle States Commission, 2003) and Figure 1.1, the Middle States Commission establishes an expectation that any learning outcome is integrated into the curriculum at the course, program, or institutional levels, and that faculty and librarians collaborate in planning, instruction, and assessment, once assessment is implemented. Various stakeholders are demanding that institutions share the data gathered during assessment. As the previous chapters indicate, however, such collaboration, assessment, and accountability and transparency are not the norm. Not all institutions of higher education are structured to support and encourage collaboration, and assessment is not widespread at many institutions. Further, many institutions fail to differentiate between evaluation and assessment when looking at student learning. For information literacy to be integrated as a learning outcome throughout the curriculum, and for collaboration between librarians and faculty to become widespread, information literacy and collaboration need to become a part of the institutional and organizational cultures. In many cases, information literacy integration will require changes to the institutional and organizational cultures, including the library culture, which presupposes widespread and high-level support for such change.

DEFINITIONS OF INSTITUTIONAL AND ORGANIZATIONAL CULTURES

Institutional culture can be defined as "the values, norms and patterns of action that characterize social relationships within a formal organization"

(Scott & Marshall, 2005, para. 1). Institutional culture is more than just policies or "the way it's done" (Lakos & Phipps, 2004, p. 348). It involves "overt and covert rules, values, and principles an organization owns that are influenced by history, custom, and practices" (Lakos & Phipps, 2004, p. 348). The shared assumptions and understandings that make up the culture of an institution guide the behaviors of individuals within that institution. An institutional culture is deeply entrenched, and often the assumptions and understandings upon which it rests are so ingrained that they are taken for granted among the individuals within the organization (Lakos & Phipps, 2004).

Each college or university has its own institutional culture, shaped in part by "the mission of the institution, as defined, articulated, and used on campus" (Association for the Study of Higher Education, 2005, p. 46), as well as institutional history and traditions, values, and the influence of founders and leaders. While the institutional culture broadly describes the college or university, each department and division within the institution has its own unique culture as well, referred to as the organizational culture. In the department or division, Julien and Pecoskie (2009) suggest that "individual conduct is associated with a specific position or set of circumstances, which provide behavioral guidelines, prescriptions, and boundaries" (p. 150). Even within a department, several cultures may exist. For instance, a library has its own organizational culture, and each department within the library has unique cultures that could vary from each other and from the larger library culture. Likewise, each academic department and program has a unique organizational culture. Rather than generalize about "the faculty" as a group, Hardesty (1995) therefore suggests that librarians must recognize that faculty come from multiple cultures. For instance, each discipline is "shaped by the inquiry paradigm in which the faculty member works" (Association for the Study of Higher Education, 2005, p. 52), with the result that patterns of belief, attitudes, and even lifestyle vary along disciplinary lines. In some instances, faculty identification with their discipline might outweigh loyalty to the institution (Knight & Trowler, 2000).

INTERACTIONS ACROSS AND AMONG CULTURES

The existence of organizational cultures within the institution adds a layer of complexity to the interactions between librarians and faculty. In addition to understanding the broader campus culture, librarians must also consider that faculty operate in a different context (Julien & Pecoskie, 2009) and that faculty are not a single group, but have many different cultures across the institution. Discussion of institutional and organizational cultures at the case study institutions was limited.

Interviewees at institution C are the only ones to use the term "institutional culture" to describe the commitment to information literacy on their campus, and indeed several people, from librarians to senior administrators, use the phrase. Two academic deans acknowledge that information literacy is discussed regularly at curriculum meetings, and insist that faculty are "very aware" of the need to incorporate learning outcomes for information literacy into their courses, with a goal to integrate it eventually at the program level. The rhetoric was supported by behaviors and classroom evidence. For instance, course pages and assignments reflected collaboration between librarians and faculty in several areas from assignment design to instruction and assessment, such as assignments scored by collaboratively developed rubrics and pre- and posttests. During the campus site visit, the librarian met with one faculty member to discuss information literacy learning outcomes for a proposed course. The two planned to meet again to talk about planning for program-level outcomes. Institution C also has a policy in place requiring new and revised courses to include outcomes for information literacy. The initiative has been in place for several years and has survived turnover in senior administration, which speaks to the degree to which it is now embedded in the institution's culture. The support for the program and the planning taking place bodes well for its future. However, further integration of information literacy, especially at the program level, is not guaranteed. To begin with, it will take more than just the efforts of the librarians and a department chair to integrate information literacy throughout a department; other faculty need to be engaged in the process for it to succeed. In addition, as is the case at other institutions, faculty and librarians at institution C sometimes confuse assessment and evaluation. In order to properly study progress toward student learning outcomes, the institution must disambiguate the terminology and implement authentic assessment measures.

While institution C has made progress in developing an institutional culture of information literacy, recognition of the organizational cultures within the institutional culture is limited throughout the case study institutions. While librarians at each institution emphasize outreach and relationship building, none of them talk about targeting their message to accommodate departmental differences. Instead, they either focus on individuals who seemed receptive to their ideas, or they take a broader perspective of reaching out to the faculty as a whole. For instance, when institutions B and D arranged focus group interviews with faculty, they do not appear to have approached faculty at a departmental or program level. Instead, they opened each section to whichever faculty would come. As a result, it seems most discussion during the focus group interviews either revolved around general information literacy competencies, or centered on the individual courses attending faculty teach, perpetuating the course-level mind-set.

This is not to suggest that librarians are unaware of, or do not understand, differences in departmental cultures. For instance, the business librarian at institution D is cognizant of the culture of the business school and believes that her own background in accounting lends her some credence with those faculty. Likewise, a librarian at institution C discusses working with individual faculty to adapt the ACRL's (American Library Association, Association of College and Research Libraries, 2000) standards for information literacy to reflect the needs, priorities, and expectations of their courses and disciplines.

What was missing in the four case study institutions, and indeed in the literature of library and information science, is a broader discussion of identifying and trying to understand the range of differences in priorities, communication styles, and work preferences within the institution, and then targeting marketing and outreach efforts at the organizational level. These observations suggest that librarians may be more successful in permeating the various organizational cultures if they approach departments in a more flexible way, with attention to the disciplinary differences and preferences. Smith (2001) underscores the need for librarians to talk with faculty to identify learning goals within the context of each program. Even if an outcome such as information literacy is cross-curricular or part of general education, not every academic department will emphasize the same learning goals for its students or approach instruction of the competency in the same way, underscoring the importance of the ACRL discipline guidelines (discussed in Chapter 8). The challenge for librarians is to change the prevailing mind-set from focusing on individual faculty members and courses toward a department- and program-level approach. None of the case study institutions appears to have a plan in place for such an approach.

IMPORTANCE OF CULTURAL SENSITIVITY

Individuals who would influence change must be aware of and understand the many coexisting cultures within an institution and adapt their style to each of the various cultures. Knight and Trowler (2000) contend that "cultural sensitivity is paramount" (p. 79), and those who would influence faculty must learn to work within the norms of each department. Kezar (2005, 2006) affirms that in working with different departments, "individual, disciplinary, and other differences need to be taken into account" (2006, p. 827), and contends that "it is important to use a variety of strategies" (2005, p. 857) when trying to build relationships or a case for a new initiative. She asserts that individuals need to keep their audience in mind, suggesting that while scientists are persuaded by empirical data, humanities faculty might prefer inspiring quotations. A single, broad approach is unlikely to achieve widespread success; rather, librarians must adapt their approach as they move in and between departments (Blackmore, 2007).

Changing or influencing existing institutional or organizational cultures is challenging, however. As Schroeder and Mashek (2007) note, initiatives such as information literacy as a student learning outcome often require a change in the cultural mind-set. At the same time, however, Lakos and Phipps (2004) warn that such change is difficult to accomplish. The behaviors and actions of individuals within the organization "are based on long-held and strongly felt attitudes and assumptions, as are attitudes about work and effectiveness, and are difficult to change" (p. 351). They maintain that for such change to occur, "the organization must either recognize a threat to its survival, or a strong, positive external pressure that calls for adaptation" (p. 349). Yet, achieving that cultural change in spite of difficulties is essential for information literacy. Bennett (2007) notes that "the key to success in programs of information literacy is that they become institutional initiatives, rather than solely library initiatives" (p. 162). In other words, faculty must agree that information literacy is important and be willing to address it within their classrooms. Likewise, deans and provosts need to develop policies and incentives that facilitate collaboration and the adoption of information literacy into the curriculum, especially at the program level.

Using data generated through information literacy workshops conducted by the Council for Independent Colleges, Bennett (2007) identified a set of contextual criteria that characterize institutions with a culture conducive to information literacy. One of the most influential factors is a commitment to collaboration, which often requires a "fundamental rethinking of roles and authority over knowledge" (p. 153). The pervasiveness of technology, and the growing expertise of other professionals in this area, may mean that faculty have to consider sharing their classroom with some of those experts. Likewise, librarians have to be ready and willing to take on professional roles that bring them out of the library and more into the classroom. Bennett (2007) also found that campus-wide issues bearing on libraries and transformative uses of technology lent themselves to increased attention to information literacy. For instance, many campuses involved in library renovations are rethinking the use of library space and considering the role and impact of technology on how information is accessed and used. In planning for such changes, many campuses are reshaping the ways in which libraries can contribute to and support the educational, and especially liberal arts, missions of their institutions, with a focus on teaching roles of librarians and using the library as a teaching or educational space. For such changes to have an impact beyond the library, however, librarians have to involve other stakeholders such as faculty and even students in the planning stages. If librarians act alone in making these decisions about space and technology, they are unlikely to gain widespread buy-in for those changes after they are implemented.

CONCLUSION

On most campuses, information literacy instruction depends on faculty invitations for one-shot sessions, and does not extend beyond the course level. The question remains, then, "How can librarians move past a handful of unconnected relationships to generate a network of faculty and administrative support?" The focus on learning outcomes, including information literacy, provides an opportunity for academic libraries to directly address and affect student learning through collaboration with faculty on instruction and assessment. To take advantage of this opportunity, librarians must develop strategies to approach and interact with various departments with attention to the individual cultures of those departments (Smith, 2001).

Because information literacy is interdisciplinary in nature and depends on cooperation and collaboration across campus for integration, developing an information literacy program at many institutions entails changes to the institutional culture. Senior administrators, including library directors, academic deans, and provosts, will have to work together with faculty and librarians to cultivate an environment that supports an outcome related to information literacy. In order to effect the necessary change, these individuals need to engage in dialogues across departments, with awareness of and sensitivity to different organizational cultures; to create a common vision of an information literacy program; and to offer incentives for implementation. In essence, campus leaders must emerge who have the influence and support to engage a base of followers to take action and implement change. The next chapter examines the role of leadership for information literacy, and the various individuals and groups across campus who might play a leadership role.

REFERENCES

American Library Association, Association of College and Research Libraries. (2000). *Information literacy competency standards for higher education.* Retrieved from http://www.ala.org/ala/mgrps/divs/acrl/standards/information literacycompetency.cfm

Association for the Study of Higher Education. (2005). Understanding institutional culture. *ASHE Higher Education Report, 31*(2), 39–54. Retrieved from Ebsco.

Bennett, S. (2007). Campus cultures fostering information literacy. *portal: Libraries and the Academy, 7*(2), 147–167. Retrieved from Project MUSE.

Blackmore, P. (2007). Disciplinary difference in academic leadership and management and its development: A significant factor? *Research in Post-Compulsory Education, 12*(2), 225–239.

Hardesty, L. (1995). Faculty culture and bibliographic instruction: An exploratory analysis. *Library Trends, 44*(2), 339–368. Retrieved from Gale.

Julien, H., & Pecoskie, J. J. L. (2009). Librarians' experiences of the teaching role: Grounded in campus relationships. *Library and Information Science Research, 31*(3), 149–154. Retrieved from ScienceDirect.

Kezar, A. (2005). Redesigning for collaboration within higher education institutions: An exploration into the developmental process. *Research in Higher Education, 46*(7), 831–860. Retrieved from Ebsco.

Kezar, A. (2006). Redesigning for collaboration and learning initiatives: An examination of four highly collaborative campuses. *Journal of Higher Education, 77*(5), 804–838. Retrieved from ProQuest.

Knight, P. T., & Trowler, P. R. (2000). Department level cultures and the improvement of learning and teaching. *Studies in Higher Education, 25*(1), 69–83. Retrieved from Ebsco.

Lakos, A., & Phipps, S. (2004). Creating a culture of assessment: A catalyst for organizational change. *portal: Libraries and the Academy, 4*(3), 345–361. Retrieved from Project MUSE.

Middle States Commission on Higher Education. (2003). *Developing research and communication skills: Guidelines for information literacy in the curriculum.* Philadelphia, PA: Author.

Schroeder, R., & Mashek, K. B. (2007). Building a case for the teaching library: Using a culture of assessment to reassure converted campus partners while persuading the reluctant. *Public Services Quarterly, 3*(1–2), 83–110. Retrieved from Ebsco.

Scott, G., & Marshall, G. (2005). Organizational culture. In *Dictionary of Sociology.* Retrieved from Oxford Reference.

Smith, K. R. (2001). New roles and responsibilities for the university library: Advancing student learning through outcomes assessment. *Journal of Library Administration, 35*(4), 29–36. Retrieved from InformaWorld.

CHAPTER 11

Leadership for Information Literacy

As the previous chapters demonstrate, proponents of information literacy face numerous obstacles to its integration beyond the course level. To advance to the program and institutional levels, campus leaders must emerge and initiate dialogues to create a vision that generates a broad base of followers who buy into and are willing to work toward achieving that vision. Further, they must develop an environment that facilitates and rewards collaboration. As the Middle States Commission (2003) acknowledges, the framework of Figure 1.1 requires a deeper level of collaboration between faculty and librarians than what currently exists on most campuses. As such, an information literacy program that conforms to that figure may require each group to rethink its roles and responsibilities in relation to information literacy.

The concept of information literacy is not always well understood by those who are expected to take part in its instruction and assessment. In addition, the term information literacy is often over-identified with library skills, reinforcing the idea that it is not the faculty's responsibility. Campus leaders need to facilitate dialogues among faculty and staff about a shared vision of an information-literate graduate in order to increase awareness and understanding of the topic, and to create a framework to which both librarians and faculty can buy in. Leaders must stress the connections among information literacy, critical thinking, communication skills, and lifelong learning. From these discussions, faculty, staff, department chairs, and senior administrators can decide where information literacy fits into programs and the larger curriculum, and which competencies to prioritize. To create that buy-in, it is essential to have leadership capable of motivating people to work together and achieve a meaningful learning goal, and to benefit from the data collected.

DEFINITIONS OF LEADERSHIP

To understand leadership in the context of information literacy, it is first necessary to address the concept of leadership. Numerous leadership theories, styles, and definitions exist. This brief introduction draws on current research relevant to higher education.[1] Early theories equate leadership with positions of power and explained leadership in terms of internal qualities or attributes that were inborn (see, e.g., Bass, 1990; Bennis & Nanus, 1985; Horner, 1997). Other conceptualizations, however, have emphasized that leadership is not necessarily role- or position-bound, and that it is a process that can be learned.

Clark (2008) suggests that leadership is a process by which a person influences others to accomplish a vision and goals, and that brings people together to make the organization more cohesive and effective in both the present and the future. He argues that leaders are defined through a combination of attributes that include values, knowledge, skills, and behaviors. In essence, what makes a person a leader is a vision, an ability to create a network of supporters who will take action to achieve their goal. Any individual within an organization can become a leader if there is a common vision that others accept and work to achieve (see, e.g., Bass, 1990; Kouzes & Posner, 2002; Northouse, 2007).

Gardner (1990) contends that leadership is "the accomplishment of group purpose" (p. 38). The behaviors and skills that leaders use to accomplish their vision change according to the situations and contexts (Saal & Knight, 1988). In other words, leaders apply different leadership styles depending on the situation. Figure 11.1 depicts the process of leadership for information literacy. Leaders should understand the institutional culture, create a shared vision of information literacy, and use relationship-building skills to create a network of followers. With these elements in place, leaders motivate action for change, which in the case of information literacy involves high levels of collaboration between faculty and librarians to integrate information literacy throughout the curriculum.

Teacher Leaders

Researchers have identified a number of the attributes that enable leaders to succeed, and some of these attributes apply to higher education and, more specifically, to educators or teachers. Leaders create a common vision around which others rally and work to achieve. When the vision centers on a concept that is not well understood, like information literacy, leaders must ensure that a common understanding of an information-literate graduate emerges around which they can expect buy-in. Kezar (2005, 2006) refers to this part of the process as the "learning" phase. Leaders must have followers. In higher education in general, and for teachers in particular, researchers have emphasized the necessity of a leader's ability to build relationships and work collaboratively in order to create a network of supporters or followers (Dozier, 2007; Fowler & Walter, 2003; Frost & Harris, 2003; Kezar, 2005, 2006; York-Barr & Duke, 2004). According to Donaldson (2007), the ability to work collaboratively with others as a means to gaining influence is so important for teachers that he calls this "relational leadership."

Another aspect commonly identified as key to the success of leaders in accomplishing change is a realistic understanding of the organizational context and culture within which they work (Horner, 1997). As catalysts for change, teacher leaders are team players who understand the context and culture of their organizations and how to work within them to get positive results. Frost and Harris (2003) term this type of understanding "situational knowledge," which involves understanding and being responsive to different environments and political climates. Teacher leaders combine their relationship-building skills and knowledge of the organization to build support systems within which they can promote a vision and influence change. Finally, leaders are willing to take risks (Mader, 1996; York-Barr & Duke, 2004). Introducing change into an organization can be difficult and could be met with resistance, but leaders who understand their organizational context also understand when to challenge other's ideas and decisions (Brown, 1995).

This chapter examines the extent to which librarians fit each aspect of this concept of leadership for information literacy. Further, it analyzes the role of faculty, senior administrators, and accreditation organizations in helping to realize the integration of information literacy within the curricula of higher-education institutions.

LIBRARIANS AND LEADERSHIP

In most colleges and universities, faculty oversee the curriculum and have autonomy within the classroom, meaning that leadership for information literacy depends on the buy-in and cooperation of faculty and senior administrators such as academic deans, library directors, and provosts. Librarians cannot integrate information literacy throughout the curriculum without faculty and administrative support. Indeed, Bloomberg and McDonald (2004) suggest that any successful proposal for change within a college or university must be "rooted in faculty support" (p. 261). On the other hand, faculty do not necessarily have to initiate the change, but can be influenced to engage in instruction for information literacy through a common vision (Fister, Hutchens, & MacPherson, 2001). It remains unclear, however, who on campus could best create that vision and attract followers to work toward it. Examining the evidence in this study in the context of Figure 11.1 reveals

Figure 11.1   Leadership for Information Literacy Leaders

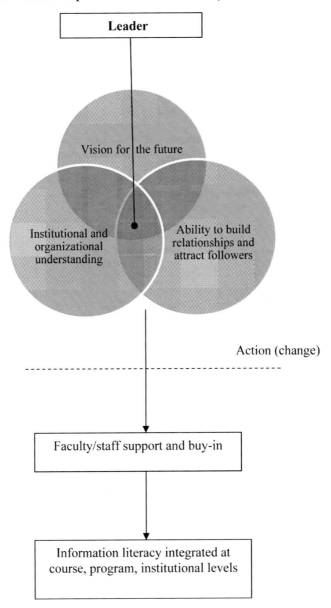

Leader

Vision for the future

Institutional and organizational understanding

Ability to build relationships and attract followers

Action (change)

Faculty/staff support and buy-in

Information literacy integrated at course, program, institutional levels

that most librarians engage almost exclusively in relationship building and have not adopted other leadership behaviors. Relationship building is an important precursor to leadership, as it enables the leader to build the critical mass of followers to work toward the shared vision (Kezar, 2005, 2006). It is not an end in itself; as the figure illustrates, relationship building is but one of the attributes associated with leadership. However, for an individual to become a leader, he or she must use those attributes to attract followers and influence them to take action. Thus far, most librarians have not accomplished this end. In fact, it is possible that front-line instruction librarians may be unable to realize a campus-wide, integrated information literacy program without leadership being demonstrated by the library director and other senior administrators such as deans and provosts (McGuinness, 2007).

Relationship Building

Much of the work done in libraries lends itself well to relationship building. Librarians interact with faculty from all departments, as well as staff in other areas of the college, on a regular basis by engaging in liaison activities, seeking input on collection development, operating copyright and digital rights clearance and reserve services, and so on. In many places, instruction librarians have already forged relationships with many faculty members through years of teaching bibliographic instruction sessions. The examples of successful collaborative projects at case study institutions, such as the team-taught chemistry course or the writing fellow initiative, show that librarians have made some inroads in building relationships with various people on their campuses. Librarians have ample opportunity to build on this foundation, and many librarians are engaged in relationship building, especially at the course level.

Librarians at the case study institutions underscore the importance they attribute to relationship building throughout their interviews. Several of them use words such as "relationship building," "boundary-spanning," and "personal diplomacy" to describe their outreach efforts, suggesting that these librarians appreciate the importance of reaching out to colleagues across campus and view themselves as ambassadors for information literacy.

A librarian at institution B was emphatic about the importance of relationship building. She used the word often in her interview, and outlined various ways in which librarians can reach out to faculty. For instance, in addition to collaborating with faculty for instruction, she suggests that librarians work with faculty to conduct evaluation research and assist them in determining the extent of citation to their own publications. During lunch with the investigator and the library director, this librarian left the table to converse with an academic dean. Upon returning, she explained that such interactions with high-level administrators help to keep the library visible, and establish connections on which librarians can call when they need support.

In addition to course collaborations, librarians at the case study institutions and self-study documents occasionally find other venues for reaching out to faculty and other colleagues. For instance, librarians at both institutions B and D conducted focus group interviews with faculty as a way of creating a dialogue on information literacy. Faculty have a chance to learn more about the library and information literacy, and to see the ways in which the goals of information literacy align with their own course and program goals, mirroring Kezar's (2005, 2006) emphasis on learning as an underpinning for change. Finally, the focus group interviews demonstrate to the various faculty that many of them share concerns with student work, and that information literacy learning goals are not systematically addressed throughout the curriculum. As such, these events provide a learning opportunity for all involved.

The librarians who conducted focus group interviews with faculty describe the events as well attended. Institution D offered a total of 12 focus group interviews, with as many as 10 faculty members attending each. Librarians could use these interviews as a springboard for further interaction and discussion with faculty, but as with course collaborations, they have not capitalized on the potential relationships these interviews offered. Indeed, two librarians at institution D acknowledge that the librarians had not followed up with faculty to let them know the results of the focus group interviews or what actions the library had taken in response to what was learned. Librarians need to do more to promote their successful projects beyond the library. In fact, during focus group interviews, librarians and faculty found they share common concerns about students, including sloppy citations, poor discrimination of information resources, and inability to employ proper search strategies to locate information. Librarians should use these concerns to continue the dialogue with faculty and develop learning outcomes related to improving student knowledge and habits in these areas. Once they establish learning outcomes, librarians and faculty can plan instruction and assessment for those outcomes.

As of yet, none of the institutions studied display evidence of integrating information literacy at the program level, despite the fact that three of the four case study institutions include information literacy in their general education curriculum, and two of those have a required, stand-alone course for information literacy. In fact, in some instances, stand-alone courses for information literacy may discourage rather than facilitate relationship building, because they tend to remain segregated from the rest of the curriculum and to reinforce the idea that faculty do not need to address information literacy topics in their own courses because they are being addressed elsewhere in the curriculum. Faculty may be less inclined to invite librarians into their classes when stand-alone courses exist. As an example, librarians at institution A indicated that they concentrate on their stand-alone courses, and do few in-class sessions for faculty in other courses. At institutions A and B, several departments offer their own information literacy courses. These courses are taught by departmental faculty, and although they address many of the same competencies as general information literacy courses, the faculty who teach them generally do not involve librarians in planning courses and assignments, nor do they invite them in to participate in instruction.

Librarians appear to have little involvement with faculty beyond the course level. While librarians work closely with individual faculty on courses and/or on campus-wide committees, there is little evidence that they interact with all or an overwhelming majority of faculty at the program level. For instance, librarians at three of the case study institutions are involved in curriculum planning at the institutional level, and work with individual faculty in planning and delivering discrete courses, but there is little evidence of their attending departmental planning meetings, or developing learning outcomes with program faculty. One exception is institution C. Although delivery of information literacy instruction still takes place primarily at the course level, as noted previously, the groundwork is being laid for integration at the program level. An institutional policy requires all new or revised courses and programs to include information literacy learning outcomes, and the librarians are working actively with faculty at all levels to address this requirement. Eventually, faculty and librarians plan to build on this foundation and introduce more advanced concepts throughout each program that align with the programmatic goals. Such integration might be based on rubrics outlining competencies that progress from novice to advanced levels. Much of the work at institution C still remains to be done, however. Although administrators support the integration of information literacy, and faculty and librarians appear to be on board, the program is still in the planning stage, and it remains to be seen if the institution will succeed in implementing its vision.

Nevertheless, institution C remains an isolated example. As one of the case study librarians explains, the type of relationship building that results in collaboration is generally "hit or miss," and depends on the individual faculty member's receptiveness. Based on the evidence from these case study institutions, librarians' relationships with faculty remain largely unconnected, and fail to involve a critical mass of individuals who are willing to work to achieve information literacy competencies. Relationships with different individuals and groups tend to remain distinct, and they have not coalesced into a base of followers, supporters, or what Kezar (2005, 2006) calls the critical mass necessary for an undertaking at the program level to become self-sustaining over time. Reports in the literature of library and information science show that the course-level relationships described in the case studies are not uncommon (see, e.g., Ferrer-Vinent & Carello, 2008; Millet, Donald, & Wilson, 2009; Stephenson & Caravello, 2007). While participants in these courses tend to describe their relationships as successful, the collaborations rarely extend beyond single courses and are not woven throughout a program. These courses have not produced a snowball effect in that they neither pique the interest of other faculty nor encourage them to seek out librarians to participate in their courses.

Librarians are engaging in a behavior that is precursory to leadership, but they cannot build on these successes to make inroads at the program level. Indeed, some front-line instruction librarians appear to believe that relationship building is an end in itself. In other words, they cultivate relationships, but they are not using those relationships to create a vision for information literacy and influence changes to integrate information literacy throughout the curriculum. As Wijayasundara (2008) comments, "enthusiasm alone is not sufficient to achieve a successful collaboration project" (p. 190). On the other hand, if librarians understand program-level assessment, they could lead faculty by modeling the action and perhaps through professional development trainings.

Institutional Understanding and Involvement

Successful leaders have a strong understanding of the larger organization in which they function. They have a vision and know the key players with whom to partner, what policies are in place to assist in carrying out that vision, and what behaviors or actions are considered acceptable (Frost & Harris, 2003; York-Barr & Duke, 2004). Kriigel and Richards (2008) emphasize the importance of such campus-level involvement for librarians for "gaining an understanding of the organizational topography" (p. 64). According to the case study institutions, some librarians are engaged in activities at a campus-wide level that should provide them opportunities to build more relationships, involve others in leadership, and create supporters in key positions. Others are frustrated in their attempts to get involved at the program and institutional level. At institutions B and C, librarians are highly involved at the institutional level, and the librarians at institution B credited their director with their involvement. The director at institution B made it a priority when she assumed her position to involve the staff in campus-wide committees, which she believes helps to raise the library's profile on campus, and to keep librarians connected to important people and issues on campus. The reference librarian at institution C indicates that all library staff are involved in at least one campus-wide committee; and she serves on the curriculum committee, which, among other things, approves new and revised courses and programs.

While these examples demonstrate involvement that could lead to greater organizational understanding, it is unclear whether librarians use that understanding to influence change. For instance, the librarian at institution C was on the curriculum committee when it developed the policy to incorporate information literacy goals into all new and revised courses. There is no indication that she or the library director helped to initiate that policy. In fact, the charge to create the policy came from the president's office, and seems to have been motivated in part by the focused self-study the institution prepared for their decennial accrediation. At institution A, librarians had previously been involved in a curriculum committee that approved discipline-specific information literacy classes, but the committee dissolved following turnover with the academic dean. The seeming ease with which that committee was disbanded suggests that the program did not have the "critical mass" of campus network support. In both situations, librarians either do not have the organizational knowledge and support to drive change, or they are failing to use it effectively.

On the other hand, librarians at institution D feel disconnected from the larger institution, and somewhat frustrated in their attempts to become more involved. These librarians contend that they have tried to be "more systematic in their outreach" and indicate that they work with academic advisors, departments with capstone projects, and the writing center to promote information literacy services. However, one librarian describes her institution as "reluctant embracers" of information literacy, suggesting that librarians are not finding willing partners. The general sense at this institution is that despite effort on the part of the librarians, outreach efforts have been ineffective.

Creating a Shared Vision

A shared vision is essential to influencing change and creating collaborative relationships (Northouse, 2007; Wijayasundara, 2008), because that vision, together with a set of common goals, motivate and inspire followers to accomplish the vision. Since librarians in the institutions included in this study have not rallied a base of supporters, it is perhaps not surprising that they have not advanced a vision of information literacy that has gained wide support. Indeed, a common vision of information literacy should result in a shared vocabulary, but several librarians interviewed in the case studies express discomfort with the term "information literacy," though they could offer no replacement term. Most contend that faculty do not understand the concept, which suggests an inability or failure to create a consensus or generate buy-in.

The dialogues initiated through focus group interviews at institutions B and D uncovered some misconceptions and areas of concern that need to be addressed before a shared vision can emerge. The focus group interviews offered a good starting point, but the dialogue needs to be sustained in order to move forward from identifying problems to finding solutions. However, this has not occurred. Indeed, a librarian from institution D commented that some of the focus group interviews centered on learning outcomes within the major. Such a conversation could have provided an opportunity for librarians to become involved at the program level if they had continued the dialogue as Smith (2001) recommends, but thus far they have not. By not following up on these initial conversations, librarians are forfeiting another leadership opportunity.

Institution C has the most fully developed and widely held vision of information literacy of the institutions included here. Throughout the institution, faculty, librarians, and administrators agree that information literacy competencies are important and necessary for all of their students. As such, they are committed to integrating learning outcomes for information literacy into courses and programs, beginning with new and revised courses as they are submitted to the curriculum committee. Librarians and senior administrators agree that faculty on their campus understand the information literacy competencies and are integrating learning outcomes for information literacy explicitly into their courses, with plans to work toward program-level integration. This institution undertook a selected topics self-study in 2002, in which the institution, with the Middle States Commission's approval, reviews in-depth two or three areas of interest, rather than a comprehensive review of the entire institution. In its 2002 study, institution C focused on information literacy, even before the current standards of the Middle States Commission went into effect, demonstrating early adoption. At the time of that self-study, the information literacy study group, comprised of faculty, librarians, and staff from across campus, developed a local definition of information literacy, which is as follows:

> Information literacy is a set of abilities people employ in situations ranging from specialized research activities to the routines of daily life. As a result, they can recognize when information is needed, and then locate, evaluate, and use effectively and ethically that information. Specifically, an information-literate person must be able to (1) determine the extent of the information needed, (2) access that information effectively and efficiently, (3) evaluate the information and its sources critically, (4) selectively incorporate the information into one's knowledge base, (5) use the information effectively to accomplish a specific purpose, and (6) understand the economic, legal, and social issues surrounding the use of information, ultimately employing it ethically and legally. In his or her research, the information-literate person will interact successfully with material available through oral, printed, visual, and electronic technologies. Information-literate individuals are also able to continually update and apply information literacy skills throughout their lifetime for both career and civic needs.

Although this definition draws heavily on the ACRL standards (American Library Association, Association of College and Research Libraries, 2000), by drafting its own definition, the institution was able to address "local concerns" and emphasize areas of importance to the college's mission. The definition therefore became a first step in creating a vision for information literacy on the campus by aligning the generic definition with the specific focuses and concerns of the institution. Institution C is the only one among the case studies at which librarians, faculty, and administrators asserted in the interviews that faculty and staff across campus understand information literacy and work to integrate it into the curriculum.

Taking Risks

There is little evidence in the case studies of librarians taking calculated risks or challenging established ideas in order to promote information literacy. The fact that most collaborations between faculty and librarians remain at the course level, and that librarians do not seem to act on what organizational knowledge they have, suggests that many of them may indeed be unwilling to venture away from the relationships and spheres of influence with which they are familiar and comfortable. Mader (1996), however, argues that the willingness to take risks is especially important for library leaders. She notes a study that surveyed librarians using a framework of leadership traits developed for corporate leaders. While librarians consider many of the proposed traits (vision, communication, self-confidence, and trust) essential, they also valued risk taking, which was not part of the corporate framework. Likewise, Mader (1996) refers to an active learning session at the 1996 LOEX conference in which librarians identified the willingness to take risks and responsibility, as well as being able to create an environment in which it is okay to fail, as the second-most important of 19 general attributes needed by instruction librarians.

Despite claiming to value risk taking, librarians do not provide many examples of it in the arena of information literacy. Rather, there are some examples of risk-adverse behavior. For instance, one librarian at institution A expresses concern over anticipated changes to information literacy policies, but appears unwilling to ask the dean directly, despite the fact that the changes directly impact her instructional activities. The librarian has strong feelings about the changes and the role of the library, but she seemed to be afraid to state her views to the dean. Ironically, she had previously stated that she had a good working relationship with the dean.

When planning focus group interviews with faculty, librarians at institution D chose not to conduct the interviews themselves, but rather coordinated them with another department. Initially, the librarians contended that they do not have experience administering focus group interviews, and for this reason, they asked the director of the writing program to be facilitator. Upon further discussion, one librarian expressed her belief that the director of the writing program has more "cachet" with faculty than do librarians. She believes the faculty accepted him more readily than they would have the librarians because he has a doctoral degree and had worked previously as a faculty member. In essence, the librarians are reluctant to engage directly with faculty on the assumption that faculty would not "accept" them. This unwillingness led to some missed opportunities during the focus group interviews. While the librarians are pleased overall with the work of the writing center director, they admit that he did not always guide the interviews as they would have liked. They indicate that several times, faculty made some point about information literacy that they would have liked to investigate further, but the writing director did not follow up on it. For his part, the director pointed out in his interview that he is not an expert on information literacy. By letting him represent the library on this topic, the librarians certainly let a leadership opportunity pass.

This same director of writing has observed risk-adverse behavior in librarians. He contends that, when faculty request the support of one of the writing fellows from his program, he "has no trouble" setting out conditions for the faculty to meet before he would grant their request. The librarians expressed surprise that he would do this, and he believes librarians and others involved in faculty support tend to rush to comply with faculty requests, and are often reluctant to set conditions or to counter with requests of their own. It appears that the librarians worry that if they do not agree to work with the faculty under the faculty's conditions, they may not be asked again. The writing director further states that "it's occurred to me more than once that librarians can afford to be more forthcoming than they sometimes are and operate from a position of greater strength regarding what they have to offer faculty and their students." Since current efforts to build a base of supporters and create a vision do not seem to be succeeding, it may be necessary for librarians to take risks to achieve their learning goals.

SUPPORT FROM ADMINISTRATORS AND FACULTY

Creating a culture that facilitates collaboration between librarians and faculty and allows for integration of information literacy into the curriculum depends on curricular and policy changes over which faculty and senior administrators have control. Finding ways to influence faculty is essential to the success of information literacy and outcomes assessment. Librarians do not have the kind of ongoing contact with students that faculty have. Even when they teach credit-bearing courses, most librarians do not have student advisory responsibilities, and the courses they teach often entail less than a full semester. Faculty have the most interactions with students. They design the assignments, and because they assign grades, faculty often have the greatest motivational influence on students. Perhaps most importantly, however, faculty have control over the curriculum. Ultimately, faculty and curriculum committees, which are comprised mostly of faculty, make decisions about the content and learning outcomes for the curriculum, and as such, their buy-in is essential for information literacy to be integrated. By engaging in relationship building and collaboration, librarians at case study institutions attempt to garner faculty support, but such efforts have not yet led to widespread success. Front-line librarians who are generally responsible for information literacy within the library do not often have the clout to make such changes, nor do they create a vision that others would follow. Rather, librarians at the case study institutions repeatedly point to high-level administrators throughout the institution as having been vital in bringing attention to information literacy.

Several librarians at institution B indicate that their current director has been instrumental in raising the profile of the library and involving library staff at the wider campus level. They credit her for getting library staff onto institutional committees, including a campus-wide curriculum committee and the faculty senate. Likewise, a librarian at institution A notes that when the stand-alone information literacy course was introduced at her institution, the dean at the time created an information literacy subcommittee of the curriculum committee that had the authority to approve any new designated information literacy courses. When that dean left, the new dean dissolved the subcommittee and does all course approval herself, underscoring the importance of support at the upper levels of administration.

Such support is widely acknowledged at institution C, where librarians credit academic deans, the provost, and the president for creating an institutional culture that supports information literacy. The president of institution C issued the initial charge to integrate information literacy into all new and revised courses, setting the course for further integration at the program level. Two academic deans participated in case study interviews and talked knowledgeably about information literacy, repeatedly commenting that it is part of the culture on their campus. That fact that institution C has made the most progress toward integrating information literacy at the program and institutional levels and is the only institution at which interviewees agree that information literacy is a part of the culture attests to the importance of strong support of the senior administrators.

Indeed, the example of institution C lends credence to the idea that front-line librarians cannot create widespread change for information literacy on their own, but need the assistance of senior administrators and faculty. As Hardesty (1995) notes, in relationships with faculty, librarians are not usually in a position of strength; and while they can offer suggestions or support, they cannot insist on change. Writing from a faculty perspective, Smith (2001) suggests that, as institutions identify and develop learning outcomes, they create an opportunity for greater librarian involvement. He contends that departmental faculty might be receptive to librarian involvement, but the onus is on librarians to approach faculty and explicitly identify how the library can support teaching, because faculty are unlikely to identify librarians as teaching partners. Still, librarians need a shared vision before they can move information literacy to program or institutional levels.

While Smith's (2001) faith in faculty responsiveness is reassuring, other writers point out that instruction librarians have worked with faculty to deliver information literacy instruction for years and yet, in the vast majority of institutions, those relationships have not progressed beyond the course level or become part of the larger curriculum (Badke, 2005; McGuinness, 2007). McGuinness (2007) is skeptical of an approach that relies on individual faculty to become "academic champions" of information literacy, and insists that librarians must work with senior administrators, including library directors, deans, and provosts, to permeate the institutional culture.

Bloomberg and MacDonald (2004) describe a successful effort to implement an assessment program at one institution. According to their approach, senior institutional administrators set the context by initiating discussion with faculty, providing opportunities for learning, and creating a shared vision for assessment. Eventually, with support from the administration, a team of faculty and staff, including the library director, convened to define a set of cross-curricular learning outcomes for students, which included information literacy. The team developed rubrics against which to measure student learning for each outcome, and then began a pilot program to integrate instruction for those outcomes into the classroom. Such collaboration and partnering could serve as a model for other organizations. However, the process that Bloomberg and Mac-Donald (2004) illustrate is time- and budget-intense, which underscores the need for senior administrators to support it and make the necessary resources available. From this perspective, it is incumbent on senior administrators to take initiative and offer a way to encourage faculty and librarians for outcomes assessment to succeed. Without that support, front-line librarians may be leaders at some level, but their efforts are unlikely to be widely successful.

The role of front-line instruction librarians might be to inform those to whom they report, directors and assistant directors, who in turn can bring issues to the attention of senior administrators and faculty. Administrators oversee the policies, procedures, and reward systems within which the institution operates, and thus their support is essential to promoting change in the organization. For instance, many institutions of higher education are structured to reward individual efforts, which creates competition among faculty and between departments. Likewise, individuals and departments wishing to collaborate may not be able to share budget money easily, or may not have access to the same technology software and support. As such, administrators may need to rework some internal infrastructure to establish and maintain a culture of collaboration (Kezar, 2005, 2006). Administrators might also offer incentives to encourage faculty to address information literacy within their courses and programs. Perhaps most importantly, however, through their actions, administrators establish the culture of the broader organization. If they treat information literacy as a priority, others are likely to follow.

Incentives and Rewards

It is important to note that, although librarians cannot change the overall reward system of an institution, some libraries have instituted their own reward and incentive system as a way of reaching out to colleagues. Indeed, four self-studies, one of which was also a case study institution, mentioned library-initiated incentives for faculty to integrate information literacy. For instance, one university library awards faculty stipends. According to the library's website, by accepting the stipends, faculty agree to collaborate with a librarian, develop information literacy learning outcomes for their course, prepare a written report for the library, and participate in a panel discussion (Weinberg Memorial Library, 2009). As of 2009, the program has been in place for five years. Kriigel and Richards (2008) describe a similar program at their institution in which a faculty member who has been a "distinguished friend of the library" is honored by a luncheon. Institution C implemented an award program for students in which the best student paper receives a monetary award. Each of these incentive and award programs brings attention to the library and helps to get other constituents involved. Further, the fact that the library is willing to put money into supporting these programs underscores its commitment.

EXTERNAL PRESSURE

In addition to leadership from individuals and groups on campus, pressure from external organizations can provide important motivation to drive wide-scale change. Kezar (2006) found that disciplinary and professional societies, grant-offering foundations, business, and government could all make an impact on institutions. She contends that "the pressure from accreditors was a major source of support for administrators and faculty ... but in particular, it held sway with administrators who saw a poor accreditation report affecting institutional reputation" (p. 825).

Interviewees at all four case study institutions indicate that external pressures such as those emanating from the Middle States Commission's standards bring attention to information literacy on their campuses. In addition, librarians and the dean of general education at institution A identify a system-wide mandate as crucial to their cause. In fact, the librarian contends that the information literacy course "would not have happened" without the impetus of the statewide mandate. Issued in 2000, the mandate outlines 10 core competencies for all students, including information literacy. With the authority of such a charge to support them, the librarians instituted a required credit-bearing information literacy course. Even when the mandate was revised, and information literacy no longer had to be addressed separately but could be integrated into general education, the original mandate created enough momentum that the institution retains its existing course.

At each of the other case study institutions, the Middle States Commission's standards offer the librarians similar leverage. Two of the institutions indicated that initial efforts at information literacy grew out of recommendations from visiting team reports during accreditation visits. In each case, once the Middle States Commission expressed concerns over the levels of information literacy and library involvement, the campus took action. At one institution, librarians were charged with developing a plan to introduce information literacy into the curriculum. In both cases, the library received more resources—either in terms of money, or through renovations—and the overall profile of the library on campus was raised.

These examples demonstrate that accreditation standards can be effective in motivating change within institutions. By setting standards and expectations, accreditation organizations might encourage reflection and dialogue across campus as constituents consider how to meet those standards. In addition, when the visiting teams representing accreditation organizations express concern over institutional performance as they did with institutions B and C, they bring the issue to the attention of senior administrators and drive them to address it. In a way, pressure from accreditation organizations may create demand for and facilitate the emergence of leaders. Ratteray (2002) notes that some librarians want the Middle States Commission to enforce collaboration and learning goals related to information literacy, thereby helping librarians to circumvent faculty reticence. However, he maintains that such enforcement is "a role the Commission does not advocate for itself except as a last resort" (p. 369). In fact, it is unclear whether such enforcement would be as effective as librarians anticipate because faculty may not be especially responsive to mandates.

Indeed, while librarians at case study institutions, and to some extent administrators including academic deans, assert that accreditation standards are a driving force, the faculty did not place much emphasis on accreditation. For instance, when asked what motivated the creation of designated information literacy courses, the faculty member teaching the East Asian course at institution A contended that the Middle States Commission standards are not a big factor. Rather, she maintains that the courses were developed in response to perceived needs on the part of students to learn these competencies. Likewise, a faculty member at institution B indicates the stand-alone information literacy course at his institution was created because faculty recognize that students need additional support for research projects. In both cases, the faculty view efforts for information literacy as self-motivated, and describe courses as a response to student needs, not compliance to a mandate.

These faculty responses align with Colbeck's (2002) findings with regard to faculty and administrator reactions to state policies in Ohio and Tennessee, both of which have enacted system-wide policies on teaching. Specifically, the Ohio Board of Regents enacted a mandate that requires institutions to increase time faculty spend teaching, while Tennessee has had a policy in place since 1979 that financially rewards institutions for successful performance across a range of indicators, including student learning and satisfaction. In comparing responses to Ohio's mandates to increase faculty teaching time with Tennessee's incentive program, which offers merit funding to high-performing institutions, Colbeck (2002) finds that external pressures and mandates can be sources of tension and lead to resistance. Mandates, she notes, require enforcement, and imply that the targeted institution can and should engage in the prescribed behavior, but will not do so unless forced. She describes mandates as inflexible and warns that they often "lead to reduced motivation to exceed minimum standards set by the policy or to outright resistance" (p. 5). In addition, Colbeck (2002) finds that mandates sometimes anger faculty, who view them as an affront to their professional expertise and authority. As such, she concludes that "faculty were not likely to be responsive to externally imposed orders" (p. 11). Further, senior administrators sometimes take steps to "buffer" faculty from the direct impact of mandates. For instance, administrators in some Ohio universities simply had staff change the way that faculty report time spent teaching—rather than changing actual time in the classroom—to conform with the mandates. Bloomberg and McDonald (2004) similarly assert that external forces such as accreditation standards are not effective motivators for faculty. They contend that faculty value student success and view issues like accreditation standards and state mandates as "peripheral" and "relegated to the 'administrative side'" (p. 259).

The implication is that accreditation organizations and senior administrators play a key role in creating a context for change within institutions, but they must find a balance between applying pressure with incentives for change and trying to force change through mandates. At case study institutions, the accreditation standards seem to bring the issue of information literacy to the attention of administrators, lending credence to librarians' promotion of the topic and influencing administrators to address information literacy with faculty and curriculum committees. Thus, external pressures function best as a way to open up dialogues on campus (Kezar, 2005, 2006). Administrators and other interested constituents can use those pressures to argue for their projects, much as Ratteray (2002) seems to intend when he stated that the Middle States Commission prefers "that institutions consistently drive their own engines for change" (p. 369). For instance, rather than arguing the importance of information literacy solely from a library perspective, librarians can point to the necessity of addressing information literacy for accreditation. They can align library goals with institutional goals and define ways that the library can support the institution in reaching those goals. In this way, accreditation standards would provide a context for librarians to reach out to faculty and begin or further discussions on information literacy. Such discussions, however, would be only a starting point for librarians to generate faculty awareness and interest in the topic of information literacy. Librarians would then need to move discussions toward creating a concrete vision which could then be put into action.

CONCLUSION

Integrating information literacy at the program and institutional levels and developing or deepening collaborative relationships between faculty and librarians often requires changes to curricula and policies that amount to changes in the institutional culture. As noted in the previous chapter, institutional cultures are deeply ingrained and difficult to change. As such, effective leaders must emerge who can rally followers around a shared vision and influence those followers to accomplish that vision. The evidence from the case studies suggests that front-line librarians do not have the status or clout to inspire such change. Although librarians have had some limited success with faculty at the course level, they have developed neither a convincing or shared vision of information literacy nor a network of followers who would work toward that vision.

Institutions that have made the most progress in developing information literacy programs, such as institution C, are those at which administrators such as academic deans and provosts have taken an interest in information literacy and have worked with faculty and librarians to create a vision and a plan for achieving integration into the curriculum. Through campus-wide dialogues, changes in policy, and the creation of incentives, administrators facilitate the adoption of information literacy and garner the buy-in of faculty. Without such high-level support, integration beyond the course level is unlikely.

Such support is not widespread, however. The issue remains that faculty and administrators on many campuses have not been persuaded of the necessity of information literacy as a learning outcome. While librarians engage in relationship building as a means to bring information literacy to the attention of faculty and administrators, most interviewees at the case study institutions insist that external pressure from accreditation organizations and statewide mandates is essential. The evidence suggests that leadership for information literacy depends on the combined efforts of senior administrators, faculty, librarians, and even external forces such as accreditation organizations.

The next chapter, the conclusion of this study, examines the influences that facilitate and discourage the integration of information literacy into campus cultures, and it suggests steps for further integration.

NOTES

1. For a more extensive discussion, see Kezar, Carducci, and Contreras-McGavin (2006).

REFERENCES

American Library Association, Association of College and Research Libraries. (2000). *Information literacy competency standards for higher education.* Retrieved from http://www.ala.org/ala/mgrps/divs/acrl/standards/information literacycompetency.cfm

Badke, W. B. (2005). Can't get no respect: Helping faculty to understand the educational power of information literacy. *Reference Librarian, 43*(89–90), 63–80. Retrieved from InformaWorld.

Bass, B. M. (1990). *Bass and Stodgill's handbook of leadership: A survey of theory and research.* New York, NY: Free Press.

Bennis, W. G., & Nanus, B. (1985). *Leaders: Strategies for taking charge.* New York, NY: Harper & Row.

Bloomberg, S., & McDonald, M. (2004). Assessment: A case study in synergy. In P. Hernon & R. E. Dugan (Eds.), *Outcomes assessment in higher education: Views and perspectives* (pp. 259–289). Westport, CT: Libraries Unlimited.

Brown, T. (1995). Great leaders need great followers. *Industry Week/IW, 244*(16), 25–29. Retrieved from Ebsco.

Clark, D. (2008). *Concepts of leadership.* Retrieved from http://www.nwlink.com/~donclark/leader/leadcon.html

Colbeck, C. L. (2002). State policies to improve undergraduate teaching: Faculty and administrator responses. *Journal of Higher Education, 73*(1), 3–25. Retrieved from Project MUSE.

Donaldson, G. A., Jr. (2007). What do teachers bring to leadership? *Educational Leadership, 65*(1), 26–29. Retrieved from Ebsco.

Dozier, T. K. (2007). Turning good teachers into great leaders. *Educational Leadership, 65*(1), 54–58. Retrieved from Ebsco.

Ferrer-Vinent, I. J., & Carello, C. (2008). Embedded library instruction in a first-year biology laboratory course. *Science and Technology Libraries, 28*(4), 325–351. Retrieved from Informaworld.

Fister, B., Hutchens, E. O., & MacPherson, K. H. (2001). From BI to IL: The paths of two liberal arts colleges. In H. Thompson (Ed.), *Crossing the divide: Proceedings of the tenth national conference of the association of college and research libraries* (pp. 203–212). Chicago, IL: Association of College and Research Libraries. Retrieved from http://www.ala.org/ala/mgrps/divs/acrl/events/pdf/fister.pdf

Fowler, C. S., & Walter, S. (2003). Instructional leadership: New responsibilities for a new reality. *College and Research Libraries News, 64*(7), 465–468. Retrieved from H. W. Wilson.

Frost, D., & Harris, A. (2003). Teacher leadership: Towards a research agenda. *Cambridge Journal of Education, 33*(3), 479–498. Retrieved from Ebsco.

Gardner, J. W. (1990). *On leadership.* New York, NY: Free Press.

Hardesty, L. (1995). Faculty culture and bibliographic instruction: An exploratory analysis. *Library Trends, 44*(2), 339–368. Retrieved from Gale.

Horner, M. (1997). Leadership theory: Past, present and future. *Team Performance Management, 3*(4), 270–287. Retrieved from Emerald.

Kezar, A. (2005). Redesigning for collaboration within higher education institutions: An exploration into the developmental process. *Research in Higher Education, 46*(7), 831–860. Retrieved from Ebsco.

Kezar, A. (2006). Redesigning for collaboration and learning initiatives: An examination of four highly collaborative campuses. *Journal of Higher Education, 77*(5), 804–838. Retrieved from ProQuest.

Kezar, A., Carducci, R., & Contreras-McGavin, M. (2006). *Rethinking the "L" word in higher education: The revolution of research on leadership.* San Francisco, CA: Jossey-Bass.

Kouzes, J. M., & Posner, B. Z. (2002). *The leadership challenge.* San Francisco, CA: Jossey-Bass.

Kriigel, B. J., & Richards, T. F. (2008). From isolation to engagement: Strategy, structure and process. In P. Hernon & R. R. Powell (Eds.), *Convergence and collaboration of campus information services* (pp. 63–79). Westport, CT: Libraries Unlimited.

Mader, S. (1996). Instruction librarians: Leadership in the new organization. *RQ, 36,* 192–197.

McGuinness, C. (2007). Exploring strategies for integrated information literacy. *Communications in Information Literacy, 1*(1), 26–38. Retrieved from http://www.comminfolit.org/index.php/cil/article/view/Spring2007AR3/14

Middle States Commission on Higher Education. (2003). *Developing research and communication skills: Guidelines for information literacy in the curriculum.* Philadelphia, PA: Author.

Millet, M. S., Donald, J., & Wilson, D. W. (2009). Information literacy across the curriculum: Expanding horizons. *College and Undergraduate Libraries, 16* (2–3), 180–193.

Northouse, P. G. (2007). *Leadership: Theory and practice* (4th ed.). Thousand Oaks, CA: Sage Publishing.

Ratteray, O. M. T. (2002). Information literacy in self-study and accreditation. *Journal of Academic Librarianship, 28*(6), 368–375. Retrieved from H. W. Wilson.

Saal, F. E., & Knight, P. A. (1988). *Industrial/organizational psychology: Science and practice.* Pacific Grove, CA: Brooks/Cole Publishing.

Smith, K. R. (2001). New roles and responsibilities for the university library: Advancing student learning through outcomes assessment. *Journal of Library Administration, 35*(4), 29–36. Retrieved from InformaWorld.

Stephenson, E., & Caravello, P. S. (2007). Incorporating data literacy into undergraduate information literacy programs in the social sciences. *Reference Services Review, 35*(4), 525–540.

Stewart, D. (1994). *Faculty responsibility and evaluation.* Retrieved from http://www.ohio.edu/POLICY/18-009.html

Tennessee Higher Education Commission. (n.d.). *Performance funding frequently asked questions.* Retrieved from http://www.tn.gov/moa/strGrp_prefFund.shtml

Weinberg Memorial Library. (2009). *Information literacy grants awarded.* Retrieved from http://academic.scranton.edu/department/wml/ARCHIVED/features/spring06s-4.html

Wijayasundara, N. D. (2008). Faculty-library collaboration: A model for University of Colombo. *International Information and Library Review, 40*(3), 188–198. Retrieved from ScienceDirect.

York-Barr, J., & Duke, K. (2004). What do we know about teacher leadership? Findings from two decades of scholarship. *Review of Educational Research, 74*(3), 255–316. Retrieved from ProQuest.

CHAPTER 12

Looking to the Future

Government, students and parents, employers, and others demand evidence that colleges and universities achieve their missions and goals, and that students graduate with the knowledge, "abilities, habits of mind, ways of knowing, attitudes, values, and other dispositions" (Maki, 2004, p. 3) they need to succeed in their work and personal lives. Institutions provide evidence of achievement by defining learning outcomes, or the knowledge, abilities, and skill sets that students demonstrate at the course, program, and institutional levels; and assessing progress toward meeting those outcomes. Institutions have different missions that shape the learning goals for that organization, and therefore have different learning goals. However, at the broadest level, several competency areas (e.g., critical thinking, quantitative reasoning, and written and oral communication) are widely recognized as important for all students to attain, regardless of major or program of study (National Leadership Council for Liberal Education and America's Promise, 2007). Information literacy is one area of outcomes assessment that is consistently identified as important for success in a knowledge economy and information-abundant environment (American Psychological Association, 2002; Lumina Foundation, 2011; National Leadership Council for Liberal Education and America's Promise, 2007; Project on Accreditation and Assessment, 2004; Schneider, 2010). Because it is just one among several competencies identified as important to all students, it remains for institutions, their faculty, and staff to decide how to prioritize information literacy among the many competing demands on their time, resources, budgets, and educational practices to ensure that students graduate with the competencies they need.

While institutions are individually responsible for their own success, accreditation organizations help ensure quality and facilitate improvement by establishing standards and requiring institutions to reflect on their practices and gather and report data that indicate how they meet specific accreditation standards and where they need to improve. In other words, accreditation organizations have a responsibility to their stakeholders, constituent institutions, and the public to facilitate and promote quality and improvement in higher education. Ewell (2001) contends that "accreditation must adopt a visible and proactive stance with respect to assuring acceptable levels of student academic achievement ... [g]iven escalating stakeholder demands, nothing less will prove sufficient to maintain the public credibility" (p. 2)

However, the extent to which stakeholder demands have influenced institutions to define and assess learning outcomes for information literacy remains unclear. Discussion of information literacy is fairly widespread in self-studies. Among the reports reviewed, more than half of the institutions mention the concept as a desirable outcome for students. Nevertheless, the language is not widely backed by action, indicating that while information literacy has entered the lexicon of higher education, it has not yet permeated the culture of most institutions. While institutions discuss information literacy in the context of their curricula and goals, few define information literacy as a separate learning outcome, or assess learning for information literacy content. While the Middle States Commission (2003) indicates that information literacy should be addressed at all levels of the curriculum, and is relevant to all disciplines and fields of study, most instruction for information literacy consists of one-shot sessions dependent on the invitation of interested faculty. As such, instructors specializing in information literacy cannot sequence offerings to build on previous skills and knowledge. This approach to information literacy is not consistent with the expectations of the Middle States Commission (2003). In fact, most of the handful of colleges and universities that have program-integrated information literacy are accredited by organizations other than the Middle States Commission. That information literacy is included in accreditation standards does not imply that all institutions need to approach information literacy in the same way. The Middle States Commission (2003) appreciates that institutional missions vary, and each institution, program, and academic discipline has different goals and expectations related to learning outcomes for information literacy depending on their missions. However, these goals need to be identified and articulated in order for institutions to prepare for systematic assessment that will help determine if the goals are achieved. Without assessment based on specific learning outcomes, institutions are not accountable for information literacy.

As a further complication, data showing the extent to which students are information literate are not easily accessible or widely disseminated. No organization collects aggregate data for learning outcomes related to information literacy, and institutional responses to requests for information were uneven. Despite public pressure for increased accountability and transparency, many institutions are unwilling to share information with the public or researchers, even with the assurance of confidentiality.

The fact that information literacy has not progressed beyond the course level at most institutions, let alone become part of the institutional culture, suggests a lack of leadership and shared vision, a failure to understand assessment, and a mischaracterization of evaluation as assessment. As defined in Chapter 8, assessment involves the systematic gathering, analyzing, and interpreting of evidence to gauge progress toward meeting a specific, measurable standard such as those set by accreditation organizations. Front-line librarians alone cannot achieve high-level integrated and collaborative instruction beyond the course level. They need support from their directors, other senior administrators, and accreditation organizations, as well as widespread buy-in and support of faculty. This realization may spur those in administrative positions to work more closely with librarians and teaching faculty to determine how to facilitate a more widespread integration of information literacy. Accreditation organizations may also reexamine their role of influencing change on campus. While many individuals view accreditation organizations as catalysts for change, the organizations themselves seem hesitant to enforce their own standards, leaving institutions with large leeway in how they implement those standards. Perhaps accreditation organizations can engage in discussions with faculty, librarians, and administrators to determine whether they can facilitate and inspire change without resorting to mandates. Such discussion might result in a companion publication to *Developing Research and Communication Skills* (Middle States Commission, 2003) and *Student Learning Assessment* (Middle States Commission, 2007). Additionally, accreditation organizations need to offer more training in assessment research to visiting team members and hold them more accountable for determining whether institutions are truly meeting their missions and goals.

Librarians and some stakeholders increasingly recognize information literacy as an essential competency to survive and succeed in an information-rich world. Institutions of higher education have a crucial role to play in ensuring that students acquire these competencies through a systematic instruction program, and have a responsibility to inform the public of the achievement gained from learning goals. This study suggests that, although some progress is being made, many institutions still have much work to attain an integrated information literacy program. Through an examination of information literacy as a learning outcome, this study draws attention to the issue as outlined by the Middle States Commission (2003). The results of this study may encourage faculty, administrators, librarians, and even accreditation organizations to reconsider the place of information literacy on campuses. While broad discussion at the regional or national level may be useful in bringing wider attention to the topic, it is critical for those involved in student learning at individual institutions to examine the role of information literacy within their own campus context, if they regard information literacy as a learning goal. In addition, these findings may spark discussion among those involved about why information literacy initiatives are stalled at the course level, as well as what steps must be taken and who must be involved to progress beyond this level. As such, this study could encourage those interested in learning outcomes for information literacy as they take steps toward implementing or expanding information literacy initiatives on their campus.

INFORMATION LITERACY IN CONTEXT

Over the last two decades, the standards of regional accreditation organizations have placed increased emphasis on information literacy as a student learning outcome (Gratch-Lindauer, 2000; Saunders, 2007). At the same time, analysis of the workplace and job ads indicates that employers value the skills, knowledge, and abilities associated with information literacy, even if they do not always use that phrase (Crawford & Irving, 2009). Klusek and Bornstein (2006) reviewed job postings from the business sector and concluded that, although they do not use the term, employers look for qualifications related to information literacy in new hires. The American Association of Colleges and Universities (AAC&U) president agrees, stating that information literacy is one of several new competencies that employers are demanding and which are essential to "success in today's workplace" (Schneider, 2010, section 2, para. 5), while the Lumina Foundation (2011) asserts that "both expressive activities and cognitive functions of analysis require students to use information resources effectively" (p. 8). The North Central Association of Schools and Colleges (2003) acknowledges the transition to a knowledge economy, where "what is valued is the knowledge worker's capacity to sift and winnow massive amounts of information to discover or create new or better understandings" (p. 3.2-12). A more recent and more high-profile acknowledgement comes from President Obama (National Information Literacy Awareness Month, 2009), who underscores his support for the concept in a presidential proclamation declaring October 2009 as National Information Literacy Awareness Month. Noting that people are bombarded with vast amounts of information, he asserts that "[r]ather than merely possessing data, we must also learn the skills necessary to acquire, collate, and evaluate information for any situation" (National Information Literacy Awareness Month, 2009, para. 1). Further, the president emphasizes the role of institutions of education in promoting information literacy, contending that "[i]n addition to the basic skills of reading, writing, and arithmetic, it is equally important that our students are given the tools required to take advantage of the information available to them" (National Information Literacy Awareness Month, 2009, para. 3).

Despite this attention to information literacy, most institutions do not engage in a coordinated and systematic approach to it. Educators recognize that students generally come to college without information literacy skills. In particular, research shows that college students are often unable to read or understand citations, do not understand methods of organizing information, and lack abilities to find and evaluate information (Asher, Duke, & Green, 2010). Still, while over half of the institutions nationwide mention information literacy in their accreditation documents, actual engagement in instruction and assessment is uneven. Nearly all instruction of information literacy happens at the undergraduate course level. Little direct assessment of information literacy occurs, with some institutions confusing course evaluations with direct assessment of student learning.

The Middle States Commission (2003) stresses the importance of collaboration between faculty and librarians for information literacy. While the self-studies refer often to collaboration, it remains largely at the course level, and partnerships of the type depicted in Figure 1.1 remain rare. Instead, much information literacy instruction takes place through one-shot sessions or credit-bearing classes that are not well integrated into the larger curriculum. In fact, when discussing information literacy, self-studies often use the word "program" to describe what is essentially an unconnected and nonsequential array of courses and in-class sessions. As such, these institutions are not yet fulfilling the Middle States Commission's standards for information literacy as a program or institutional learning outcome.

The current state of information literacy in the institutions examined here stands in stark contrast to the emphasis that stakeholders place on the concept. Despite the consistent recognition of its importance by stakeholders, this inability to achieve integrated information literacy suggests a vacuum of leadership for information literacy in these institutions. Indeed, Todd (1999) notes the impact that new technologies and the explosive increase in information production have had on society, and he suggests that restructuring education to meet these challenges "may be the key leadership challenge of education for the next millennium" (p. 4).

CURRENT ISSUES

The question remains, "Why is the concept of information literacy not addressed more consistently and thoroughly within higher education?" It may be that programs and institutions focus on other learning outcomes, (e.g., global citizenry, critical thinking, or problem solving), and do not view information literacy as a high priority. Institutions that do want to increase attention to information literacy face two main barriers to integrating it: a confusion over ownership, and a leadership vacuum. The self-studies and case studies show no clear agreement on who should be responsible for information literacy within the institution, nor have leaders emerged who influence individuals at the broad program and institutional levels to work toward an integrated information literacy program built around a shared vision. As a result, most information literacy programs have not gone beyond the course level.

Ownership and Information Literacy

Librarians have long promoted and championed information literacy, and the concept is heavily associated with librarianship. Several of the competencies associated with information literacy, such as the ability to locate and access information, are rooted in traditional bibliographic instruction in which librarians have been engaged at least since the early twentieth century. As attention to information literacy from accreditation organizations increases, some librarians see information literacy as an opportunity for academic libraries to raise their profile and perhaps regain centrality on their campuses (Badke, 2005; Owusu-Ansah, 2007; Smith, 2001). While many librarians seek to take advantage of the opportunities to engage in instruction and curriculum planning, they may unintentionally reinforce the view that information literacy is nothing more than library skills. The association between information literacy and libraries may lead many faculty to believe that information literacy is not their purview but that it can be addressed entirely by librarians, despite strong assertions that the responsibility must be shared.

The Middle States Commission (2003) asserts that information literacy is a much larger concept than library skills or bibliographic instruction. To fully address the six competencies of information literacy identified by both the Middle States Commission (2003) and ACRL (American Library Association, Association of College and Research Libraries, 2000), institutions cannot rely solely on librarians (Middle States Commission, 2003; Ratteray, 2002; Stanger, 2009). By believing that faculty and librarians share joint responsibility for information literacy instruction and assessment (see Figure 1.1), the Middle States Commission (2003) implies that faculty and librarians share ownership of the concept. Likewise, ACRL (American Library Association, Association of College and Research Libraries, 2000) underscores the importance of collaboration for information literacy, stating that "incorporating information literacy across curricula, in all programs and services, and throughout the administrative life of the university, requires the collaborative efforts of faculty, librarians, and administrators" (section 3, para. 3).

Indeed, faculty involvement is the lynchpin of integration for information literacy. Faculty own the curriculum at most colleges and universities, and without their support, information literacy will be treated as an add-on or an afterthought. Asher, Duke, and Green (2010) underscore the importance of collaboration for information literacy, stating it is necessary because of "librarians' structural placement as marginal to students' academic world" (section 7, para. 6). In fact, they find that librarians are chronically overlooked by students and conclude that "professors play a central role in brokering the relationship between students and librarians" (Asher, Duke, & Green, 2010, section 7, para. 5). Ratteray (2005) affirms the centrality of faculty to information literacy when he states that "faculty and students are at the center of this learning universe, and librarians are important supporters and facilitators" (para. 3). Further, he contends that the "real" meaning of information literacy goes "way beyond anything having to do with a library or 'research' in its technical library-based sense" (para. 3), and that information literacy is in fact "75% or more about teaching and learning and only about 25% or less about anything the library or information professionals bring to the mix" (Ratteray, 2008, section 5, para. 3).

Many librarians espouse the same view. Stanger (2009) contends that much of the ACRL (2000) framework for information literacy "falls under the instructional control of disciplinary faculty" (p. 4). Likewise, Fister, Hutchens, and MacPherson (2001) assert that "the main goal is to hand over ownership of information literacy to the faculty because for the most part its success is in their hands. The librarians will help—as they have for decades—but the faculty are the ones who will work most closely with the students on the whole [educational] process" (p. 208). These authors reaffirm the importance of moving information literacy from a "library-based program into a cross-campus enterprise with wider ownership, seeking not just buy-in but leadership and engagement beyond the walls of the library" (p. 204). The practice on most campuses, however, rarely reflects such collaboration and faculty centrality.

Most faculty are not engaged in information literacy. Bruce (2001) notes that higher-education journals outside the discipline of library and information science (LIS) rarely address information literacy. She suggests that "the transformation of the information literacy agenda from a library-centered issue to a mainstream educational issue is only beginning" (p. 113). Simply stated, faculty do not always view "their instructional territory as explicitly including the dimensions of information literacy delineated by ACRL" (Stanger, 2009, p. 3). In fact, the broad definition and emphasis on cross-curriculum application of information literacy may be a barrier to integrating it. The generic nature of the competencies may persuade faculty that information literacy falls outside of their disciplines and therefore should be addressed elsewhere (Snavely & Cooper, 1997; Stanger, 2009). ACRL maintains that the framework does not need to be accepted as a whole but can be refined as needed, by picking out selected competency areas. Further, ACRL tries to assist in the process of refining the generic standards by offering discipline-specific versions (discussed in Chapter 8), but these have not been widely recognized yet outside of LIS.

Another reason that faculty may not claim ownership of information literacy is that the concept continues to be over-identified with library skills. Ratteray (2008) laments that the word information literacy is too "library-centric" (section 5, para. 3). Some librarians agree with him. For instance, librarians at institution D expressed discomfort with the phrase information literacy because they believe that faculty associate it with the library, and thus assume it is the library's responsibility. Baker (2005) notes that most of the literature devoted to information literacy is written by librarians and is "library-centric in philosophy" (para. 2), perpetuating the notion that it is synonymous with library skills. Faculty responses to the phrase information literacy suggests that librarians and even accreditation organizations might be more successful if they discussed the relevant outcomes of finding, using, and evaluating information without using the actual words information literacy. Nevertheless, no one has proposed a viable alternative term that is widely accepted.

The issue of ownership is further compounded by the fact that some librarians see information literacy as their purview, and do not want to partner with teaching faculty (Julien & Given, 2002/2003). In direct contrast to Ratteray (2005), Owusu-Ansah (2007) argues strenuously that libraries should be central to the instruction of information literacy. He decries solutions that "subordinate the library to the activities and concessions of those who have come to be accepted as the mainstream teachers on campus—the faculty" (p. 416). Indeed, he objects to any approach to information literacy instruction that "removes control from the library" (p. 419). Similarly, while Badke (2005) does not oppose collaboration, he maintains that "librarians trump faculty" when it comes to teaching the competencies of information literacy. Finally, Eland (2005) challenges "the faculty/librarian dichotomy that [Ratteray] continues to perpetuate" (para. 2). In his estimation librarians and libraries contribute to student learning by functioning as a gateway to information whether they are actively involved in teaching or not, and as such they should be regarded as faculty. These discussions support Baker's (2005) comment that "librarians, as a profession, guard the IL [information literacy] turf pretty jealously" (para. 3). Indeed, Julien and Given (2002/2003) find such opinions widely held on library listservs, and warn that by "positioning themselves as owners of the library territory . . . librarians may actually further entrench the existing polarities that appear to define their relationships with faculty" (p. 80). Such attitudes run counter to the model of information literacy proposed by the Middle States Commission (2003), and as such do not fulfill the standards as they are written. The Middle States Commission emphasizes that neither faculty nor librarians are solely responsible for information literacy, and that the competencies are best addressed by both librarians and faculty together. However, Ratteray (2002, 2005) stresses that faculty are central to all learning, and librarians, while important, essentially lend support. Julien and Given (2002/2003) suggest librarians will make progress by "eliminating the discourse of power and control, and promoting a discourse of equivalence (i.e., where librarians and faculty can learn from and guide each other)" (p. 76).

Smith (2001), who acknowledges the contribution that librarians can make through information literacy services, points out that increased focus on learning outcomes offers librarians new opportunities to align their services with the institution's mission and goals and to demonstrate how the library supports achievement of that mission and related learning goals. He states "faculty play an especially important role [regarding learning outcomes assessment], but assessment questions can't be fully addressed without participation of student affairs educators, librarians, administrators, and students" (p. 32). Faculty are central to the process, but librarians and others involved in the educational process have important supporting roles. As a result, instead of trying to assert ownership, librarians should engage with faculty in assessment for information literacy.

A final factor contributing to confusion surrounding the ownership of information literacy rests with the fact that, in a majority of the institutions reviewed, information literacy is often placed in the context of general education. Fifty-eight self-studies (59.8%) from institutions accredited by the Middle States Commission and 64 institutions (27.9%) from the other regions mention it as part of general education. However, few of these institutions specified how it is addressed within the general education curriculum. If institutions indicate that information literacy is part of the first-year program, they often do not explain whether it is incorporated through a one-shot library session, addressed through a collaborative effort by librarians and some faculty members, or through some other means. For example, one institution identifies specific courses within the general education program designed to address certain competencies, such as math, quantitative reasoning, and writing skills. When discussing information literacy, however, this institution reports that the topic is addressed by all courses at all levels. Such vague statements suggest that information literacy is probably not explicitly covered in these courses, and it is therefore difficult to assess learning in relation to it.

Like information literacy, general education programs are often orphaned within the larger curriculum. Because general education emphasizes broad, basic skills rather than specialized knowledge, faculty often view it as peripheral to their own discipline and research interests (Freake, von Hammerstein, & Goodstein, 2008; Snavely & Cooper, 1997; Stevens, 2001). Yet, faculty engagement is crucial because "general education only works well when there is broad-based faculty engagement in and ownership of general education" (Point Loma Nazarene University, n.d., para. 4). By making learning outcomes for information literacy part of the general education curriculum without extending them to the majors and programs as well, institutions reinforce the idea that information literacy is peripheral to disciplinary studies.

What all involved in this debate must recognize is that ownership of information literacy is not mutually exclusive. While faculty involvement is essential, it does not imply that librarians should be excluded from the process. Just as Figure 1.1 suggests, librarians and faculty can share the responsibility for instruction and assessment. In order to achieve a partnership, however, faculty must be willing to integrate information literacy into their courses and programs as appropriate, and librarians have to be willing to collaborate rather than looking for control (Breivik, 1989; Snavely & Cooper, 1997). As the original champions of information literacy, librarians have not yet emerged as campus leaders who move the concept to the program and institutional level and gain the widespread participation and buy-in of faculty and administrators. Librarians must "intentionally step back and share ownership" (Fister et al., 2001, p. 205), but find ways to fill the leadership vacuum.

Leadership and Information Literacy

Instruction librarians have been reaching out to faculty and collaborating on a limited scale for decades, but their work has not generated widespread buy-in from faculty, and they have been unable to extend information literacy to the program level (Badke, 2005; McGuinness, 2007; Owusu-Ansah, 2007). Librarians themselves are limited to the course level, either teaching stand-alone courses or offering in-class instruction at the course level as requested by faculty. In fact, front-line librarians do not appear to have the level of influence necessary to move information literacy to a higher level. This indicates leadership must come from higher up, within either the library or the broader institution.

The most likely candidates for such a leadership role are senior administrators, which includes library directors. Snavely and Cooper (1997) acknowledge the importance of garnering support of administrators, stating that efforts by librarians are bound to be "relatively inconsequential unless the goal of the university and its upper-level administrative staff is to ensure that this is an institutional goal as well" (p. 57). Indeed, they warn that "the climate for implementation of an information literacy program may not be favorable unless implemented carefully and as part of the deans' and department chairs' agendas, not the librarians' " (p. 55). McGuinness (2007) asserts the importance of involving senior administrators in order to permeate the wider institutional culture. Administrators can support curricular changes that will integrate information literacy and librarians more fully into the curriculum, and promote interaction between students and librarians (Asher, Duke, & Green, 2010). Librarians will continue to experience limited success with the current approach of reaching out to individual faculty members and hoping that these faculty members will become academic champions for information literacy on the campus (McGuinness, 2007).

This is not to suggest that administrators should try to force curricular change through a top-down approach. In fact, such an effort is unlikely to succeed, given the culture of faculty autonomy in most institutions

(Fister et al., 2001). Rather, administrators can create the opportunities for discussion and put in place incentives that can encourage faculty participation. For instance, Fister et al. (2001), and Bloomberg and McDonald (2004), describe situations in which administrators help set a context by drawing faculty into discussions, listening to their concerns, and providing opportunities and incentives for them to learn more about outcomes assessment and related topics. This approach builds consensus and a sense of ownership among the faculty, and encourages them to act on the context established by the administrators. As Fister et al. state, it is important "that motivated faculty be the ones that take the lead and that the process be at the grassroots for it to be accepted" (p. 208).

In fact, the few institutions that seem to be creating a culture of information literacy demonstrate this approach. North Georgia College and State University, North Carolina Wesleyan College, and Institution C, for instance, all engaged in campus-wide discussions around the implementation of an information literacy program. In other words, faculty and administrators were involved early on in the process, and thereby likely feel ownership in the plan and a stake in its outcome. In each case, the discussions resulted in a local definition of information literacy, which might serve as a sort of shared vision, one of the precursors of leadership described in Chapter 11. Even if, as is often the case, locally developed definitions closely resemble the ACRL standards, the evidence suggests that the process is what is important. A local definition that grows organically from conversations across the institution is likely to garner more buy-in and be more widely understood by those involved in its implementation than a definition imposed or adopted from outside. Indeed, the librarian at institution C notes that this is the case on her campus, and that all faculty know what information literacy is and how it needs to be addressed. The common vocabulary, shared understanding, and buy-in resulting from this process should make taking action to integrate information literacy easier.

Administrators, including library directors, play a crucial role in creating a context in which a formal information literacy program can take root. They can initiate campus-wide dialogues by bringing together faculty and librarians to discuss the issue and its role in the curriculum. They can develop incentives to influence faculty and librarians to work together to implement an assessment plan such as those described by Maki (2002) and López (2002). Librarians at the case study institutions consistently point to individual senior administrators as strong library supporters and credit them with furthering the development of information literacy on their campuses. Nevertheless, even with that upper-level support, only a handful of institutions are making progress toward program-level integration, including institution C and the two SACS-accredited institutions with the QEP focused on information literacy. While these preliminary steps establish an environment that is conducive to information literacy integration, faculty ownership ultimately drives change. Indeed, their support "is essential to the success of the program and ultimately will make or break it" (Snavely & Cooper, 1997, p. 57).

ASSESSMENT

Assessment is the cornerstone of quality, improvement, and accountability. Through assessment, institutions can understand how well students achieve learning goals, and can enact policies that improve the learning experience. As Maki (2004) explains, assessment "enables us to determine the fit between what we expect our students to be able to demonstrate or represent and what they actually do demonstrate and represent" (p. 2). Further, assessment reveals "how well we translate our intentions into multiple, varied, and frequent opportunities for students to learn" (p. 3). When assessment results reveal gaps between the expectations and actualities, institutions can implement improvements to foster better learning. In addition, assessment offers evidence of quality. Accreditation organizations use the results of assessment as a measure of how well institutions meet accreditation standards. In sharing assessment results, institutions make themselves accountable by "providing substantive evidence that their investment yields significant results" (Suskie, 2004, p. 13). For libraries, assessment offers evidence of the impact the library has on student learning and, by extension, achievement of the institutional mission. To be effective, however, such evidence must be "systematic, coherent, and connected" (Oakleaf, 2010).

Despite its importance, many institutions apparently do not engage in widespread or systematic assessment activities for information literacy. Indeed, assessment practices in general may not be very widespread. While a report from the National Institute for Learning Outcomes Assessment (Kuh & Ikenberry, 2009) indicates that 92 percent of colleges and universities use at least one assessment tool to measure student learning, and two-thirds of institutions use three or more, the same report indicates that the vast majority of assessment is indirect (as defined in Chapter 11). For instance, national surveys and standardized tests, respectively, are the most widely used tools. As discussed in Chapter 11, surveys and interviews rely on self-reporting and do not directly measure student learning. Institutions reported heavy use of other indirect measures such as focus group interviews with students and employers, and alumni surveys. Indeed, such methods are incorrectly categorized as assessment, since they really evaluate perceptions and opinions over student learning. On the other hand, tests offer insight into what students know or have learned, but they typically measure more memorization and rote learning than higher-order thinking. Authentic assessments such as portfolios are employed at only about 8 percent of institutions, and assessment of the portfolios or other capstone projects is rarely linked to rubrics, or pre- and posttesting over the duration of a program.

Bloomberg and McDonald (2004), Maki (2004), and Suskie (2004, 2009, 2010) underscore the importance of making assessment part of the institutional culture, meaning it is a core activity, and that processes and policies are in place to support it. Each of these authors offers guidelines for implementing assessment plans. As Maki explains, "some campuses may embed or weave this institutional commitment into existing institutional structures and practices ... [while] others may develop new ways of behaving that accommodate the depth and breadth of this commitment" (p. 3). Faculty and staff directly involved in teaching design the assignments and interact with the students whose work will be assessed. The buy-in and support of these faculty and staff is essential for a successful assessment program, and Suskie (2004) advocates structuring assessment to empower faculty to take a leadership role. At the same time, however, senior administrators play an important role in facilitating a culture of assessment. Administrators can help to ensure faculty support by involving them in the planning stages, listening to their needs and concerns, and rewarding their efforts (Maki, 2004; Suskie, 2004). Indeed, Suskie (2004) notes that few institutions have widespread and successful assessment programs without the support of those in top-level positions. She laments the fact that many institutions do not provide incentives for faculty and staff to use assessment data in this way, and notes that "if there's little incentive to change or be innovative, there's little reason to assess how we're keeping our promises" (Suskie, 2010, para. 10).

The framework for achieving a culture of assessment set out by these authors mirrors that for information literacy. In each case, senior administrators set the context by involving the campus in a dialogue and by creating the environment and incentives that encourage participation in the project. Through involvement in the planning stages, and with support from administrators, faculty and staff need to take ownership of the initiative and carry out the goals. Assessment is essential for faculty and librarians to gauge how well students are learning and for improving learning related to information literacy. In order to be successful as initiatives, both assessment and information literacy must be integrated into institutional cultures through supportive administrators and involved faculty and staff.

As discussed in Chapter 8, assessment for information literacy may focus on student outcomes and student learning outcomes, and it may be direct or indirect. Assessment of learning outcomes, whenever possible, should use direct methods such as those described by Oakleaf (2008, 2009), and focus on changes in student knowledge and behavior as a direct result of program-wide instruction. For instance, the LIS literature describes a range of measures including tests, portfolios, capstone projects, and reviews of bibliographies for term projects (see e.g., Diller & Phelps, 2008; Katz, 2007; Scharf, Elliot, Huey, Briller, & Joshi, 2007; Sharma, 2007), with similar measures reported in self-studies. Ideally, when assessing projects or portfolios, faculty and librarians use rubrics that delineate the skills and abilities for each competency at novice, intermediate, and proficient levels (Oakleaf, 2009). In addition to what students learn, however, institutions and stakeholders are also interested in student outcomes such as levels of engagement, persistence rates, and graduation rates. Student outcomes with regard to information literacy have not been widely developed and researched. However, some authors have reported that instruction for information literacy may increase student engagement (Flaspohler, 2003; Gratch-Lindauer, 2007; Kuh & Gonyea, 2003), while other authors claim that students who elect to take information literacy courses have greater persistence than their counterparts (Selegean, Thomas, & Richman, 1983).

Assessment for Improvement

While it is concerning that so little assessment for student learning outcomes that cover information literacy takes place, there is a further consideration as well. Collecting and reporting assessment data relates to one of the purposes of assessment: accountability. By offering evidence of student learning through assessment data, institutions indicate how they are meeting their own missions as well as accreditation standards and stakeholder demands. Assessment has another equally important purpose, however, which is improvement of teaching and learning. In other words, institutions should use assessment data to inform decision making and identify ways to ensure that students are learning effectively (Maki, 2010; Suskie, 2009, 2010). As noted in Chapter 8, institutions should engage in assessment "for the purposes of judging (and improving) overall instructional effectiveness" (Ewell, 2001, p. 7). Suskie (2010) suggests that assessment is "a vital tool to help us make sure that we fulfill the crucial promises we make to our students and society" (para. 7). Evidence suggests, however, that even where assessment is taking place, it is not necessarily followed by action for improvements in teaching and learning (Ewell, 2009; Jaschik, 2009; Suskie, 2010).

According to the national survey of chief academic officers completed by the National Institute for Learning Outcomes Assessment, the two most common uses of assessment data are to prepare self-studies for regional accreditation and self-studies for program accreditation. In other words, institutions are documenting assessment activities, many of which are actually evaluation activities, in order to report to accreditation organizations and satisfy compliance requirements; but they are not necessarily using the data generated by assessment to make curricular changes. In fact, this survey indicates that the use of assessment data for revising learning goals or modifying the general education curriculum is less frequent than accreditation reporting. Similarly, other uses that might be related to improving teaching and learning are even less frequently reported. For instance, the uses of assessment data for evaluating teaching faculty and staff for promotion or merit increases are two of the three lowest-reported activities. The survey indicates that assessment data are used to adjust admissions criteria and make determinations for entry to upper-level classes slightly more often than evaluation of faculty (Jaschik, 2009; Kuh & Ikenberry, 2009). Low engagement in such activities directly related to teaching and learning indicates that institutions are not following through to close the assessment cycle by using data to inform decisions that will improve those areas. Instead, many institutions seem to separate assessment activities from the improvement of teaching and learning (Suskie, 2010).

The general findings of the National Institute for Learning Outcomes Assessment (Kuh & Ikenberry, 2009) align with those of this study. Only a few institutions explicitly indicate that they use assessment data to make changes to teaching and learning. For instance, two self-studies note using data from SAILS to inform changes to library instruction. One notes that the SAILS test showed students did not have a strong understanding of plagiarism or of how to search databases. In response, librarians changed the curriculum for the required information literacy course to spend more time on these two areas. The examples of implementing changes as a result of direct assessment, however, are few. Other institutions seem to rely more on indirect measures. For instance, one institution reports using a survey that revealed students do not have a strong grasp of the differences between catalogs and databases, or how to use Boolean operators in searching. As a result, the librarians plan to make changes to improve learning based on these survey results, although the self-study does not indicate that any changes have been implemented yet. Another institution reports the use of a survey and focus groups to identify ways to improve the introductory library sessions. Several other institutions state that they use assessment data to make changes to the information literacy curriculum, but specify neither the methods used to collect the data nor the changes made as a result of data analysis.

The fact that some institutions are using data, be it from direct or indirect measures, to make changes and inform decision making is positive. It indicates that these institutions understand that the purpose of assessment goes beyond reporting and accountability, and encompasses changes to improve teaching and learning. These institutions, however, appear to be the exception. The majority of the institutions did not specify changes made in response to assessment data, but simply state that the data are used to inform decision making. As the report from the National Institute for Learning Outcomes Assessment concludes, "American higher education is far from where it needs to be in assessing student learning and in using the results to improve outcomes" (Kuh & Ikenberry, 2009, p. 28).

It is possible that the process of accreditation, with its dual focus on accountability and improvement, subtly discourages institutions from directing attention to improvement, at least with regard to accreditation reports. To assess for improvement requires that institutions find flaws or problems in order to fix them, and institutions are not likely to highlight deficiencies for their accreditation organizations. Rather, when attempting to demonstrate accountability to accreditation organizations, institutions try to demonstrate high levels of achievement in areas like learning outcomes, suggesting there is no need for improvement (Ewell, 2009; Suskie, 2010). Thus, institutions are faced with a tension between a focus on what they are doing well for accountability, or what they are doing less well for improvement, and in this situation "accountability wins" (Ewell, 2009, p. 8). This tension points to a possible role for visiting teams. When conducting campus visits, visiting team members should look not only for evidence of assessment activities, but also indications that assessment data are being used to improve teaching and learning. In this way, accreditation organizations can hold institutions accountable not only for achievement, but also for improvement through effective use of assessment data. Likewise, institutions must promote a culture of assessment by engaging faculty in assessment planning from the initial stages and developing incentives and rewards for faculty who participate in assessment activities (Ewell, 2009; Suskie, 2010).

Moving Forward

Achieving an integrated information literacy program as outlined in Figure 1.1 involves progress and changes in several areas. The first step for most institutions is to move from evaluation to assessment of learning outcomes. Faculty and librarians must stop relying almost exclusively on evaluative methods such as course evaluations, bibliography reviews, and self-reporting surveys, which do not uncover changes in student knowledge or progress in learning. Making such a change requires new knowledge and understanding. Faculty and librarians must learn to disambiguate between the evaluation and assessment approaches, and must understand direct and indirect methods, before they can properly implement authentic assessment tools that offer real insight into student learning.

Once they implement consistent use of assessment, faculty and librarians must focus on moving instruction for information literacy upward from the course level to the program and institutional levels. Again, this will require that librarians and faculty obtain new knowledge as they come to a shared vision of information literacy, learn to collaborate on deeper levels, and inspire support throughout the institution. After they define learning outcomes for information literacy at the program and institutional levels, they must implement the assessment tools to gauge student learning at these levels.

While faculty and librarians gain knowledge and understanding through their own effort and professional development, the Middle States Commission and other accreditation organizations should provide learning opportunities for them. Since the Middle States Commission (2002, 2003) stresses the importance of student learning outcomes in its standards, it must assist institutions to learn how to apply those outcomes to demonstrate achievement of improved learning over time. At this point, the Middle States Commission does not offer clear distinctions between evaluation and assessment methods, or guidance on how to choose the appropriate method for reviewing student learning. Rather, it contributes to the confusion over these methods by mixing them together within *Developing Research and Communication Skills* (Middle States Commission, 2003) and *Student Learning Assessment* (Middle States Commission, 2007). As institutions plan and implement programs to assess student learning outcomes, accreditation organizations must provide more learning opportunities for faculty and staff around assessment. Further, they must ensure that the visiting teams that represent them clearly understand assessment and can recognize when it is properly used.

THE ROLE OF ACCREDITATION

Ultimately, institutions are responsible for setting and achieving goals for student learning. If a collaborative and integrated information literacy program requires fundamental change at some universities and colleges, administrators, faculty, and librarians must work together to make those changes to set and meet their learning goals. However, accreditation organizations can influence institutions and create pressure that may fuel the discussions and work that will accomplish change. In fact, the National Institute for Learning Outcomes Assessment (Kuh & Ikenberry, 2009) contends that accreditation is a primary driver for assessment and improvement in higher education. In a presentation to the North Central Association of Colleges and Schools describing how they successfully engaged faculty in assessment on their campus, officials from Blackburn College claim they "used pressure from the college's accreditor ... as a 'stick' that helped them argue that 'there was a fairly firm mandate that we had to achieve' " (Lederman, 2010, para. 17). The findings of this study confirm this view. As noted, several of the interviewees at case study institutions acknowledged that accreditation review was one of the motivating forces behind changes to their approaches to information literacy. Similarly, the two SACS-accredited institutions with QEP focused on information literacy are among the few institutions in this study that seem to be moving toward program integration and a culture of information literacy, and those proposals grew out of the accreditation review requirements.

As discussed in Chapter 2, the role of accreditation organizations in American higher education is to ensure quality and improvement by requiring institutions to demonstrate achievement of student learning through assessment and accountability for the mission. However, despite the fact that information literacy in the vast majority of institutions has not extended beyond the course level, and assessment largely focuses on indirect measures, accreditation organizations do not appear to be demanding change. In other words, accreditation organizations appear not to be strongly enforcing their own standards, since they appear to accept course-level instruction and high use of indirect assessment or even the substitution of evaluation methods as assessment. The question is, "Is the Middle States Commission taking action to spur change within these institutions?"

The Middle States Commission (2003, 2009) has the most extensive and detailed set of standards in relation to information literacy, and it emphasizes the applicability of information literacy across disciplines and at all levels of education. In addition, the commission acknowledges the importance of assessment, through both direct and indirect measures and at the course, program, and institutional levels, to improve student learning. Finally, it emphasizes the centrality of faculty to information literacy instruction, and strongly emphasizes partnerships between faculty and librarians for instruction and assessment of information literacy, as depicted in Figure 1.1. Nevertheless, the evidence gathered for this study indicates that institutions whose reports were examined are largely not meeting these expectations. This is perhaps nowhere better reflected than in the fact that the few institutions that demonstrate evidence of program-integrated information literacy fall outside of the purview of the Middle States Commission. Granted, there are several institutions within the Middle States Commission's region with proposals or future recommendations that outline a move toward integration beyond the course level; but these are all still in the planning stages, while a handful of institutions outside of the region have already instituted such programs.

Accreditation organizations have come under widespread criticism recently. Badke (2005) suggests that accreditation standards currently lack "teeth" (p. 77) and as such, librarians cannot rely on them as agents for change. Ratteray (2002) states that accreditation organizations do not want to be enforcers because they would rather institutions take responsibility for themselves. Indeed, that officials from Blackburn College would describe accreditation standards as a "fairly firm" (Lederman, 2010, para. 17) mandate further suggests that institutions do not necessarily regard accreditation organizations as strict enforcers of change, a position seconded by the Center for College Affordability and Productivity, which asserts that accreditation organizations do not provide sufficient means for assuring quality and improvement (Gillen, Bennett, & Vedder, 2010). Further, Bloomberg and McDonald (2004) contend that accreditation standards are not viewed as immediate to the classroom and thus do not motivate change among faculty. Still, accreditation organizations have a responsibility to ensure quality and facilitate the improvement of learning. Since visiting teams represent the accreditation organizations and have direct contact with the institution, they must be trained to recognize appropriate uses of assessment, and must be held accountable for their review of institutions. By not being more forceful in requiring institutions to meet standards for information literacy, the accreditation organizations may be contributing to a sense that institutions do not have to be accountable in this respect. Baker (2005) underscores this sentiment. In discussing current approaches to information literacy, she acknowledges that "it isn't the kind of broadly-based programming that Ratteray and his colleagues promote. But if our own accreditors don't bark, where's the harm?" (para. 5). This posting strongly suggests that, even though administrators, faculty, and librarians may have to make change happen, they often need a push from external forces to begin.

Currently, external forces may be prolonging the status quo rather than facilitating change. In particular, financial constraints resulting from the economic recession of 2008–2009 present challenges for starting new initiatives. Certainly, higher education faces enormous pressure right now, and information literacy is not necessarily a priority at all institutions. The economic downturn and the resulting loss of endowment and funds means that many institutions may not have the resources to make substantial changes (Kuh & Ikenberry, 2009; Lederman, 2009; Lombardi, 2009). The value of endowments declined 23 percent from 2008–2009, while the average investment return was -18.7 percent, making this the worst fiscal year for colleges and universities since the Great Depression (Blumenstyk, 2010). In addition to budget constraints, information literacy competes for faculty time and attention with various other literacies and competencies, including critical thinking, global citizenry, media literacy, and visual literacy (Snavely & Cooper, 1997). Faculty have to choose among the many learning outcomes considered essential, and in some cases, they may not consider information literacy a top priority. Further, some faculty resist outcomes assessment in general (Hutchings, 2010; Tener, 1999; Weiss, Habel, Hanson, Cosbey, & Larsen, 2002).

Despite these constraints, institutions have a responsibility to keep achieving and maintaining the quality of student education. As the National Institute for Learning Outcomes Assessment (Kuh & Ikenberry, 2009) notes, "ultimately, access and affordability are empty gestures in the absence of evidence of accomplishment" (p. 5). Since assessment is essential for understanding student learning (Maki, 2004), institutions must develop learning goals and an assessment plan. Too often, institutions adopt a "compliance approach" (Maki, 2002, p. 8) to assessment, beginning assessment only when preparing for an accreditation visit. Maki (2002, 2004) outlines an approach to developing an assessment plan. In addition to defining learning goals and choosing appropriate measures, she suggests that institutions "need to identify if, in fact, they provide sufficient educational opportunities inside and outside the classroom to develop the desired outcomes they assert they teach or develop" (2002, p. 8). This approach hearkens to the assessment cycle depicted in Figure 8.1, which suggests that the first step in assessment is to inventory current practices and identify what learning and assessment activities are already underway.

Whether the motivation is internal or external, the commitment to quality must be maintained. As an arbiter of quality and a primary driver for assessment, accreditation organizations are uniquely positioned to ensure that institutions remain focused on their commitment. Indeed, accreditation organizations have a responsibility to promote quality improvement, and stakeholders such as the federal government have increased scrutiny of the role of accreditation organizations recently. While defenders contend that accreditation organizations are responsible for increases in attention to and assessment of student learning, critics are not satisfied with the extent or rate of change (Bennett, 2010; Eaton, 2010; Gillen, Bennett, & Vedder, 2010). In particular, stakeholders criticize accreditation organizations for "being too secretive about how they assess colleges and using outmoded standards that don't give enough weight to measuring student learning" (Kelderman, 2010, para. 1). These stakeholders call for accreditation organizations to be more transparent and to provide more information to the public about the quality of the institutions they accredit (Gillen, Bennett, & Vedder, 2010). In the face of such criticism, the future of accreditation may lie in "strengthening accountability and enhancing service to the public while maintaining the benefits of quality improvement and peer review" (Eaton, 2010, para. 7). To satisfy stakeholders, "accreditation must adopt a visible and proactive stance with respect to assuring acceptable levels of student academic achievement. Given escalating stakeholder demands, nothing less will prove sufficient to maintain the public credibility of our voluntary peer-based system" (Ewell, 2001, p. 2).

FURTHER RESEARCH

As an exploratory study, this research only begins to probe the complex issues underlying the integration of information literacy as a student learning outcome into higher-education curricula. As such, it suggests many possible avenues for further research. First, this study focused most attention on institutions under the aegis of the Middle States Commission on Higher Education, one of six regional accreditation organizations in the United States. For instance, all case study institutions are from this region. While the self-studies provide valuable insight into institutional treatment of information literacy, they are limited in their perspective. As noted in Chapter 5, the regional accreditation organizations vary in their level of attention to and emphasis on information literacy, and this is reflected to some extent in the self-studies. Institutions may be involved in information literacy to a greater extent than is reflected in their self-studies, but might not address it in their self-studies because information literacy is not a focus of the standards with which they are complying. The case studies and campus visits offer much more context, and it was through the case studies of the four institutions accredited by the Middle States Commission that the five themes emerged. More case studies might be performed at institutions within the other five regions, and their results compared to this study to examine similarities and differences in institutional responses to information literacy standards across regions. This study establishes a baseline look at the state of information literacy in relation to accreditation standards. Since reaffirmation of accreditation takes place on a 10-year cycle, with institutions applying for reaffirmation at different times, this study could be repeated, perhaps on a 5-year cycle, to track changes and developments in accreditation standards and institutional responses to information literacy over time.

In addition, many program accreditation organizations have standards regarding information literacy. Another study could examine the extent to which programs such as engineering, psychology, or accounting are implementing information literacy. Finally, this study focused exclusively on non-profit institutions. For-profit colleges and universities are growing rapidly and gaining accreditation, and a future study could examine their information literacy activities to compare with traditional nonprofit institutions.

Much of the data for this study was gathered through examination of self-study documents, which have inherent limitations. These documents, produced for decennial accreditation visits, generally are very broad in scope. Each institution must make decisions about what to include and exclude when preparing these studies. As such, some institutions may possibly have information literacy programs that extend beyond what the data examined here reveal, but were not included in the self-study. A future study might probe other institutional documents (e.g., library self-studies, curriculum maps, or course materials) for a different perspective on information literacy on these campuses. Finally, this study represents a cross-section in time. Many of the documents examined had been written prior to the current Middle States Commission's standards. Others included future plans and recommendations for growing or implementing information literacy activities. A future study might revisit the institutions to see what changes have occurred, and if there is greater transparency.

Assessment of learning outcomes for information literacy is not widespread beyond some individual courses, and is often accomplished through indirect methods. Yet, assessment is crucial to an institution's understanding of its own achievements, and also indicates areas for improvement. A future study might investigate assessment to determine if the self-studies accurately portray campus activities, or if assessment for information literacy is underreported.

Discussions with faculty and librarians might reveal a different picture for information literacy assessment. The study could extend to other learning outcomes to allow for comparisons between assessment for information literacy and those learning outcomes.

While the perspective on information literacy of most stakeholders is known or available, little has been written about the perceptions of teaching faculty with regard to information literacy. Since faculty support is essential to the success of information literacy programming, future research could elicit responses from faculty across disciplines to see what importance they attribute to information literacy, and how they envision the breakdown of responsibilities for instruction and assessment of information literacy. In light of the discussion regarding institutional and organizational cultures, the study could compare faculty reactions across disciplines to see if organizational culture of different departments and programs affects perceptions of information literacy, as well as how they handle other outcome areas such as critical thinking. Similarly, since the ACRL has published several sets of discipline-specific standards for information literacy (see Table 12.1), a study might examine the application of these standards in departments and programs and see how helpful they have been in creating a vision and moving beyond that vision to implementation of program-level assessment.

The leadership vacuum is an important finding of this study. Future research might study the context of leadership for information literacy on campuses to see what factors contribute to or inhibit the emergence of leaders. This study identified possible positions that might lend themselves to leadership. A study might investigate the willingness and ability of library directors and others on campus to assume leadership for information literacy, build a shared vision, and motivate others to follow.

Table 12.1   ACRL Discipline-Specific Standards for Information Literacy

Title	Date Issued	URL
Science and engineering/technology	2006	http://www.ala.org/ala/mgrps/divs/acrl/standards/infolitscitech.cfm
Literatures in English	2007	http://www.ala.org/ala/mgrps/divs/acrl/standards/researchcompetenciesles.cfm
Anthropology and sociology	2008	http://www.ala.org/ala/mgrps/divs/acrl/standards/anthro_soc_standards.cfm
Political science	2008	http://www.ala.org/ala/mgrps/divs/acrl/standards/PoliSciGuide.pdf
Psychology	2010	http://www.ala.org/ala/mgrps/divs/acrl/standards/psych_info_lit.cfm

Finally, this study uncovered differing opinions about the importance of external pressures such as accreditation standards in influencing widespread campus change. While individual librarians and administrators believe accreditation organizations are important catalysts, some writings mention that faculty are more impervious to outside pressure. In addition, how accreditation organizations define their own role for motivation or mandating remains unclear. A study might probe these questions to see how different outside influences impact change on campus, compared to internally motivated change. In particular, future research could investigate the work of visiting teams. Such a study might examine how team members are trained and prepare for their visits and how knowledgeable they are about assessment, and perhaps interview former team members about the process. Clearly, team members themselves might be the focus of the investigation.

EXPECTATIONS AND REALITY

A gap exists between the stated expectations for information literacy of the Middle States Commission (2003) and other regional accreditation organizations on one hand, and the reality on many of the campuses studied on the other. While many institutions claim to be integrating information literacy into their curricula, and use the word "program" to describe their efforts, virtually all instruction and assessment of information literacy takes place at the course level. Collaboration is likewise heavily concentrated at the course level. Further, what some institutions characterize as collaboration is often nothing more than a traditional one-shot session. Perhaps most importantly, however, the levels of assessment are paltry. Few institutions are engaging in assessment for information literacy at all. Those that do assessment rely heavily on indirect measures, and occasionally mischaracterize evaluation tools as assessment. While these activities do not align with the standards and expectations of the Middle States Commission (2003), neither do they seem to cause concern among visiting teams, the Middle States Commission, and perhaps other accreditation organizations.

If accreditation organizations such as the Middle States Commission want to change this mind-set and influence change, they might reconsider how they prepare for and approach institutional reviews for accreditation. As discussed in Chapter 8, many faculty, librarians, and others mischaracterize certain tools such as surveys and interviews as assessment. If the visiting teams, which are often made up of faculty, staff, and perhaps librarians from peer institutions, are not aware of the differences between evaluation and assessment, they may approve institutional approaches to assessment that do not meet the requirements of assessment as defined in Chapter 8. The fact that many institutions are retaining accredited status despite confusion over assessment and evaluation suggests that visiting teams are not prepared to identify and address the issue. By not disambiguating the terms, and by presenting evaluation and assessment methods together in its publications, the Middle States Commission further confuses the issue.

In order to combat such misrepresentations, the Middle States Commission and other accreditation organizations need to emphasize outcomes and learning outcomes assessment in visiting teams training, so that team members are better equipped to recognize and distinguish between evaluation and assessment. The Middle States Commission holds an annual conference and offers workshops throughout the year for member institutions. Perhaps it should develop programs and training sessions that define assessment, distinguish between direct and indirect measures, and guide participants in choosing and implementing assessment tools. Such training is warranted, as misunderstandings and mischaracterizations of assessment prevail in many self-studies. The Middle States Commission must also better differentiate between evaluation and assessment in its documentation. In *Developing Research and Communication Skills* (Middle States Commission, 2003) and *Student Learning Assessment* (Middle States Commission, 2007), the commission uses the terms assessment and evaluation interchangeably, and presents both approaches as assessment. The commission must revise its texts to be clearer about what comprises assessment, and to guide institutions in choosing and implementing appropriate methods. Accreditation organizations have a responsibility for ensuring that institutions are accountable, and assessment is an important tool in answering calls for accountability. However, those involved must have a clear understanding of what assessment entails in order to use it properly. Accreditation organizations must ensure that both the visiting team members who represent the organization and constituent institutions have the training and support they need to understand and use assessment for student learning. If visiting team members do not have a clear understanding of the difference between evaluation and assessment, how can the Middle States Commission expect institutional faculty and staff to do so?

Mischaracterizations of assessment and evaluation are not uncommon. Sakai and Ichiko (2008) contend that increased participation in LibQUAL+, a survey to evaluate service quality in libraries, is an indicator of progress in the area of assessment. For instance, the University of Texas at Austin (2008) claims that questions from its LibQUAL survey such as "the library aids my advancement in my academic discipline or work" and "the library helps me to distinguish between trustworthy and untrustworthy information" (p. 35) measure information literacy outcomes. In fact, like all other questions on the survey, the five questions listed as "information literacy outcomes" questions actually measure participants' desired and perceived levels of service and thus measures service quality. In fact, LibQUAL+ is not associated with any learning outcome or rubric. Likewise, a librarian at institution B mentions the results of the National Survey of Student Engagement (NSSE) when discussing assessment for information literacy. This librarian acknowledges that NSSE does not specifically address information literacy, but he implies that perhaps the results could be used as assessment if it goes unquestioned during a review. In fact, while NSSE has a broad base of supporters who assert the reliability and validity of the instrument (Kuh, 2004), some critics question NSSE's overall validity as an assessment tool (Schneider, 2009). Schneider (2009) notes that most of NSSE's claims to validity rest on correlational studies that are more than 30 years old, stating that "scant empirical evidence exists to link NSSE scores to student learning outcomes," (para. 7) and "many of NSSE's assertions have not been subject to rigorous analysis" (para. 6). Nevertheless, NSSE is a popular tool not only for internal assessment, but also for cross-institutional comparisons. In fact, NSSE scores make up a large portion of the information reported on websites such as College Navigator. As such, institutions are using NSSE scores as a means of raising the institutional transparency.

Transparency, or the public dissemination of information, is related to accountability. In order to demonstrate accountability to stakeholders beyond campus, institutions must share assessment information. However, the levels of transparency among institutions included in this study are uneven. Many institutions are unwilling to share accreditation documents, even when they are assured of confidentiality and privacy. As part of their role in promoting accountability, accreditation organizations could also promote transparency in constituent institutions. Currently, accreditation organizations such as the Middle States Commission claim to encourage institutions to share information with the public. However, little evidence of such encouragement exists. Rather, the accreditation organizations stress institutional privacy and ownership of information (Gillen, Bennett, & Vedder, 2010), which allows institutions large leeway in refusing to share information. As one of the external forces influencing institutions of higher education, accreditation organizations have an opportunity to facilitate accountability and transparency.

CONCLUSION

The discussion of information literacy as a learning outcome begs the question of how institutions implement and assess other broad-based learning outcomes, and whether they engage in higher levels of assessment for those other outcomes. It is possible that information literacy is not a high priority for many institutions, and that other learning outcomes (e.g., critical thinking) are more systematically integrated into the curriculum and more widely and directly assessed. On the other hand, unlike many of the other learning outcomes (e.g., critical thinking and global citizenry), information literacy has a widely agreed-upon definition and set of learning goals as well as a framework for implementation (see Figure 1.1). The existence of such frameworks might arguably make it easier for institutions to address, since much of the work of defining learning outcomes has already been done, and faculty, librarians, and administrators need only to adapt the framework to fit their institution and to relate them to rubrics. If all of the guidelines, definitions, and accreditation standards do not spur institutions to action, what will?

Information literacy is a complex topic, crossing disciplines and encompassing a wide range of knowledge, abilities, and skills, and thus achieving integration of information literacy may be a challenge. It seems that a coordinated effort, both internal and external to the institution, may be necessary to achieve a program in which information literacy is integrated and distributed across the curriculum at the program and institutional levels. Although they may prefer not to act as "deus ex machina" (Ratteray, 2002, p. 369), accreditation organizations need to be more proactive in ensuring that institutions gather evidence of student learning through valid assessment measures, and actually using the data for improvement. In particular, accreditation organizations must offer better training for institutions and visiting teams, and be more explicit about the distinction between evaluation and assessment. They need to clarify what constitutes assessment as opposed to course evaluation, and to guide institutions in the proper use of assessment tools to document change. By establishing clear guidelines of what constitutes assessment and expectations for documenting progress in learning outcomes, accreditation organizations might influence changes in institutional and organizational culture toward greater assessment. Finally, accreditation organizations could increase expectations and demand that institutions be more transparent with assessment data related to student outcomes and student learning outcomes.

Ultimately, however, institutions are responsible for student learning. Accreditation standards are interpreted through individual institutional missions, meaning that accreditation organizations and the visiting teams that represent them take the mission into account when reviewing an institution. Institutions must decide what their priorities are, and advance ways to facilitate and support those priorities. Continuation of information literacy largely at the course level must be resisted. Librarians need to partner with faculty and redirect their resources and energies to the program and institutional levels. Currently, most initiatives for information literacy are stalled at the course level. Librarians and faculty must make an effort to move information literacy to other levels of the curriculum, which may require rethinking the roles, responsibilities, and modes of interaction for both groups. Still, the emergence of information literacy at the program and institutional levels will not happen until administrators and key faculty become champions for assessment and integration into the institutional culture, and inspire follow-through for improving learning. Integrating information literacy into the curriculum and assessing student learning for information literacy represents both a challenge and an opportunity. While many obstacles exist to achieving a fully integrated program, those faculty and librarians who take the initiative to overcome those barriers and demonstrate student gains in "the knowledge leading to understanding but also abilities, habits of mind, ways of knowing, attitudes, values, and other dispositions" (Maki, 2004, p. 3) will contribute to institutional goals of improved learning. Student outcomes assessment represents "an important opportunity to make the library an even more central part of . . . [academe]" (Smith, 2001, p. 36).

REFERENCES

American Library Association, Association of College and Research Libraries. (2000). *Information literacy competency standards for higher education.* Retrieved from http://www.ala.org/ala/mgrps/divs/acrl/standards/information literacycompetency.cfm

American Psychological Association. (2002). *The assessment cyberguide for learning goals and outcomes.* Retrieved from http://www.apa.org/ed/governance/bea/assessment-cyberguide-v2.pdf

Asher, A., Duke, L., & Green, D. (2010, May 17). *The ERIAL project: Ethnographic research in Illinois academic libraries.* Retrieved from http://www.academic commons.org/commons/essay/erial-project

Badke, W. B. (2005). Can't get no respect: Helping faculty to understand the educational power of information literacy. *The Reference Librarian, 89–90,* 63–80. Retrieved from InformaWorld.

Baker, C. (2005, November 21). Re: What we do vs. what we call it (Electronic mailing list message). Retrieved from http://lists.ala.org/sympa/arc/ili-l/2005-11/msg00120.html

Bennett, D. C. (2010, January 26). Going public. *Inside Higher Ed.* Retrieved from http://www.insidehighered.com/views/2010/01/26/bennett

Bloomberg, S., & McDonald, M. (2004). Assessment: A case study in synergy. In P. Hernon & R. E. Dugan (Eds.), *Outcomes assessment in higher education: Views and perspectives* (pp. 259–289). Westport, CT: Libraries Unlimited.

Blumenstyk, G. (2010). Average return on endowment investments is worst in almost 40 years. *Chronicle of Higher Education.* Retrieved from http://chronicle.com/article/Average-Return-on-Endowment/63762/

Breivik, P. S. (1989). Information literacy: Revolution in education. In G. E. Mensching Jr. (Ed.), *Coping with information illiteracy: Bibliographic instruction for the information age.* Ann Arbor, MI: Pierian Press.

Bruce, C. (2001). Faculty-librarian partnerships in Australian higher education: Critical dimensions. *Reference Services Review, 29*(2), 106–116. Retrieved from Emerald.

Crawford, J., & Irving, C. (2009). Information literacy in the workplace: A qualitative exploratory study. *Journal of Librarianship and Information Science, 41* (1), 29–38. Retrieved from Sage.

Diller, K. R., & Phelps, S. F. (2008). Learning outcomes, portfolios, and rubrics, oh my! Authentic assessment of an information literacy program. *portal: Libraries and the Academy, 8*(1), 75–89. Retrieved from Project MUSE.

Eaton, J. (2010, January 18). Accreditation 2.0. *Inside Higher Ed*. Retrieved from http://www.insidehighered.com/views/2010/01/18/eaton

Eland, T. (2005, November 21). RE: What to call what we do: Information literacy or research fluency (Electronic mailing list message). Retrieved from http://lists.ala.org/sympa/arc/ili-l/2005-11/msg00118.html

Ewell, P. T. (2001). *Accreditation and student learning outcomes: A proposed point of departure*. Washington, DC: Council for Higher Education Accreditation. Retrieved from http://www.chea.org/award/StudentLearningOutcomes 2001.pdf

Ewell, P. T. (2009). *Assessment, accountability, and improvement: Revisiting the tension*. Urbana, IL: University of Illinois and Indiana University, National Institute of Learning Outcomes Assessment (NILOA).

Fister, B., Hutchens, E. O., & MacPherson, K. H. (2001). From BI to IL: The paths of two liberal arts colleges. In H. Thompson (Ed.), *Crossing the divide: Proceedings of the tenth national conference of the association of college and research libraries* (pp. 203–212). Chicago, IL: Association of College and Research Libraries. Retrieved from http://www.ala.org/ala/mgrps/divs/acrl/events/pdf/fister.pdf

Flaspohler, M. (2003). Information literacy program assessment: One small college takes the big plunge. *Reference Services Review, 31*(2), 129–140. Retrieved from Emerald.

Freake, H., von Hammerstein, K., & Goodstein, L. (2008). *Faculty ownership of general education: Teaching what excites you!* (PowerPoint slides). Retrieved from http://74.125.93.132/search?q=cache:ZkhypK9ygawJ:www.aacu.org/meetings/generaleducation/gened2008/documents/CS4.ppt+%22general+education%22 +ownership&cd=2&hl=en&ct=clnk&gl=us&client=firefox-a

Gillen, A., Bennett, D. L., & Vedder, D. (2010). *The inmates running the asylum? An analysis of higher education accreditation*. Washington, DC: Center for College Affordability and Productivity. Retrieved from http://www.centerforcollege affordability.org/uploads/Accreditation.pdf

Gratch-Lindauer, B. (2000). Comparing the regional accreditation standards: Outcomes assessment and other trends. *Journal of Academic Librarianship, 28* (1–2), 14–25. Retrieved from H. W. Wilson.

Gratch-Lindauer, B. (2007). Information literacy–related student behaviors: Results from the NSSE items. *College and Research Libraries News, 68*(7), 432–436, 441. Retrieved from H. W. Wilson.

Hutchings, P. (2010). *Opening doors to faculty involvement in assessment*. Champaign, IL: National Institute for Learning Outcomes Assessment. Retrieved from http://learningoutcomesassessment.org/documents/PatHutchings_001.pdf

Jaschik, S. (2009, October 26). Assessment vs. action. *Inside Higher Ed*. Retrieved from http://www.insidehighered.com/news/2009/10/26/assess

Julien, H., & Given, L. M. (2002–2003). Faculty-librarian relationships in the information literacy context: A content analysis of librarians' expressed attitudes and experiences. *Canadian Journal of Information & Library Sciences, 27* (3), 65–87. Retrieved from Ebsco.

Katz, I. R. (2007). Testing information literacy in digital environments: ETS's iSkills assessment. *Information Technology and Libraries, 26*(3), 3–12. Retrieved from ProQuest.

Kelderman, E. (2010, January 26). Education department official calls for more transparency in accreditation. *Chronicle of Higher Education*. Retrieved from http://chronicle.com/article/Education-Department-Offici/63730/

Klusek, L., & Bornstein, J. (2006). Information literacy skills for business careers: Matching skills to the workplace. *Journal of Business and Finance Librarianship, 11*(4), 3–21. Retrieved from InformaWorld.

Kuh, G., & Ikenberry, S. (2009). *More than you think, less than we need: Learning outcomes assessment in American higher education.* Urbana, IL: University of Illinois and Indiana University, National Institute for Learning Outcomes Assessment (NILOA).

Kuh, G. D. (2004). *The national survey of student engagement: Conceptual framework and overview of psychometric properties.* Retrieved from http://nsse.iub.edu/2004_annual_report/pdf/2004_Conceptual_Framework.pdf

Kuh, G. D., & Gonyea, R. M. (2003). The role of an academic library in promoting student engagement and learning. *Journal of Academic Librarianship, 64*(4), 256–282. Retrieved from H. W. Wilson.

Lederman, D. (2009, June 29). The economy's large shadow. *Inside Higher Ed.* Retrieved from http://www.insidehighered.com/news/2009/06/29/nacua

Lederman, D. (2010, May 28). The faculty role in assessment. *Inside Higher Ed.* Retrieved from http://www.insidehighered.com/news/2010/05/28/assess

Lombardi, J. V. (2009, August 3). The next big thing: Crisis and transformation in American higher education. *Inside Higher Ed.* Retrieved from http://www.insidehighered.com/blogs/reality_check/the_next_big_thing_crisis_and_transformation_in_american_higher_education2

López, C. (2002). Assessment of student learning: Challenges and strategies. *Journal of Academic Librarianship, 28*(6), 356–367. Retrieved from H. W. Wilson.

Lumina Foundation. (2011). *The degree qualifications profile.* Indianapolis, IN: Author. Retrieved from http://www.luminafoundation.org/publications/The_Degree_Qualifications_Profile.pdf

Maki, P. (2002). Developing an assessment plan to learn about student learning. *Journal of Academic Librarianship, 28*(1–2), 8–13. Retrieved from H. W. Wilson.

Maki, P. (2004). *Assessing for learning: Building a sustainable commitment across the institution.* Sterling, VA: Stylus.

Maki, P. (2010). *Assessing for learning: Building a sustainable commitment across the institution* (2nd ed.). Sterling, VA: Stylus.

McGuinness, C. (2007). Exploring strategies for integrated information literacy. *Communications in Information Literacy, 1*(1), 26–38. Retrieved from http://www.comminfolit.org/index.php/cil/article/view/Spring2007AR3/14

Middle States Commission on Higher Education. (2003). *Developing research and communication skills: Guidelines for information literacy in the curriculum.* Philadelphia, PA: Author.

Middle States Commission on Higher Education. (2007). *Student learning assessment: Options and resources.* Philadelphia, PA: Author. Retrieved from http://www.msche.org/publications/SLA_Book_0808080728085320.pdf

Middle States Commission on Higher Education. (2009). *Characteristics of excellence in higher education: Requirements of affiliation and standards for accreditation.* Philadelphia, PA: Author. Retrieved from http://www.msche.org/publications/CHX06_Aug08REVMarch09.pdf

National Information Literacy Awareness Month, 74 Fed. Reg. 51445 (2009).

National Leadership Council for Liberal Education and America's Promise. (2007). *College learning for the new global century.* Washington, DC: Association of American Colleges and Universities.

North Central Association of Schools and Colleges, Higher Learning Commission. (2003). *Handbook of accreditation* (3rd ed.). Chicago, IL: Higher Learning Commission. Retrieved from http://www.ncahlc.org/download/Handbook03 .pdf

Oakleaf, M. (2008). Dangers and opportunities: A conceptual map of information literacy assessment approaches. *portal: Libraries and the Academy, 8*(3), 233–253. Retrieved from Project MUSE.

Oakleaf, M. (2009). Using rubrics to assess information literacy: An examination of methodology and interrater reliability. *Journal of the American Society for Information Science and Technology, 60*(5), 969–983.

Oakleaf, M. (2010). *The value of academic libraries: A comprehensive research review and report.* Chicago, IL: American Library Association. Retrieved from http://www.acrl.ala.org/value/

Owusu-Ansah, E. K. (2007). Beyond collaboration: Seeking greater scope and centrality for library instruction. *portal: Libraries and the Academy, 7*(4), 415–429. Retrieved from Project MUSE.

Point Loma Nazarene University. (n.d.). *General education administration.* Retrieved from http://www.pointloma.edu/Academics/SpecialPrograms/ GeneralEducationProgram/GeneralEducationAdministration.htm

Project on Accreditation and Assessment. (2004). *Taking responsibility for the quality of the baccalaureate degree.* Washington, DC: Association of American Colleges and Universities.

Ratteray, O. M. T. (2002). Information literacy in self-study and accreditation. *Journal of Academic Librarianship, 28*(6), 368–375. Retrieved from Ebsco.

Ratteray, O. M. T. (2005, 20 November). Re: What to call what we do: Information literacy or research fluency? (Electronic mailing list message). Retrieved from http://lists.ala.org/sympa/arc/ili-l/2005-11/msg00117.html

Ratteray, O. M. T. (2008, 17 July). Information literacy and faculty summary of responses (Electronic mailing list message). Retrieved from http://lists.ala.org /sympa/arc/ili-l/2008-07/msg00093.html

Sakai, Y., & Ichiko, M. (2008). Building a culture of assessment: A report from the second library assessment conference. *Journal of College and University Libraries, 84*, 9–14.

Saunders, L. (2007). Regional accreditation organizations' treatment of information literacy: Definitions, collaboration, and assessment. *Journal of Academic Librarianship, 33*(3), 317–326. Retrieved from H. W. Wilson.

Scharf, D., Elliot, N., Huey, H. A., Briller, V., & Joshi, K. (2007). Direct assessment of information literacy using writing portfolios. *Journal of Academic Librarianship, 33*(4), 462–477. Retrieved from H. W. Wilson.

Schneider, C. G. (2010, June 3). *The three-year degree is no silver bullet.* Retrieved from http://www.aacu.org/about/statements/2010/threeyears.cfm

Schneider, M. (2009, November 24). Assessing NSSE. *Inside Higher Ed.* Retrieved from http://www.insidehighered.com/views/2009/11/24/schneider

Selegean, J. C., Thomas, M. L., & Richman, M. L. (1983). Long-range effectiveness of library use instruction. *College and Research Libraries, 44*(6), 476–480.

Sharma, S. (2007). From chaos to clarity: Using the research portfolio to teach and assess information literacy skills. *Journal of Academic Librarianship, 33*(1), 127–135. Retrieved from H. W. Wilson.

Smith, K. R. (2001). New roles and responsibilities for the university library: Advancing student learning through outcomes assessment. *Journal of Library Administration, 35*(4), 29–36. Retrieved from InformaWorld.

Snavely, L., & Cooper, N. (1997). Competing agendas in higher education. *Reference and User Services Quarterly, 37*(1), 53–63. Retrieved from ProQuest.

Stanger, K. (2009). Implementing information literacy in higher education: A perspective on the roles of librarians and disciplinary faculty. *LIBRES: Library and Information Science Research Electronic Journal, 19*(1), 1–6. Retrieved from Ebsco.

Stevens, A. H. (2001). The philosophy of general education and its contradictions: The influence of Hutchins. *JGE: The Journal of General Education, 50*(3), 165–191. Retrieved from Project MUSE.

Suskie, L. (2004). *Assessing student learning: A common sense guide*. Bolton, MA: Anker Publishing.

Suskie, L. (2009). *Assessing student learning: A common sense guide* (2nd ed.). San Francisco, CA: Wiley & Sons.

Suskie, L. (2010, October 26). Why are we assessing? *Inside Higher Ed*. Retrieved from http://www.insidehighered.com/views/2010/10/26/suskie

Tener, R. K. (1999). Outcomes assessment and the faculty culture: Conflict or congruence? *Journal of Engineering Education, 88*(1), 65–73. Retrieved from ProQuest.

Todd, R. (1999). Transformational leadership and transformational learning: Information literacy and the World Wide Web. *NASSP Bulletin, 83*(605), 4–12. Retrieved from ProQuest.

University of Texas at Austin. (2008). *LibQUAL+ 2008 survey*. Retrieved from http://lib.utexas.edu/sites/default/files/vprovost/2008_LibQUAL_Institution-Results.pdf

Weiss, G. L., Habel, S. K., Hanson, C. M., Cosbey, J. R., & Larsen, C. (2002). Improving the assessment of student learning: Advancing a research agenda in sociology. *Teaching Sociology, 30*(1), 63–80. Retrieved from ProQuest.

BIBLIOGRAPHY

Abbott, J. C. (1957). *Raymond Cazallis Davis and the University of Michigan general library 1877–1905*. Retrieved from Proquest Research.

Accardi, M. T., Drabinski, E., & Kumbier, A. (2010). *Critical library instruction: Theories and methods*. Duluth, MN: Library Juice Press.

Accrediting Council for Independent Colleges and Schools. (2008). *History of accreditation*. Retrieved from http://www.acics.org/accreditation/content .aspx?id=2258

Adelman, C. (2008). *Learning accountability from Bologna: A higher education policy primer*. Washington, DC: Institute for Higher Education Policy. Retrieved from http://www.ihep.org/assets/files/publications/g-l/Learning_Accountability _from_Bologna.pdf

Albitz, R. S. (2007). The what and who of information literacy and critical thinking in higher education. *portal: Libraries and the Academy, 7*(1), 97–109. Retrieved from Project MUSE.

Albrecht, R., & Baron, S. (2002). The politics of pedagogy: Expectations and reality for information literacy in librarianship. *Journal of Library Administration, 36*(1–2), 71–96. Retrieved from Haworth Press Journals.

Alfino, M., Pajer, M., Pierce, L., & Jenks, K. O. (2008). Advancing critical thinking and information literacy skills in first year college students. *College and Undergraduate Libraries, 15*(1–2), 81–98. Retrieved from H. W. Wilson.

Allen, E. E. (1995). Active learning and teaching: Improving postsecondary library instruction. *Reference Librarian, 51–52*, 89–103. Retrieved from Haworth Press Journals.

Allen, J. (2004). The impact of student learning outcomes assessment on technical and professional communication programs. *Technical Communication Quarterly, 13*(1), 93–108. Retrieved from ProQuest.

Alstete, J. W. (2004). *Accreditation matters: Achieving academic recognition and renewal*. San Francisco, CA: Jossey-Bass.

American Council of Trustees and Alumni. (2005). *Governance in the public interest: A case study of the University of North Carolina system.* Washington, DC: Author. Retrieved from https://www.goacta.org/publications/downloads/ NCReportFinal.pdf

American Council of Trustees and Alumni. (2007). *Why accreditation doesn't work and what policymakers can do about it.* Retrieved from https://www.goacta .org/publications/downloads/Accreditation2007Final.pdf

American Council of Trustees and Alumni. (2009). *What will they learn?* Washington, DC: Author. Retrieved from https://www.goacta.org/publications/downloads/ WhatWillTheyLearnFinal.pdf

American Council on Education. (2008). *ACE analysis of higher education act reauthorization.* Retrieved from http://www.acenet.edu/AM/Template.cfm?Section =Home&TEMPLATE=/CM/ContentDisplay.cfm&CONTENTID=29218

American Library Association. (1989). *Presidential committee on information literacy: Final report.* Chicago, IL: Author. Retrieved from http://www.ala.org/ala/ mgrps/divs/acrl/publications/whitepapers/presidential.cfm

American Library Association. (2008). *ALA council adopts revised standards for application.* Retrieved from http://www.ala.org/Template.cfm?Section=archive &template=/contentmanagement/contentdisplay.cfm&ContentID=171135

American Library Association, American Association of School Librarians, and Association for Educational Communications and Technologies National Guidelines Vision Committee. (1998). *Information literacy standards for student learning.* Retrieved from http://www.ala.org/ala/mgrps/divs/aasl/aaslarchive/ pubsarchive/informationpower/InformationLiteracyStandards_final.pdf

American Library Association, Association of College and Research Libraries. (2000). *Information literacy competency standards for higher education.* Retrieved from http://www.ala.org/ala/mgrps/divs/acrl/standards/informationliteracy competency.cfm

American Library Association, Association of College and Research Libraries. (2001). *National information literacy survey.* Retrieved from http://www.ala .org/ala/mgrps/divs/acrl/issues/infolit/professactivity/survey/index.cfm

American Library Association, Association of College and Research Libraries. (2003). *Assessment issues.* Retrieved from http://www.ala.org/ala/mgrps/ divs/acrl/issues/infolit/infolitresources/infolitassess/assessmentissues.cfm

American Library Association, Association of College and Research Libraries. (2006). *Science and technology information literacy guidelines.* Retrieved from http://www.ala.org/ala/mgrps/divs/acrl/standards/infolitscitech.cfm

American Library Association, Association of College and Research Libraries. (2007). *Research competency guidelines for research in English literature.* Retrieved from http://www.ala.org/ala/mgrps/divs/acrl/standards/research competenciesles.cfm

American Library Association, Association of College and Research Libraries. (2007). *Standards for proficiencies for instruction librarians and coordinators.* Retrieved from http://www.ala.org/ala/mgrps/divs/acrl/standards/ profstandards.cfm

American Library Association, Association of College and Research Libraries. (2008). *Information literacy standards for anthropology and sociology students.* Retrieved from http://www.ala.org/ala/mgrps/divs/acrl/standards/anthro_soc_standards.cfm

American Library Association, Association of College and Research Libraries. (2008). *Political science research competency guidelines.* Retrieved from http://www.ala.org/ala/mgrps/divs/acrl/standards/PoliSciGuide.pdf

American Library Association, Association of College and Research Libraries. (2009, January 14). *OnPoint: "What really are student outcomes?"* Retrieved from http://www.ala.org/ala/mgrps/divs/acrl/events/onpoint/archives/2009-01-14.cfm

American Library Association, Association of College and Research Libraries, Task Force on Information Literacy Standards. (2000). Information literacy competency standards for higher education: The final version, approved January 2000. *College and Research Libraries News, 61*(3), 207–215. Retrieved from H. W. Wilson.

American Psychological Association. (2002). *The Assessment Cyberguide for learning goals and outcomes.* Retrieved from http://www.apa.org/ed/governance/bea/assessment-cyberguide-v2.pdf

Amudhavalli, A. (2008). Information literacy and higher education competency standards. *DESIDOC Journal of Library and Information Technology, 28*(2), 48–55.

Angelo, T. A., & Cross, K. P. (1993). *Classroom assessment techniques: A handbook for college teachers* (2nd ed.). San Francisco, CA: Jossey-Bass.

Asher, A., Duke, L., & Green, D. (2010, May 17). *The ERIAL project: Ethnographic research in Illinois academic libraries.* Retrieved from http://www.academic commons.org/commons/essay/erial-project

Associated Colleges of the South. (2006). Information fluency working definition. Retrieved from http://www.colleges.org/techcenter/if/if_definition.html

Association of American Colleges and Universities. (2008). *New leadership for student learning and accountability.* A joint report with the Council for Higher Education Accreditation. Retrieved from http://www.chea.org/pdf/2008.01.30_New_Leadership_Statement.pdf

Association of American Colleges and Universities Board of Directors. (2004). *Our students' best work: A framework for accountability worthy of our mission.* Washington, DC: Association of American Colleges and Universities.

Association for the Study of Higher Education. (2005). Understanding institutional culture. *ASHE Higher Education Report, 31*(2), 39–54. Retrieved from Ebsco.

Babbie, E. R. (2002). *The basics of social research* (2nd ed.). Belmont, CA: Wadsworth Thomson Learning.

Badke, W. B. (2005). Can't get no respect: Helping faculty to understand the power of information literacy. *Reference Librarian, 43*(89), 63–80. Retrieved from Informaworld.

Baker, C. (2005, 21 November). RE: What we do vs. what we call it (Electronic mailing list message). Retrieved from http://lists.ala.org/sympa/arc/ili-l/2005-11/msg00120.html

Baker, R. L. (2004). Keystones of regional accreditation: Intentions, outcomes, and sustainability. In P. Hernon & R. E. Dugan (Eds.), *Outcomes assessment in higher education: Views and perspectives* (pp. 1–16). Westport, CT: Libraries Unlimited.

Barratt, C. C., Nielsen, K., Desmet, C., & Balthazor, R. (2009). Collaboration is key: Librarians and composition instructors analyze student research and writing. *portal: Libraries and the Academy, 9*(1), 37–56. Retrieved from Project MUSE.

Bass, B. M. (1990). *Bass and Stodgill's handbook of leadership: A survey of theory and research*. New York, NY: Free Press.

Benjamin, R. (2008). The case for comparative institutional assessment of higher-order thinking skills. *Change, 40*(6), 50–56. Retrieved from ProQuest.

Bennet, O., & Gilbert, K. (2009). Extending liaison collaboration: Partnering with faculty in support of a student learning community. *Reference Services Review, 37*(2), 131–142. Retrieved from Ebsco.

Bennett, D. C. (2008). Templates galore: New approaches to public disclosure. *Change, 4*(6), 36–42. Retrieved from ProQuest.

Bennett, D. C. (2010, January 26). Going public. *Inside Higher Ed*. Retrieved from http://www.insidehighered.com/views/2010/01/26/bennett

Bennett, S. (2007). Campus cultures fostering information literacy. *portal: Libraries and the Academy, 7*(2), 147–167. Retrieved from Project MUSE.

Bennis, W. G., & Nanus, B. (1985). *Leaders: Strategies for taking charge*. New York, NY: Harper & Row.

Beno, B. (2007). *C-RAC letter on negotiated rule making*. Washington, DC: Council of Regional Accrediting Commissions. Retrieved from http://www.ncahlc.org /download/CRAC_Negreg.pdf

Bhavnagri, N. P., & Bielat, V. (2005). Faculty-librarian collaboration to teach research skills: Electronic symbiosis. *Reference Librarian, 43*(89), 121–138. Retrieved from Haworth Press Journals.

Birmingham, E., Chinwongs, L., Flaspohler, M. R., Hearn, C., Kvanvig, D., & Portmann, R. (2008). First-year writing teachers, perceptions of students' information literacy competencies, and a call for a collaborative approach. *Communications in Information Literacy, 2*(1), 6–24. Retrieved from H. W. Wilson.

Blackmore, P. (2007). Disciplinary difference in academic leadership and management and its development: A significant factor? *Research in Post-Compulsory Education, 12*(2), 225–239.

Bloland, H. G. (2001). *Creating the Council for Higher Education Accreditation (CHEA)*. Phoenix, AZ: Oryx Press.

Bloom, B. S. (1956). *Taxonomy of educational objectives: The classification of educational goals*. New York, NY: McKay.

Bloomberg, S., & McDonald, M. (2004). Assessment: A case study in synergy. In P. Hernon & R. E. Dugan (Eds.), *Outcomes assessment in higher education: Views and perspectives* (pp. 259–289). Westport, CT: Libraries Unlimited.

Blumenstyk, G. (2010). Average return on endowment investments is worst in almost 40 years. *Chronicle of Higher Education*. Retrieved from http://chronicle.com/ article/Average-Return-on-Endowment/63762/

Bodi, S. (1990). Teaching effectiveness and bibliographic instruction: The relevance of learning styles. *College and Research Libraries, 51*, 113–119. Retrieved from H. W. Wilson.

Bok, D. (2005). *Our underachieving colleges: A candid look at how much students learn and why they should be learning more*. Princeton, NJ: Princeton University Press.

Bowers, C. V. M., Chew, B., Bowers, M. R., Ford, C. E., Smith, C., & Herrington, C. (2009). Interdisciplinary synergy: A partnership between business and library faculty and its effects on students' information literacy. *Journal of Business and Finance Librarianship, 14*(2), 110–127. Retrieved from InformaWorld.

Boyer Commission on Educating Undergraduates in the Research University. (1998). *Reinventing undergraduate education: A blueprint for America's research universities.* Stony Brook, NY: State University of New York.

Breivik, P. S. (1989). Information literacy: Revolution in education. In G. E. Mensching Jr. (Ed.), *Coping with information illiteracy: Bibliographic instruction for the information age.* Ann Arbor, MI: Pierian Press.

Breivik, P. S. (2000). Information literacy and lifelong learning: The magical partnership. Paper presented at the *International Lifelong Learning Conference,* Central Queensland University, Queensland: Australia. Retrieved from http://hdl.cqu.edu.au/10018/3916

Breivik, P. S. (2000). Information literacy and the engaged campus. *AAHE Bulletin, 53,* 3–6. Retrieved from http://www.aahea.org/bulletins/articles/nov2000_1.htm

Breivik, P. S. (2005). Twenty-first century learning and information literacy. *Change, 37*(2), 20–27. Retrieved from Ebsco.

Breivik, P. S., & Gee, G. E. (1989). *Information literacy: Revolution in the library.* New York, NY: MacMillan.

Brough, K. (1972). *Scholar's workshop: Evolving conceptions of library service.* Boston, MA: Gregg Publishers.

Brown, A. G., Weingart, S., Johnson, J. A. J., & Dance, B. (2004). Librarians don't bite: Assessing library orientation for freshmen. *Reference Services Review, 32*(4), 394–403. Retrieved from Emerald.

Brown, T. (1995). Great leaders need great followers. *Industry Week/IW, 244*(16), 25–29. Retrieved from Ebsco.

Bruce, C. (1997). *The seven faces of information literacy.* Adelaide, Australia: Auslib Press.

Bruce, C. (2001). Faculty-librarian partnerships in Australian higher education: Critical dimensions. *Reference Services Review, 29*(2), 106–116. Retrieved from Emerald.

Budd, J. M. (2008). Cognitive growth, instruction, and student success. *College and Research Libraries, 69*(4), 319–330. Retrieved from H. W. Wilson.

Business Higher Education Forum. (1997). *Spanning the chasm: Corporate and academic cooperation to improve work-force preparation.* Washington, DC: Author.

Business Higher Education Forum. (1999). *Spanning the chasm: A blueprint for action. Academic and corporate collaboration: Key to preparing tomorrow's high-performance workforce.* Washington, DC: Author.

Business Higher Education Forum. (2004). *Public accountability for student learning in higher education: Issues and options.* Retrieved from http://www.bhef.com/publications/documents/public_accountability_04.pdf

Carey, K. (2007). Truth without action: The myth of higher-education accountability. *Change, 39*(5), 24–29. Retrieved from Ebsco.

Carey, K. (2010). That old college lie. *Democracy: A Journal of Ideas, 15,* online. Retrieved from http://www.democracyjournal.org/15/6722.php

Carey, K., & Alderman, C. (2008). *Ready to assemble: A model state higher education accountability system.* Washington, DC: Education Sector. Retrieved from http://www.educationsector.org/usr_doc/HigherEdAccountability.pdf

Carnegie Corporation of New York. (2003). *A short history of Carnegie Corporation's library program.* Retrieved from http://carnegie.org/publications/carnegie-reporter/single/view/article/item/100/

Carnegie Foundation for the Advancement of Teaching. (2007). *The Carnegie classification of institutions of higher education.* Retrieved from http://www.carnegiefoundation.org/classifications/

Church, R. L., & Sedlak, M. W. (1989). The antebellum college and the academy. In L. S. Goodchild & H. S. Wechsler (Eds.), *The history of higher education* (pp. 95–108). Needham Heights, MA: Ginn Press.

Christoforou, A. P., & Yigit, A. S. (2008). Improving teaching and learning in engineering education through a continuous assessment process. *European Journal of Engineering Education, 33*(1), 105–116. Retrieved from Ebsco.

Clark, D. (2008). *Concepts of leadership.* Retrieved from http://www.nwlink.com/~donclark/leader/leadcon.html

Colbeck, C. L. (2002). State policies to improve undergraduate teaching: Faculty and administrator responses. *Journal of Higher Education, 73*(1), 3–25. Retrieved from Project MUSE.

Commission on Collegiate Nursing Education. (2008). *Standards for accreditation of baccalaureate and graduate degree nursing programs.* Retrieved from http://www.aacn.nche.edu/accreditation/pdf/standards.pdf

Commonwealth Foundation. (2008). High costs of higher education: Reforming how Pennsylvania taxpayers finance colleges and universities. *Commonwealth Policy Brief, 20*(6), 1–14. Retrieved from http://www.commonwealthfoundation.org/docLib/20090904_HigherEdPB.pdf

Costello, B., Lenholt, R., & Stryker, J. (2004). Using blackboard in library instruction: Addressing the learning styles of generations X and Y. *Journal of Academic Librarianship, 30*(6), 452–460. Retrieved from H. W. Wilson.

Council for Higher Education Accreditation. (2003). *Statement of mutual responsibilities for student learning outcomes: Accreditation, institutions, and programs.* Washington, DC: Author. Retrieved from http://www.chea.org/pdf/StmntStudentLearningOutcomes9-03.pdf

Council for Higher Education Accreditation. (2006). *Accreditation and accountability: A CHEA special report.* Washington, DC: Council for Higher Education Accreditation. from http://www.chea.org/pdf/Accreditation_and_Accountability.pdf

Council for Higher Education Accreditation. (2006). *CHEA at a glance.* Washington, DC: Council for Higher Education Accreditation. Retrieved from http://www.chea.org/pdf/chea_glance_2006.pdf

Council for Higher Education Accreditation. (2006). *Fact Sheet #5.* Washington, DC: Council for Higher Education Accreditation. Retrieved from http://www.chea.org/pdf/fact_sheet_5_operation.pdf

Council for Higher Education Accreditation. (2008, September 19). Accreditation and the Higher Education Opportunity Act of 2008. *CHEA Update,* 45. Retrieved from http://www.chea.org/Government/HEAUpdate/CHEA_HEA45.html

Council of Independent Colleges. (2004). CIC endorses ACRL Information literacy competency standards. *Independent Online Newsletter.* Retrieved from http://www.cic.edu/publications

Crawford, J., & Irving, C. (2009). Information literacy in the workplace: A qualitative exploratory study. *The Journal of Librarianship and Information Science, 41*(1), 29–38. Retrieved from Sage.

Creswell, J. W. (2003). *Research design: Qualitative, quantitative, and mixed methods approaches.* Thousand Oaks, CA: Sage Publications.

Davis, R. C. (1986). Teaching bibliography in colleges. In L. L. Hardesty, J. P. Schmitt, & J. M. Tucker (Eds.), *User instruction in academic libraries: A century of selected readings* (pp. 35–45). Metuchen, NJ: Scarecrow Press.

Dawson, M. M., & Overfield, J. A. (2006). Plagiarism: Do students know what it is? *Bioscience Education e-Journal, 8*(1). Retrieved from http://www.bioscience. heacademy.ac.uk/journal/vol8/beej-8-1.aspx

Devlin, F. A., Burich, N. J., Stockham, M. G., Summey, T. P., & Turtle, E. C. (2006). Getting beyond institutional cultures: When rivals collaborate. *Journal of Library Administration, 45*(1), 149–168. Retrieved from Informa-World.

Dickson, L. (2008). Economic inequality and higher education: Access, persistence, and success. *Industrial and Labor Relations Review, 61*(3), 427–429. Retrieved from Ebsco.

Diller, K. R., & Phelps, S. F. (2008). Learning outcomes, portfolios, and rubrics, oh my! Authentic assessment of an information literacy program. *portal: Libraries and the Academy, 8*(1), 75–89. Retrieved from Project MUSE.

Domonkos, L. S. (1989). History of higher education. In L. S. Goodchild & H. S. Wechsler (Eds.), *The history of higher education* (pp. 3–24). Needham Heights, MA: Ginn Press.

Donaldson, G. A., Jr. (2007). What do teachers bring to leadership? *Educational Leadership, 65*(1), 26–29. Retrieved from Ebsco.

Dougherty, R. M. (2009). Assessment + analysis = accountability. *College and Research Libraries, 70*(5), 417–418. Retrieved from H. W. Wilson.

Downey, A., Ramin, L., & Byerly, G. (2008). Simple ways to add active learning to your library instruction. *Texas Library Journal, 84*(2), 52–54. Retrieved from H. W. Wilson.

Doyle, C. S. (1992). *Final report to the National Forum on Information Literacy.* Syracuse, NY: ERIC Clearinghouse on Information and Technology.

Dozier, T. K. (2007). Turning good teachers into great leaders. *Educational Leadership, 65*(1), 54–58. Retrieved from Ebsco.

Dugan, R. E., & Hernon, P. (2002). Outcomes assessment: Not synonymous with inputs and outputs. *Journal of Academic Librarianship, 28*(6), 376–380. Retrieved from H. W. Wilson.

Dugan, R. E., & Hernon, P. (2006). Institutional mission-centered student learning. In P. Hernon, R. E. Dugan, & C. Schwartz (Eds.), *Revisiting outcomes assessment in higher education* (pp. 1–12). Westport, CT: Libraries Unlimited.

Duncan, A. (2009). *What I really want to say . . .: Education secretary Arne Duncan's 21st century vision.* Retrieved from http://www.plotkin.com/blog-archives/ 2009/10/education_secre.html

Dwyer, P. M. (2006). The learning organization: Assessment as an agent of change. In P. Hernon, R. E. Dugan, & C. Schwartz (Eds.), *Revisiting outcomes assessment in higher education* (pp. 165–180). Westport, CT: Libraries Unlimited.

Eaton, J. (2007). Nationalization and transparency: On our own terms. *Inside Accreditation, 3*(1). Retrieved from http://www.chea.org/ia/IA_10807.htm

Eaton, J. (2010, January 18). Accreditation 2.0. *Inside Higher Ed*. Retrieved from http://www.insidehighered.com/views/2010/01/18/eaton

Eaton, J. S. (2007). Assault on accreditation: Who defines and judges academic quality? *Liberal Education, 93*(2), 2–3. Retrieved from Ebsco.

Eaton, J. S. (2007). Federal policy events and reflections on the accreditation-government relationship: Four points. *Inside Accreditation, 3*(4). Retrieved from http://www.chea.org/ia/IA_08-13-07.html

Eaton, J. S. (2007). Nationalization and transparency: On our own terms. *Inside Accreditation, 3*(1). Retrieved from http://www.chea.org/ia/IA_10807.htm

Educational Testing Service. (2009). *iCritical thinking powered by ETS*. Retrieved from http://www.ets.org/

Edzan, N. N. (2008). Analysing the references of final year project reports. *Journal of Educational Media and Library Sciences, 46*(2), 211–231. Retrieved from Ebsco.

Eisen, A., Hall, A., Lee, T. S., & Zupko, J. (2009). Teaching water: Connecting across disciplines and into daily life to address complex societal issues. *College Teaching, 57*(2), 99–105. Retrieved from Gale.

Eisenberg, M., Lowe, C. A., & Spitzer, K. L. (2004). *Information literacy: Essential skills for the information age*. Westport, CT: Libraries Unlimited.

Eland, T. (2005, November 21). RE: What to call what we do: Information literacy or research fluency (Electronic mailing list message). Retrieved from http://lists.ala.org/sympa/arc/ili-l/2005-11/msg00118.html

Elmborg, J. (2006). Critical information literacy: Implications for instructional practice. *Journal of Academic Librarianship, 32*(2), 192–199. Retrieved from H. W. Wilson.

Epstein, J. (2010, June 18). Method to Miller's madness. *Inside Higher Ed*. Retrieved from http://www.insidehighered.com/news/2010/06/18/credithour

Ewell, P. T. (1997). Accountability and assessment in a second decade: New looks or the same old story? In *Assessing Impact: Evidence and Action, Presentations from the 1997 AAHE Conference on Assessment and Quality* (pp. 7–21). Washington, DC: American Association of Higher Education.

Ewell, P. T. (2001). *Accreditation and student learning outcomes: A proposed point of departure*. Washington, DC: Council for Higher Education Accreditation. Retrieved from http://www.chea.org/award/StudentLearningOutcomes2001.pdf

Ewell, P. T. (2009). *Assessment, accountability, and improvement: Revisiting the tension*. Urbana, IL: University of Illinois and Indiana University, National Institute of Learning Outcomes Assessment (NILOA).

Ewell, P. T., & Jones, D. P. (2006). State-level accountability for higher education: On the edge of transformation. *New Directions for Higher Education, 135*, 9–16. Retrieved from Ebsco.

Farber, E. I. (2004). Working with faculty: Some reflections. *College and Undergraduate Libraries, 11*(2), 129–135. Retrieved from InformaWorld.

Ferrara, H. (2007). *Accreditation as a lever for institutional change: Focusing on student learning outcomes.* Retrieved from ProQuest Digital Research. (AAT 3255872)

Ferrer-Vinent, I. J., & Carello, C. (2008). Embedded library instruction in a first-year biology laboratory class. *Science and Technology Libraries, 28*(4), 325–351. Retrieved from Informaworld.

Fister, B., Hutchens, E. O., & MacPherson, K. H. (2001). From BI to IL: The paths of two liberal arts colleges. In H. Thompson (Ed.), *Crossing the divide: Proceedings of the tenth national conference of the association of college and research libraries* (pp. 203–212). Chicago, IL: Association of College and Research Libraries. Retrieved from http://www.ala.org/ala/mgrps/divs/acrl/events/pdf/fister.pdf

Flaspohler, M. (2003). Information literacy program assessment: One small college takes the big plunge. *Reference Services Review, 31*(2), 129–140. Retrieved from Emerald.

Florida State University. (n.d.). *Instruction at FSU.* Retrieved from http://learningforlife.fsu.edu/ctl/explore/onlineresources/i@fsu.cfm

Ford, L. E. (2006). *Assessment from the inside out: How we used a student's experience in the major as a way to examine our own teaching, judge student learning outcomes, and reevaluate our goals.* Paper presented at the annual meeting of the American Political Science Association, Marriott, Philadelphia, PA. Retrieved from http://www.allacademic.com/

Fowler, C. S., & Walter, S. (2003). Instructional leadership: New responsibilities for a new reality. *College and Research Libraries News, 64*(7), 465–468. Retrieved from H. W. Wilson.

Freake, H., von Hammerstein, K., & Goodstein, L. (2008). *Faculty ownership of general education: Teaching what excites you!* (PowerPoint slides). Retrieved from http://74.125.93.132/search?q=cache:ZkhypK9ygawJ:www.aacu.org/meetings/generaleducation/gened2008/documents/CS4.ppt+%22general+education%22+ownership&cd=2&hl=en&ct=clnk&gl=us&client=firefox-a

Frost, D., & Harris, A. (2003). Teacher leadership: Towards a research agenda. *Cambridge Journal of Education, 33*(3), 479–498. Retrieved from Ebsco.

Furno, C., & Flanagan, D. (2008). Information literacy: Getting the most from your 60 minutes. *Reference Services Review, 36*(3), 264–271. Retrieved from Emerald.

Gardner, J. W. (1990). *On leadership.* New York, NY: Free Press.

Gelmon, S. B. (1997). Intentional improvement: The deliberate linkage of assessment and accreditation. In *Assessing impact: Evidence and action, Presentations from the 1997 AAHE Conference on Assessment and Quality* (pp. 51–65). Washington, DC: American Association of Higher Education.

Gilchrist, D. L. (2007). *Academic libraries at the center of instructional change: Faculty and librarian experience of library leadership in the transformation of teaching and learning.* Retrieved from ProQuest Research.

Gillen, A., Bennett, D. L., & Vedder, D. (2010). *The inmates running the asylum? An analysis of higher education accreditation.* Washington, DC: Center for College Affordability and Productivity. Retrieved from http://www.centerforcollege affordability.org/uploads/Accreditation.pdf

Given, L. M., & Julien, H. (2005). Finding common ground: An analysis of librarians' expressed attitudes toward faculty. *Reference Librarian, 89*(90), 65–87. Retrieved from Haworth Press Journals.

Glenn, D., & Fischer, K. (2009, August 31). The canon of college majors persists amid calls for change. *Chronicle of Higher Education.* Retrieved from ProQuest.

Grassian, E. S., & Kaplowitz, J. R. (2001). *Information literacy instruction: Theory and practice.* New York, NY: Neal-Schuman.

Grassian, E. S., & Kaplowitz, J. R. (2005). *Learning to lead and manage information literacy instruction.* New York, NY: Neal-Schuman.

Gratch-Lindauer, B. (2002). Comparing the regional accreditation standards: Outcomes assessment and other trends. *Journal of Academic Librarianship, 28* (1–2), 14–25. Retrieved from H. W. Wilson.

Gratch-Lindauer, B. (2007). Information literacy–related student behaviors: Results from the NSSE items. *College and Research Libraries News, 68*(7), 432–436, 441. Retrieved from H. W. Wilson.

Gruber, C. S. (1989). Backdrop. In L. S. Goodchild & H. S. Wechsler (Eds.), *The history of higher education* (pp. 181–196). Needham Heights, MA: Ginn Press.

Guskin, A. E., & Marcy, M. B. (2003). Dealing with the future NOW. *Change, 35* (4), 10–22. Retrieved from Ebsco.

Happel, S. K., & Jennings, M. M. (2008). An economic analysis of academic dishonesty and its deterrence in higher education. *Journal of Legal Studies Education, 25*(2), 183–214. Retrieved from Ebsco.

Hardesty, L. (1995). Faculty culture and bibliographic instruction: An exploratory analysis. *Library Trends, 44*(2), 339–368. Retrieved from Gale.

Hardesty, L. L., Schmitt, J. P., & Tucker, J. M. (1986). *User instruction in academic libraries: A century of selected readings.* Metuchen, NJ: Scarecrow Press.

Harrod, T. (2008). *Where is information literacy in life sciences outcomes assessment?* Retrieved from http://www.aacu.org/meetings/engaging_science/Poster 3parta.pdf.pdf

Hawkins, H. (1989). University identity: The teaching and research functions. In L. S. Goodchild & H. S. Wechsler (Eds.), *The history of higher education* (pp. 265–279). Needham, MA: Ginn Press.

Hayward, F. (2002). *Glossary of key terms.* Washington, DC: Council for Higher Education Accreditation. Retrieved from http://www.chea.org/international/ inter_glossary01.html#qa

Hearn, J. C., & Holdsworth, J. M. (2002). Influences of state-level policies and practices on college students' learning. *Peabody Journal of Education, 77*(3), 6–39. Retrieved from Ebsco.

Hearn, M. R. (2005). Embedding a librarian in the classroom: An intensive information literacy model. *Reference Services Review, 33*(2), 219–227. Retrieved from Emerald.

Hemming, W. (2005). Online pathfinders: Toward an experience-centered model. *Reference Services Review, 33*(1), 66–87. Retrieved from Emerald.

Hernon, P., & Dugan, R. (2009). Assessment and evaluation: What do the terms really mean? *College & Research Libraries News, 70*(3), 146–149. Retrieved from H. W. Wilson.

Hernon, P., & Powell, R. R. (2008). Introduction. In P. Hernon & R. R. Powell (Eds.), *Convergence and collaboration of campus information services* (pp. 1–31). Westport, CT: Libraries Unlimited.

Higher Education Opportunity Act of 2008, P.L. 110-315. Retrieved from http://purl.access.gpo.gov/GPO/LPS103713

Holmes, K. E. (2003). A kaleidoscope of learning styles: Instructional supports that meet the diverse needs of distant learners. *Journal of Library Administration, 37*(3–4), 367–378. Retrieved from Haworth Press Journals.

Horner, M. (1997). Leadership theory: Past, present and future. *Team Performance Management, 3*(4), 270–287. Retrieved from Emerald.

Houlson, V. (2007). Getting results from one-shot instruction: A workshop for first-year students. *College and Undergraduate Libraries, 14*(1), 89–108. Retrieved from Informaworld.

Humphreys, D., & Porter, R. (2008). *Major higher education associations pledge new leadership for student learning and accountability at CHEA Annual Conference*. Press Release Memo. Retrieved from http://www.chea.org/pdf/2008.01.30_Leadership_Statement_News_Release.pdf

Hutchings, P. (2010). *Opening doors to faculty involvement in assessment*. Champaign, IL: National Institute for Learning Outcomes Assessment. Retrieved from http://learningoutcomesassessment.org/documents/PatHutchings_001.pdf

Institutional eligibility under the Higher Education Act, as amended, and the secretary's recognition of accreditation agencies; Final rule. 34 C.F.R. § 602 (2009).

Ironside, P. M. (2004). "Covering content" and teaching thinking: Deconstructing the additive curriculum. *Journal of Nursing Education, 43*(1), 5–12.

Ivey, R. T. (1994). Teaching faculty perceptions of academic librarians at Memphis State University. *College and Research Libraries, 55*(1), 69–82. Retrieved from H. W. Wilson.

Jacobs, J. A., & Frickel, S. (2009). Interdisciplinarity: A critical assessment. *Annual Review of Sociology, 35*, 43–65. Retrieved from Annual Reviews.

Jacobson, T. E., & Germain, C. A. (2006). A campus-wide role for an information literacy committee. *Resource Sharing and Information Networks, 17*(1–2), 111–121. Retrieved from H. W. Wilson.

Jaschik, S. (2008, November 17). Accountability system launched. *Inside Higher Ed.* Retrieved from http://www.insidehighered.com/news/2007/11/12/nasulgc

Jaschik, S. (2009, September 9). (Not) crossing the finish line. *Inside Higher Ed.* Retrieved from http://www.insidehighered.com/news/2009/09/09/finish

Jaschik, S. (2009, October 26). Assessment vs. action. *Inside Higher Ed.* Retrieved from http://www.insidehighered.com/news/2009/10/26/assess

Johnson, A. M. (2003). Library instruction and information literacy. *Reference Services Review, 31*(4), 385–418. Retrieved from H. W. Wilson.

Johnstone, D. B. (1998). The financing and management of higher education: A status report on worldwide reforms. Retrieved from http://www.fel-web.org/fel/bolonia/noabolonia.es/bancomundial.pdf

Jones, E. A. (1995). *National assessment of college student learning: Identifying college graduates' essential skills in writing, speech and listening, and critical thinking*. Washington, DC: National Center for Education Statistics.

Julien, H., & Given, L. M. (2002–2003). Faculty-librarian relationships in the information literacy context: A content analysis of librarians' expressed attitudes and experiences. *Canadian Journal of Information and Library Sciences, 27* (3), 65–87. Retrieved from Ebsco.

Julien, H., & Pecoskie, J. J. L. (2009). Librarians' experiences of the teaching role: Grounded in campus relationships. *Library and Information Science Research, 31*(3), 149–154. Retrieved from ScienceDirect.

Kanter, R. M. (1994). Collaborative advantage: The art of alliances. *Harvard Business Review, 4,* 96–108. Retrieved from Ebsco.

Katz, I. R. (2007). Testing information literacy in digital environments: ETS's iSkills assessment. *Information Technology and Libraries, 26*(3), 3–12. Retrieved from ProQuest.

Kearns, K., & Hybl, T. T. (2005). A collaboration between faculty and librarians to develop and assess a science literacy laboratory module. *Science and Technology Libraries, 25*(4), 39–56. Retrieved from Haworth Press Journals.

Kelderman, E. (2009, October 26). Competition, not accreditation, pushes up law school cost, GAO survey says. *Chronicle of Higher Education.* Retrieved from ProQuest.

Kelderman, E. (2010, January 26). Education department official calls for more transparency in accreditation. *Chronicle of Higher Education.* Retrieved from http://chronicle.com/article/Education-Department-Offici/63730/

Kells, H. R. (1994). *Self-study processes: A guide for postsecondary and similar service-oriented institutions and programs.* Phoenix, AZ: Oryx Press.

Keyser, M. W. (1999). Active learning and cooperative learning: Understanding the difference and using both styles effectively. *Research Strategies, 17*(1), 35–44.

Kezar, A. (2005). Redesigning for collaboration within higher education institutions: An exploration into the developmental process. *Research in Higher Education, 46*(7), 831–860. Retrieved from Ebsco.

Kezar, A. (2006). Redesigning for collaboration and learning initiatives: An examination of four highly collaborative campuses. *Journal of Higher Education, 77*(5), 804–838. Retrieved from ProQuest.

Kezar, A., Carducci, R., & Contreras-McGavin, M. (2006). *Rethinking the "L" word in higher education: The revolution of research on leadership.* San Francisco, CA: Jossey-Bass.

Kingsbury, A. (2007). The measure of learning. *U.S. News and World Report, 142* (9), 52–57. Retrieved from Ebsco.

Klein, A. (2006). Accountability key, groups tell colleges. *Education Week, 25*(32), 9. Retrieved from ProQuest.

Klusek, L., & Bornstein, J. (2006). Information literacy skills for business careers: Matching skills to the workplace. *Journal of Business and Finance Librarianship, 11*(4), 3–21. Retrieved from InformaWorld.

Knapp, P. (1966). *The Monteith College library experiment.* New York, NY: Scarecrow Press.

Knight, L. A. (2006). Using rubrics to assess information literacy. *Reference Services Review, 34*(1), 43–55. Retrieved from Emerald.

Knight, P. T., & Trowler, P. R. (2000). Department level cultures and the improvement of learning and teaching. *Studies in Higher Education, 25*(1), 69–83. Retrieved from Ebsco.

Kouzes, J. M., & Posner, B. Z. (2002). *The leadership challenge.* San Francisco, CA: Jossey-Bass.

Kriigel, B. J., & Richards, T. F. (2008). From isolation to engagement: Strategy, structure and process. In P. Hernon & R. R. Powell (Eds.), *Convergence and collaboration of campus information services* (pp. 63–79). Westport, CT: Libraries Unlimited.

Krippendorff, K. (1980). *Content analysis: An introduction to its methodology.* Beverly Hills, CA: Sage Publications.

Kuh, G., & Ikenberry, S. (2009). *More than you think, less than we need: Learning outcomes assessment in American higher education.* Urbana, IL: University of Illinois and Indiana University, National Institute for Learning Outcomes Assessment (NILOA).

Kuh, G. D. (2007). Risky business: Promises and pitfalls of institutional transparency. *Change, 39*(5), 30–35. Retrieved from ProQuest.

Kuh, G. D., & Gonyea, R. M. (2003). The role of an academic library in promoting student engagement and learning. *Journal of Academic Librarianship, 64*(4), 256–282. Retrieved from H. W. Wilson.

Kuh, G. D. (2004). *The national survey of student engagement: Conceptual framework and overview of psychometric properties.* Retrieved from http://nsse.iub.edu/2004_annual_report/pdf/2004_Conceptual_Framework.pdf

Kuhlthau, C. C. (1993). *Seeking meaning: A process approach to library and information services.* Norwood, NJ: Ablex Publishing.

Kuntner, M., Greenberg, E., Jin, Y., Boyle, B., Hsu, Y., & Dunleavy E. (2007). *Literacy in everyday life: Results from the 2003 National Assessment of Adult Literacy.* Washington, DC: National Center for Education Statistics.

Kwon, N. (2008). A mixed methods investigation of the relationship between critical thinking and library anxiety among undergraduate students in their information search process. *College and Research Libraries, 69*(2), 117–131. Retrieved from H. W. Wilson.

Kwon, N., Onwuegbuzie, A. J., & Alexander, L. (2007). Critical thinking disposition and library anxiety: Affective domains on the space of information seeking and use in academic libraries. *College & Research Libraries, 68*(3), 268–278. Retrieved from H. W. Wilson.

Lakos, A., & Phipps, S. (2004). Creating a culture of assessment: A catalyst for organizational change. *portal: Libraries and the Academy, 4*(3), 345–361. Retrieved from Project MUSE.

Leckie, G. J., & Fullerton, A. (1999). Information literacy in science and engineering undergraduate education: Faculty attitudes and pedagogical practices. *College and Research Libraries, 60*(1), 9–29, Retrieved from H. W. Wilson.

Lederman, D. (2007, September 17). College accountability movement moves on-line. *Inside Higher Ed.* Retrieved from http://www.insidehighered.com/news/2007/09/17/adult

Lederman, D. (2008, August 18). Let the assessment PR wars begin. *Inside Higher Ed.* Retrieved from http://www.insidehighered.com/news/2008/08/18/cla

Lederman, D. (2009, June 24). Advice for U.S. on accreditation. *Inside Higher Ed.* Retrieved from http://www.insidehighered.com/news/2009/06/24/naciqi

Lederman, D. (2009, June 29). The economy's large shadow. *Inside Higher Ed.* Retrieved from http://www.insidehighered.com/news/2009/06/29/nacua

Lederman, D. (2009, August 24). Carrying out the Higher Ed Act. *Inside Higher Ed*. Retrieved from http://www.insidehighered.com/news/2009/08/24/rules

Lederman, D. (2009, December 18). Scrutiny for an accreditor. *Inside Higher Ed*. Retrieved from http://www.insidehighered.com/news/2009/12/18/hlc

Lederman, D. (2010, April 13). No letup from Washington. *Inside Higher Ed*. Retrieved from http://www.insidehighered.com/news/2010/04/13/hlc

Lederman, D. (2010, March 9). Unwelcome "help" from the Feds. *Inside Higher Ed*. Retrieved from http://www.insidehighered.com/news/2010/03/09/accredit

Lederman, D. (2010, May 28). The faculty role in assessment. *Inside Higher Ed*. Retrieved from http://www.insidehighered.com/news/2010/05/28/assess

Leef, G. (2003). *Becoming an educated person*. Retrieved from https://www.goacta.org/publications/downloads/BEPFinal.pdf

Levine, M. (2007). The essential cognitive backpack. *Educational Leadership, 64*(7), 16–22. Retrieved from Ebsco.

Leonhardt, D. (2009, September 8). Colleges are failing in graduation rates. *New York Times*. Retrieved from http://www.nytimes.com/2009/09/09/business/economy/09leonhardt.html

Leonhardt, T. W. (2004). Faculty status. *Technicalities, 24*(4), 3–5. Retrieved from H. W. Wilson.

Lindauer, B. G. (2004). The three arenas of information literacy assessment. *Reference and User Services Quarterly, 44*(2), 122–129. Retrieved from H. W. Wilson.

Lingenfelter, P. E. (2003). Educational accountability. *Change, 35*(2), 18–24. Retrieved from ProQuest.

Linville, D. J. (2009). Assessing assessment. *Language Arts, 86*(5), 396. Retrieved from ProQuest.

Lloyd, A. (2005). Information literacy: Different contexts, different concepts, different truths? *Journal of Librarianship and Information Science, 37*(2), 82–88. Retrieved from Emerald.

Lombardi, J. V. (2006, August 10). Virtues and vices of "value added." *Inside Higher Ed*. Retrieved from http://www.insidehighered.com/views/2006/08/10/lombardi

Lombardi, J. V. (2009, August 3). The next big thing: Crisis and transformation in American higher education. *Inside Higher Ed*. Retrieved from http://www.insidehighered.com/blogs/reality_check/the_next_big_thing_crisis_and_transformation_in_american_higher_education2

Lopéz, C. (2002). Assessment of student learning: Challenges and strategies. *The Journal of Academic Librarianship, 28*(6), 356–367. Retrieved from H. W. Wilson.

Lopéz, C. L. (2004). A decade of assessing student learning: What we have learned, and what is next. In P. Hernon & R. E. Dugan (Eds.), *Outcomes assessment in higher education: Views and perspectives* (pp. 29–72). Westport, CT: Libraries Unlimited.

Lorenzen, M. (2001). A brief history of library information in the United States of America. *Illinois Libraries, 83*(2), 8–18. Retrieved from H. W. Wilson.

Lumina Foundation. (2011). *The degree qualifications profile*. Indianapolis, IN: Author. Retrieved from http://www.luminafoundation.org/publications/The_Degree_Qualifications_Profile.pdf

Macklin, A. S., & Culp, F. B. (2008). Information literacy instruction: Competencies, caveats, and a call to action. *Science & Technology Libraries, 28*(1), 45–61. Retrieved from InformaWorld.

Mader, S. (1996). Instruction librarians: Leadership in the new organization. *RQ*, 36, 192–197.

Maki, P. (2002). Developing an assessment plan to learn about student learning. *The Journal of Academic Librarianship*, 28(1/2), 8–13. Retrieved from H. W. Wilson.

Maki, P. (2004). *Assessing for learning: Building a sustainable commitment across the institution*. Sterling, VA: Stylus.

Maki, P. (2010). *Assessing for learning: Building a sustainable commitment across the institution* (2nd ed.). Sterling, VA: Stylus.

Manuel, K. (2004). Generic and discipline-specific information literacy competencies: The case of the sciences. *Science and Technology Libraries*, 24(3–4), 279–308. Retrieved from Haworth Press Journals.

Manuel, K., Beck, S. E., & Molloy, M. (2005). An ethnographic study of attitudes influencing faculty collaboration in library instruction. *Reference Librarian*, 43(89), 139–161. Retrieved from Haworth Press Journals.

Marklein, M. B. (2007, January 11). Panel urges collegians to focus on liberal arts. *USA Today*. Retrieved from Ebsco.

Martin, L. M., & Jacobson, T. E. (1995). Reflections on maturity: Introduction to "Library instruction revisited: Bibliographic instruction comes of age." *Reference Librarian*, 51–52, 5–13. Retrieved from Haworth Press Journals.

McGuinness, C. (2007). Exploring strategies for integrated information literacy. *Communications in Information Literacy*, 1(1), 26–38. Retrieved from http://www.comminfolit.org/index.php/cil/article/view/Spring2007AR3/14

McGuinness, C., & Brien, M. (2007). Using reflective journals to assess the research process. *Reference Services Review*, 35(1), 21–40. Retrieved from Emerald.

Middle States Commission on Higher Education. (2002). *Characteristics of excellence in higher education*. Philadelphia, PA: Author. Retrieved from http://www.msche.org/publications/CHX06_Aug08REVMarch09.pdf

Middle States Commission on Higher Education. (2002). *Designs for excellence: Handbook for institutional self-study*. Philadelphia, PA: Author. Retrieved from http://www.umaryland.edu/self_study/documents/middles_%20states_%20designs.pdf

Middle States Commission on Higher Education. (2003). *Developing research and communication skills: Guidelines for information literacy in the curriculum*. Philadelphia, PA: Author.

Middle States Commission on Higher Education. (2005). *Assessing student learning and institutional effectiveness*. Philadelphia, PA: Author. Retrieved from http://www.msche.org/publications/Assessment_Expectations051222081842.pdf

Middle States Commission on Higher Education. (2007). *Self-study: Creating a useful process and report*. Philadelphia, PA: Author. Retrieved from http://www.msche.org/publications/SelfStudy07070925104848.pdf

Middle States Commission on Higher Education. (2007). *Student learning assessment: Options and resources*. Philadelphia, PA: Author. Retrieved from http://www.msche.org/publications/SLA_Book_0808080728085320.pdf

Middle States Commission on Higher Education. (2009). *Characteristics of excellence in higher education: Requirements of affiliation and standards for accreditation*. Philadelphia, PA: Author. Retrieved from http://www.msche.org/publications/CHX06_Aug08REVMarch09.pdf

Middle States Commission on Higher Education. (2009). *Mission, vision, and core values*. Philadelphia, PA: Author. Retrieved from http://www.msche.org/?Nav1=ABOUT&Nav2=MISSION

Middle States Commission on Higher Education. (n.d.). *Public communication in the accrediting process*. Philadelphia, PA: Author. Retrieved from http://www.msche.org/?Nav1=POLICIES&Nav2=INDEX

Miller, C. (2008). The new higher education act: Where it comes up short (Commentary). *Chronicle of Higher Education, 54*(48), A19–A20. Retrieved from ProQuest.

Miller, C. (n.d.) *Accountability/consumer information*. Retrieved from http://www.ed.gov/about/bdscomm/list/hiedfuture/reports/miller.pdf

Miller, C., & Malandra, G. (n.d.). *Accountability/assessment*. Retrieved from http://www.ed.gov/about/bdscomm/list/hiedfuture/reports/miller-malandra.pdf

Miller, M. (1997). Looking for results: The second decade. In *Assessing impact: Evidence and action, Presentations from the 1997 AAHE Conference on Assessment and Quality* (pp. 23–30). Washington, DC: American Association of Higher Education.

Millet, M. S., Donald, J., & Wilson, D. W. (2009). Information literacy across the curriculum: Expanding horizons. *College and Undergraduate Libraries, 16* (2–3), 180–193.

Morley, L. & Aynsley, S. (2007). Employers, quality, and standards in higher education: Shared values and vocabularies or elitism and inequalities? *Higher Education Quarterly, 61*(3), 229–249. Retrieved from Ebsco.

Mounce, M. (2009). Academic librarian and English composition instructor collaboration: A selected annotated bibliography 1998–2007. *Reference Services Review, 37*(1), 44–53. Retrieved from Emerald.

Munro, K. (2006). Modified problem-based library instruction: A simple reusable instructional design. *College and Undergraduate Libraries, 13*(3), 56–61. Retrieved from Haworth Press Journals.

Murray, M., Perez, J., & Guimaraes, M. (2008). A model for using a capstone experience as one method of assessment of an information systems degree program. *Journal of Information Systems Education, 19*(2), 192–208. Retrieved from Ebsco.

National Council for Accreditation of Teacher Education. (2008). *NCATE to develop options within the accrediting process*. Retrieved from http://www.ncate.org/Public/Newsroom/NCATENewsPressReleases/tabid/669/EntryId/72/NCATE-to-Develop-Options-within-Accrediting-Process.aspx

National Information Literacy Awareness Month, 74 Fed. Reg. 51445 (2009).

National Leadership Council for Liberal Education and America's Promise. (2007). *College learning for the new global century*. Washington, DC: Association of American Colleges and Universities.

National Research Council. (2001). *Knowing what students know: The science and design of educational assessment*. J. Pellegrino, N. Chudowsky, & R. Glaser (Eds.). Washington, DC: National Academy Press. Retrieved from ebrary.

Neal, A. D. (2008). Seeking higher-ed accountability: Ending federal accreditation. *Change, 40*(5), 24–31. Retrieved from ProQuest.

Nealy, M. J. (2009). Report: College graduation rates could dramatically decline. *Diverse Issues in Higher Education, 26*(11), 8. Retrieved from ProQuest.

Neely, T. Y. (2006). *Information literacy assessment: Standards-based tools and assignments*. Chicago, IL: American Library Association.

New England Association of Schools and Colleges. (2005). *Standards for accreditation*. Bedford, MA: Author. Retrieved from http://www.neasc.org

New England Association of Schools and Colleges. (2008). *FAQs*. Retrieved from http://cihe.neasc.org/information_for_the_public/faq_about_accreditation

New England Association of Schools and Colleges. (2008). *Student success S-series*. http://cihe.neasc.org/standards_policies/commission_policies/

Noland, B. E., Johnson, B. D., & Skolits, G. (2004). *Changing perceptions and outcomes: The Tennessee performance funding experience*. Retrieved from http://tennessee.gov/thec/Divisions/AcademicAffairs/performance_funding/Research%20Noland%20DandridgeJohnson%20Skolits%202004.pdf

North Carolina Wesleyan College. (2009). *GIST: Getting information skills today*. Retrieved from http://ncwc.libguides.com/data/files5/146960/QEP_Document_Aug_2009.pdf

North Central Association of Schools and Colleges, Higher Learning Commission. (2003). *Handbook of accreditation* (3rd ed.). Chicago, IL: Higher Learning Commission. Retrieved from http://www.ncahlc.org/download/Handbook03.pdf

North Central Association of Schools and Colleges, Higher Learning Commission. (2010). *Academic quality improvement program (AQIP)*. Retrieved from http://www.ncahlc.org/aqip-home/

North Georgia College and State University. (2007). *IL=IL: Information literacy = Informed leaders: North Georgia College and State University Quality Enhancement Plan*. Retrieved from http://www.northgeorgia.edu/sacs/documents/

Northouse, P. G. (2007). *Leadership: Theory and practice* (4th ed.). Thousand Oaks, CA: Sage Publishing.

Northwest Commission on Colleges and Universities. (2003). *Accreditation handbook*. Redmond, WA: Author. Retrieved from http://www.nwccu.org

Oakleaf, M. (2008). Dangers and opportunities: A conceptual map of information literacy assessment approaches. *portal: Libraries and the Academy, 8*(3), 233–253. Retrieved from Project MUSE.

Oakleaf, M. (2009). The information literacy instruction assessment cycle: A guide for increasing student learning and improving librarian instructional skills. *Journal of Documentation, 65*(4), 539–560. Retrieved from Emerald.

Oakleaf, M. (2009). Using rubrics to assess information literacy: An examination of methodology and interrater reliability. *Journal of the American Society for Information Science and Technology, 60*(5), 969–983.

Oakleaf, M. (2010). *The value of academic libraries: A comprehensive research review and report*. Chicago, IL: American Library Association. Retrieved from http://www.acrl.ala.org/value/

Office of the Governor, Rick Perry. (2004). *Governor Rick Perry directs university regents to set accountability standards*. Retrieved from http://governor.state.tx.us/news/press-release/4327/

O'Hanlon, N. (2007). Information literacy in the university curriculum: Challenges for outcomes assessment. *portal: Libraries and the Academy, 7*(2), 169–189. Retrieved from ProjectMUSE.

Olsen, J. K., & Coons, B. (1989). Cornell University's information literacy program. In *Coping with information illiteracy: Bibliographic instruction for the information age*. Papers presented at the 17th national LOEX library instruction conference held in Ann Arbor, Michigan, May 4–5, 1989.

Oklahoma State Regents for Higher Education. (2008). *Brain gain 2010*. Retrieved from http://www.okhighered.org/studies-reports/brain-gain

Owusu-Ansah, E. K. (2003). Information literacy and the academic library: A critical look at a concept and the controversies surrounding it. *Journal of Academic Librarianship, 29*(4), 219–230. Retrieved from H. W. Wilson.

Owusu-Ansah, E. K. (2004). Information literacy and higher education: Placing the academic library in the center of a comprehensive solution. *Journal of Academic Librarianship, 30*(1), 3–16. Retrieved from H. W. Wilson.

Owusu-Ansah, E. K. (2005). Debating definitions of information literacy: Enough is enough! *Library Review, 54*(6), 366–374. Retrieved from Emerald.

Owusu-Ansah, E. K. (2007). Beyond collaboration: Seeking greater scope and centrality for library instruction. *portal: Libraries and the Academy, 7*(4), 415–429. Retrieved from Project MUSE.

Peterson, L. M. (2007). Articulating the future through collaboration. *New Directions for Higher Education, 138*, 95–102. Retrieved from Ebsco.

Point Loma Nazarene University. (n.d.). *General education administration*. Retrieved from http://www.pointloma.edu/Academics/SpecialPrograms/GeneralEducationProgram/GeneralEducationAdministration.htm

Poll, R., & Payne, P. (2006). Impact measures for libraries and information services. *Library Hi Tech, 24*(4), 547–562. Retrieved from Emerald.

Prince, M., & Felder, R. (2007). The many faces of inductive teaching and learning. *Journal of College Science Teaching, 36*(5), 14–20. Retrieved from Ebsco.

Project on Accreditation and Assessment. (2004). *Taking responsibility for the quality of the baccalaureate degree*. Washington, DC: Association of American Colleges and Universities.

Project SAILS. (2009). *Project SAILS*. Retrieved from https://www.projectsails.org/

Radcliff, C. J. (2007). *A practical guide to information literacy assessment for academic librarians*. Westport, CT: Libraries Unlimited.

Rader, H. B. (2004). Building faculty-librarian partnerships to prepare students for information fluency: The time for sharing information expertise is now. *College and Research Libraries News, 65*(2), 74–76, 80, 83, 90. Retrieved from H. W. Wilson.

Ratteray, O. M. T. (2002). Information literacy in self-study and accreditation. *Journal of Academic Librarianship, 28*(6), 368–375. Retrieved from H. W. Wilson.

Ratteray, O. M. T. (2005, November 20). Re: What to call what we do: Information literacy vs. research fluency (electronic mailing list message). Retrieved from Information Literacy Listserv, http://lists.ala.org/wws/arc/ili-l

Ratteray, O. M. T. (2008, July 17). Information literacy and faculty: Summary of responses (electronic mailing list message). Retrieved from http://lists.ala.org/sympa/arc/ili-l/2008-07/msg00093.html

Redden, E. (2008, July 28). On accountability, consider Bologna. *Inside Higher Ed*. Retrieved from http://www.insidehighered.com/news/2008/07/28/bologna

Reindl, T. (2007). *Hitting home: Quality, cost and access challenges confronting higher education today*. Indianapolis, IN: Lumina Foundation. Retrieved from http://www.eric.ed.gov/PDFS/ED497037.pdf

Remler, N. L. (2002). The more active the better: Engaging college English students with active learning strategies. *Teaching English in the Two Year College, 30*(1), 76–81. Retrieved from ProQuest.

Rice, R. E. (2006). Enhancing the quality of teaching and learning: The U.S. experience. *New Directions for Higher Education, 133*, 13–22. Retrieved from ProQuest.

Rockman, I. F. (2002). Strengthening connections between information literacy, general education, and assessment efforts. *Library Trends, 51*(2), 185–198. Retrieved from H. W. Wilson.

Rossin, D., Ro, Y. K., Klein, B. D., & Yi, M. G. (2009). The effects of flow on learning outcomes in an online information management course. *Journal of Information Systems Education, 20*(1), 87–98. Retrieved from Ebsco.

Rothstein, S. (1955). *The development of reference services through academic traditions, public library practice, and special librarianship.* Chicago, IL: Association of College and Reference Librarians.

Ruediger, C., & Jung, D. (2007). When it all comes together: Integrating information literacy and discipline-based accreditation standards. *College and Undergraduate Libraries, 14*(1), 79–87. Retrieved from Ebsco.

Saal, F. E., & Knight, P. A. (1988). *Industrial/organizational psychology: Science and practice.* Pacific Grove, CA: Brooks/Cole Publishing.

Sakai, Y., & Ichiko, M. (2008). Building a culture of assessment: A report from the second library assessment conference. *Journal of College and University Libraries, 84*, 9–14.

Salony, M. F. (1995). The history of bibliographic instruction: Changing trends from books to the electronic world. *Reference Librarian, 51–52*, 31–51. Retrieved from Haworth Press Journals.

Saunders, L. (2007). Regional accreditation organizations' treatment of information literacy: Definitions, collaboration, and assessment. *Journal of Academic Librarianship, 33*(3), 317–326. Retrieved from H. W. Wilson.

Saunders, L. (2009). The future of information literacy: A Delphi study. *portal: Libraries and the Academy, 9*(1), 99–114. Retrieved from Project MUSE.

Saunders, V. (2007). *Does the accreditation process affect program quality? A qualitative study of perceptions of the higher education accountability system on learning.* Retrieved from ProQuest Digital Research. (AAT 3268202)

Scales, J., Matthews, G., & Johnson, C. M. (2005). Compliance, cooperation, collaboration, and information literacy. *Journal of Academic Librarianship, 31* (3), 229–235. Retrieved from H. W. Wilson.

Scharf, D., Elliot, N., Huey, H. A., Briller, V., & Joshi, K. (2007). Direct assessment of information literacy using writing portfolios. *Journal of Academic Librarianship, 33*(4), 462–477. Retrieved from H. W. Wilson.

Schneider, C. G. (2010, June 3). *The three-year degree is no silver bullet.* Retrieved from http://www.aacu.org/about/statements/2010/threeyears.cfm

Schneider, M. (2005). *2003 National Assessment of Adult Literacy (NAAL) results.* Retrieved from http://nces.ed.gov/whatsnew/commissioner/remarks2005/12_15_2005.asp

Schneider, M. (2009, November 24). Assessing NSSE. *Inside Higher Ed.* Retrieved from http://www.insidehighered.com/views/2009/11/24/schneider

Schroeder, R., & Mashek, K. B. (2007). Building a case for the teaching library: Using a culture of assessment to reassure converted campus partners while persuading the reluctant. *Public Services Quarterly, 3*(1–2), 83–110. Retrieved from Ebsco.

Schroeder, U., & Spannagel, C. (2006). Supporting the active learning process. *International Journal on E-Learning, 5*(2), 245–265. Retrieved from Gale.

Schulte, S. J., & Sherwill-Navarro, P. J. (2009). Nursing educators perceptions of collaboration with librarians. *Journal of the Medical Library Association, 97*(1), 57–60. Retrieved from Ebsco.

Scott, G., & Marshall, G. (2005). Organizational culture. In *Dictionary of Sociology*. Retrieved from Oxford Reference.

Selegean, J. C., Thomas, M. L., & Richman, M. L. (1983). Long-range effectiveness of library use instruction. *College and Research Libraries, 44*(6), 476–480.

Senge, P. (1990). *The fifth discipline: The art and practice of the learning organization*. New York, NY: Doubleday.

Sharma, S. (2006). From chaos to clarity: Using the research portfolio to teach and assess information literacy skills. *Journal of Academic Librarianship, 33*(1), 127–135. Retrieved from H. W. Wilson.

Shaw, C. B. (1928). Bibliographic instruction for students. *Library Journal, 53*, 300–301.

Shupe, D. (2007). Significantly better: The benefits for an academic institution focused on student learning outcomes. *On the Horizon, 15*(2), 48–57. Retrieved from ProQuest.

Simmons, M. H. (2005). Librarians as disciplinary discourse mediators: Using genre theory to move toward critical information literacy. *portal: Libraries and the Academy, 5*(3), 297–311. Retrieved from Project MUSE.

Smith, F. A. (2007). Perspectives on the . . . pirate-teacher. *Journal of Academic Librarianship, 33*(2), 376–388. Retrieved from H. W. Wilson.

Smith, G. A. (2009). Retooling the profession: Librarianship in an era of accountability and competition. *Christian Librarian, 52*(3), 76–84. Retrieved from Ebsco.

Smith, K. R. (2001). New roles and responsibilities for the university library: Advancing student learning through outcomes assessment. *Journal of Library Administration, 35*(4), 29–36. Retrieved from Informaworld.

Snavely, L., & Cooper, N. (1997). Competing agendas in higher education. *Reference and User Services Quarterly, 37*(1), 53–63. Retrieved from ProQuest.

Sonley, V., Turner, D., Myer, S., & Cotton, Y. (2007). Information literacy assessment by portfolio: A case study. *Reference Services Review, 35*(1), 41–70. Retrieved from Emerald.

Sonntag, G. (2008). We have evidence, they are learning: Using multiple assessments to measure information literacy learning outcomes. *IFLA Conference Proceedings*, pp. 1–14. Retrieved from Ebsco.

Southern Association of Colleges and Schools. (2008). *Principles of accreditation: Foundations for quality enhancement*. Decatur, GA: Author. Retrieved from http://www.sacscoc.org/pdf/2008PrinciplesofAccreditation.pdf

Southern Association of Colleges and Schools. (2010). *Principles of accreditation: Foundations for quality enhancement*. Decatur, GA: Author. Retrieved from http://www.sacscoc.org/pdf/2010principlesofacreditation.pdf

Stamatoplos, A. (2009). The role of academic libraries in mentored undergraduate research: A model of engagement in the academic community. *College and Research Libraries, 70*(3), 235–249. Retrieved from H. W. Wilson.

Stanger, K. (2009). Implementing information literacy in higher education: A perspective on the roles of librarians and disciplinary faculty. *LIBRES: Library and Information Science Research Electronic Journal, 19*(1), 1–6. Retrieved from Ebsco.

Stassen, M. L. A., Doherty, K., & Poe, M. (2001). *Program-based review and assessment.* Amherst, MA: University of Massachusetts, Amherst. Retrieved from http://www.umass.edu/oapa/oapa/publications/online_handbooks/program_based.pdf

Stephenson, E., & Caravello, P. S. (2007). Incorporating data literacy into undergraduate information literacy programs in the social sciences. *Reference Services Review, 35*(4), 525–540.

Stevens, A. H. (2001). The philosophy of general education and its contradictions: The influence of Hutchins. *JGE: The Journal of General Education, 50*(3), 165–191. Retrieved from ProjectMUSE.

Stewart, D. (1994). *Faculty responsibility and evaluation.* Retrieved from http://www.ohio.edu/POLICY/18-009.html

Stokes, P. J. (n.d.). Hidden in plain sight: Adult learners forge a new tradition in higher education. Retrieved from http://www.ed.gov/about/bdscomm/list/hiedfuture/reports/stokes.pdf

Stoops, J. A., & Parsons, M. D. (2003). Higher education and accreditation. In J. W. Guthrie (Ed.), *Encyclopedia of education* (2nd ed., Vol. 1, pp. 28–35). New York, NY: MacMillan Reference. Retrieved from Gale Virtual Reference Library.

Suskie, L. (2004). *Assessing student learning: A common sense guide.* Bolton, MA: Anker Publishing.

Suskie, L. (2006). Accountability and quality improvement. In P. Hernon, R. E. Dugan, & C. Schwartz (Eds.), *Revisiting outcomes assessment in higher education* (pp. 13–38). Westport, CT: Libraries Unlimited.

Suskie, L. (2009). *Assessing student learning: A common sense guide* (2nd ed). San Francisco, CA: Wiley & Sons.

Suskie, L. (2010, October 26). Why are we assessing? *Inside Higher Ed.* Retrieved from http://www.insidehighered.com/views/2010/10/26/suskie

Swanson, T. (2005). Teaching students about information: Information literacy and cognitive authority. *Research Strategies, 20*(4), 322–333.

Swartz, P. S., Carlisle, B. A., & Uyeki, E. C. (2007). Libraries and student affairs: Partners for student success. *Reference Services Review, 35*(1), 109–122. Retrieved from Emerald.

Taylor, M. C. (2009, April 27). End the university as we know it. *New York Times.* Retrieved from Lexis-Nexis.

Tener, R. K. (1999). Outcomes assessment and the faculty culture: Conflict or congruence? *Journal of Engineering Education, 88*(1), 65–73. Retrieved from ProQuest.

Tennessee Higher Education Commission. (n.d.). *Performance funding advisory committee.* Retrieved from http://www.tn.gov/moa/strGrp_prefFund.shtml

Terrell, K. (2009). Harvard and Princeton top the U.S. News college rankings. *U.S. News and World Report.* Retrieved from http://www.usnews.com/articles/education/best-colleges/2009/08/19/harvard-and-princeton-top-the-us-news-college-rankings.html

Thomas, M. K. (2009). Time for higher ed to survive crisis and thrive. *New England Journal of Higher Education, 23*(3), 11.

Thompson, G. B. (2002). Information literacy accreditation mandates: What they mean for faculty and librarians. *Library Trends, 51*(2), 218–241. Retrieved from H. W. Wilson.

Todd, R. (1999). Transformational leadership and transformational learning: Information literacy and the World Wide Web. *NASSP Bulletin, 83*(605), 4–12. Retrieved from ProQuest.

Trow, M. (1994). Managerialism and the academic profession: The case of England. *Higher Education Policy, 7*(2), 11–18.

Trussell, A. (2004). Librarians and engineering faculty: Partnership opportunities in information literacy and ethics instruction. *IATUL Proceedings*, 1–8. Retrieved from H. W. Wilson.

Tunon, J. (2003). The impact of accreditation and distance education on information literacy. *Florida Libraries, 46*(2), 11–14. Retrieved from H. W. Wilson.

University of Central Florida. (2008). *Program assessment handbook.* Orlando, FL: University of Central Florida. Retrieved from http://oeas.ucf.edu/doc/acad_assess_handbook.pdf

University of Minnesota. (2007). Consortium on fostering interdisciplinary inquiry. Retrieved from https://www.myu.umn.edu/metadot/index.pl?id=1562406

University of Texas at Austin. (2008). *LibQUAL+ 2008 survey.* Retrieved from http://lib.utexas.edu/sites/default/files/vprovost/2008_LibQUAL_Institution-Results.pdf

US Department of Education. (2006). *A test of leadership: Charting the future of U.S. higher education.* Washington, DC: Author. Retrieved from http://www.ed.gov/about/bdscomm/list/hiedfuture/reports/final-report.pdf

US Department of Education. (2008). *Glossary.* Retrieved from http://studentaid.ed.gov/PORTALSWebApp/students/english/Glossary.jsp

US Department of Education, Accreditation Team. (2009). *Negotiated rulemaking for higher education. Session III, issues and draft regulatory language.* Retrieved from http://www.ed.gov/policy/highered/reg/hearulemaking/2009/accreditation.html

US Department of Education, Office of the Inspector General. (2009, December 14). *Review of the Middle States Commission on Higher Education's standards for program length.* Retrieved from http://www.ed.gov/about/offices/list/oig/aireports/i13j0005.pdf

US Department of Education, Office of the Inspector General. (2009, December 17). *Alert memorandum.* Retrieved from http://www.ed.gov/about/offices/list/oig/auditreports/AlertMemorandums/l13j0006.pdf

US Department of Labor. (1991). *What work requires of schools.* Washington, DC: Author. Retrieved from http://wdr.doleta.gov/SCANS/whatwork/whatwork.pdf

US Government Accountability Office. (2009). Higher education: Issues related to law school cost and access. Retrieved from http://www.gao.gov/new.items/d1020.pdf

Vance, K. (2008). The value of stepping outside your normal role: Lessons learned from serving on cross-disciplinary teams. *Business Communications Quarterly, 71*(2), 226–231. Retrieved from Ebsco.

VanderPol, D., & Taranto, C. (2002). Information literacy: A new tune for library instruction to music students. *Music Reference Services Quarterly, 8*(2), 15–24. Retrieved from H. W. Wilson.

Van der Wende, M. (2000). The Bologna declaration: Enhancing the transparency and competitiveness of European higher education. *Higher Education in Europe, 25*(3), 305–310. Retrieved from Ebsco.

Vedder, R. K. (2008). Colleges should go beyond the rhetoric of accountability. *Chronicle of Higher Education, 54*(42), A64. Retrieved from Ebsco.

Walsh, A. (2009). Information literacy assessment: Where do we start? *Journal of Librarianship and Information Science, 41*(1), 19–28. Retrieved from Sage.

Walsh, D. C., & Cuba, L. (2009). Liberal arts education and the capacity for effective practice: What's holding us back? *Liberal Education, 95*(4), 32–38. Retrieved from ProQuest.

Walter, S. (2008). Librarians as teachers: A qualitative inquiry into professional identity. *College and Research Libraries, 69*(1), 51–71. Retrieved from H. W. Wilson.

Wang, P. (2009). Rein in the cost of higher ed. *Money, 38*(8), 18. Retrieved from Ebsco.

Ward, D. (2006). Revisioning information literacy for lifelong meaning. *The Journal of Academic Librarianship, 32*(4), 396–402. Retrieved from H. W. Wilson.

Weinberg Memorial Library. (2009). *Information literacy grants awarded.* Retrieved from http://academic.scranton.edu/department/wml/ARCHIVED/features/spring06s-4.html

Weiner, S. G. (2005). The history of academic libraries in the United States: A review of the literature. *Library Philosophy and Practice, 7*(2), 1–12. Retrieved from Ebsco.

Weiss, G. L., Habel, S. K., Hanson, C. M., Cosbey, J. R., & Larsen, C. (2002). Improving the assessment of student learning: Advancing a research agenda in sociology. *Teaching Sociology, 30*(1), 63–80. Retrieved from ProQuest.

Welch, J. M. (2006). Loosening the ties that bind: Academic librarians and tenure. *College and Research Libraries, 67*(2), 164–176. Retrieved from H. W. Wilson.

Wellman, J. (1998). *Recognition of accreditation organizations.* Washington, DC: Council for Higher Education Accreditation. Retrieved from http://www.chea.org/pdf/RecognitionWellman_Jan1998.pdf

Western Association of Schools and Colleges Accrediting. (2001). *Handbook of accreditation.* Alameda, CA: Author. Retrieved from http://www.wascsenior.org/

Western Association of Schools and Colleges Accrediting. (2008). *Handbook of accreditation.* Alameda, CA: Author. Retrieved from http://www.wascsenior.org/

Western Cooperative for Educational Telecommunications. (2009). *College choices for adults.* Retrieved from http://www.collegechoicesforadults.org/

Wheelan, B. S. (2009). Colleges and universities must not rest on their laurels. *Diverse Issues in Higher Education, 26*(9), 66. Retrieved from ProQuest.

Wiggins, G. (1997). Feedback: How learning occurs. In *Assessing impact: Evidence and action, Presentations from the 1997 AAHE Conference on Assessment and Quality* (pp. 31–39). Washington, DC: American Association of Higher Education.

Wijayasundara, N. D. (2008). Faculty-library collaboration: A model for University of Colombo. *International Information and Library Review, 40*(3), 188–198. Retrieved from ScienceDirect.

York-Barr, J., & Duke, K. (2004). What do we know about teacher leadership? Findings from two decades of scholarship. *Review of Educational Research, 74*(3), 255–316. Retrieved from ProQuest.

Young, E. (2009). *Policy briefs: Are Texas universities making the grade in accountability?* Retrieved from http://www.texaspolicy.com/pdf/2009-06-PB17-HE-transparency-ey.pdf

Yudof, S., & Ruberg, C. (2007). *Secretary Spellings encourages greater transparency and accountability in higher education at the national accreditation meeting* (Press Release). Retrieved from http://www.ed.gov/news/pressreleases/2007/12/12182007.html

Zmuda, A. (2008). Springing into active learning. *Educational Leadership, 66*(3), 38–42. Retrieved from Ebsco.

Zurkowski, P. B. (1974). *The information service environment relationships and priorities.* Washington, DC: National Commission on Libraries and Information Science.

INDEX

About the Author

LAURA SAUNDERS is an assistant professor in the Graduate School of Library and Information Science at Simmons College. Dr. Saunders has written articles for the *Journal of Academic Librarianship* and *College and Research Libraries*, and her article "Regional Accreditation Organizations' Treatment of Information Literacy" was recognized as one of the 20 best articles of the year by ALA's Library Instruction Round Table.

Edwards Brothers, Inc.
Thorofare, NJ USA
February 20, 2012